The Culture and Art
of Death in 19th
Century America

The Culture and Art of Death in 19th Century America

D. TULLA LIGHTFOOT

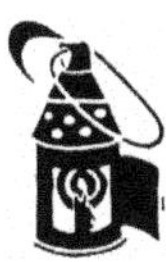

McFarland & Company, Inc., Publishers
Jefferson, North Carolina

Names: Lightfoot, D. Tulla, author.
Title: The culture and art of death in 19th century America /
D. Tulla Lightfoot.
Description: Jefferson, North Carolina : McFarland & Company, Inc., 2019. |
Includes bibliographical references and index.
Identifiers: LCCN 2019000489 | ISBN 9781476665375 (paperback :
acid free paper) ♾
Subjects: LCSH: Death in art. | Death—United States—History—19th
century. | Bereavement—United States—History—19th century.
Classification: LCC NX650.D4 L55 2019 | DDC 700/.4548—dc23
LC record available at https://lccn.loc.gov/2019000489

ISBN (print) 978-1-4766-6537-5
ISBN (ebook) 978-1-4766-3518-7

Front cover image © 2018 iStock

Printed in the United States of America

*McFarland & Company, Inc., Publishers
Box 611, Jefferson, North Carolina 28640
www.mcfarlandpub.com*

Table of Contents

Preface

I remember being a child of five or six and being taken to the funeral of a favorite great-uncle where my grandmother became hysterical and cried and screamed so much that she had to be dragged away from the grave. When we visited the grave a year later, there was a depression in the earth at least 6 inches deep showing the sad, rectangular shape of his coffin, as if the whole world shrank a little because of the loss of this man.

Not long after this, I remember sitting on a rocking chair next to my grandfather on the porch of his house and wanting to ask him if he was afraid to die. My grandfather smoked too much, had an enlarged heart and looked like one of the oldest people in the world. Of course, I didn't ask him this question. I didn't have the nerve to ask, although the words were so loud in my head that I wondered why he couldn't hear or sense my thoughts. Today we are still fascinated with death. We may not wear black dresses and mourning veils, but death awaits us all. It is mysterious. It lies at the end of the journeys of all of our lives.

A few years ago, I prepared a lecture for a conference on the topic of artists' responses to death in 19th century America. No one else in my department at the university wanted to tackle what they saw as a very unpleasant topic, and whenever I mentioned my research my colleagues reacted by expressing their distaste with a resounding "Yuck!" This led me to believe that our modern aversion to anything dealing with death kept scholars of art away from approaching serious research in this field.

So, when an editor who had seen my presentation contacted me about writing this book, I took him up on the deal. Preparing my presentation, I had discovered that most books on death in the Victorian era were either short, with little information, or too focused on just one topic. The short books reported on what people wore, how long periods of mourning were, and mourning etiquette, but didn't explain why the people acted the way they did or why these practices developed at this time. To me these books were unsatisfactory. They didn't describe the people who made the artifacts used in the mourning process with enough depth. They didn't discuss the effects mourning customs had on the larger world, and they didn't mention the scientific or technological discoveries that made these practices seem logical. They also didn't mention the changes in religious thought that helped explain why people mourned this way. The 19th century Victorians were portrayed as being quaint, scary, or weird. These were people who created rigid rules for mourning for seemingly no reason and then followed them to a tee.

The books I found on a single topic had depth, but they didn't mention how the pieces fit together to form a larger whole. The authors stayed inside their areas and shut out information about the rest of this society. Often, they came up with theories that didn't give the reader a larger understanding of who these grieving Victorians were. In this work I am trying to rectify these omissions. I am trying to make these people, our ancestors, seem less crazy and weird, and more human and rational.

Through my research I became amazed at how much we have learned and changed in a short period of time—about a hundred or a hundred and fifty years. I was amazed to learn how little people understood about health and the causes of diseases in the 19th century. I came to understand how things we now take for granted, like the creation of a lighting system and new means of transportation, radically changed the way our great- or great-great-grandparents lived. The nineteenth century was an age of rapid development. Religion, political systems, and societies in the Western world had no choice but to respond to these changes. Sometimes they responded for the better, but sometimes they responded for the worse and dissolved into chaos and war.

Can we learn anything from the past? I believe that we can. Study of this turbulent time can help us navigate the changes that we find in our own time. This is why having a broader view of why Victorians created their mourning rituals and mourning artifacts is important. It can give us important insight into our own lives and changes taking place in our own time.

It is vital for the reader to understand that each section of this book represents an entire field of study populated by academics who spent or spend their entire careers researching a topic. Other sections, such as the one on mortuary statues, have been neglected, with hardly any serious study being conducted on the topic at all. It is my hope that this book will spur some of you to explore these topics and add to our understanding of the people and practices of this time. I have included a bibliography of the articles, books, newspapers, journals, and electronic information I have used. Some of the books were written in Victorian times. In many cases the reason for this inclusion is that no current information could be found on these topics. In other cases, information from books written in the 19th century is included because they were read and believed by the Victorians. My hope is that the information I include from these sources gives us a better understanding of the mindset of these people.

In addition to researching written material, I also became a reporter and investigated organizations founded during this time. I became a volunteer librarian for the South Florida chapter of the Theosophy Society. I studied books written by its leaders: Madame Helena P. Blavatsky, Henry Steel Olcott, Annie Besant and Charles Webster Leadbeater. I attended classes on Rudolph Steiner's anthroposophy, and pored over drawings he and Theosophists made of the sacred geometry and the appearance of our auras, and descriptions of the many levels of the afterlife. This knowledge is imperative in understanding the artistic movements that developed during this period. In addition, I took classes on how to read the Akashic Record, Buddhist beliefs, Jewish beliefs about death, and Hinduism. I studied works from the Puritans and the Catholic and Methodist churches. I read work by the spiritualist Andrew Jackson Davis; manifestos written by artists such as Kandinsky and Mondrian; the journal written by Paul Gauguin; and letters from Vincent van Gogh, his brother Theo and other family members in hopes that my work would give you a broader understanding of these times.

Today, death is not a popular subject of discussion. Research on traditional artists' work on the theme of death has been neglected. The great artists of this time were affected by the death they saw all around them. This was evident in their writings and in their art. The great artists of the 19th and early 20th centuries were also knowledgeable about the religious and philosophical thought of their times, including the idea from occult philosophies and spiritualism that death was not an end to existence. This fact has largely been excluded from mention in art history texts and needs to be included to fully understand abstraction and minimal art. But the response to death made artists out of others who are not well known and who never appear in art history books. Craftsmen, designers, architects, and jewelers were inspired by death. They found patrons in grief-stricken mourners and created important work. Landscape artists, photographers and sculptors were spurred to develop new skills as memorial art was commissioned to adorn garden cemeteries and document the dead lying in battlefields. Do-it-yourselfers created their own relics and artwork, learning techniques from patterns found in books and magazines, and then creating meaningful work from their own imaginations. Death was the impetus for creativity in the Victorian age. Affecting everyone, death encouraged deep emotions that were expressed through art.

Now, older than my grandfather was when I sat with him on the porch, I have experienced the death of my mother, the death of my father and the deaths of various cousins, aunts and uncles. Neighbors have succumbed to death's grasp, as have friends, acquaintances and countless pets. Their loss is shocking in its permanence. Throughout our lives we will all experience this loss. We will have a short time off from work, and then go back, expected to function at the same level as before.

The Victorians reacted differently. They turned themselves into walking symbols of their grief. The creativity, artistry and inventiveness behind this is what I hope this book will bring to life.

<h1 style="text-align:center">1</h1>

The Victorian Age

Named for Queen Victoria of the United Kingdom and Ireland, and Empress of India, the Victorian Age began with her birth in 1837 and ended in 1901, the year of her death. During this period, American and European amateur and professional artists created works dealing with death more than at any other time. These works still exist, and modern people find themselves fascinated with them, as well as with the era.

While the nineteenth century is the focus of this story, and the time of Queen Victoria is the best time to begin, the roots of these practices lie in older time periods. Some of these art practices continue to have effects on the art and society of modern times. Because of this, the book does not stop with the death of the queen. Instead, it continues the saga up until modern times in an attempt to explain the importance the art and ideas had both for our ancestors and our contemporary lives.

The nineteenth century was an dynamic time for art. It was a time of great change. At the start of the century, artists such as Jacques-Louis David and Jean Ingres painted in an austerely realistic neoclassical style that reflected the no-nonsense philosophy of the French Revolution. Reacting to the invention of photography in the 1830s, artists such as Eugene Delacroix and J. M. W. Turner began adding their emotional interpretations to scenes that often contained blurred areas in a style we now call Romantic. Photography, the record of actual light on objects, is the epitome of realism. As it gained in popularity and availability, artists had to redefine what they did. To be relevant, they had to do things that the camera could not do, and they reinvented themselves in an expanding pantheon of styles from Impressionism to Post-Impressionism to Symbolism, Expressionism and beyond, often writing long manifestos explaining why they were doing what they did. Artists also sought new inspirations for their art. Turning away from traditional themes of religion and historical events, and portraits of rich customers, they found inspiration in the ordinary people that surrounded them. Their artwork proudly showed their hand and their vision. Their art intentionally depicted a world interpreted by their minds, their abilities and their emotions—things lacking in realistic photographs.

While artists of the nineteenth century were redefining the parameters of art and reinventing their role in society, conditions for the people of Europe and the United States were rapidly changing, too, but were often harsh and severe. The century between 1800 and 1900 was one of constant war and the inevitable loss of life war brought. Imperialist nations fought to claim territory and extend their spheres of influence. Subjugated peoples rose up to fight their conquerors time and time again in Asia, Africa, New Zealand, and North America. Nations fought nations, and Napoleon tried and failed to dominate the world.

The United States was not spared involvement in deadly conflict. At the beginning of the century Americans were recovering from the estimated 4,500 deaths resulting from the long Revolutionary War, which began in 1775 and ended in 1783. Shortly after the start of the century another estimated 2,200 died as a result of the War of 1812, which ended in 1815. More than 11,000 lives were lost as a result of the Mexican-American War of 1846–1848, and thousands of lives were lost as Native Americans fought to reclaim their land ("America's War").

Soldiers do not die only in battle. They die from other causes such as injuries, incarceration, poor living conditions and contraction of disease, making the total death rate for all these wars much higher. But it was the War Between the States, or the Civil War, that had the greatest effect on the American population. The Civil War began in 1861 and ended in 1865. The Office of Veteran Affairs estimates that a total of 214,938 soldiers died in battle with an additional 283,394 dying in the theater of operations making the total loss of life 498,332 individuals. The U.S. National Park Service states that the total number of soldiers killed in the Civil War is 620,000 (Faust). As a result of the Civil War, one quarter of all soldiers, one out of every sixteen men aged 13–43 (2 percent of the entire American population) died either in combat, from injuries sustained during battle, or from diseases that spread through the regiments (Laderman, 97). More than 3 million soldiers fought in this war. Few could avoid contact with the deceased or the stench of decaying bodies. As the battles raged across farmland, cities and towns, an estimated 50,000 civilians met their ends (Faust). This loss of life affected every American family and greatly influenced the culture of the country.

War was not the only reaper of lives. People also fought disease. As the Industrial Revolution took hold, more people lived and worked in close proximity to each other. Diseases spread. Without a clear understanding of the causes of a disease, there was no effective way to combat it. The leading cause of death from disease in nineteenth century America was tuberculosis, but typhoid fever, typhus, small pox, cholera, diphtheria, pneumonia and tetanus carried death sentences, too, and children were the most vulnerable of all. In her book *Women at Home in Victorian America*, Ellen M. Plante (75) admitted that statistics for the early 1800s are scarce, but she believed that in the last quarter of the 19th century one out of every ten infants died before the age of one. In 1900, 30 percent of all deaths in the United States occurred in children under five years of age. Pneumonia, tuberculosis, diarrhea and enteritis (an inflammation of the small intestines) were their killers, but cholera was not far behind. Major cholera epidemics occurred in the United States in 1832, 1849, 1866 and late 1879. In the outbreak of 1849, St. Louis, Missouri, lost one out of every eleven citizens to the disease. The popular treatment for disease, call the "Heroic" method of medicine and used by physicians until the mid–1800s, consisted of excessive blood-letting, induced sweating, vomiting and purging, along with blistering of the skin (Burns, chronology, 1793). Blisters were created by applying a burn agent to the skin, such as a secretion of the blister beetle, or Spanish fly. When the blister formed, it was punctured so that the fluid, thought to contain the inflammation, drained from the skin. More often than not these treatments contributed to the death of the patients rather than curing them.

Medicine was at its infancy in the hundred years from 1800 to 1900. Medical procedures, including childbirth, were very dangerous. In the middle of the 19th century a woman's chance of dying during childbirth was 1 in 30 (Burns, caption to 76). American medical professionals often scoffed at and were slow to adopt life-saving techniques developed and tested in Europe. Sophisticated surgery couldn't be performed because there wasn't a way to allow patients to sleep through the pain. The development of anesthesia wasn't begun until the English chemist Humphrey Davy performed experiments with nitrous oxide in 1799. In 1846 Scottish surgeon Robert Liston experimented with ether. Shortly afterwards, in 1847, another Scott, James Simpson, discovered chloroform's power to put patients to sleep. Since the needed dose was unknown, this method unfortunately killed as well as anesthetized.

As could be expected, hospitals in Europe and in the United States were seen as places to fear, and in 1800 were only established by charities as places where the less fortunate went to die. As late as 1870, only 100 hospitals existed in the United States (Husband and O'Loughlin, 220). It was not until the 1900s, when hospitals became safer, that their creation was seen as being useful, and state and local governments recognized their responsibility to establish them. Before then, doctors came to the house, where people were born and where people died.

Doctors didn't understand how diseases spread. The need to wash their hands or sterilize their medical instruments when examining patients was unknown to them. Even when performing surgery, doctors didn't wash their hands or change their clothing. To the contrary, they proudly wore dirty aprons stained with the blood of former patients in an attempt to impress new customers with their prowess. Instead of healing the sick, doctors often turned patients into victims by spreading infection and disease. This was especially true in the case of "childbirth fever." Despite the fact that the German doctor Ignaz Semmelweis reported as early as 1795 that the practice of scrubbing the hands of visitors and doctors (especially those doctors coming from the dissection room) with chloride of lime before entering the maternity ward significantly reduced the death rate from childbirth, his paper was not read in Britain until 1848 (Flanders, 56). His findings were not believed in the United States until several years later. Doctors instead believed that childbirth fever was an emotional illness caused by the overexcitement of the mother. The culture combined this idea with biblical morality, saying that women were made to suffer for the sins of Eve. If a woman exhibited symptoms of the disease, she was given opium, brandy and champagne. Her relatives were told to pray and hope for the best. Puerperal (childbirth) fever, now called septicemia, caused ⅓ to ½ of all deaths after childbirth (56).

The English doctor Edward Jenner created the first vaccine against smallpox in 1796, but it was not until 1861 that Frenchman Louis Pasteur proved the relationship between puerperal fever and spores of living organisms (streptococcus). This slowly led to the understanding that germs caused diseases and that germs were distributed in the air or spread by dirty hands, instruments, or contaminated surfaces. But it wasn't until 1867 that Joseph Lister, a British surgeon, used Pasteur's ideas to create the antiseptic principle in the practice of surgery. Lister used carbolic acid, a corrosive substance that damaged the skin, to kill germs (Burns, 1867). Unfortunately, despite numerous publications and a visit to the United States in 1876, his ideas were deemed insignificant to American doctors as late as the 1890s. Steam sterilization began being practiced in Europe in 1886. By 1888 some forward-thinking American practitioners had begun boiling instruments to sterilize them. This was followed shortly after by the practice of alcohol sterilization in 1894 and iodine sterilization in 1908; however, many practitioners in the United States continued to doubt that these "new-fangled" techniques were worthwhile.

Without a clear understanding of the causes of disease, people were unable to combat it or even comprehend it. The death of loved ones and family members was a constant in their lives. In the United States, it is estimated that as many as two hundred out of every thousand infants died shortly after birth (Nugent, quoted in Laderman, 25). More than 16 percent of all children born did not live to see their first birthday. Judith Flanders, in her book *Inside the Victorian Home*, estimated that by age five every child had contracted at least one and possibly a combination of diseases such as scarlet fever, diphtheria, smallpox, measles, whooping cough, typhus or typhoid fever, any of which could prove fatal (Flanders, 880). The most fatal of these were scarlet fever, diphtheria and "summer diarrheas" (Burns, 1736). Epidemics of cholera, typhoid fever, and dysentery were caused by infected milk and infected water. Since people did not understand how diseases spread, major epidemics swept the country over and over again. Without common medicines such as acetylsalicylic acid, or aspirin (not for sale until 1899), even common illnesses such as chicken pox and mumps could kill.

Twenty to thirty percent of all children died before reaching ten years of age. Of the remainder, eight to ten percent died before reaching their twentieth birthday. The rate of deaths for those born in American cities was greater because of urbanization (Burns, 1825–1850). If one made it to adulthood in 1849, the life expectancy was less than forty years for the gentry class. Life expectancy was significantly less for working class individuals (Laderman, 24).

The way people lived was also dangerous to their continued existence. The flush toilet was invented in 1596 by John Harington but was not common until being introduced to the general public in London's Great Exhibition of 1851, where an estimated 827,000 used them to relieve themselves, encouraging the creation of municipal sewage systems (Flanders, 324). Before that humans living in rural environments sat in an outhouse (called a "privy" in England) and dropped their waste into a hole in the ground called a cesspit. At regular intervals, a material such as quicklime, fireplace ashes or yeast was poured down the hole to help break down the waste and lessen the smell. When the hole was filled, the waste was shoveled out, composted, and used as fertilizer, or the hole was covered up and the outhouse moved to a different spot. If the outhouse was located too near a well or source of drinking water, disease occurred and spread. In urban Europe, common folk relieved themselves in chamber pots and threw the waste into street gutters, which carried it to a cesspit where liquid waste was allowed to seep into the ground and contaminate area wells. English cesspits were irregularly cleaned, once every eight to ten years. The noxious gases that resulted from fermented solid excrement caused infections and asphyxiated unlucky cesspit cleaners. The London typhus outbreak of 1837 killed 16,000 people each year for four years. Scarlet fever killed another 20,000 in 1840. In 1848 there were 30,000 deaths from typhoid in Britain, another 13,000 from influenza and 50,000 from cholera in 1850. Flanders (336) wrote: "It was thought that for every person who died of old age or violence, another eight died of disease."

While the spread of disease was not fully understood, it was recognized that poor sanitation was a contributing factor. Cesspools were created, which contained liquid waste, but these continued to be a hazard to one's health. Cesspools were difficult to clean. They frequently overflowed and the liquid eventually found its way to the Thames. Of the 4,363 people killed by London's cholera epidemic of 1866, 93 percent drank water supplied by East London Water Company, which used improperly filtered water from the Thames that also contained offal from slaughter houses, industrial waste and dead dogs and cats. It wasn't until the construction of the sewage system on the Thames, completed in the 1870s, that waterborne epidemics became a thing of the past (Flanders, 339).

Even houses and apartments were a danger to one's survival. Advances in lighting technology changed home and social life, allowing people to be active after dark. Unfortunately, oxygen was lost in poorly ventilated rooms that used gas lighting. Kerosene, which was distilled from coal, was used in lamps that were cheaper than using candles. However, these lamps were not safe and could explode (Flanders, 201). Inhaling fumes and particulates from kerosene lamps was the equivalent of smoking two packs of cigarettes a day and caused lung cancer. Poor ventilation and fuel-based lighting also caused respiratory infection, influenza and pneumonia ("Impact of Lighting Poverty on Children"). As of 2015, poor illumination continues to kill approximately 1.5 million people annually.

Flanders (304) noted that 19th century children were "smothered in clothes." Infants wore a binder called a "bellyband," a strip of flannel or linen swathed around their stomachs to keep their "bowels warm and spines firm" (61). Babies and toddlers up to the age of 3 or 4 wore petticoats and dresses. After this age, boys wore jackets, waistcoats, stockings, knickerbockers, hats, and boots that buttoned to the ankles. Girls dressed as women and wore vests, chemises, stockings, drawers, petticoats, frocks and pinafores. They donned coats and mufflers when they went out of doors. When a girl reached puberty, she began to wear a corset. Metal eyelets were fabricated in the 1820s, which allowed the corsets to be pulled tightly without tearing the fabric. Winter clothes were made of flannel or wool. In the summer, children wore the same amount of clothes, but they were fashioned out of cotton or linen. Flanders (306) estimates that a fashionable adult woman carried thirty-seven pounds of clothing on her back. In comparison, today our outfits weigh no more than two.

A woman's appearance and dress were deemed important indications of her character. Dresses covered the feet and dragged on the street and sidewalk, causing another author on Victorian America to write: "One shudders to think of the pollution gathered up by a skirt that not merely touches but drags on the sidewalk, gathering up microbes by the hundred, and bringing into a clean house dirt of every description" (Erbsen, 176).

Proper ideas of what women should wear and how women should act adversely affected their health. Appropriately dressed women wore a chemise (a knee length shirt) under a corset, then a camisole shaped to the waist, petticoats, and crinolines, over which was an ornamental petticoat and then the overskirt. The numerous petticoats and support material made their waists look so large that the corset needed to be pulled tightly. Corsets were pulled tighter and tighter as the century progressed despite warnings from the medical field. They eventually were so tight that they restricted breathing and caused ribs to overlap, jeopardizing women's internal organs. Women were "shut up in the too hot or too cold parlor with uncomfortable, restrictive and often injurious clothing" (Plante, 185). Another cause of poor health was the notion that it was improper for women to engage in active exercise.

Ideas of childrearing also contributed to the high death rate among children of the Victorian age. Girls were put into corsets at the onset of menstruation. Their diets were restricted to low-protein and bland foods, and physical activity was curtailed. Babies were given medicines containing opium, chloral hydrate and cannabis, and mothers were advised to have their children wash these down with brandy, possibly causing death from narcotic overdoses. Teething was seen as a serious illness that could cause a baby's death. Mothers were encouraged to stop feeding teething infants milk and instead give them opium syrup accompanied by a liberal dose of castor oil. Teething babies were put into hot baths, and in extreme cases, their gums were lanced (Flanders, 79).

The mid–1800s saw the mass production of baby bottles and the idea that breast-feeding was not as nutritious as bottle-feeding. Unfortunately, there may have been some truth to this because mothers from lower economic classes suffered from poor nutrition, and it is believed that rickets and curvature of the spine in babies may have been the result. These bottles were designed so that infants could independently feed without supervision, freeing the caretaker for more important work. The rubber nipple was not perfected until the 1900s (Flanders, 57–58). Before this time, nipples, or teats, for bottles were made from different materials including rags, wood and even calf teats. These were bought at the chemists and fastened to the bottle with a metal ring. Baby bottles and teats proved difficult or impossible to clean. Mothers were even discouraged from washing the nipples altogether because the importance of sterilization to human health was not understood until the 1890s. Contaminated bottles and nipples contributed to high infant mortality. Contaminated or infected milk caused typhus, typhoid fever and dysentery. If a disease didn't kill your infant, dehydration from diarrhea might. The necessity of fluid replacement was not understood and as a result, tens of thousands of infants and children died.

Expectant mothers also put their health at risk because of the fashion of the day. Pregnancy was a condition to be concealed as long as possible, and women were encouraged to wear corsets throughout their pregnancy. After 1840 steel stays were replaced by the more flexible whalebone for pregnant women. These stays were taken off during labor, replaced by a large bandage that extended from the chest to the lower abdomen (Flanders, 51).

Food could also be toxic in the Victorian age because there were few regulations or standards in the 1800s. Britain passed the "Sale of Goods Act" in 1885, but before then an article in *The Lancet*, a British medical journal, exposed the addition of alum, lime, chalk and even plaster of Paris to commercially produced bread. Potato flour, carbonate of soda and caustic lime were found to be added to lard, and red oxide of lead was commonly used as a popular food coloring. Chromate of lead was used in candy (Flanders, 282).

Until the second half of the 19th century, recipes for cures and treatments were handed down from family elders or found in popular women's magazines. An example of these "home remedies" was a prevention for cholera: "three castor beans, strung on a silk thread and hung around your neck"; if the thread was drawn tight enough, it was thought to ward off the disease (Erbson, 59). Two calves' feet baked in two pints of water and 2 pints of new milk for 3½ hours, then cooled and the fat removed, was believed to cure common women's ailments such as dyspepsia, modern-day indigestion. The symptoms of this disease were lack of appetite, heartburn, stomach pains or diarrhea (Plante, 182).

Disease could strike anyone at any time, for no apparent reason, and there was little understanding of how to combat it. Death also came as a result of war, bad habits, primitive technology and societal conventions. During the Victorian age and most of the nineteenth century, death occurred at home with family, friends, the doctor, and the minister in attendance. If someone had the misfortune of dying somewhere else, a great effort was made to bring the body back home so it could be tended to and buried in the prescribed way. Today there are professionals who deal with the remains of our loved ones, but this industry did not exist in the nineteenth century. Families handled their corpses themselves and had an intimate relationship with and responsibility to the dead. Death was an omnipresent part of life in the Victorian age, and no one, no matter how young or old, rich or poor, escaped the effects of having someone close to them pass away. It was no wonder that people used their creativity to create objects to help them cope with their loss, and it was no wonder that artists and craftspeople emerged to cater to those grieving.

2

Psychic Artists, Performance Art and Death

The Afterlife

In response to the great increase in deaths in the 19th century, people's ideas about God changed. Instead of the fierce God of the Puritans, who believed that punishment for original sin would be the fires of hell after death, gentler and kinder beliefs emerged to temper religious thoughts of the afterlife. One philosophy was formalized into a religion called Spiritualism, which was spread by believers and performance artists who called themselves "mediums." The artists entertained clients in small group settings called "séances." They also performed in large theaters or auditoriums in front of hundreds of people at once. Hundreds if not thousands of people discovered that they were mediums, and millions of people came to believe in "continuous life" and human communication with angels, demons and spirits of the dead. Most of the mediums, but not all, were debunked; discovered to have employed devious methods to produce the illusion that they communicated with heavenly beings or spirits of the dead. Some of these debunked mediums continued to insist that they actually possessed clairvoyance and mediumistic abilities but resorted to tricks when their powers failed so as not to disappoint their audiences. The religion of Spiritualism continues to exist today. Mediums amaze us on television, on the Internet and in Spiritualist camps. More importantly, the philosophy of spiritualism has mingled with those of traditional religious thought to forever change ideas about death and the afterlife.

The belief that each of us possess something—a spirit or a soul—that continues after the death of our physical body is an ancient one. In some cultures, the final destination for this spirit depended on our actions in this life. The souls of worthy ancient Egyptians traveled to Sekhet-Aaru, the heavenly reed fields, where they lived forever in paradise. Greek and Roman souls left their bodies at the exact time of death and traveled to the underworld ruled by the god Hades. If lucky and righteous, they continued onward to the Elysium Fields, or paradise. The souls of the Celtic people of Ireland travelled to Tir na nÓg—a place somewhere across the English Channel on the mysterious European continent, and the souls of select dead Norse warriors travelled to Valhalla, the banquet hall of their chief god, Odin. Depending on their beliefs, other Norse thought that their souls would inhabit Helgafjell—the holy mountain and home of the goddess Hel, or dwell in Fólkvangr—the field of the people. The concept of an afterlife was not unique to Europeans. As one example, in 2007 Chinese archeologists discovered a 2,500-year-old tomb containing nearly 4 dozen victims who had been sacrificed. These victims were servants, concubines or even relatives of an elite individual. They were killed so they could accompany and attend to their master's needs in the afterlife. This concept of an afterlife is found in most cultural groups spaced widely across the earth, including the pre-colonial civilizations of North America, the aboriginal peoples of Australian, and the tribes of Africa.

Coupled with the belief in an afterlife was the widespread practice of what we now call ancestor worship. This is the belief that the deceased not only exist but continue to take interest in their living relatives and may even influence events in their descendants' lives. Religions that incorporated ancestor worship contained practices to guarantee that the dead remained happy. For example: ancient Egyptians buried their dead with essential items to ensure their prosperity in the afterlife. Modern people also continue the practice of ancestor worship to an extent. Mexicans continue to observe the pre–Columbian holiday of El Día de los Muertos, or the Day of the Dead, but tie it to the Catholic Church's All Souls Day celebrated on November 1. This is the day when the souls of departed family members return to earth and are visited in the cemetery. Buddhists of Japan celebrate Obon, the days when believers invite their ancestors into their houses with special food. At the end of the holiday, they burn paper lanterns to send the spirits back to their resting places. Jews light candles for dead relatives on anniversaries of their deaths and pray to redeem them and honor them in heaven. Jews also place written prayer requests on tombstones of saintly rabbis in hopes that they will act as intermediaries with God to grant their prayers. The Catholic Church also believes that the dead can hear our prayers. While it forbids necromancy, communication with the dead, practitioners may pray to those who have been canonized as saints and ask them to offer their prayers to the divine.

While ordinary people can to pray or talk to the dead, the dead do not regularly answer back. In the past, those claiming to be able to have a conversation with a spirit, such as the Oracle of Delphi, were honored, cherished or feared by their communities. But with the expanding influence of the Judeo-Christian and Muslim religions, people who communicated with spirits or ghosts became suspect, even though both the Old and the New Testaments contain stories of ghosts and spirits (1 Shmuel/Samuel 28 and Luke 24:37–40). In Deuteronomy 18:9–12 we are told that speaking to the dead is an abomination practiced by the original settlers of the promised land. Abominations such as this, and such as sacrificing their sons and daughters, were the reasons God took away their land and gave it to the Israelites. The Bible takes calling up the dead very seriously and warns that it might lead to idol worshiping. Muslims, too, believe that the soul, or *ruh*, of a person, especially that of a righteous person, exists after death and can hear and observe the living. But most Muslims believe that calling up the dead, an angel, a devil or a jinn for help or intercession is an act of *shirk*—a sin. The thing to note here is that these religions do not deny the possibility of communication with the dead. Instead, they believe so strongly in it that they warn against even attempting it.

Throughout time, however, there have been those who practiced this form of the occult arts—knowledge hidden from most of us and known only to a select few. In the early 1600s, the legendary Christian Rosenkreuz supposedly founded the Rosicrucian Order, now known as the Ancient Mystical Order of the Rose Cross (AMORC). The Order came to prominence with the anonymous publication, in Germany, of its manifestos,

Fama Fraternitatis, printed in 1614, and *Confessio Fraternitatis,* first printed in 1615. AMORC claims that its roots date from Egypt of 1500 BCE and Pharaoh Thutmose III, and that these teachings were introduced to Europeans in the time of Charlemagne (742–814 CE) by the French philosopher Arnaud ("The Ancient and Mystical Order Rosae Crucis"). This secret society did not follow any organized religion but used metaphysics and mysticism to experience direct conscious union with what they call the "Absolute Divine Mind." Followers believe that humans are immortal spirits made in the image of God, sent to this life to acquire knowledge. When the physical body is worn out, it is discarded, and after a while, the spirit is reborn. However, before this reincarnation, there is a period of time when the soul is in the land of the "living dead," and during this time, it can communicate with loved ones still alive (Heindel, 7–8). In the American colonies, this group had ties to the rites of the Freemasons—a tolerant organization that accepted occult ideas found in pre–Christian religions. Several leaders of our country were members of the Masons, and their ideology of tolerance was reflected in the founding documents that established our government.

Slave owners may also have been more receptive to the possibility of communication with the dead, especially if their slaves came from the Caribbean Islands or Africa, where religions encouraged people to see themselves as spirits and believe that the spirits of their deceased ancestors affected their earthly lives. Despite the conversion of slaves to Christianity, these old ideas persisted and influenced those with whom they lived. European colonists also came into contact with Native Americans, whose religions included a belief in active relationships with spirits of the dead. This is reflected in the words of Chief Si'ahl (1780–1866), known in English as Chief Seattle, of the Duwamish Tribe. His famous speech, given in 1854, was translated by Dr. Henry A. Smith and reprinted in the *Seattle Sunday Star* newspaper:

> Our dead never forget the beautiful world that gave them being. They still love its winding rivers, its great mountains and its sequestered vales, and they ever yearn in tenderest affection over the lonely hearted living and often return to visit and comfort them…. The white man will never be alone. Let him be just and kindly deal with my people, for the dead are not powerless. Dead—I say? There is no death. Only a change of worlds [*Seattle Sunday Star*].

* * *

The 1700s and 1800s saw the rise of American esoteric religions that firmly asserted the human ability to communicate directly with the dead, with angels, or with God. Many of these sprang up in a part of North America historians call the "burned-over district." Located in the western and central parts of New York State, the area is so named because of the intense religious fervor that occurred there at the end of the eighteenth century during the Protestant evangelical movement called the Second Great Awakening. One of these religions was the United Society of Believers in Christ's Second Appearing, more commonly known as Shakers. This group was founded by Anna Lee (1735–1784), who led her followers from Manchester, England, to New York in 1774 (Horowitz, 11). A proponent of celibacy and equal rights for men and women, Mother Ann was thought by her believers to be the second coming of Christ in female form. As part of their charismatic religious practice, Shakers not only danced, shook and shouted, they also prophesied and saw visions of the dead. Some even claimed that the spirit of Mother Ann returned from death to guide her flock as they spread across the frontier into Kentucky.

Jemima Wilkinson (1752–1819), a Quaker, became the avatar of God in 1776. Born in Cumberland, Rhode Island, she contracted typhoid fever and almost died. When she recovered she believed that she actually was dead and had passed into the world of angels. What remained on earth was no longer Jemima, but Christ Himself, who had entered her body, causing her to become neither man nor woman but the holy vessel of God. Known forever more as "The Publick Universal Friend," she traveled around North America giving public sermons and was the first woman preacher many had ever seen. The Publick Universal Friend eventually founded the Society of Universal Friends in 1783 and a colony in upper New York State.

Although Joseph Smith (1805–1844) was born in the newly formed state of Vermont, he and his family moved to Palmyra, New York, when he was 12. This was a time when the burned-over district was experiencing an intense period of revitalization. Joseph Smith used a "seer stone" with magic symbols on it to gain second sight. He also communicated with God the Father, Jesus Christ and the angel Moroni to uncover a book of golden plates (Horowitz, 24). In 1830 he translated and published the plates as the *Book of Mormon*. This same year, Smith also founded the Church of Christ, now called the Church of Jesus Christ of Latter-day Saints. Mormons believe that the dead exist in the afterlife as conscious spirits that can be offered salvations by being baptized by proxy if they had not been baptized in life. The deceased, residing in the afterworld, can accept or decline this baptism.

One influence on these zealous theologians may have been the respected Swedish philosopher, writer and scientist Emanuel Swedenborg (1688–1772), who also communicated with spirits. Swedenborg started his career as a scientist studying, among other things, neurons and the brain. God chose to speak to Professor Swedenborg while he was dining in a London restaurant, and he experienced an awakening. This awakening enabled Swedenborg to travel to heaven and hell, where he talked to angels and demons. He also continued his conversations with God, who explained the meaning of the Bible. In his book *Heaven and Hell,* published in 1758 and translated from the original Latin into several modern languages, he wrote that heaven was divided into two kingdoms, that there were three heavens, and that each heaven consisted of innumerable societies. He knew this intimately because he had visited heaven several times with the help of angels, although he warned others that communication with spirits could be dangerous (Tuchman, 386).

Swedenborg believed that the world was entering a new spiritual age based on divine love and universal acceptance. Contradicting contemporary Christian beliefs, he denied that our souls would face a judgment day. To what should be our great relief, God revealed to Swedenborg that judgment day had already come and passed in 1757. This meant that the ideas of the Second Coming, Resurrection, and the Day of Judgment were passé. After death, our spirits retained our human form and personality, leaving nothing behind except our earthy bodies. After death our spirits continued to learn and gain self-awareness with the help of angels.

Several groups formed during his lifetime to discuss his ideas, giving him a great influence on intellectuals such as English artist and poet William Blake (1757–1827) and New England transcendentalist Ralph Waldo Emerson (1803–1882). Swedenborg also influenced John Chapman (1774–1845), better known as Johnny Appleseed. Johnny not only planted apple seeds wherever he went, but also passed out literature and preached the ideas of the Church of New Jerusalem and Swendenborg to anyone who would listen to him, including Native Americans (Horowitz, 39–40). Today, several churches such as the General Church of New Jerusalem, the New Church, and the Swedenborgian Church base their beliefs on Swendenborg's revelations. Swedenborg was a respected scientist and the publisher of *Daedalus Hyperboreus*, a journal that recorded scientific discoveries. His scientific interests lay in anatomy, physiology and metallurgy. However, in midlife Swedenborg's interests turned to spiritual concerns and he searched to locate the part of the human anatomy that housed our soul.

Scientific advancement in the 1800s—including discoveries of electricity and magnetism—tended to support a belief in the existence of spirits of the dead. The fact that not everyone could see or communicate with ghosts did not mean they did not exist. Electricity and magnetism were also unseen forces that existed, and it was proven that humans contained these mysterious energies. Simple observations showed that certain animals, such as eels, could discharge an electric shock, and in 1791 Italian scientist Luigi Galvani (1737–1798) published the results of his experiments on bio-electromagnetics. Galvani demonstrated that he could make the leg muscles of a frog contract by touching its nerves with metal charged from a Leyden jar. From his experiments, which included observations of suspended frog parts during lightening storms, and making a frog's muscles move by touching them with the nerves of a different frog, the doctor deduced that animals produced and transmitted electricity on their own. He called this phenomenon "animal electricity." His experiments led to the knowledge that nerves are electrical conductors carrying electricity that is used to pass signals to muscles. This knowledge created the fields of neurophysiology and neurology and proved that unseen and insubstantial parts of our bodies created electric energy (Whittaker, 67).

The younger Alessandro Volta (1745–1827) disagreed with Galvani's conclusions. In fact, Volta created the voltaic pile (which will be discussed in a later chapter) to prove this theory wrong (Whittaker, 70). But Galvani was not wrong, and he was not disheartened by Volta's argument. He enlisted the aid of his cousin Giovani Aldini and together, in 1794, they proved that his original conjecture was true. Animal and human tissue are a source of electricity, and human nerves are electrical conductors.

Volta's experiments eventually led to the invention of the telegraph, which allowed people to communicate with each other over long distances. If humans possessed souls that continued to exist after death, it was only logical to assume that human souls were made out of material similar to Galvani's animal electricity. The assumption that the living could communicate with spirits of the deceased did not seem that farfetched. So it was no surprise that people reacted with great enthusiasm when two children, Margaretta (Margaret or Maggie) Fox, aged 15, and Cathie (Kate) Fox, aged 12, residents of the famed burned-over district of New York, claimed to do just that in 1848.

* * *

The Fox sisters were the last children of John Fox, a poor blacksmith, and his wife Margaret, who rented a reputedly haunted house in the small town of Hydesville, New York, about 20 miles from Rochester. Almost as soon as the family moved in they began to hear strange knocking noises in the night and the sounds of furniture moving about. According to testimony signed by Mrs. Fox shortly after the famous events, the youngest child, Kate, began communicating with the spirit she named "Mr. Splitfoot" by first snapping her fingers and then clapping her hands (Horowitz, 54). The spirit responded with knocking sounds that came to be known as "rapping." Communication began in earnest on the eve of April Fools' Day, when Margaret began clapping, and the knocking noises followed the rhythms she made. Mrs. Fox, a kind but naïve woman, assumed that the sound was made by the ghost and asked if it could tell her the ages of her children. When it did, she asked if the noisemaker was a human but got no response. When she asked if it was a wounded spirit, she suggested a two-knock response if the answer was true and a one-knock response for a no. The family eventually worked out a code enabling them to communicate with what they came to believe was the spirit of a 31-year-old peddler who had been murdered in the house. Through this rapping communication, they were informed that his body was still buried in the cellar.

News of this communication with a ghost spread quickly. Visitors came to calm the spirit with prayer, but the noises continued. Neighbors even dug up the basement trying to uncover the skeleton of the ghost, but none was found. In fact, the skeleton was not discovered until 1904, when the cellar wall fell down revealing a secondary wall. Excavations then discovered the entire skeleton and, some say, the murdered peddler's tin box (Maynard, 6).

Many Americans of 1848 wholeheartedly believed that spirits of the dead communicated with these girls. Those who had immigrated from England knew that the ghost of Anne Boleyn had been haunting the country since her execution in 1536, and the ghosts of her successors, Jane Seymour and Katherine Howard, reportedly roamed the halls of their former palace, Hampton Court. In the late 1700s communication was attempted with London's famous Cock Lane ghost. This ghost inhabited the bedroom of Elizabeth Parsons near St. Paul's Cathedral in 1762. After a code was agreed upon, with one knock from the ghost meaning yes and two knocks meaning no, it was revealed that the specter was the deceased sister-in-law and lover of William Kent, an innkeeper and moneylender who had become involved with her and may have poisoned her after his wife's death.

America was primed for communication with spirits, although not all of these spirits were thought to be benign. The slave Tituba confessed to seeing and communicating with a demon, or perhaps the devil himself, during the Salem witch trials of 1692. In 1817, a ghost referred to as the Bell Witch of Tennessee haunted the home of farmer John Bell in Tennessee. The ghost, an old woman whom humans called Kate, pulled the bed sheets of the family's children, sang unintelligently and made tapping sounds. As time went by Kate grew bolder. She pounded on their cabin walls, attacked one of the farmer's nine children, Betsy, and threatened to kill John Bell. The three oldest Bell children, who had served under General Andrew Jackson during the battle of New Orleans, told him about their family's distress. With the intent of vanquishing the poltergeist, the future president of the United States rode to the Bell homestead intending to expel the spirit. Scared out of his wits by the ghost on the very first night, the general and his frightened troops left defeated the very next day (Cellania).

Americans believed in ghosts. Besides the religious testaments of the Shakers and the Quakers, and works of Emmanuel Swedenborg, ghosts were part of popular culture through literature. American author Washington Irving had published his story "The Legend of Sleepy Hollow" in 1820; and *A Christmas Carol* by Charles Dickens had been published in 1843 after a visit was made to the country by the author in 1842. To the dismay of Dickens, British copyright laws were not upheld in the United States, so Americans could read his work for free. Soon after the report of the Fox girls' communication skills, hundreds accepted that the rapping sounds were made by spirits of the dead, and the fact that such extraordinary abilities belonged to Maggie and Kate Fox, regular children born to ordinary parents, made advocates believe that spirits might communicate with anyone, even them.

Mesmerism as Performance Art

Another big reason why so many in America and the rest of the world accepted that the Fox children communicated with ghosts stemmed from the work a hundred years earlier by Franz Anton Mesmer (1734–1815) and his discovery and exploitation of hypnosis. At the same time Galvani and Volta were engrossed with electricity, Franz Anton Mesmer, a physician living in what we now call Germany, was studying the ability of magnetism to heal illness. Mesmer had studied medicine at the University of Vienna. After graduation he stayed in that city, built his practice and developed an interest in astronomy. Through astronomy he met Friar Maximillian Hell (1730–1792), a Jesuit healer and the director of the Vienna observatory. Hell supposedly cured people using a magnetized steel plate. In time, Mesmer came to believe that human beings contained magnetic fields caused by an invisible magnetic fluid. He hypothesized that the sun and the moon influenced the fluid in our bodies just as they created tides in the sea. Mesmer believed that illness was caused by a disharmonious flow of this force, and that by controlling the internal tide and restoring the balance of this fluid, he could promote health.

At first Mesmer had patients swallow a drink laced with iron, which he then manipulated from outside their bodies with magnets. When he had more patients than he could handle at one time, the doctor built wooden tubs called *baquets* (the French word for tub), and filled them with materials such as iron filings, broken glass and magnetized water. Cut into the lid of each *baquet* were holes from which protruded bent iron rods. Each patient grabbed a rod and placed it on the affected area of his or her body. They then joined hands while Mesmer manipulated their animal magnetism by pointing to them or bombarding them with his stares, which he believed contained magnetic rays. Patients would gasp, shake, or go into a trance as obstructions were released, allowing the magnetic fluid, or life force, to flow freely. This often appeared as a crisis, after which the patient was cured.

As time went by, Mesmer realized that certain people, such as himself, could control their own magnetic fluid and the magnetic fluid of others. He called this ability "animal magnetism." He believed that he could transfer his own animal magnetism to his patients and enhance the experiences they were having when holding onto the *baquet*. To heighten the mood, Mesmer decorated his *baquet* rooms with astrological signs and figures, had what he thought was celestial music played in the background, and dressed in the lilac-colored costume of a magician. The lights were dimmed as he walked around his patients, transferring his animal magnetism to them with a whack of his metal wand or the laying on of his hands. Mesmer became a dramatic showman—some would even say a performance artist. Even without the *baquet* he could free blocked magnetic fluid with wild hand motions and the movement of his eyes. Sometimes all he needed to do was stare at a patient, his hands creating the shape of a pyramid, for the patient to go into convulsions and be cured.

Mesmer was forced to leave Vienna when he could not cure a blind musician with his methods. He and his wealthy wife moved to Paris, where he became popular with

Queen Marie Antoinette and members of the French court. He was eventually investigated by a committee formed by the French Academy of Sciences on the request of the queen's husband, King Louis XVI. The American statesman and scientist Benjamin Franklin was appointed to this committee. Because of Franklin's ill health, he invited the other members and a representative of Mesmer to his residence, where a demonstration of mesmerism took place. The committee concluded that they could find no evidence of "magnetic fluid" or "animal magnetism," but they could not doubt that a good number of Mesmer's patients went into a trance during the process and appeared to be cured (Horowitz, 31). Mesmer died in 1815, never fully understanding how important the induced trance state was, but others took notice and continued to research it. Calling themselves "magnetizers," these practitioners used Mesmer's techniques to relieve pain and cure hysteria.

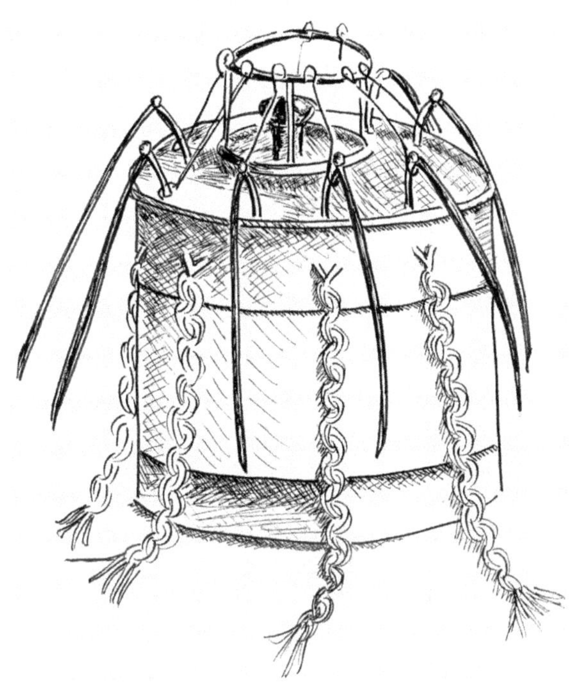

Mesmer, "Baquet" (drawing by the author).

Performance artists such as Charles Lafontaine (1803–1892) recognized the theatrical opportunities to be had by mesmerizing groups of people and took their acts to the stage. A stage mesmerizer might call a person in the audience up to the stage, then begin by waving his hands in front of the subject's face and asking him or her to relax. The mesmerizer would then get in touch with the subject's animal magnetism, and the subject, often times a woman, would be put under his "spell." Lafontaine made quite a name for himself by mesmerizing a lion in the London Zoo and drew large crowds to his shows. Copycats sprang up. These stage mesmerizers realized that they could suggest things to subjects that would amuse a paying audience, such as have them speak in "foreign tongues," bark like a dog, or not feel pain when being pinched, prodded or poked with pins. Crowds flocked to these shows to see their relatives and friends transformed right before their eyes.

Not all those interested in mesmerism were performers. Scottish physician James Braid (1795–1860) attended several of Lafontaine's travelling shows in 1841. Convinced that these effects were real, Braid devoted a year of earnest research to Mesmer's techniques. Braid discarded the concepts of magnetic fluid and animal magnetism and renamed the phenomenon "hypnosis." Although accused of being in league with Satan by the curate of St. Jude's Church of Liverpool, Braid lectured and published papers claiming that hypnosis was a peculiar but normal physiological state. Braid's experiments proved that trance could be induced by eye fixation rather than hand motions or the theatrics of the mesmerist. Under hypnosis a patient could be made to perform a task set by the mesmerizer and even be given posthypnotic suggestions.

But strange things seemed to happen to subjects when in a trance state. Some of them were able to diagnose themselves. Some even diagnosed other people, indicating that they possessed extra sensory perception, or ESP. Braid's objective look at the trance phenomena couldn't stop patients from believing that what possessed them when in trance was spiritual rather than physical, and that when in trance they were actually getting in touch with spirits of the dead, angels, or God. The Chevalier de Barberini believed that when he was in the magnetic state he could feel the illness in the patients he and his colleagues were treating. In 1784 he formed a magnetic group called La Concorde. His powers were tested in 1784 at the Lyon Veterinary College when he correctly diagnosed an ailing horse. Under hypnosis, patients of the La Concorde group saw spirits of their departed friends and family and described "lucids," scenes and people in the other world.

Charles Poyen Saint Sauveur, possibly born on the island of Guadeloupe, was a French doctor who had received magnetic treatments for his digestive and anxiety conditions. He came to America and toured the New England states in 1836–7 (DeVoll, 101). He demonstrated Mesmer's techniques by diagnosing and inducing trances in audience volunteers. Saint Sauveur trained American mesmeric physicians who set up shop or travelled the new country healing and doing demonstrations of their own. In France, mesmerism was for the aristocracy, but in the United States it became a popular movement, embraced by the middle class. Louisa May Alcott's father, Bronson Alcott, was cured of a Typhus fever with mesmeric cures, as was Nathaniel Hawthorne's fiancée, Sophia Peabody (cured of headaches), and Margaret Fuller, the transcendentalist (cured of blinding headaches and back pain) (DeVoll, 103). Traditional medicine of the time was crude and offered nothing better in its stead. People with headaches, liver ailments, back pain, rheumatism, nervous conditions and the like flocked to mesmerists for cures. In Boston alone there were 200 mesmerists in 1843 (102).

In the same year, Andrew Jackson Davis (1826–1910) attended a lecture on mesmerism by Doctor James Stanley Grimes from Castleton Medical College. Davis was a 17-year-old apprentice to a cobbler. Davis understood that becoming a mesmerist would offer him a better life. At home, a local tailor, William Livingston, had been experimenting with this form of hypnotism and found that Davis could easily fall into a trance, or the mesmerized state. Davis became an excellent subject and felt that while in trance state he glowed with light and was weightless, and that his mental powers increased (Horowitz, 35).

Andrew Jackson Davis became a champion of Spiritualism and is credited with formulating Spiritualist beliefs. He described the afterlife and was convinced that spirits of the dead were in communication with spirits of the living on a higher sphere. His background and childhood were similar to that of the Fox sisters. He was born into poverty in the burned-over Hudson Valley of New York state, had little schooling, and was the son of a shoe mender who, like John Fox, reportedly drank too much. In 1839 Davis and his family moved to Poughkeepsie, New York, where the boy was enrolled in a Quaker school. He then followed in his father's footsteps by apprenticing as a cobbler. After attending Dr. Grimes' lecture, Davis continued working with Livingston and discovered that he was able to maintain consciousness while in a magnetized trance state. He was also able to hear his deceased mother speak to him and in time connected with the spirit of the Greek physician Galen, from Pergamon. From 1844 to 1847 Davis toured the region lecturing on mesmerism. During his lectures he communicated with Galen to heal members of the audience by diagnosing and prescribing cures while in trance.

Davis moved to Manhattan in 1845, where he was called the Poughkeepsie Seer and where he conducted public trance sittings. The young journalist Edgar Allen Poe attended one and was so inspired by the event that he wrote the story "Mesmerism in America." In this tale a man is placed under hypnosis at the time of his death and remains in this state for seven months. When he is awakened, he dissolves into a puddle of putrefied goo. Poe failed to mention that the story, one of his most widely read tales, was fiction, and many readers believed that it was a scientific report.

Davis continued to earn money by diagnosing diseases, but while in trance he began communicating with Emanuel Swedenborg, whose work had been translated and made available in America in 1845. The spirit of Swedenborg told Davis, "By thee will a new light appear." (Horowitz, 36). This encouraged the teenager to use trance states to reach the afterworld as Swedenborg himself had done. Davis spent 15 months in a trance dictating *The Principles of Nature, Her Divine Revelations and a Voice to Mankind* to his scribe, the Reverend William Fishbough. In this work Davis dictated his version of the creation of the universe, reinterpreted the Old and New Testaments, and wrote that Jesus was a great reformer, but not divine. Davis affirmed that there was a mother as well as a father god, foresaw the discovery of Neptune and Pluto, and predicted that higher realms of knowledge were available to all through the trance state.

The 800-page book was a great success. Published in 1847, it sold 900 copies the very first week (Horowitz, 36). Of particular interest was his description of the afterlife, which he called the "Summerland," and his explanation of Swedenborg's ideas that souls passed through spheres of existence after death. In addition to ideas from Swedenborg, Davis blended ideas of mesmerism with those of a utopian socialist society proposed by French philosopher, Charles Fourier (1772–1837) (Isaacs, quoted in Kerr and Charles, 81). Davis's work affirmed that through trance, the living could communicate with the dead, and that the dead were benevolent, having been enlightened by the love and light of heaven. These ideas paved the way for a new religion that was to be called "Spiritualism." They also defined the role of the "sensitive" or "medium," and "trance" in spirit communication.

Séance as Performance Art

Soon after the occurrence of the rapping sounds, neighbors of the Fox clan started behaving differently towards them. Some believed that the girls were divinely inspired, but others believed them to be witches. Things got so emotional that the Reverend George York, the minister of the church the family attended, feared that they were in league with the devil and asked the Fox family to leave the congregation. Kate Fox was sent to Rochester to live with their much older sister, Leah Fox Fish, and Leah's daughter Lizzy. Mrs. Fox and Margaret soon joined them with hopes that the spirit would be left behind. But according to Leah's memoirs the rapping, rather than stopping, continued. It got even stronger and mixed with stomping sounds. Worse of all, objects began to float in the air.

The family held sessions in Leah's rented apartment, which coincidentally was located near a Rochester graveyard. As their abilities became known, the family were sometimes invited to hold sessions in the houses of others. The format of these performance pieces, which became known as séances, were strongly influenced by Leah, who supported her family by giving piano lessons. The Fox family did not charge anyone a fee for attending their séances, but occasionally the spirits mentioned to the "guests" that the girls needed certain items, like new shoes or new dresses, and the family gladly accepted gifts.

The rapping noises and other phenomena occurred only when Maggie or Kate were present, but Leah made herself an integral part of the performance by becoming the one who interpreted the messages using a system that included an alphabet board. The Universalist minister the Reverend Charles Hammond described an early séance at the Fox apartment in Rochester. He, the three Fox sisters, and their mother sat around a large table that held a lit candle. The rapping began immediately, coming from every corner of the room; then the table rose from the ground. The Reverend Hammond pressed on it to keep it down, but it rose "a full six feet." The noises grew louder. He also felt fingers pull his hair and tap his knee, then something shook his shoulders (Isaacs, 86).

Leah encouraged her Quaker friends Amy and Isaac Post to witness these spirit communications. The Posts became convinced of the reality of the phenomena and were early enthusiasts of the girls, introducing them to several of their wealthy friends. The couple had recently lost their only daughter, a child of four. To them these séances gave proof of the immortality of the human soul. While many people, especially those of the clergy, remained skeptical that the Fox sisters were communicating with the dead, a growing number of influential people became convinced they were legitimate, having witnessed effects similar to those the Reverend Hammond had. Most importantly, the spirits revealed private information that only the deceased would know. The Fox children's direct communication with the dead offered hope of reunion in heaven with loved ones. Grief could now be replaced with celebration. Death could be seen as birth in a new, spiritual life.

As news of the séances spread, many townspeople grew leery of the mediums' ability to communicate with the dead, and Leah's music business waned, which meant that she needed to earn a living from the spiritual work. Eliab Wilkinson Capron, a newspaper editor from nearby Auburn, New York, heard about the spirit rapping and invited the girls to lead a séance at his home. During the session the spirits communicated that the group should rent the large auditorium in Rochester called Corinthian Hall and charge the public admission to view demonstrations of the sisters' abilities. Capron and George Willets (who also believed in the girls' powers) jumped at the chance to participate. Willets acted as business manager, and Capron would act as the emcee. Capron also set to work writing a pamphlet about the girls that would go on sale after their last appearance in the hall.

The first public demonstration of the Fox sisters occurred on November 14, 1849. In all, 400 people, including several members of the press, paid 25 cents each night to stare at Leah and Margaret, who sat on a platform set on the stage. The first event began with Capron's lecture on the history of the spirit noises, followed by the rapping sounds themselves, barely audible in the large, crowded room. Sensing that much of the audience was skeptical, Capron announced that he would create a five-person committee to examine the Fox sisters and report any improprieties back to an audience the following night. Amy Post stood near the podium and accompanied the sisters as they disrobed. The committee of examiners checked for signs of a hoax but were unable to discover any deceit. Many people believed that the girls made the noises by cracking the bones of their toes, and committee members held the girls' feet, but the noises continued and no trick could be found. When the committee reported this finding to a paying audience on the following night, the crowd demanded that another committee be formed of more skeptical inquirers. This second committee was more rigorous. The men's wives strip-searched the Fox sisters to make sure they weren't hiding noisemakers on their bodies or in their clothes. When the committee members delivered the news in Corinthian Hall that no fraud could be detected, some audience members grew so hostile that police had to be called to escort the family to safety. The uproar was covered by several newspapers. The story of the spirit rappings increased newspaper sales and made the girls famous. Capron's pamphlet quickly went on the market and, at 25 cents a copy, sold well. The notoriety of the Fox girls increased.

Horace Greeley, the respected and influential editor of the *New-York Tribune*, a daily paper, and a weekly national newspaper called the *Weekly Tribune*, wrote a three-column editorial reviewing Capron's book. In response, letters to the editor suggested that spirits might be using electricity to make the knocking sounds. Those who attended the séances in Rochester responded, noting the link between spirit communication and mesmerism. Others reminded readers of the biblical warning that not all spirits were good. Articles by and about "anti-spiritualists" sold papers, too. Stanley Grimes, the country's leading lecturer on mesmerism, believed in clairvoyance, the ability to know things beyond normal sensory contact, and at first believed the Fox sisters might have this psychic ability. However, after attending a séance he decided they were cleverly committing fraud, although he didn't know how (Chapin, 93). Grimes put himself in the middle of the controversial debate on spiritualism as did C. Chauncey Burr, the editor of the *Nineteenth Century Review*. Burr held the belief that the mesmeric powers of suggestion could lead some to imagine they heard the rapping sounds. Both Grimes and Burr toured the lecture circuit, including anti-spiritualism as a topic they knew would draw an audience.

Horace Greeley invited the Fox family to his house for three days to further investigate the phenomena surrounding them. During his investigation the girls were tied up so they couldn't possibly operate hidden mechanisms, as well as made to undress so they could be searched. As before, no trickery could be found. Greeley, mourning the loss of his own son, was convinced of the Fox girls' sincerity. His editorials in which he stated his conviction that the girls did not commit fraud increased their fame.

When Andrew Jackson Davis heard of the girls' ability to channel spirits, he invited them to his Manhattan home. Their spirit communication gave him proof of the righteousness of his visions. Spiritualism was on its way to become a religion, offering proof to millions of the existence of a higher power, of an afterlife, and of the continuous existence of the human spirit after death. Unlike Davis, the Fox sisters never claimed to have divine powers and did not know that they were the start of a new religion. They just were conduits used by the spirits to communicate to the living—they were living, breathing telegraph machines. As such, they were criticized for the mundane messages they relayed. The fact that spirits existed was a powerful affirmation of a higher power. But the question was then, why didn't the spirits have loftier messages to give? And why did they make themselves known to these uneducated, naïve girls?

* * *

As soon as word got out about the Rochester rappings, others discovered that they had mediumistic powers, too. By 1850 there were 100 mediums in Auburn, New York, alone (Isaacs, 86). They used rapping, speaking through the medium, and clairvoyance to communicate. Some mediums got the spirits to play guitars, trumpets, drums or other musical instruments. In 1851 Burr advertised that in his course of study of the phenomenon of spirit communication he investigated forty-seven "mediums" and discovered "seventeen different ways by which mediums in different places produce the sounds" (Chapin, 108). Most followed a standard séance format with guests seated around a table, and most began the session with a prayer. Usually guests would sing a hymn, join hands to "raise the vibrations," and then wait in silence for the spirit to communicate. In a Fox séance, one of the younger sisters, either Maggie or Kate, would fall into a dream state or trance at this point. Other mediums followed suit. The rappings would begin, and someone, possibly the medium, would interpret the communication. Psychic artists, or spirit mediums, also went on tour; their performances filled lecture halls. Magicians and jugglers also went on tour during this time, but these performers had to take out and pay for licenses. Spiritualists could claim that they were scientists demonstrating phenomena and so avoid paying license fees.

Spiritualism was one of the few professions in which women outnumbered the men. The majority of mediums were poor, teen-aged girls like the Fox sisters and Cora Hatch. Hatch was described by popular writer Nathaniel Parker Willis as being seventeen or eighteen, with long, loose hair falling over her shoulders. Despite the "biblical injunction against women preaching" Hatch stood in a pulpit and "a church full of people listening attentively while she prayed" (Braude, 94). Hatch combined the beauty of a young female with the spirit of the male who spoke through her. Men paid to listen to this delicate blond teenager at a time when other women speaking for abolition of slavery and equal voting rights couldn't get an audience. Spiritualism became a venue for women to become leaders, religious or otherwise. Trance medium Victoria Woodhull even became the nation's first female presidential candidate in 1872. She was able to address a joint committee of Congress, the first woman to do so, because the words she spoke came to her in a dream of a Greek elder, the spirit guide she had had since she was a little girl (Horowitz, 62).

By 1853 an editorial in the *Daily National Intelligencer* newspaper condemned spirit rapping, not because it was fraudulent but because belief in spirit communication was having dire consequences to some. The paper reported that several hundred people had to be institutionalized in insane asylums because of what the spirits said to them, and at least seventeen others had committed suicide to join deceased loved ones because they no longer feared death. As time went by, some people committed murder, convinced that the spirits ordered them to do so. Because of the negative depiction of the consequences of believing in spirit communication, mainstream media declined further mention of the topic, forcing devout spiritualists such as Davis to publish their own journals such as the *Banner of Light* and the *Spiritual Telegraph*. Spiritualists organized and joined private spirit circles. They then organized conventions where the faithful openly discussed topics important to them. Soon there were spiritualists churches, spiritualist summer camps and spiritualist Sunday schools. For the most part these were based on Davis' description of the Summerland. In time, more formal organizations formed such as the New England Spiritualists' Association (NESA), which in 1854 proclaimed: "Our creed is simple. Spirits do communicate with man—that is the creed" (Kaplan, 5).

Spiritualism as a religious philosophy was codified by the French educator known as Allan Kardec (1804–1869). Kardec's name at birth was Hippolyte León Denizard Rivail. He was well educated, with several university degrees, and he became interested in séances when mediums first appeared in France. He interviewed ten mediums, asking them a series of questions about spirit communication, the spirit world and the meaning of life, and found that they all had a similar voice—one very different from that of the medium. He believed that these spirits were speaking specifically to him and believed that what they said was a philosophy that he named "Spiritism." Writing under the name of Kardec, his first book on the subject was *Le Livre des Esprits,* or *The Spirits' Book*, written in 1857, which he claimed had been dictated to him through spirit-teaching. The topics in the book included the immortality of the soul, the nature of spirits and their relationship with men, the moral law, the present life, the future life, and the destiny of the human race. As new information was revealed to him by the spirits, he revised his work. This book became the recognized book of spiritualist philosophy and was so popular that Kardec founded the Parisian Society of Psychologic Studies, becoming its president until his death. Kardec also wrote *The Mediums' Book* in 1861, *The Gospel as Explained by Spirits* in 1864, *Heaven and Hell* in 1865 and *Genesis* in 1867. Two of his pamphlets are "What is Spiritism?" and "Spiritism Reduced to its Simplest Expression." Although he himself was not a medium, his group held séances at his house every Friday night until he died. Kardec's ideas traveled to Latin America, where they are venerated. His image on devotional candles can be bought in the United States (Horowitz, 64–65).

Performing Medium: Performance Art

Mrs. Benedict and Mrs. Tamlin, who attended the Fox sister séances, discovered that they also possessed mediumistic powers, but this was not the case for everyone. While spiritualists believed that spirits could come to anyone, they discovered that not everyone had the ability to be a medium, a person able to communicate between the living and the dead. A great number of mediums turned out to be poor, young or sick, which caused their reliability and intentions to be questioned. As Harry Houdini, the famous magician and spiritualist debunker, noted several years after the birth of spirit communication, acting as a medium was a magical way for these unfortunates to attain affluence and attention. Many of the mediums were poor and orphans from the burned-over district of upstate New York.

Some mediums held séances and performed for small audiences, while performance artists such as Ira and William Davenport, whose father was a policeman, exhibited their abilities before large audiences. The Davenport brothers held public and private séances from the 1850s to 1877. Ira reported to Houdini that the brothers earned $40,000 in eight months performing in Mexico and South American in 1876 (Houdini, Exposes, 28). This was a huge sum and the equivalent of $850,000 in 2016 currency. Ira Davenport offered to go on the same tour with Houdini in 1910, telling him that it would be much easier now that there were railroads instead of mules for transportation (Houdini, *Exposes*, 28). The Davenport brothers also toured Europe in 1864–68 and again in 1874–1877. Neither of the brothers claimed to be mediums, but they called their performances séances and let the audiences determine their authenticity.

The Davenport brothers were considered "performing mediums," and they introduced the use of a cabinet into their act. Members of the audience tied the brothers' hands and ankles, proving that they were unable to move on their own. Then they were placed in a large cabinet—a wardrobe—in which musical instruments hung from the top. When the cabinet was shut, rappings sounds could be heard, and the instruments played, supposedly by spirit manipulation. Sometimes a hand appeared at the opening of the cabinet door, yet when completely opened the brothers were found in the same position, still securely bound. The cabinet, they said, was needed to exclude distractions from the audience, allowing the brothers to concentrate and direct their energy towards the spirits. The Davenport brothers were fifteen and thirteen when their father began managing their careers.

At the same time spirits began communicating with the Fox sisters, Daniel Dunglas Home (1833–1886), considered by some to be one of the greatest mediums who ever lived, also summoned spirits to play a musical instrument—this time the accordion. Unlike the Fox girls, Home was never publicly accused of fraud, although some believed that the tricks he used were unveiled in private. The great magician Harry Houdini related that the poet Robert Browning attended one of Home's séances, where the medium materialized the face of Browning's dead son. Browning revealed to Houdini that no son of his had ever died, and that when he grabbed the ghostly face, he discovered that he was actually holding the medium's foot (Houdini, *A Magician*, 41). Houdini also wrote that Home once dematerialized emeralds and when asked to rematerialize them again said he couldn't because they had gone to the "Spirit Land." When a policeman found them in the medium's coat pocket, Home insisted that an evil spirit had put them there.

Having impeccable manners, Daniel Dunglas Home was thought to be an aristocrat, the illegitimate son of an Earl of Home. Despite these occasional minor transgressions, Home made the spiritualist séance fashionable. Born in Scotland in 1833, he died from tuberculosis in 1886. In his book *Incidents in My Life*, Home explained that he was raised by his aunt and uncle and had emigrated with them to America when he was nine years old. Admittedly a child of delicate health, he claimed that he saw the spiritual presence of a deceased friend in a "cloud of brightness" when he was just thirteen. This was a year before the Fox girls began their own spirit communications. Four years later, Home prophesized the death of his mother, who he believed had been "a seer throughout her life" (Home, 20). On the day of his mother's death, a bust of her head appeared to Home solemnly telling him the exact time of her passing—12 o'clock. A few months later, loud rapping and knocking sounds disturbed his Connecticut house. Soon after, furniture began moving and levitating on its own. The rapping sounds followed the teenager when he visited the home of another aunt. Here he was able to communicate with the spirit and discovered it to be his mother speaking to him from beyond the grave: "'Daniel, fear not, my child, God is with you, and who shall be against you? Seek to do good: be truthful and truth-loving, and you will prosper, my child. Yours is a glorious mission—you will convince the infidel, cure the sick, and console the weeping.' This was the first communication I ever received" (Home, 26).

Home's aunt and uncle made him leave their house soon after this communication, believing that he had been speaking to the devil. The town's Methodist minister believed it was the devil, too, but the Congregationalist minister prayed with the teen. Each time a prayer mentioned God or Jesus, gentle raps sounded on their chairs. This convinced Home that although he hadn't sought to have these unusual abilities, they were approved of by the Lord, and he vowed to continue developing his abilities no matter what hardships they might bring.

Living with friends in upstate Connecticut, Home conducted séances in which he healed the sick and communicated with the dead using the Fox sisters' alphabet code, which by then had been published and was well known to all (Home, 27). Although he was only 18 years old, all sorts of people flocked to him—some to get help and consolation, and some to investigate his honesty—putting enormous amounts of pressure on him and making him feel that he didn't have a moment's privacy. People reported that spirits tapped out messages during his séances, heavy tables moved about the room on command in broad daylight, and phosphorescent lights gleamed on the walls. Often the séance table would rise and float in midair. Home never said that the force behind these phenomena proved the existence of life after death. He admitted that he himself was perplexed about what would cause them. He denied he had any strange powers and explained that there was nothing special about him except for the fact that he had always had very bad health.

Respected men such as William Cullen Bryant, the editor of the *New York Evening Post*, Dr. David Wells, a professor at Harvard University, and John Worth Edmonds, a New York Supreme Court judge, were convinced of Home's sincerity and abilities. Home worked on developing his skills until he was able to lie on a chair and have the chair removed from under him so that he floated on air. In this state, he was able to elongate his body and, in front of witnesses, float headfirst out of one window and into the window of another room (Houdini, *A Magician*, 47–48). In 1851 Home was advised to travel to Europe for his tuberculosis. There he met men such as Sir William Crookes, the scientist who pioneered the invention of the vacuum tube. In Europe he performed for leaders including Napoleon III and Queen Sophia of the Netherlands. Crookes became convinced that he saw Home levitate from the ground, although Houdini noted that Crookes was extremely nearsighted and hadn't put on his glasses until after the event (Houdini, *A Magician*, 43).

Home never charged for his services but performed them as a guest of his hosts. If he had charged for communication with the dead, he might have been accused of the crime of fraud. To raise money, Home tried to found a séance group he named the Spiritual Athenaeum. Membership in this group would cost 5 pounds a year and would go to him as his income. Unfortunately for him, the group idea failed and, as did other mediums, he continued to rely on the spirits to suggest that his believers give him "gifts" to meet his needs. This didn't always turn out well for Home. In 1866 the spirit of her deceased husband told Jane Lyon, a wealthy widow, to adopt Home and give him 60,000 pounds. She later changed her mind and sued. The court ruled that Home had defrauded the old woman and made him pay her back (Houdini, *A Magician*, 43).

Early in Home's career Mrs. Maria Hayden (1826–1883) and her husband, William, invited him to hold a séance in their house in Hartford, Connecticut. Soon afterwards an article appeared in the press stating that during the séance participants saw a table move without anyone touching it. Mrs. Hayden began practicing table rapping on her own, and in October 1852 the couple felt sufficiently successful to set sail for England to lecture on the science of what they called "electro-biology." Unfortunately, Mrs. Hayden's lecture was not a success; however, her presentation was followed by another by a Shaker, Mr. David Richmond, who introduced table-turning to the British. This kind of communication with spirits did not require a paid professional and was more closely related to mesmerism and animal magnetism. Table-turning became a popular pastime in Britain and in France despite disclaimers by scientists such as Michael Faraday that table-turning was caused by the unconscious muscular action of séance attendees. By 1855 invitations for "tea and table-turning" became quite common in Britain, and Mr. David Weatherhead, a grocer, started what was to become the *British Spiritual Telegraph*, a magazine that published articles about spiritual phenomena. Spiritualism was the first movement exported from the United States to Europe (Horowitz, 64). There was little entertainment at that time; not everyone could play a musical instrument or sing. Speaking to the dead proved even more popular than watching a demonstration of magnetism or electricity.

It has been reported that besides Napoleon III of France, another leader of a country, Queen Victoria, tried to communicate with the dead and practiced table-turning. In the United States there were rumors that Mary Todd Lincoln invited the medium Nettie McGarvie to the White House to hold séances that were attended by her husband, the president. Abraham and Mary Lincoln had lost their son Willie in 1861. Believing that her son continued to exist brought comfort to his mother and possibly to the president as well. In 1862 Nettie wrote in her autobiography that a strong, masculine spirit spoke through her and told the president not to delay the Emancipation Proclamation (Maynard, 65). In 1863 Abraham Lincoln attended another séance in Georgetown. Nettie's "familiar" spirit, Dr. Bamford, spoke through her, telling the president that the northern soldiers were disheartened and ready to give up. He advised the president to go to the front with his family to rally and unite the troops. At another of Nettie's séances, President Lincoln also witnessed a piano "waltzing around the room" in time to the music (Maynard, 79). The president sat on the piano as did others, but the force was so strong that the piano continued to move. Nettie believed that Lincoln was in communication with numerous mediums such as Charles Foster, Charles Colchester, Mrs. Lucy A. Hamilton and Charles Redmond. As a youth Lincoln reportedly consulted fortune tellers and was criticized in Cleveland's *Plain Deal* newspaper for having consulted with "spooks" (Maynard, 85).

Sir Arthur Conan Doyle, the creator of the Sherlock Holmes mystery series, was a firm believer in spiritualism. Raised as a Catholic, Conan Doyle earned a degree in medicine from Edinburgh University. Skeptical of spiritualism at first, he came to be its most ardent supporter by 1917, especially after the death of his own son. He likened his belief in spirits to his belief in lions. He had never seen a lion, but he believed that they existed. He grew to be certain that intelligence could exist apart from the human body (Polidoro, *Charlie, Charlie*, 19). Conan Doyle, an expert on the subject, described D. D. Home as being unusual for having four distinct types of mediumships: trance, clairvoyance, direct voice, and physical.

While in trance, a trance medium lets his or her consciousness step aside so that the spirits can speak through her or him. Nettie McGarvie had several spirits talk through her, and she claimed she had no memory of what was said afterwards. Nettie also had a little messenger named "Pinkie" who gave her messages when she was not in a trance. Physical mediums also needed to be in a trance state. While the mediums were in trances, the spirits used their energy to do things such as manipulate objects, make rapping or knocking sounds, levitate objects, produce smells, cause drafts, or create lights. Clairvoyant mediums possessed extrasensory perception. They could tell the future or diagnose an illness, and they were fully conscious. "Direct voice" mediums had enough energy that the spirits could create a voice independent of the medium. The medium was not in a trance and could even have a conversation with the spirit. This was very difficult to do. It was thought that the dead functioned at a higher "vibration" level than the living. To communicate with them, the living need to do something to raise their level of vibration like pray, sing, or laugh. Enjoying nature could also raise one's vibrations. Conversely, the dead had to do something on their side to lower their vibrations. This was thought to be why not every spirit or person could communicate between worlds.

These four types mentioned by Conan Doyle do not encompass all of the shenanigans going on at séances in the late nineteenth and early twentieth centuries. The eventual husband of Kate Fox, Henry D. Jencken, a London legal scholar and advocate, described what could be expected from a medium in 1869: levitation of objects and of the medium; sounds of knocks or raps; sounds of words, music, birds, etc.; the playing of musical instruments; spirit writing; elongation of the medium's body; fluids held in the air without containers; aroma of flowers; the appearance of fruit and vegetables; and the appearance of body parts or spirit forms (Pearsall, 81).

Kate Fox was hired by the inventor Horace H. Day to give private sittings in 1854. She was then hired by Charles F. Livermore, a rich banker from New York, to do the same. She was said to have held 400 sittings from 1860 to 1866. Kate began these séances by interpreting rapping noises but then developed the ability of "spirit writing." On the 43th sitting for Livermore a substance rose from the floor, illuminated by psychic light. This formed into the shape of a human head that was believed to be Estelle, Livermore's deceased wife. While Kate's hands were held, writing appeared on cards in Estelle's own script (Isaacs, 100). Kate was also able to conjure the spirit of Benjamin Franklin for Livermore. Franklin was the most sought-after spirit by mediums of the day because he had discovered electricity. After several years, Estelle decided she had had enough and declared that she would no longer appear. Livermore remarried and paid for Kate to travel to London, England, where she continued to hold séances, was married, and had children. In trance, Kate produced automatic writing with either her left or right hands, and sometimes both at once.

Home was also able to materialize hands and faces of the spirits. The American medium Mrs. Nelson Holmes had this same ability; she arrived in London in the 1870s. Author and actress Florence Marryat (1833–1899) and her childhood friend Anne paid ten shillings each to attend her séance. It was the first one Marryat had ever attended, and she was so impressed that she wrote about the effects in her book *There Is No Death* (1891). Mrs. Holmes opened the folding door to two rooms and placed a square of black fabric with a hole in its center over the opening. Marryat and Anne went into the back room to make certain that the door was locked and that no one was inside. Then they went back to the front room and sat down. It was a cold February night and they were the only ones in the séance circle. They waited past nine p.m. and were just about to give up when they saw a white, indistinct cloud materialize and then disappear. The white mass did this several times and finally hovered on the fabric, where the face of Anne's deceased mother appeared, wearing the cap she had been buried in. Anne asked the spirit several questions, and the spirit nodded yes or no. Anne then saw a former boyfriend who had died in a sudden accident. The spirit still had a clot of blood on his face and hair from his fatal fall. Marryat saw the face of a dearly departed friend but didn't recognize him at first. When she finally did, she ran towards him, but the phantom quickly vanished, never to return, while Anne's mother and friend came back several times. Finally, Anne saw the eyes and nose of a little girl. Again she didn't recognize them, but she realized later that they belonged to her dead baby, who had lived for only ten days (Marryatt, 9). To Florence Marryat this proved that the dead continued to age in the afterlife, as described by Henry Wadsworth Longfellow in his poem "Resignation" about his beloved lost child, Fanny:

> Not as a child shall we again behold her;
> For when with raptures wild
> In our embraces we again enfold her,
> She will not be a child;
> But a fair maiden, in her father's mansion,
> Clothed with celestial grace;
> And beautiful with all the soul's expansion
> Shall we behold her face!

Marryat went on to become a medium herself and wrote convincingly of the existence of the spirit after death in her book.

Professor Johann Carl Friedrich Zöllner, the chair of astrophysics at Leipzig University and a colleague of Crooke, wrote impressively about the psychic phenomena he had witnessed in 1877–78 in his work *Transcendental Physics,* which was translated into English in 1880. The psychic artist Henry Slade (1840–1905) led séances for Zöllner where spirits tied knots into a rope made of hemp that Zöllner held. The rope was tied at one end with a knot to form a loop. In broad daylight, Zöllner placed the rope on the table and held his fingers over the knot, letting the rest of the loop fall to his lap. Zöllner (18) attests that Slade's hands were on the table and visible at all times. To his amazement, and the amazement of his friends, many of them professors and scientists, the rope was knotted several times. Zöllner and Slade repeated this phenomenon, always with the same results.

While the knot trick impressed some, Slade's most important contribution to the psychic arts was his invention of slate writing, or communicating with spirits through the written word. In a session described by Zöllner that took place in the scientist's home, Slade placed a clean, newly purchased slate and pencil above the head of one of the circle members, Professor Braune. As soon as he did, the scratching of the pencil could be heard. When they looked at the slate there was writing on it. At the same time Zöllner's bed, also in the room but behind a screen, moved at least two feet from the wall. Zöllner and his friends asked Slade what this meant, but the medium shrugged and said he didn't know (Zöllner, 32). At another session a few days later Zöllner's screen dividing his room completely broke apart with a loud bang, frightening the group. Slade placed a newly cleaned folding slate on the table, keeping both his hands in sight. Again the noise of a slate pencil was heard. When it stopped, Slade picked up the slate and found this message written on it: "It was not our intention to do harm: forgive what has happened" (35).

Under the eyes of Zöllner and his colleagues, Slade's spirits played the accordion, rang bells and briefly showed their small, red hands. Around the circle, spirits would touch participants, grasp or pinch them. Sometimes they left wet spots on the slates. Zöllner recorded that strange things were happening around, and to, Slade. The medium was sometimes but not always able to move the needle of a compass with the wave of his hands, and while Slade was a guest at Zöllner's house, forces around Slade caused pieces of wood and coal to fall from the ceiling. A pocket knife even flew out of Zöllner's suit, sailed through the air and struck another guest. The spirits continued to write on slates, but skeptics criticized the messages contained in the writing and called it "commonplace, and so completely within the compass of human knowledge" (Zöllner, 116). People expected genius from the deceased, or, at the very least, good spelling. Both of these were sadly lacking.

Perhaps the strangest manifestation of spirit by psychic performance artists was "ectoplasm"—a sticky white substance that seeped from the orifices of mediums such as Eva Carrière (born in 1886) and the womb of Kathleen Goligher (born in 1898.) The word *ectoplasm* was coined by the French spiritualist Charles Richet in 1903. In Victorian English it was called *teleplasm* or *ideoplasm*. Ectoplasm, first thought to be invisible to the naked eye, was sometimes captured on photographic plates. Rods of the stuff were thought to protrude so far out from the body of the medium that sounds were made as it banged into the far corners of the room. Belief in this substance moved the mediums further and further away from proving the continued existence of the soul after death and closer to the X-rated performances of burlesque.

Eva Carrière's name at birth was Marthe Beraud. She began holding séances in Algeria, where her father was stationed when she was 19. Here she materialized the spirit of a 300-year-old Indian Brahman called Bien Boa. However, others claimed that Boa was one of her hired hands, a living, breathing person dressed up to play the part. These accusations didn't deter the lovely Eva, and she and her various companions traveled to Europe to perform. Eva mixed spiritualism with pornography by beginning her sessions in the nude and having someone inspect her internally to show that she had nothing hidden either on or in her body. She was then sewn into tights with a net covering her face. She entered a cabinet while participants in her séance sat around a table repeating, "*Donnez, donnez,*" the French word for "give." Fully prepared, participants urged the ectoplasm to enter her from the great beyond. Her sessions began at 7:30 p.m. and could last hours past midnight. When she emerged from her cabinet, streams of ectoplasm were found inside the netting. Described as looking like plaster or froth, the stuff covered her eyes or nose. Eva even pulled the rubbery ectoplasm out of her mouth. In the folds of the ectoplasm were terra-cotta-colored faces of those who had passed away (Polidoro, 42).

Although this was later than Victorian times, Sir Arthur Conan Doyle thought the ectoplasm thrilling when he attended a session in the early 1920s in France. On examination of the substance he thought it felt like an umbilical cord, but wider and softer, and it disappeared when examined with an electric torch. Conan Doyle thought the manifestation crude, but still a sign of the forces beyond this life, but then Conan Doyle had recently lost his son in World War I and went on to believe in the existence of the Cottingley fairies after seeing photographs taken of drawings by Elsie Wright, age 16, and Frances Griffith, aged 9. (The children did not want to hurt Conan Doyle's feelings, so they kept the origin of their photographs a secret until 1981.)

When Eva Carrière arrived in London, she and her accomplice were investigated by a committee set up to expose fraudulent mediums, and Harry Houdini was one of the men chosen by the Society of Psychical Research to examine her. He wrote that Eva was stripped and searched and then made to drink coffee to discolor anything she might be hiding in her stomach. Eva put on tights and a black lace bag was sewn around her to ensure that she couldn't put anything into her mouth. Her accomplice, Mme. Bisson, put Eva into a hypnotic sleep and guests repeated the word *donnez* in unison for a quarter of an hour when they were told that she would "bring forth" the ectoplasm. After a three-hour wait, the medium was unwrapped. Houdini admitted that he saw something he described as white plaster come from her nose with a cartoon face colored on it. She then took a "load" out of her mouth. The magician believed that it was a trick, and the ectoplasm was inflated rubber that Eva regurgitated. When the substance disappeared, he felt sure it was because of sleight of hand (Houdini, *A Magician*, 170).

Houdini, Conan Doyle and Twentieth Century Investigations

Eva wasn't the only medium investigated by a committee. From the beginning of spirit contact, committees of investigators and individuals such as Harry Houdini were more interested in disproving the tricks used by the mediums than in the messages they had to tell. These investigators were generally skeptics who chose not to believe in spirits no matter what and took part in séances only with the intent of proving the mediums to be frauds. True believers such as Florence Marryat and Sir Arthur Conan Doyle felt that these skeptics scattered the good will around the table (Polidoro, *Final Séance*, 87). They believed the spirits could feel the negative energy these investigators brought, making spirit communication difficult or even impossible.

The Fox sisters were examined by faculty at the University of Buffalo Medical School in February 1851. Doctors noticed that Margaret's face showed effort when the rappings occurred and deduced that she must have been creating the noises with "voluntary muscular contractions" of her skeleton (Maynard, 92). These doctors noted that a different woman could make snapping noises with her dislocated knee joints. They conjectured that these muscular contractions also made the furniture move and jarred the doors and séance table. The sounds coming from different parts of the room were produced by ventriloquism or by delusion on the part of the guests. For proof, Dr. Lee, one of the examiners, had the girls sit with their legs out in front of them, resting on cushions, and noted that no noises were made; but the older sister, Leah, argued that the reason the spirits didn't appear was the harsh treatment the girls endured. Houdini, writing about the girls years later, agreed with the doctors' findings. As a contortionist, he thought that the ability to make rapping sounds with the joints of one's toes was easily developed by children younger than twelve and that with practice could continue throughout their lives. He wrote in his investigative book *A Magician Among the Spirits* (1924) that Kate and Maggie Fox were led like lambs by their sister Leah, who was more than 20 years older than they. As for the messages the spirit raps related that were so personal and irrefutable, Houdini concluded that Leah secretly signaled the girls to tell them what to communicate.

In the 1860s and 1870s mediums were subjected to severe indignities. They were inspected, handcuffed, their necks put in metal collars and their feet tied. Others welcomed inspections; Henry Slade advertised that he would give $1,000, an enormous sum at the time, to anyone who could prove him a fraud. At the height of his popularity, Slade was a millionaire.

In England, the London Dialectical Society was formed in 1867, created to investigate these spiritual manifestations and report back to the public. Their report was completed in 1870. The society did not choose to publish it, but the committee members did. The thirty-three-member committee heard testimonies from thirty-one witnesses and discovered that circumstances for séances varied. Not all séances were successful and certain people hindered communication altogether. But witnesses stated that among the phenomena, they heard sounds and saw bodies rise in the air. Hands and fingers appeared and touched them, and musical pieces played without instruments. Three out of the thirty-one witnesses informed the committee that red hot coals were applied to them and they were unharmed. Eight were given information at a séance that turned out to be a correct prophesy of future events and only one reported receiving information that turned out to be false.

In 1884 Henry Seybert left the University of Pennsylvania funds to establish a committee to investigate mediums, named the Seybert Commission. The ten committee members included the university provost, a paleontologist, a chemist, and a medical doctor. The commission examined Henry Slade, who had recently returned to the United States from Germany. In their report, published in 1887, the committee denounced him for using sleight of hand and foot to accomplish his feats. The committee found that the commotion the psychic artist caused by his convulsive movements hid some of the tricks he used. They also discovered that he substituted slates that he had previously written on for clean ones during the séance. When the examiners watched his prepared slates too carefully, no spirit writing occurred. Slade had already been proven to be a trickster when he moved to London in 1876. A skeptical inquirer wrestled a slate from his hands before a sitting and found that it was already filled with writing. Slade was arrested for fraud and the case went to trial. The star witness was a British magician, John Nevil Maskelyne, who duplicated all of Slade's effects for the court. Slade was found guilty and sentenced to prison for three months, but escaped to France and then to Germany (Houdini, *A Magician*, 79).

The Seybert committee also investigated another slate medium, Mrs. Patterson. Her spirit "control" was not able to produce slate writing when given a sealed package containing a slate and a pencil. The chairman of the committee, sympathetic to spiritualism, was so eager to have her prove her abilities that he let her take another sealed package of slate and pencil home with her. The committee was excited when she reported days later that the pencil was now on top of the slate, the signal that the spirits had come. They realized that they undertook a grave responsibility in obtaining proof of the afterlife. Unfortunately, when they investigated the sealed slate, they found that the wooden frame did not fit properly and allowed a knife to push the pencil out of the package. When they opened the package and looked at the slate, there was nothing written on it except scratches made when the pencil was pushed out, and the wood was discolored from the rust of the knife. The committee also noted that there were very few mediums whom the spiritualists themselves believed were honest all the time. Spiritualists brushed this aside by saying that the mediums were only human and acted fraudulently at times when the spirits weren't cooperating so as not to disappoint their customers.

At the height of Spiritualism's popularity there were eight million to eleven million people who identified themselves as Spiritualists—believers in communication with the dead. Marcellus Ayer started the First Spiritualist Temple in the 1880s when he heard the voices of his family member at a séance. Ayer (1838–1921) was born in Maine and served in the Union army during the Civil War. He founded a lucrative grocery business and was a man of means. He was disappointed that Spiritualism did not live up to its potential and believed that the medium should not be more important than the message he or she delivered. Worship services were devoted to God and not to communication with the spirits, but followers practiced trance mediumship, also known as channeling, which supposedly requires the strongest degree of control. In Ayers' vision, the group was not a new religion but a way for all faiths to find common ground. The First Spiritualist Temple and Ayer Institute is located today in Brookline, Massachusetts. One of its beliefs is that mediumship and channeling are ways to bridge the worlds of spirit and flesh. Other groups formed and are still in operation such as the Cassadaga Spiritualist Camp in Central Florida, founded in 1895, and the Lily Dale Assembly, the world's largest center for the religion of spirituality. Spiritualists have been meeting in that area of New York since 1877.

Because many mediums were accused and found guilty of fraud, belief in communication with spirits waned. In 1886 Margaret Fox Kane (she claimed she had married the famous Arctic explorer Elisha Kent Kane before he died in 1857), held a lecture at the New York Academy of Music. She told the audience, which numbered in the thousands, that she wanted to repent for all the evil she had done, and she admitted that she had make the rapping sounds first with an apple tied to a string and then with her foot. Three doctors came on stage to examine her and verify that the sounds were made by the action of the first joint of her big toe. This lecture was also published in the Sunday edition of the *New York World* newspaper (Polidoro, *Final Séance*, 116).

Time had not been kind to the medium. She had converted to Catholicism because of her husband, and when he died, his family denied that the marriage had actually taken place. They refused to give her the annuity she claimed he left her. Without this money she was penniless and was forced to go back to work as a medium for the next thirty years, a thing that she hated to do. Alcoholic and penniless, Margaret was paid $1,500 to lecture and help Reuben Briggs Davenport write a memoire entitled *The Death-Blow to Spiritualism: Being the True Story of the Fox Sisters,* in which she confessed that communication with the spirits was a hoax and that her sister Leah had been in on the deception in 1888 (Isaac, 103).

Margaret's denial-of-spiritualism lecture tour turned out to be a failure and was cancelled. No one knew what to think about her confession. Isaac K. Funk, a spiritualist clergyman and the founder of Funk and Wagnall's Company, publisher of religious books and then the encyclopedia and dictionary, wrote that Margaret had by this time sunk so low that for $5 she would have said anything; therefore her words of denial could not be believed. Other spiritualists thought that evil spirits had caused her to make this false confession. She and her sister Kate were well-known alcoholics. Houdini believed that the reason for Margaret's drunkenness was that her hypocrisy had proved too much for her, and she couldn't stand living a lie (Houdini, *Exposes*, 9). Margaret recanted her confession the following year and resumed her life as a medium. When she died in 1893, thousands of spiritualist mourners attended her funeral.

The aftermath of World War I, a war that left more than 17 million dead soldiers, saw a resurgence of psychic performances. The thought of an afterlife was comforting to those who had lost so much. Arthur Conan Doyle grew to be the great defender of spiritualism, as was his friend, the physicist Sir Oliver Lodge (1851–1940), who held important patents on radio technology. He was a member of a paranormal investigative organization called the Ghost Club, and another one called London's Society for Psychical Research. His studies on electromagnetic radiation made him believe that the universe was filled with ether, and that this was where the spirits lived. This was all explained in his book *Survival of Man,* written in 1909. After his son died in World War I he attended séances with the medium Gladys Osborne Leonard and wrote a book of these experiences entitled *Raymond, or Life and Death,* published in 1916. In it he related the description the spirit of his son gave him of an afterlife full of trees, cigars and whiskey. Considered insane by fellow scientists, Lodge continued to lecture and write books such as *Why I Believe in Personal Immortality* in 1927 and *The Reality of the Spiritual World,* published in 1930.

Like Lodge, Conan Doyle was a member of the Ghost Club and joined London's Society for Psychical Research in 1887; he was also a Freemason. He published books on the topic of spiritualism such as *The New Revelation: What Is Spiritualism?* in 1918 and *The Wanderings of a Spiritualist* in 1921.

For a while Conan Doyle and Harry Houdini shared an interest in the psychical arts. Harry Houdini was born in Budapest, Hungary, in 1874. He immigrated to the United States with his family when he was 4 years old. His father, Samuel Weiss, was a rabbi who died in 1892. His mother, Cecelia Weisz, lived until 1913. The magician had a very close bond with his mother and was devastated when she died. Conan Doyle's second wife, Jean, claimed to have mediumistic ability and could communicate with the dead through the power of the written word. Finding themselves in Atlantic City at the same time as Houdini, the Conan Doyles invited him to attend a séance where Lady ConanDoyle claimed she was in contact with Houdini's mother. In front of the magician, the medium was taken over by the spirit and wrote furiously. When she handed him the letter Houdini saw that it was in English, a language his mother never learned to read or write. The letter also addressed him as "Harry" when his mother called him by his birth name, "Ehrich." Houdini turned away from the Conan Doyles and came to believe that spiritualism was dangerous. In his book, he quoted from an article that appeared on February 9, 1920, in the *Daily Sketch* newspaper that reported a famous mental specialist saying that thousands of people had been driven to insane asylums because of spiritualism (Houdini, *A Magician*, 143). He declared that mediums only wanted money. They were fakers who would go so far as to remove the fingers of the dead, and make rubber molds of them, in order to place fingerprints on objects to make relatives believe their departed loved ones still existed in the spirit world. Houdini, the consummate magician, analyzed reports of mediums and deduced fantastic ways used to accomplish their tricks. These entailed accomplices, trap doors, spasms, convulsions, and hypnotism. He noted that there was usually a time period of days between the initial contact with a medium and a scheduled séance. This would allow these conniving crooks to bribe telephone operators for information, attend funerals, talk to the client's prostitutes, open and then reseal letters, pick the pockets of unsuspecting clients, talk to disgruntled employees, and even enroll spies in private schools to talk to the children of the deceased—all to discover supposedly "private" information they could use during future séances to make the unsuspected believe they were communicating with the dead. Lady Conan Doyle had spent the afternoon previous to Houdini's séance talking to Houdini's wife, Bess. The magician believed that this was how she gained the private information contained in the letter she wrote for him.

As a young magician, Houdini himself had led séances, calling them "intercommunication between the dead and the living." He admitted that he used tricks and planted accomplices in the audience to gather information. He didn't see any problem with this until he lost loved ones of his own. Then he understood how serious tricking people to believe in spirits was. To Houdini, it should have been a crime. In the foreword to his book *A Magician Among the Spirits*, he claimed that he firmly believed in a "Supreme Being and in the hereafter and that ... [his] mind has always been open and receptive and ready to believe," but after years of research and investigation, he was further from believing in spirits than at the start. He followed this statement with the warning that belief in spirits of the dead could result in suicide or even the murder of innocent children. In his opinion spiritualism had swept the world off its feet by 1924, and he deemed it a threat to health and sanity.

Houdini claimed to have attended more than 100 séances for the purpose of investigation. He also conferred with the most famous mediums of his time. He read everything he could about the topic and had resources dating back to the 1400s in his library. In his 35-year investigation he found not one experience that he believed was genuine; all were fraudulent. But sharp mediums, such as the famous mystic Edgar Cayce, could fool even brilliant men like Thomas Edison, who admitted in the October 1920 issue of the *American Magazine* the he had "been at work for some time building an apparatus to see if it is possible for personalities which have left this earth to communication with us."

Houdini thought that those who believed communication with the dead was happening either had "deluded brains" or were anxious to believe (Houdini, *Magician*, foreword). As to the proponents of Spiritualism, especially the scientists and famous people such as Sir Conan Doyle and Edison, he believed that they were sincere in their beliefs and as such even more dangerous because they caused thousands of others to believe in this dishonesty. Houdini was so convinced of the dangers of false mediums that he testified before the U.S. House of Representatives in February 1926 in favor of passing the "Anti Fortune Telling" bill. The magician wanted to be clear that he was not attacking Spiritualism as a religion, but only the part where the medium interacted with the dead. In his speech before Congress Houdini said: "[It] is a fraud from start to finish. There are only two kinds of mediums, those who are mental degenerates, and who ought to be under observation, and those who are deliberate cheats and frauds. … In 35 years I have never seen one genuine medium. Millions of dollars are stolen every year in American, and the Government has never paid any attention to it, because they look upon it as a religion" (Polidoro, *Final Séance*, 188).

The anti-spiritualist campaign reached its peak in March 1926 in Chicago. Houdini was not the only magician to debunk mediums, and the names of those who were proven to be fakes were made public for all to see. Some mediums, such as Mrs. Benninghoefen, who used the name of Anna Clark, were remorseful. Mrs. Benninghoefen was not only a medium but also taught several others the ropes of the psychic arts. Wanting to come clean, she performed at a press conference arranged by Houdini and admitted: "I really believed in Spiritualism all the time I was practicing it." She confessed that she would "help" the spirits out by moving objects and pretending they spoke through her. "I thought I was justified in trickery because through trickery I could get more converts to what I thought was a good and beautiful religion" (Polidoro, *Final Séance*, 187).

Some thought Houdini himself had psychic power to open locks, handcuffs, and straight jackets, or that he dematerialized to escape. And when he was having difficulty, his assistant, his wife Bess, would whisper that he should call on the spirits to help him. But the magician wrote, "I accomplish my purpose purely by physical, not psychical means. The force necessary to 'shoot a bolt within a lock,' is drawn from Houdini the living human being and not a medium" (Houdini, *A Magician*, 211) During his later performances he spent more and more time exposing the secrets of the mediums and less time on his physically exhausting escapes. Medium after medium was offered huge sums of money by *Scientific American* magazine if they were found to have real powers by an investigative committee including Houdini, but he debunked them all—some by very complicated means. Conan Doyle believed that Houdini always found objections to any medium because it kept him constantly in the public's eye.

The public was addicted to spirit communication as an alcoholic was to alcohol. Houdini described spiritualism as "mental intoxication" and wrote that it was always fatal to the human mind. Houdini toured with a lecture he called "Do the Dead Come Back?" and offered a $10,000 challenge to anyone he could not prove to be a fraud. He became a sensation in the news, which was good for him because in his 50s he was getting too old and physically damaged to perform as he once did. He was an anti-spiritualist in the decade of the 1920s—the time of President Calvin Coolidge and the prohibition of alcohol.

In the mid–1920s angry spiritualists and mediums such as Mina Crandon, a.k.a. the medium Margery, began predicting Houdini's death, but he was not alarmed. They had been predicting it for a decade. After he died in 1926 from peritonitis spread by his burst appendix, his wife continued to offer the $10,000 as a reward to any medium who could tell her the secret code words Houdini promised he would say from the afterlife. It wasn't until the words "Rosabelle believe" were published in the public press that mediums started to receive them from the other side.

* * *

The beliefs in communication with the dead that flourished during this time forged a new religion, Spiritualism, that still exists today. Although this religion's members are not as numerous as they used to be, the religion's ideas have changed the way traditional religions approach the ideas of God, heaven, hell and death. According to many religions, we possess a soul, and we will not have to wait for the end of days but rather will go directly to heaven for our rewards. It is not unusual to believe, as modern psychic artists would have it, that the souls of the dead watch over us and are there for the important times of our lives. These souls gain knowledge and continue to grow after death. Some believe that the spirits of the dead become angels and that God calls us to him because of his love. Author Mitch Horowitz wrote in his work *Occult America* that spirit communication revives after major upsets or wars, and with these revivals come people who either believe that they have special powers to communicate with spirits or who recognize an opportunity for economic gain though convincing others that they do.

But not everyone can afford to go to a medium or psychic, and for a while mediums were replaced by the Ouija board, based on the homemade talking boards that became popular in the 1850s. Instead of raps on a table, the spirits would communicate directly and spell out their messages by pointing to letters on a board using a three-legged pointer with a hole in the center called the *planchette*. They could also move the planchette directly to the word "yes" or "no." William Fuld patented a new version of the talking board in 1892, and while the name sounds ancient, and possibly Egyptian, he explained that he invented it from the French word *oui*, meaning yes, and the German word ja, also meaning yes. Fuld made at least one million dollars from the device, and he and his family manufactured it during World War II and the Korean War. Parker Brothers bought the rights to the Ouija board from the Fuld family in 1966 just when the Vietnam War was escalating. In 1967 sales of the board topped two million dollars. While most people consider the Ouija board a harmless game, others believed and still believe today that with it, one can contact spirits—benign and evil. Horowitz informs us that the board inspired writers such as Sylvia Plath, Ted Hughes and James Merrill in their work. Merrill (1926–1995) won prestigious prizes for his epic poem *The Changing Light at Sandover* and for *The Book of Ephraim,* both based in part on messages he received from spirits using the Ouija board.

Demonstrations of communication with the dead by psychic artists continue to this day. In 2011 Horowitz gave a presentation with Paul Selig, a "spiritual channel," at the

Observatory in Brooklyn, New York; they called the session "Mediumship: Its History and Today." Selig claims that he has been channeling spirits for at least 20 years. He held channeling workshops at the Esalen Institute in California, Edgar Cayce's Association for Research and Enlightenment in New York, and the Jungian Institute in Vermont.

Joseph Ross, a psychic astrologer, worked with Jeffrey Vallance on a performance piece entitled *Ghost Writers,* performed at the CBI Gallery in Los Angeles in 2015. The actor and director, Paul Williams, captured a digital image of the spirit of his mother an hour and forty-five minutes after she died. The book he wrote about this photograph, *Image of a Spirit,* was published in 2015. The forward of his book was written by Gary Schwartz, who is a professor of psychology, medicine and neurology and the director of the Laboratory for Post-Materialist Science and Spirituality at the University of Arizona in Tucson, Arizona. Schwartz claims that he can prove that the dead communicate with us through human mediums. He is author of *The Afterlife Experiments, The G.O.D. Experiments* and *The Sacred Promise.*

Despite Houdini's warnings, the psychic arts are alive and well today, as are those who practice them, the psychic artists. Many of these are members or attend workshops and lectures at Lily Dale Assembly in Chautauqua County, in upstate New York. Instead of burning at the stake people who claim to communicate with the dead, we pay to attend psychic artists' readings and watch John Edwards and Teresa Caputo, the Long Island Medium, on the television or on the internet. But just as there are psychic artists, there are those who continue to debunk them. In 1976 the Committee for Scientific Investigation of Claims of the Paranormal (CSICOP) was formed by the magician James Randi, the popular science writer Martin Gardner, and others in response to the self-proclaimed psychic Uri Geller's claims that he could bend spoons using only his mind. James Randi believed that Geller bent the spoons when no one was looking, and he foiled the psychic when he was demonstrating his powers on Johnny Carson's *Tonight Show.* Randi heads the James Randi Foundation, which hosted the Amazing Meeting, an annual conference for scientists, skeptics and magicians from 2003 through 2015. The foundation offered $1,000,000 to anyone who demonstrated a true supernatural ability under test conditions. Called the "One Million-Dollar Paranormal Challenge" all seven challengers attempting to win failed. This was perhaps because they knew that they could not pass the test, or because they feared the skeptical and negative energy of the organization would skew their results.

3

Traditional Artists and Death

Nineteenth Century Visual Artists

Celebrated visual artists of the nineteenth century couldn't help but be affected by the escalating death rate of their times. An example is Jacques-Louis David (1748–1825), who was a child of only nine years when his father was killed in a duel. David became the official painter of Napoleon I and trained many of the great European artists of the early 19th century. These artists influenced important American artists who, because of the lack of professional art schools in the new country, had to study abroad.

As a young man David won a state scholarship to travel to Rome, where he studied ancient as well as Renaissance masterpieces. His five-year stay, and his embrace of the Enlightenment philosophy, inspired him to reject the highly decorative Rococo art style so popular in France at the time and embrace the newer neoclassical style. David's canvases are orderly and rational. The backgrounds are deemphasized, allowing him to focus on the theme of his work with laser-like precision. To add emotional depth to his work, he often chose to paint scenes of impending death.

In his hugely successful work *Oath of the Horatii*, 1784, David painted the ancient legend of the three Horatii brothers accepting arms from their father while vowing to sacrifice their lives to end a Roman war. Viewers knowledgeable about the outcome knew that only one of the brothers would survive and that his survival depended on his ability to kill his sister's betrothed, who fought for the other side. This brother returns triumphantly to his family but kills his sister because she is crying at the death of her fiancé. David's *Death of Socrates*, painted in 1787, showed the execution of the great Roman teacher and philosopher. The artist painted Socrates with gray hair and wrinkled face but gave him the muscular arms and legs of a strong and powerful man. Socrates is the only figure sitting erect, posed as if lecturing to his students for the very last time. Unafraid of death, he reaches for the fatal poison he must drink. Emotions from horror to sadness to despair are painted on the faces of the surrounding figures. The austere surroundings and muted colors add to the hopelessness of the scene.

David's greatest and most famous work is *The Death of Marat*, painted in 1793–94 soon after the murder of the radical revolutionary. Stabbed to death in his bathtub by Charlotte Corday (who hoped his death would end France's Reign of Terror), David chose to depict the man nude, just moments before life ebbed from his body (Gombrich, 365). Marat's face and chest, half submerged in his bath, are illuminated by an otherworldly light made even more dominant by the contrast of the stark black background.

39

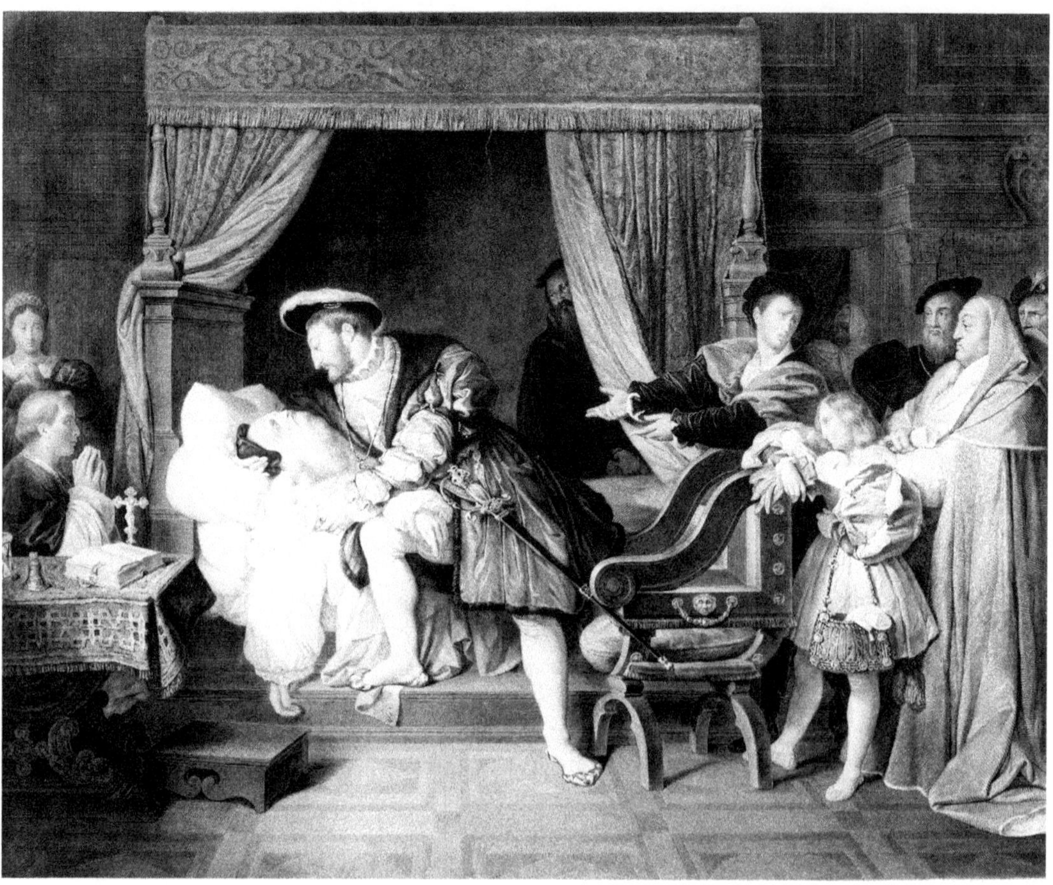

Jean-August-Dominique Ingres, *Death of Leonardo da Vinci*, 1818, oil on canvas, 40 × 50.5 cm (courtesy Petit Palais Musée des Beaux-Arts de la Ville de Paris Collection, © Roger-Viollet).

When Napoleon fell in 1815, David was exiled to Brussels. He died ten years later from injuries he sustained after being hit by a carriage, but his student, Jean-Auguste-Dominique Ingres (1780–1867), became a famous artist and teacher. Known for portraits and abstracted female nudes, Ingres also painted themes of death in his historical works. One of these, *The Death of Leonardo da Vinci*, painted in 1818, depicts a scene written by artist and art historian Giorgio Vasari in his seminal work *The Lives of the Most Excellent Painters, Sculptors and Architects*. In Ingres' painting, the King of France, Francis I, cradles the old man in his arms and serenely watches as Leonardo breathes his last breath. The king's face is close enough to breathe in air from the dying man's lungs. Metaphorically speaking, this depicts the transfer of the spirit of great art from Italy to France.

But death was also commercially important to Ingres when, in 1841, he painted a portrait of Prince Ferdinand-Philippe, Duc d'Orléans. The young royal was the eldest son of King Louis-Philippe d'Orléans and heir to the throne of France. He was also Ingres' patron and was well loved by the people of his country. Ferdinand-Philippe posed several times for this full-length work but tragically died soon after its completion when his carriage overturned. It had been assumed that the young prince, only 32 years old, would ascend to the throne. His untimely death sent the country into deep mourning. Ingres' portrait, painted so near to the prince's end, became a treasured item, and the need for duplications of this likeness kept Ingres busy and well paid.

The royal family paid the artist to design the stained glass windows for the prince's tomb. They also paid him to complete several copies of the portrait as posthumous remembrances. One full length portrait was used to decorate the prince's memorial chapel. A three-quarter length work was commissioned by the minister of the interior to be used as a model for other paintings that would hang around the realm. Besides these, Ingres painted at least five known portraits of the prince's head and shoulders, and possibly as many as nineteen. Several of these were sewn onto larger canvases and filled in by his apprentices or other painters.

In Spain, Francisco de Goya (1746–1828), an artist of the royal court, painted portraits in a way that mocked the elegance of those who sat for him (Gombrich, 365). With his revolutionary work known as *El Tres de Mayo de 1808* (The Third of May, 1808), painted in 1814, he became the first major artist to paint the brutality of war. This painting portrays Spanish resistance to Napoleon's overthrow of their monarch and the installation of his brother, Joseph Bonaparte, as king of Spain. Commissioned by the provisional government after the defeat of Napoleon, the painting commemorated the execution of hundreds of resistance fighters in Madrid. Goya's work depicts an early morning firing squad facing a disorganized group of ordinary and homely men, standing on the red puddle of blood from victims executed before them. The main figure, dressed in a bright white shirt and yellow pants, stands with his arms and legs forming the letter X, as if defiantly showing the soldiers the target of his heart. His right hand, projected towards the viewer, is scarred with stigmata, an obvious comparison of his martyrdom to the martyrdom of Christ.

From 1810 to 1820, Goya also created a series of more than eighty prints that are now entitled *Los Desastres de la Guerra* (The disasters of war). Goya did not take political sides in the Spanish resistance to the French, but his subject matter showed his rejection of French Neoclassicism and the embrace of a new style we now call Romantic. Depicting a world that was out of control, Goya filled his prints with emotion. Using minimal amounts of religious and mythic iconography, Goya drew and then printed scenes that many believe he witnessed as the war raged around him in Madrid. These scenes showed how his countrymen and women fought, but also how they were starved, raped, executed, and forced to kill. Although Goya had created this new, realistic style of art, the prints were not made public during his lifetime and were virtually unknown until thirty-five years after his death when in 1863 the Royal Academy of San Fernando in Madrid published them.

Other artists also rejected the orderliness of Neoclassicism, just as they rejected the ideas of the Enlightenment after the revolutions in France, to work in this Romantic style. Work by Eugene Delacroix (1798–1863), born after the French Revolution in France, and Joseph Mallord William Turner (1775–1851) in Britain was characterized by sensationalism and deep emotion. Their artwork showed a world that was unpredictable and chaotic—a world that could be turned upside down by forces of nature or the forces of man. Only his second major painting in oils, the *Massacre at Chios; Greek Families Awaiting Death or Slavery*, painted in 1824, made Delacroix an overnight success. Based on an actual military attack on the Greek island of Chios in 1822 by the Turkish fleet during the Greek war for independence against the Ottoman Empire, the work was exhibited opposite neoclassical work by Ingres in the French Salon exhibition of 1824. This work made Delacroix the leader of the new Romantic style.

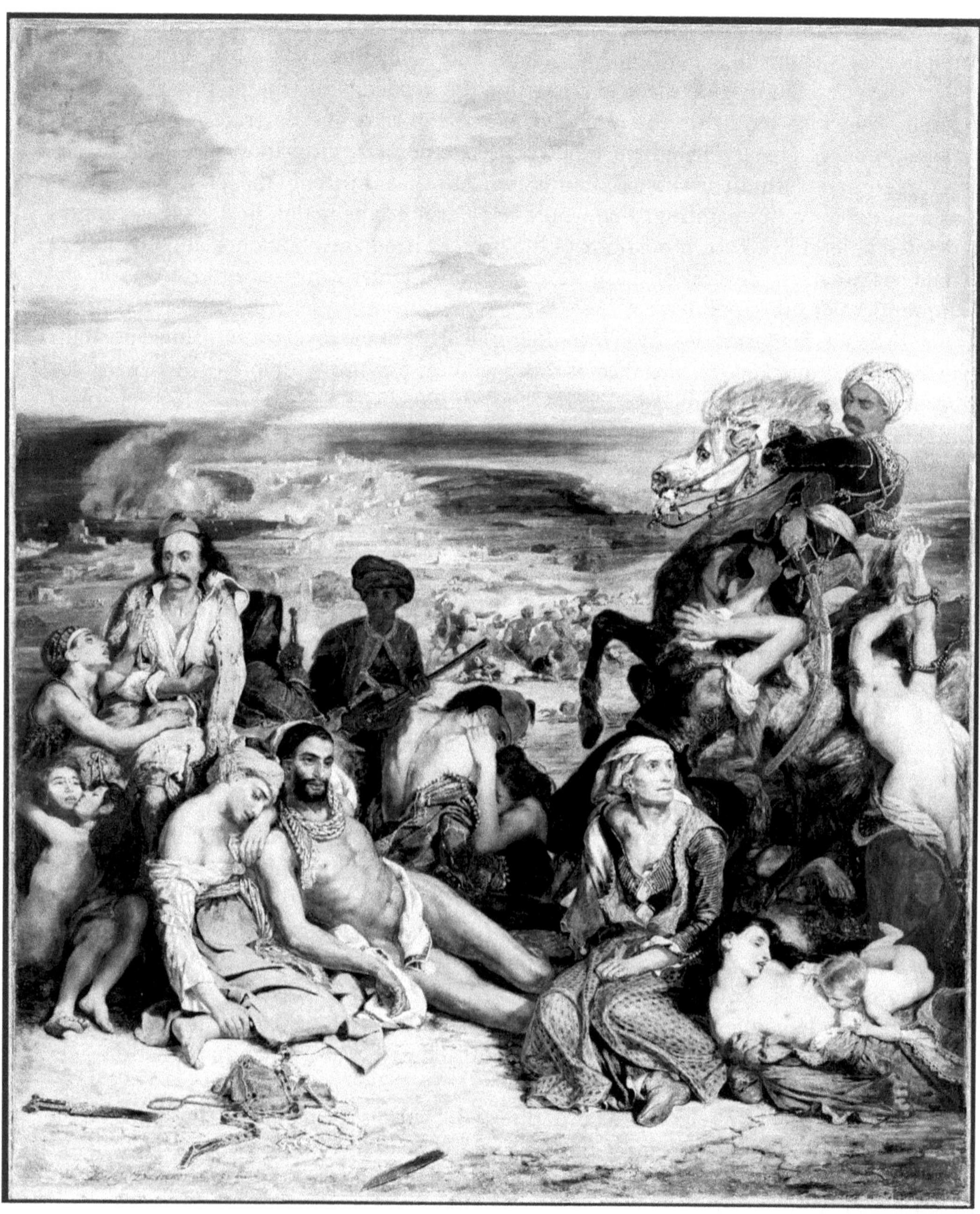

Eugene Delacroix, *Massacre at Chios*, 1824, oil on canvas (Musée du Louvre, courtesy Art Resource).

The actual attack resulted in several tens of thousands of deaths and the enslavement of the remaining seventy thousand inhabitants of the island. Delacroix depicted the horror of this genocide by painting the dead, the dying and the defeated against a background of the chaos of war. While the faces of the fallen are not grisly or distorted, and there is very little blood, the artist stirs our emotions by the interactions of the figures.

In the bottom right hand corner of the painting an infant desperately tries to gain comfort from his unresponsive, dead mother. Above him is a puddle of blood and severed body parts. On the left side of the work a naked girl kisses an unresponsive youth whose half-closed eyes look to heaven. Above them another woman reaches for a wounded man who does not have the strength to defend her or even hold her hand. Delacroix is deliberately using death to shock us and make us feel sympathy for the victims. Work like this had never been seen before and, at the time, art critics censured the artist for showing only the suffering of the defeated while ignoring the glory and heroism of the victors.

As his career continued, Delacroix was often inspired by death and disaster as is seen in the titles of his work: *Orphan Girl at the Cemetery*, 1824; *Death of Sardanapalus*, 1827; *A Mortally Wounded Brigand Quenches His Thirst*, 1825; *Hamlet and Horatio in the Graveyard*, 1839; and *Liberty Leading the People*, 1830. While the victims were depicted as relatively intact, their placement and surroundings evoke our emotions and our empathy.

Turner, who rejected detail in his dramatic landscape and seascape paintings and used light as a symbol of spirituality, served as inspiration for the Impressionist artists who followed. Yet he also depicted the dead and the dying, especially when recreating battle scenes. In his work *The Battle of Trafalgar*, 1822, the artist painted a lifeless corpse in the foreground of the work and other men frantically try to stay afloat in a sinking ship. In *Field of Waterloo*, painted first in watercolor and once again in oil in 1818, the dead lie in a heap, immersed in a golden light on the bottom of the picture plane, a scene that is both shocking and descriptive of war. Bodies are absent in the artist's *Slavers Throwing Overboard the Dead and Dying—Typhoon Coming On*, painted in 1840. Instead, hands, still in chains, reach up from the depths of the water roiled by frantically feeding fish.

After the French Revolution of 1848, which forced King Louis-Phillippe to abdicate his throne and live in exile in Great Britain, artists under the leadership of Gustave Courbet (1819–1877) embraced a new style of art named Realism (Gombrich, 383). Instead of painting historical work, these artists found inspiration in the lives of everyday people and sought truth, not prettiness. One of Courbet's first masterpieces in this genre was *A Burial at Ornans* (1849–50). In it, the artist recorded 45 actual people standing around the freshly dug grave of his great-uncle on a dark and dreary day, waiting for the ceremony to begin. The faces of the women and men, all dressed in black, show various expressions of grief and concern. A few of the women hold handkerchiefs to their faces to stifle their sobs while the priest leafs through his Bible, searching for the proper passage. The colors of the work are muted, and the figures hug the horizon line. The only thing rising above it is a staff topped by a cross adorned with the crucified figure of Christ. The size of the painting, ten feet by twenty-two feet, gives it heroic proportions that were previously used only for major works of historical or religious events. This artwork complemented the revolution occurring in French literature with authors such as Emile Zola and Honoré de Balzac. In such uncertain times, this painting was considered politically subversive and was refused for exhibition at the annual French Salon.

The Pre-Raphaelite Brotherhood of painters, in England, rejected ideas of Renaissance artist Raphael and tried to link the Romantic movement in literature with art while paying attention to the details of nature (Gombrich, 384). The painting *Ophelia* by John Everett Millais (1829–1896), completed in 1851, is a perfect example of this style of work. Millais' painting shows the young ingénue of Shakespeare's play *Hamlet*, moments before she drowns. She is floating on her back in a river. Her eyes and mouth are half closed, while her arms open feebly at her sides in a position of acceptance. She has either fallen or plunged into the river while picking flowers. Her dress eventually fills with water and drags her down to a "muddy death" (*Hamlet* 4:7).

The heir to Realism was Edouard Manet (1832–1883), who painted a work titled *The Dead Christ with Angels* in 1864. Although the artist was able to exhibit this work in France, it was disliked by art critics who thought that it was unseemly to portray Christ as a corpse. Manet was not so lucky in exhibiting several prints and paintings created from 1867 to 1869, inspired by the execution of Emperor Maximilian by a Mexican firing squad. This work was only shown in New York after the artist's death. The emperor had been installed in Mexico by Napoleon III but was overthrown and executed by Mexican patriots. Reminiscent of the 1814 painting by Francisco de Goya of the *Execution of the Third of May 1808*, Manet pictured the soldiers shooting their victim while standing in a firing squad. The soldiers' backs are towards us so we do not see the expressions on their faces. They are anonymous, dressed alike in uniform. The sergeant looks down on the ground while the emperor's pale face is surrounded by smoke from the fired weapons.

Portraits of the Deceased

For most of the nineteenth century, artists believed that for a work to be great it needed to be of an important historical event; but the demand for these large heroic works was limited. For most artists, portrait painting paid the bills, and a portrait was even more valued when the loss of a loved one was imminent. Artists were commonly employed (by families who could afford them) to capture the likeness of their loved ones either right before or right after they passed. These likenesses could be either large paintings or miniatures. The genre grew in popularity from 1830 to 1860 among the American upper class, who got this idea from their European counterparts.

Most American painters did this kind of work, and some even concentrated on it. An example was Raphaelle Peale (1774–1825,) son of the more famous artist Charles Willson Peale. Raphaelle promoted himself as an artist specifically able to paint a corpse. Dying before the invention of photography, Peale advertised that this type of painting was his specialty, boasting that he approached painting the deceased the same way one would paint any still life, a genre for which he was also well known. Working from the actual corpse, Peale followed the tradition of the time in portraying the dead as if they were still living, transforming "the ugliness of the corpse into the beauty of a memory-image, helping to console, relieve, and revitalize the grieving relations" (Laderman, 77).

Many portraits of children from this time are posthumous ones. These can be identified by a variety of symbols. In a time before universal literacy, pictorial symbols were well understood. For example, very young girls and boys were dressed alike, so a part in the middle of the child's hair indicated that the child was female while a part on the side or no part at all indicated it was male. Other symbols signified death. Among these were Greek columns, white flowers with missing petals, ships leaving the harbor, and dark clouds overhead. A portrait of a young boy painted in 1856 by the itinerant artist James B. Read hangs in the Minneapolis Institute of Art and shows some of these symbols. The child is dressed in his very best clothes, a signal of burial attire. The artist uses a heavy pallet of red, white and black, all traditional colors of mourning. In Read's portrait, the child holds his hat in his hands as if saying goodbye, and vines crawl up the porch column, signifying the survivors' attachment to the deceased. Portraits such as these would hang in a prominent place in the homes of the deceased individuals and be formally viewed by the family members on their birthdays, or on the anniversaries of their death.

If a family was not able to afford a portrait, they could purchase a print of a deathbed scene such as the popular one created from a painting by Samuel Luke Fildes. Fildes was a British artist who, in 1890, was commissioned by Sir Henry Tate (who established the Tate Gallery in London) to create a work of his own choosing. Given free reign, the artist chose as his inspiration the death of his first son, Phillip. In this 5-foot by 7-foot painting titled *The Doctor*, Fildes created a touching portrait of a concerned and dedicated doctor who sits close to and stares intensely at his patient, a young child, resting on a makeshift bed of two wooden chairs in a rustic cottage. The mother of the child has collapsed with emotion and rests her head on the table, while the father looks on helplessly at her side. A jar of medicine, a cup and spoon, a basin and pitcher surround the patient and doctor, as if to show that there was nothing more that medicine could do. The doctor can only watch and wait as light from a lamp illuminates his face and the face of the child. Some believe that the pale light coming in from the window shows that it is dawn, giving hope that the child might recover. But in real life the boy died from tuberculosis on Christmas Day in 1877. This painting was exhibited to great success in England at the Royal Academy show of 1891. An engraving of the work was quickly made, and over one million copies of it were sold in the United States alone.

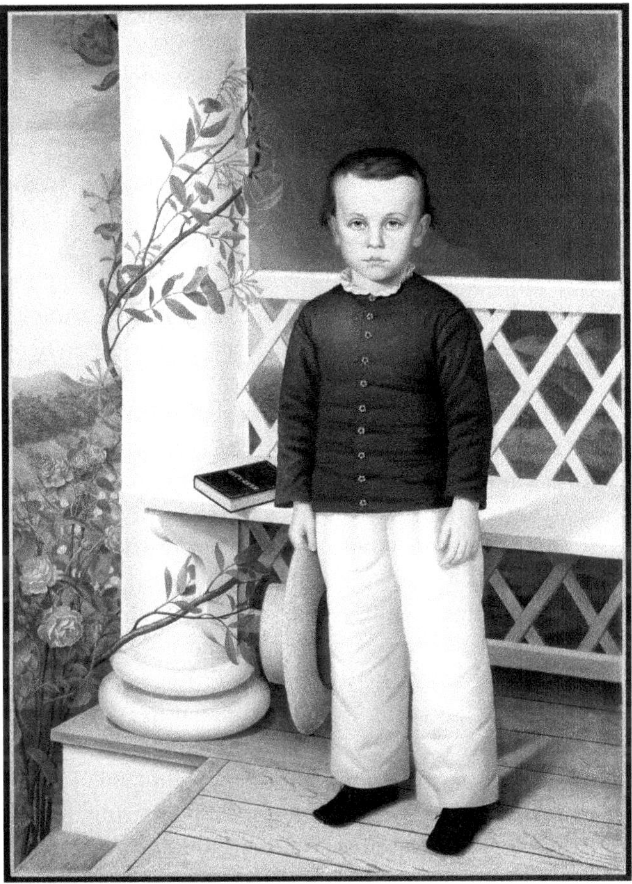

James B. Read, *Portrait of a Boy*, 1856, oil on canvas (Minneapolis Institute of Arts; gift of Mr. and Mrs. Patrick Butler; Bridgeman Images).

Spirit Painting

Humans were not the only ones to create art in the 19th century. Soon after Maggie and Kate Fox heard strange rapping sounds in 1848 and were proclaimed to be mediums, many others "developed" this mystical power. In some séances, spirits of the dead spoke in code, moved furniture around, played musical instruments, or diagnosed disease. But some spirits of the dead created artwork, or they helped humans create artwork. Some spirits have even been credited with the invention of abstract art. Such was the case with Georgiana Houghton, a British artist who lived from 1814 to 1884.

Born in the Canary Islands, Houghton spent most of her life in London; there she began training to be an artist, but she gave it up in 1851 when her sister died (Oberter, 221). Hearing news about spirit communication in America, Houghton decided to develop mediumistic talents of her own in the U.K. At first she held séances with her mother and practiced contacting the dead in 1858 and 1859; finally, her brother's spirit answered her. He put her in touch with another ghost, Henry Lenny, who, when alive, had been an artist, but deaf and mute. Houghton allowed Henry's spirit to possess her, and he guided her hands in creating artwork, using first a small board on casters called a planchette, then with a pencil, and then with watercolor paints.

Houghton continued to create artwork and was eventually able to contact the spirits of Renaissance painters such as Titian and Correggio. These great artists took possession of her body and drew through her, creating mostly nonrepresentational work consisting of spirals, thin lines, blocks and waves of color. They rejected realistic imagery in order to depict the less tangible planes of the afterlife. Also while Houghton was in trance, the spirits had her write extensive explanations on the back of each work describing what each painting meant in the process called "automatic writing" (Oberter, 224). Houghton believed that she was having a religious experience, and she understood her artwork to be dealing with Christian ideas. Other mediums merely proved that spirits of the dead existed. Georgianna Houghton meant her watercolor paintings to show that these spirits had a relationship to the Christian god and the Christian religion. Houghton gave her work titles such as *The Glory of the Lord* (1861), *The Eye of God* (1862), and *The Sheltering Wing of the Most-High*. The automatic writing delved into concepts like the Trinity, saints and the omnipresence of God. Houghton wanted to show how Spiritualism enriched Christianity rather than replaced Christianity with a new religion. Georgiana Houghton wrote this on the back of her painting, *Glory Be to God*:

In the first place I wished to show forth The Glory of The Lord in His Great Power by forming a Wing of vivid orange yellow, which Wing filled the side of the drawing, to express that His shelter is sufficient for all. Then the tender cloud like forms, to show His Softening Spirit: the upper red ones being worked over in loving circles round the little dots, to represent The Care taken of each separate individual; however small or insignificant he may be. Then was carried up another Wing to the right, in vivid green, to express that The Lord is The Father of all, and that they must look up to Him with filial love and affection, not as to a stern Judge. The same is inferred by the green and pink sevenfold cluster at the bottom of the drawing to the left, which means that all must be filled with filial love, more especially when they contemplate, symbolised a little above, on the right, the Power and Glory resigned by The Lord of life for suffering and a Crown of Thorns, for the sake of His sinful creatures: to which Crown all must look, as leading them to their own crown of glory through tribulations and crosses upon earth.

Above The Crown is The Hand of The Trinity: that of the Father symbolised in yellow; of The Holy Ghost in red; and of The Son in white, emblematic of purity; He Who without sin was numbered with

Opposite: Georgiana Houghton painting, *Glory Be to God*. The image lender cautions: "In viewing this image please take into account its limitations. Imagine seeing a black and white image of a rainbow and compare it in your mind with the real thing. This image cannot compare with the vibrancy and complexity of the original" (published with the compliments of the Victorian Spiritualist Union, Melbourne, Aus.).

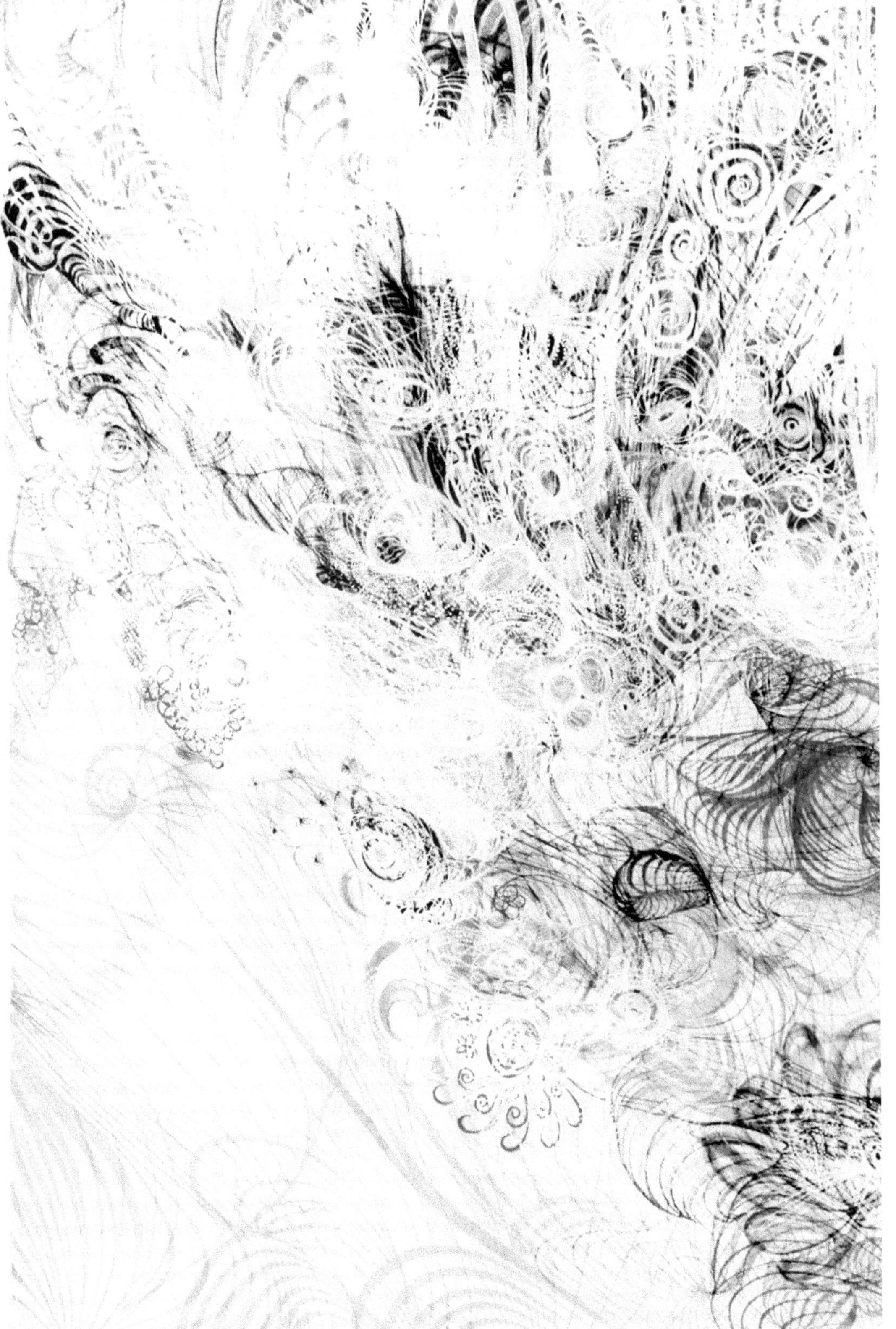

the transgressors: Whose Hand is again typified above that, in decisive blue, holding the stars of the seven first Christian churches. A little below to the right are two symbols of The Trinity Then The Ear and various symbols showing The Love and Might of The Lord; but the principal one is that on the right of the drawing, pourtraying The Shield of The Lord in sevenfold tenderness protecting and guarding his faithful servants. Above it The Arm of The Lord waves down, as if to support The Shield over those who in Faith, Hope and Charity strive to pursue a straight course; typified by those straight lines of mingled tints along the lower part of the drawing.

This drawing was finished January 4th, 1864*

Houghton held Wednesday afternoon receptions in her house during which she shared her work and the automatic writing of the spirits. But in 1871 Houghton boldly exhibited 155 of her works at the New British Gallery on Old Bond Street in London. She wrote in her autobiography: "The chief object aimed at in this Exhibition, was not so much to display the wondrous powers of the unseen intelligences, as to manifest unflinchingly to the world that true Spiritualism [is] inextricably bound up with the religion of the Sacred Scriptures" (Houghton, quoted in Oberter, 228).

Houghton wrote an extensive catalog for this exhibition. She also attended the show herself from 10:00 a.m. to 5:30 p.m. and preached to any and all who would listen to her. At a time when few women were allowed to preach, she compared herself to a clergyman and her exhibition in the gallery to a church (Oberter, 228). Unfortunately, critics dismissed her as an amateur, and spiritualist journals were confused about her work. The show was a financial disaster; she only sold one piece. However, she continued to be an ardent supporter of spiritualism and persisted in holding séances until her death. She also became involved with Frederick Hudson, a notorious British spirit photographer, who was thought to have used a trick camera but was never caught or arrested for fraud (Buck, "Without Parallel").

Although directed by spirits, Houghton never denied that she painted the work herself. However, the Hett Art Gallery and Museum of Camp Chesterfield in Indiana displays portraits not created by human hands but painted by spirits summoned by the Bangs sisters during trance. Beginning in 1894, guests at the Bangs' séances placed their hands palm down on a table. Canvas was set on top and a container of paints of many colors was placed nearby. Either Elizabeth or Mary Bangs would then go into a trance. Both sisters remained in their seats as the painting emerged, appearing before the eyes of many witnesses. Some séance guests said that the work, called *spirit paintings*, took up to 15 to 20 minutes to form. Witnesses said that some paintings were even completed in broad daylight.

Other people were able to get spirits to create artwork, too. The Campbell brothers, Allan B. Campbell and Charles Shourds (who assumed the surname of Campbell), summoned their spirit guide, Azur, and had him and other ghosts create work using pastels and oils. These are on display in the Lily Dale Museum in New York state. Guests of the séance would sign or put their marks on blank canvas and witness the gradual development of the work, which took up to 90 minutes, sometimes more. In *Precipitated Spirit Painting*, Ron Nagy states that aside from the museum at Lily Dale, one can view these paintings at the Maplewood Hotel, the Marion Skidmore Library and the office of the National Spiritualist Association of Churches (NSAC) on Cottage Row of the psychic *town of Lily Dale. Nagy had the opportunity to examine work by the Campbell brothers and claimed that the paint was still wet after more than 100 years.

I David was assisted in the execution of this drawing by many saints also by Gabriel the messanger of the Lord.

In his book *A Magician Among the Spirits*, Harry Houdini wrote that James Sauter and the infamous Ann O'Delia Diss Debar each professed to have the ability to summon spirits who made spirit paintings. Sauter primarily earned his living by being an astrologer and palm reader, but on occasion was able to produce what he called "spook pictures." The February 18, 1891, edition of the *True Republican* newspaper reported that Mrs. Beach, wife of Alfred E. Beach, the editor of *Scientific America* magazine, had acquired a rough drawing of Cassandra from Sauter, much to her husband's chagrin.

Diss Debar, born Ann O'Delia Saloman, was a notorious medium who was often in trouble with the law. She did not think highly of Sauter's work because his spirits only produced drawings while hers produced paintings. Diss Debar's abilities rose to notoriety when she claimed that one of her clients was the famous industrialist, politician and founder of Stanford University, Leland Stanford. She boldly advertised that he had offered to pay her a huge sum of money to produce a spirit painting for him. When Stanford heard about the claim on March 31, 1888, he issued a denial saying that he had never even met the woman. Soon after this, on April 11, 1888, Diss Debar and her husband were arrested for conspiracy to defraud an old man, Luther R. Marsh, of his money and property (Houdini, 71). Diss Debar, claiming to be Princess Editha Lolita Montez and Countess of Langfeldt, met the elderly lawyer when he began investigating the authenticity of her spirit paintings. The prosecution believed that Diss Debar purchased ordinary paintings from a local gallery and covered them with chalk so that in the dim light of the séance room they appeared to be untouched white canvas. According to this theory, the canvases were secretly covered with chalk to appear white. During the proceedings of the séance when the medium shook and convulsed while in trance, the chalk flaked off and the paintings were revealed. Many spiritualists, on the other hand, believed that the spirit paintings were real manifestations of the spirits of the dead, and that Diss Debarr was a true and powerful medium.

At first, Marsh, a partner in former president Chester A. Arthur's law firm, was skeptical that the paintings were real, but he became so impressed with them that he wrote an article that was published in several newspapers. He also bought some of these paintings for great amounts of money. His article alerted the old man's family and raised the suspicions of the New York Bar Association. An investigation was made that determined that Marsh not only had given Diss Debar a lot of his money but also had given her his valuable house on Madison Avenue in New York City. He did this because the medium had received messages from his newly departed wife and his daughter, Eva. It was Eva, through the medium, who suggested that the old man give Diss Debar his house, which the medium immediately mortgaged to the max. The Marsh family took the medium and her husband to court in 1888 (Houdini, *A Magician*, 70–71).

Judge Gildersleeve, who presided over the case, told the countess that her defense would be much improved if she could create a spirit painting for the jury. Unfortunately, the spirits would not cooperate, and no attempt was made. Diss Debar and her husband were found guilty, but the jury recommended clemency, and the couple served only six months in the jail at New York City's Blackwell's Island (Houdini, *A Magician*, 77).

After release, Diss Debar took her spirit paintings on the lecture tour, but things did not go well, and she and her husband were soon in debt. They disappeared from America to reappear in England in the 1890s, calling themselves Laura (the Swami) and Theodore (Horos) Jackson. Here they started a cult called "Theocratic Unity," which provided religious and educational instruction for young girls. Sadly, Horos could not resist the students in his charge, and in 1901 the couple were arrested again for fraud and also rape. The swami was sentenced to seven years in prison while her husband was sentenced to 15. After Diss Debar's release, Harry Houdini reported that she was seen practicing the occult in South Africa, Florida, and Cincinnati, Ohio, before permanently dropping out of sight (Houdini, *A Magician*, 78).

Post-Impressionists and Death

Some Impressionist painters, such as Claude Monet (1840–1926) and Pierre-Auguste Renoir (1841–1919) in France, and William Merritt Chase (1849–1916) and Maurice Prendergast (1858–1924) in America, turned their attention to scenes that celebrated life rather than those that explored what lies beyond death's door. But Spiritualism was an international religion, and it is difficult to believe that these artists had never attended a séance nor were aware of the trance state that Franz Mesmer had discovered and that was made respectable by the Marquis de Puységur, the French aristocrat, and the Scottish physician, James Beard, both researchers in mesmerism. Influenced by the Impressionist style, Vincent Van Gogh (1853–1890) also painted still lives, portraits and landscapes, but in his work we see a different goal than that of celebrating reality. We see his attempt to depict the "spirit" behind the person or the material object he drew or painted. Portraying the "spirit" of a thing became more and more important to artists as the century drew to a close and a new century began.

Van Gogh had a brief artistic career that was marked by a one-year stay in an insane asylum and death by probable suicide. He suffered from periodic attacks of hallucinations and partial seizures, leaving him depressed and in physical pain. He also fasted, smoked, and drank more absinthe than he should have. When liquor was withheld from him in the asylum, he ate his paints and drank turpentine and kerosene, making his condition even worse ("The Letters"). His placement in the asylum occurred because the artist deliberately cut off most of his ear after a fight with his roommate, the artist Paul Gauguin. Gauguin had been staying with him in hopes of becoming the director of a new art school that was to be funded by Van Gogh and his brother.

Some art historians questioned whether the artist actually cut off his ear, or if his roommate Gauguin did this accidentally in a drunken brawl. Gauguin was considered a suspect by the local police when he showed up at the residence the next day. In his journal Gauguin denied the charge and wrote that earlier in the day he had told Van Gogh that he didn't want to work there anymore. While Gauguin was taking a walk, Vincent came after him with a razor but was scared away. Gauguin claims that he did not return to the residence but slept that night in a hotel. He only discovered what Van Gogh had done the next day, and he immediately left for Paris.

Van Gogh was admitted to the local Hotel Dieu Hospital in Arles for his severed ear and was treated by Dr. Félix Rey, who believed the artist had some form of psychosis caused by epilepsy, which just happened to be the topic of his friend's recent thesis. Rey urged his patient to seek treatment for his mental condition with a specialist, and Van Gogh had his brother, Theo, sign him into the Maison de Santé Saint-Paul de Mausole mental hospital in Saint-Rémy-de-Provence.

Sadly, mental problems were common among Van Gogh's siblings, which leads Wilfred Niels Arnold ("Illness of Vincent van Gogh") to believe there was a congenital condition that created a toxic psychosis affecting them all. (Arnold [30] suggests that this disorder might be Acute Intermittent Porphyria [AIP], a blood disorder that causes neurological symptoms. Attacks caused by this condition are exacerbated by lifestyle choices such as fasting, absinthe abuse, the use of camphor as a sleeping aid, smoking—all found in Vincent's behavior.) Vincent's brother Cornelius committed suicide in 1900. His sister, Willemien, spent the last four decades of her life in an asylum (1902–1941). In 1891, a mere six months after Vincent's death, his brother Theo died in a mental hospital in the town of Den Dolden, in the Dutch province of Utrecht. Theo was diagnosed with dementia paralytica, a condition caused by syphilis or by the mercury used in treating syphilis. That he contracted so serious a phase of syphilis in so short a time seems unlikely; Theo may also have been suffering from the family's congenital disease.

While Vincent and Theo do not mention specific treatment techniques for his condition in their letters other than hydrotherapy (two-hour baths taken twice a week), we must remember that Franz Mesmer practiced his type of medicine in Paris beginning in 1778 and up until at least 1801. At the end of the century France became home to the two great schools of psychotherapy: the Nancy School, in the northeast of the country, and the Salpêtrière School of Hypnosis, located in the country's capital, Paris. It is highly likely that Vincent was hypnotized while he was a mental patient being treated for auditory and visual hallucinations in 1889. Even Sigmund Freud, the father of psychotherapy, studied hypnotism at these two great schools and used this technique with his patients from 1886 to 1896 (Bachner-Melman, "Freud's Relevance," 38). Being hypnotized would have made Van Gogh aware of the trance state, the alternate state of consciousness used by mediums to contact spirits of the dead.

Belief in spirits would not have been an alien concept to the artist. Van Gogh was a deeply religious man raised in the Dutch Reform Church. Both his grandfather and father were ministers, and the artist had served as a missionary, despite the difficulty he had following church rules. Van Gogh believed in the Holy Spirit of God and must have believed each human possessed a soul or spirit that survived and would be revived after death, or on judgment day. While he did not mention Spiritualism (*spiritism* in French) in the letters he wrote to his brother while in the institution, he did write that he was defining his religious beliefs and was open to change. In a letter to his brother Theo Vincent wrote, "Religions pass, but God remains" (Maurer, "*Pursuit*," 4).

After Van Gogh left this institution, he was under the care of Dr. Paul-Ferdinand Gachet, who had treated artists such as August Renoir, Paul Cézanne and Édouard Manet. Gachet also treated the writer and artist Victor Hugo, who developed an interest in spiritualism because of the death of his daughter in 1843. Hugo regularly held séances in which spirits told him what to write and what to draw. He also studied the writings of Swedenborg and the Cabala, an ancient Jewish system of mysticism and magic (Tuchman, *Spiritual in Art*, 32). Even if he was not hypnotized, Van Gogh was an avid reader and familiar with works by Hugo, Balzac, Maupassant, Whitman and Tolstoy. All of these writers were influenced by popular occult ideas and wrote about mystical phenomena in their work.

* * *

In the middle of the 19th century, other artists found inspiration in a competing style to Impressionism, that of the Symbolist movement. This was started by the French poet Charles Baudelaire, who was inspired by the macabre tales of American writer Edgar Allan Poe. Paul Gauguin was part of a group of artists, along with Odilon Redon, Edvard

Munch, and the American James Abbott McNeill Whistler, who attended receptions held each week by Stéphane Mallarmé, a major French Symbolist poet. Symbolist painters came to believe that artists had the ability to reveal the truth in the religious, the occult, the mystical, and the dream world. They rejected naturalism and used their "inner vision" to express psychological and spiritual reality.

Other examples of artists influenced by this style were the Austrian Gustave Klimt (1862–1918) and the Norwegian artist Edvard Munch (1863–1944). Klimt, who explored female sexuality, did not paint his award-winning masterpiece *Death and Life* until 1911. Unfortunately, the artist died from complications of the Spanish Influenza epidemic of 1918.

Death haunted Edvard Munch, who depicted feelings of isolation and anxiety emblematic of the modern world. He depicted the death of his sister in six works from 1885 to 1923 that were all titled *The Sick Child*. The 1885 version shows a frail, red-headed girl propped up with pillows in her deathbed, staring at a black curtain while a dark-haired woman sits beside her, her head bowed in grief. These works sold well and, after the death of his father, allowed Munch to support his younger siblings and assume the role of head of the family. *Girl and Death*, a lithograph created in 1894, shows a vigorous young woman embracing a skeletal figure whose bony arms feebly, yet completely, encircle her waist. In his painting *Death in the Sickroom*, 1895 (Munch Museum), Munch does not show an image of death, or the dead person; instead we see the overwhelming grief the death has caused the others in the room. Tuberculosis ravaged Norway at the time, inspiring other artists from that country, such as Hans Heyerdahl and Christian Krohg, to also use the sick or dying child as a subject for their work. Death was no stranger to Munch, who at the age of 26 had lost his mother, sister, grandfather and finally his father. He himself suffered from tuberculosis, too. All of this contributed to his tragic outlook on life, shown in his best-known work entitled *The Scream of Nature* (*Der Schrei der Natur* in German). Munch painted four versions and made lithographs of this Symbolist work, making visible what he sensed was a sound emanating from nature.

* * *

Born almost a generation before Munch, Gauguin went beyond the Symbolist tradition and created new realities influenced by his ideas of the spirit world. Gauguin and his friend Emile Schuffenecker, who painted and exhibited his artwork with Gauguin, named the new approach to painting "Synthetism." An important contemporary art critic, Achille Delarouche, wrote this about Gauguin's work: "Here appears definitely the goal toward which the different arts are tending, the place where they will meet perhaps: the future city of the spiritual life" (Gauguin, 54).

Gauguin's childhood was unconventional. He recalled that his mother—originally from an aristocratic family related to the House of Borgia, with wealthy relatives living in Peru—dressed in Peruvian costume, was a feminist, and was a childhood friend of the writer George Sand. He described his grandmother, Flora Tristan, as being a socialist and anarchist, and claimed that she spent her entire fortune on workers' causes. He also believed that she had founded a new religion with the French social reformer Barthélemy Prosper Enfantin. "The religion was named 'Mapa' in which Enfantin was the god 'Ma' and she the goddess 'Pa'" (Gauguin, *Intimate Journals*, 153). Gauguin did not explain what the tenets of this religion were.

The death of family members played an important part in Gauguin's early life. When he was only three years old, his father died during the family's voyage to Peru. This caused his immediate family to move into the great mansion of his wealthy uncle in Lima, where they lived for four years. One of his uncle's offspring was José Rufino Etchenique, who was president of Peru; Gauguin remembered the president's residence quite well when he wrote about it in his journal years later. The idyllic days in Lima ended when his paternal grandfather died and his mother and siblings returned to Paris to settle their inheritance. Soon after their arrival in France the rich Peruvian uncle also died. Without his support, the family could not return to South America, and their fortunes were radically reduced.

Gauguin became a merchant marine, then married and had five children, settling down to life as a stock broker. During this time, he also met Émile Schuffenecker, who had given up his own job as a stock broker to become an artist, art teacher and one of the founding members of the Theosophical movement in France. This movement sprang from spiritualism in that it asserted that humans possessed occult psychological powers including the ability to communicate with spirits, but it differed in attempting to reconcile the scientific method to theological mysteries. Never claiming that it was a religion, the Theosophical Society claimed that no one person or religion had the truth about the meaning of the universe and life, but that through study and group discussion, modern people could attain "ancient wisdom," the archetypal religion that had been lost over time. Gauguin left his wife and children and moved in with Schuffenecker, from whom he absorbed Theosophical ideas.

An inheritance allowed Gauguin to move to Tahiti, where he was appalled by the cruelty of Catholic missionaries who not only tried to wipe out other forms of worship, but also tried to wipe out "superb native artistic traditions" that they thought offensive to a Christian god (Maurer, 3). Gauguin, raised a Catholic, tried to reconcile Catholicism to the scientific ideas of his time in a work called *L'esprit modern et le catholicisme*, or in English, *The Modern Spirit and Catholicism*, written in 1897–98. In this hundred-page manuscript Gauguin wrote that God created the universe but then either stepped away from it or died. He also claimed that Jesus never existed but was meant to be a metaphor of pure spirituality. Not surprisingly, this work was poorly received by his Tahitian bishop, and Gauguin broke away from the church, believing that Catholicism was not rational. To Gauguin, Christ confirmed a strong belief in science by saying, "There is nothing hidden now which will not become perfectly plain … there are no secrets now which will not become as clear as daylight" (Mark 4:22). In his journals, Gauguin mentioned reading the ancient books of the Hindus, and Confucius. In his Synthetic paintings such as *The Yellow Christ* and *Jacob Wrestling with the Angel* he used flat planes of color and geometric shapes to represent spirits, in an attempt to turn natural forms into sacred symbols.

While staying in an artist colony in Brittany, Gauguin became popular with a group of students from the Académie Julian, including Paul Serérusier. Gauguin and Serérusier named this group the "Nabis" after the Hebrew word for "prophet," believing that artists were like priests or prophets. In a letter published in 1888 Gauguin wrote, "Art is Abstraction" and "creating, like our Divine Master, is the only way of rising toward God" (Moffett, 16). The Nabis artists met weekly with Gauguin or in artist Paul Ranson's atelier in Paris. Seeing spiritualist overtones in Gauguin's artwork, they drew inspiration from it. They also studied ancient symbols such as pyramids, crosses, zodiac symbols, and pentagons, which they included in their own work to create equilibrium. They also read occult literature including the popular work of Édouard Schuré (1841–1929), *Les Grands Inities,* or in English, *The Great Initiates: A Study of the Secret History of Religions*, published first in Paris in 1889. Schuré was a member of the Theosophical Society. The influence of the society on the development of art in the late 1800s and on the development of abstract art cannot be ignored.

* * *

The Theosophical Society was founded in New York City by Helena P. Blavatsky (1831–1891) and Colonel Henry Steel Olcott (1837–1907) in 1875. Blavatsky first believed in spiritualism but rejected it as a religion as more and more mediums were exposed as frauds. She also did not believe that all of the spirits being contacted were benevolent. The same year she arrived in America, 1874, she attended a séance held by the mediums William and Horatio Eddy in Vermont. There she met Colonel Henry Steel Olcott, an attorney and investigative correspondent for the *New York Graphic,* who become her partner in creating the new society (Henry Ridgely Evans, 8). A student of the occult, Blavatsky quickly began leading her own séances in New York City. Her followers convinced her and Olcott to form a new group separate from spiritualism. Someone suggested the name of "Theosophy," from the Greek roots *theo* (meaning divine or god) and *sophia* (meaning wisdom), and the society was born. The founders never claimed that the group was a religion, and neither one of them claimed to be a priest or minister. Instead they saw the society as being a movement that bonded people together. Olcott was the president and Blavatsky the corresponding secretary. In this movement they combined a belief in spirits with a study of the teachings of ancient religions, especially Hinduism and Buddhism. By applying the scientific method to their studies, they hoped to uncover "ancient wisdom"—the basis of all modern creeds. Still in existence today, the Theosophical Society is regarded as the origin of popular New Age movements of modern times.

The ideas of the society struck a chord with a receptive crowd of mourners, including artists, who had lost loved ones and wanted to believe in life after death but had been made skeptical of spiritualism by Harry Houdini and the others who constantly debunked mediums and the methods they used. More and more people in the United States and abroad joined the Theosophy Society as the rate of deaths escalated due to constant military conflicts at the end of the 19th century, World War I at the beginning of the 20th century, and the devastating influenza outbreak of 1918. Members paid dues and gained comfort from the Theosophical Society's beliefs in spirits of the dead, and also karma and rebirth, with reincarnation leading to the continued evolution of human beings.

Madame Blavatsky wrote her first work, *Isis Unveiled: A Master-Key to the Mysteries of Ancient and Modern Science and Theology,* in 1877. Her second book, *The Secret Doctrine,* was published in 1888. She claimed that she had not written these works alone but was helped by the supernatural consciousness of the Masters. In these works, she explained that humans have limited consciousness, modern religions were degenerated and unreliable, and that "modern day people—even those living in India—were ignorant of the true content of their religions" (Kraft, 150). She explained her belief that the human mind must be transcended in order to recognize that everything is part of the Absolute Being. If not, knowledge of the ancient wisdom could be a dangerous thing.

Despite there being over 600 studies about Madame Blavatsky, no trustworthy biography has ever been written. Little is known about her before she came to the United States in 1873, and many find it impossible to believe the stories she told of her young adulthood. She allegedly was born into an aristocratic Russian family, traveled the world and met the Masters of ancient wisdom, who sent her to Tibet where—under the instruction of the mahatmas "Morya" and "Koot Hoomi"—she developed her own psychic powers and was told that she would bring a new philosophy to the world (Theosophical Society). More current historians believe that when she was 17 she married a man more than 20 years older than she was and worked as a mesmerer's "sensitive" in Paris in 1849 and in Cairo in 1870 (Lavoie, 221). She is believed to have married two others while keeping the Blavatsky name. Despite her marriages, she insisted that she remained a virgin her entire life.

Olcott had been a farmer during the Civil War. He became a lawyer and journalist and was called upon to investigate the murder of President Abraham Lincoln. He developed an interest in spiritualism after seeing Andrew Jackson Davis go into a trance and diagnose illness in an audience member by merely holding onto a lock of his hair. As a mature investigator, Olcott directed his attention to claims of communication with the dead and traveled to Vermont to study the Eddy brothers' assertion that they could levitate and cause ghosts to emerge from a wooden cabinet. Olcott's book on the subject, *People from the Other World*, revealed a man who truly believed in spirit communication and psychic abilities. Olcott met Madame Petrovna Blavatsky at the Eddy séance and believed her when she denounced spiritualism for tricky mediums and lying spirits. He also believed her when she told him that she was led by the mahatmas, or the "Great White Brothers" (white meaning purity) to place spiritualism on a higher plane and reform it by linking it to ancient religions and to beliefs in reincarnation and the evolution of the human mind.

Blavatsky and Olcott did not stay in the United States to nurture the new society but left it in the hands of Abner Doubleday (the inventor of baseball). They moved to India in December 1878. There they read Hindu holy texts and allied themselves with the Indian independence movement. Seeing that Christian missionaries were attempting to destroy native religions, Olcott and Blavatsky went to Sri Lanka in 1880. Olcott ignited a Buddhist revival by writing a Buddhist "catechism." This codification of the religion gave it important recognition as a viable creed and helped believers fight the pressure of Christian missionaries to convert from their faith.

Blavatsky increasingly suffered from ill health and accepted the offer to live with British social reformer and activist Annie Besant. A controversial figure, Besant was the first woman to graduate from the University College in London in science. She wrote for *National Reformer* newspaper and collaborated with Charles Bradlaugh, her editor and the president of the National Secular Society, in publishing *The Fruits of Philosophy: or The Private Companion of Young Married People*. A controversial book written by Charles Knowlton, it gave working-class women forbidden advice on birth control. The publication of this book resulted in the law case *The Queen vs. Charles Bradlaugh and Annie Besant*. At the trial, Besant gave an impassioned speech that increased her fame (Kumar, 512). Both were found guilty of publishing what was considered to be a lewd book and given a sentence of six months in prison that was reversed on appeal. Besant continued to be an activist and published her own book on birth control called *The Laws of Population*, which resulted in her losing custody of her daughter, Mabel.

Besant was elected to the London School Board and initiated several important reforms, but after meeting Madame Blavatsky in 1890 she devoted more and more of her efforts to the Theosophical Society and traveled to India several times. Besant eventually joined the Indian National Congress and launched the India Home Rule League. Before

Blavatsky died from influenza in 1891, she appointed Besant the head of the European headquarters of the movement. By this time the Theosophical Movement had grown, numbering over 100,000 members worldwide. Members included Gauguin's friend Schuffenecker, Modhandas (Mahatma) Gandi, and the founders of abstract art, Wassily Kandinsky, Piet Mondrian, Kazimir Malevich and František Kupka. Besant continued to lead the Theosophical Society, along with Olcott. At his death in 1907, she took over as president.

Theosophy, the Anthroposophy Society, Rudolph Steiner and Abstract Art

Theosophy was not as sensational as spiritualism. Instead of paying to sit at a séance, or in an audience, and watch a demonstration of antics performed by ghosts of the dead, members of the movement were urged to pay dues, read, study, and discuss ancient texts on the occult. This made it popular with intellectuals at the latter part of the nineteenth century and the beginning of the next. Because of the society's belief that art could be used to visualize Theosophical truths, artists gained the courage to create abstract and even non-representational work. Hidden in Blavatsky's book *The Secret Doctrine* was information relevant to artists about the "sacred geometry." This was the ancient belief that geometric shapes have meaning and exist as "thought forms" of the creator of the universe, or God (Blavatsky, *Secret Doctrine*, vol. 1, bk. 2, ch. 2). Second-generation theosophists Annie Besant and Charles W. Leadbeater believed in the power artists had to understand these thought forms and wrote, "Nature manifests itself rhythmically in geometric structure, which, being a thing of beauty, can be discovered by an artist endowed with intuition" (Guggenheim, 4). In later books the two delved into explaining the specific meanings of color and form.

Charles Webster Leadbeater (1854–1934) left his position as a priest in the Anglican church to become a high-ranking member of the Theosophical Society. Deeply affected by losing his father to tuberculosis when he was only eight years old, Leadbeater developed an interest in spiritualism and in the medium Daniel Dunglas Home, but was led to Theosophy by A. P. Sinnett's work *The Occult World*. This book was dedicated to Blavatsky's teacher, Mahatma Koot Hoomi. Sinnett and his wife, Patience, lived in India, where he met Blavatsky and Olcott. Sinnett mentioned Blavatsky's belief in the "Maitreya." This was a World Teacher, or Christ, who periodically came to earth to guide human evolution to a higher realm (both the Buddha and Jesus were believed to be his incarnations). Leadbeater became Blavatsky's pupil and moved to India to receive information from the Masters of Ancient Wisdom. He also accompanied Olcott to Burma and Sri Lanka and served as the first headmaster of the English Buddhist Academy, still in existence today and now called Anada College.

To Leadbeater, the dead are not lost to us. They exist in the astral plane called Kâmaloka (Leadbeater, *The Astral Plane*, introduction). They cannot see our physical bodies like the living can, but they perceive our astral bodies. The dead can feel our emotions and can speak to us when we are asleep. Leadbeater admitted that he was clairvoyant. His eyes were "fully opened," which allowed him to see the astral plane. In 1895 he published *The Astral Plane: Its Scenery, Inhabitants and Phenomena*. Leadbeater asserted that he did not write the manual himself, but was a "servant of the Masters who are the Elder

Brothers of our race," who told him what to write (Leadbeater, preface). This was first in a series of his works that had a huge influence on the pioneers of abstract art. Leadbeater stated, and believed, that clairvoyance was not a unique ability. He encouragingly declared that even beginning students of Theosophy could soon acquire this skill.

In this complex manual, the author explained that the astral plane, the fourth dimension, or *Kâmaloka* in Sanskrit, is the second great plane of nature, the next above the physical world that we know and see, and the place where we go to after death and before rebirth. Leadbeater wrote that Kâmaloka has seven subdivisions and that each subdivision becomes less and less material (or realistic) and more "withdrawn from our lower world and its interests"—simplified or abstract (Leadbeater, *The Astral Plane*, 8). An example Leadbeater gave was that of a solid glass cube. A normal, or untrained, person will see this cube in 3-dimensional perspective. A clairvoyant looking at the same glass cube sees the outside as well as the inside, and the object appears to be flat. Disregarding the rules of perspective, showing objects from different points of view, and flattening space all are hallmarks of abstract art.

Leadbeater claimed that possession of clairvoyance or "astral sight" allows one to see auras, which are invisible forms of matter, such as the particles composing the atmosphere. As the author wrote: "[These are] various emanations which are always being given out by everything that has life" (Leadbeater, *Man Visible and Invisible*, 9). To the clairvoyant, all things, even inorganic objects, are surrounded by an egg shaped "aura," a unique atmosphere of "luminous mist of a highly complex structure" that vibrates and interpenetrates everything (Leadbeater, 9). An example of this is seen in Leadbeater's discussion of a common rock. An untrained person sees only an inert mass of a certain size and shape. But a clairvoyant sees that both the physical and the astral particles of the stone are constantly in motion and universal life circulates through and radiates from it. To a clairvoyant, everything, even a rock, is surrounded by an aura, and this "appropriate elemental essence" (Leadbeater, *Man Visible and Invisible*, 21) actively fluctuates throughout. Astral sight, attainable to even beginners, enables one to see this "etheric" double of a being. Similar to Mesmer's electro-magnetism, the etheric double is the "actual manifestation of the Ego on their respective planes" (Leadbeater, *Man Visible and Invisible*, 11).

Leadbeater's book must have been inspirational to artists like Hilma af Klint (1862–1944), who lived in Sweden and was a member of the Swedish branch of the Theosophical Society. She studied Theosophical literature, attended lectures and discussions, and made contact with spirits with names such as "Amaliel" and "Gregor," who had her painting on the "astral plane" as early as 1896 (Fant, 156). Trained as an artist at the Royal Academy of Art in Stockholm, Sweden, she was so respected by her professors that she was honored by being awarded a studio of her own.

Af Klint's interest in the occult started when her ten-year-old sister died from the flu in 1880. She went on to develop her own mediumistic abilities and conducted weekly séances from 1892 to 1906, acting as medium for four other women artists who called themselves the Friday Group, or "da Fem," or in English, The Five. Professionally, she was known for her portrait and landscape work, but the spirits urged her to reject these genres in order to paint what they said would be a "message to the world." From 1905 to 1915, spiritual forces worked through her while she was in a trance state in the process known as automatic painting. The media she used were oils and tempera paint.

Af Klint's work was large. Some paintings measured ten feet high. Measuring only five feet tall herself, she worked on the floor; one painting has her footprint on it ("Hilma af Klint"). She named her bodies of work "Drawings for the Temple" and "Ten Large Series." Like that of Georgiana Houghton, the work was non-representational and contained spirals and thin lines set against flat backgrounds of a solid color. To represent the immortal aspects of man, af Klint used Rosicrucian and Theosophical symbols such as the "ultimate atom" shape, dots, horizontal lines, crosses, circles, ovals, and other geometric forms rendered in various tints of different hues. Unlike Houghton, she was a trained artist who had studied color and form. Despite this, she did not change any errors she recognized in what she created while in her unconscious trance state. Af Klint claimed to have become clairvoyant in 1915. No longer needing a spirit guide, she traveled the astral plane on her own. Her abstract work depicted visualizations of things appearing in the fourth dimension that Leadbeater had described.

Art was important to the Theosophical Society. Curated exhibitions always accompanied the annual national or international conventions each branch held. For example, in 1910 the branch of the Theosophical Society of the Netherlands devoted its entire national convention to the topic of "Theosophy and Art." It is very probable that af Klint put her work in group shows at these conventions and had them exhibited for emerging artists in the society to see. It is possible that her work inspired other artists and became the beginning vocabulary used by the pioneers of abstract art.

Af Klint read and attended lectures by Rudolf Steiner (1861–1925), an Austrian philosopher, architect, artist and social reformer who never officially joined the society but lectured extensively in European Theosophical Society functions. Steiner did not lead séances but admitted to having contact with the dead, claiming that at the young age of nine he was able to see the spirit of his deceased aunt. He alleged that the spirit world was something the mind intrinsically knew and perceived, and like Leadbeater, believed that most people could develop mediumistic powers of their own.

In Steiner's opinion, auras could not be seen with our eyes because sensing them was a spiritual and inner phenomenon. Auras were seen by the soul of a sensitive person who perceived them as a cloud of different colors. Using a blackboard and colored chalk, he drew intricate patterns illustrating his ideas. While his early blackboard drawings were erased, his later students thought to cover the blackboard with black paper, and many of these drawings remain.

Steiner was appointed leader of the Theosophical Esoteric Society for Germany and Austria and was held in high esteem until the leaders of the society declared that the "Maitreya," or avatar of God, had come to earth and was the fourteen-year-old son of the society's clerk, named Jiddu Krishnamurti. Believing that the second coming of Christ would be a spiritual awakening and not a physical embodiment, Steiner broke from Theosophy and formed his own society of "spiritually dedicated people" (Goetheanum). This group was located in Dornach, Switzerland, and was called the Anthroposophical Society—still in existence today. Unlike Theosophy, which was influenced by eastern religions, Steiner's group looked favorably on Christianity and searched for universal truths in Western traditions.

Thrilled when the great man came to Sweden to lecture, af Klint invited him to her studio and showed him her spirit paintings, but this meeting did not go well. Steiner's charismatic personality encouraged supporters but antagonized others, some of whom became his fierce enemies. Some of his neighbors in Dornach feared the desire for knowledge of the spirit world that he and his followers sought. One even set fire to the innovative main building of his complex, named the Goetheanum, in 1923.

The Goetheanum was completed in Dornach, Switzerland, in 1913. This was to be the centerpiece of the Anthroposophical Society. The design for this building was based on the sacred geometry of the sphere. It did not have any corners, and it embodied Goethe's and Steiner's world conception. Those seeking knowledge of the spirit world, including artists, were drawn to the site, which unfortunately was viewed with suspicion and loathing by some of the local residents. The building was eventually destroyed by arson on New Year's Eve in 1923. It was redesigned by Steiner and rebuilt using poured concrete. However, the new building was not completed until after the architect's death. Perhaps, because of this act of intimidation, Steiner came to believe that humans were not yet ready to understand the spiritual concepts so important to him, and that they needed at least another 50 years to evolve. He convinced af Klint that the world was not ready to see her paintings either and that she should not exhibit them anywhere for the next 50 years (Tuchman, 157–158). Af Klint died 30 years after her meeting with Steiner, in 1944. Following the advice of the great man, she stipulated in her will that her 100 papers and over 1,200 paintings should not be shown until 20 more years had elapsed ("Hilma af Klint").

It is interesting that work of both both Houghton and af Klint has recently been exhibited in contemporary galleries. Af Klint was brought to world attention by Åke Fant for the exhibition called "The Spiritual in Art: Abstract Painting 1890–1985." This was organized by Maurice Tuchman of the Los Angeles County Museum in 1986. In 2013 af Klint's work was displayed in Stockholm's Moderna Museet in a show called "Pioneer of Abstraction." In 2016, af Klint's work was brought to England and exhibited in London's Serpentine Gallery. Her work is held in the Hilma af Klint Foundation outside of Stockholm, Sweden. In 2016, Houghton's work was exhibited in the Courtault Gallery in London. The Victorian Spiritualists' Union in Melbourne, Australia, acquired 35 of Houghton's drawings in 1910.

Clairvoyance and Abstract Art

It is possible that af Klint's work was never displayed in the private venues of Theosophical Society conventions and did not influence future abstract artists enough to try their hands at the style, but the leaders of the society encourage abstraction on their own. Leadbeater and Besant continued to focus their attention on color and form in a book that they co-authored, *Thought Forms* (Theosophical Publishing House, 1901). This short book discusses auras more thoroughly. It also expands ideas of Swedenborg, that thoughts and emotions cause vibrations producing visual manifestations in the physical world that clairvoyant people can see. Leadbeater continued his descriptions of thought forms and auras in his work *Man Visible and Invisible: Examples of Different Types of Men as Seen by Means of Trained Clairvoyance* (1902). Aside from pages of text, this book contains diagrams and colored illustrations.

These books point out that one's aura is a different color depending on the development of the individual. The more refined a person, the more beautiful their aura; or, as Leadbeater described it, a "higher type" of person possesses finer qualities of astral matter and rippling fine, clear colors. The aura of a "gross" person would be dense and a dull brown, green or red. According to Theosophical ideas, humans have several bodies. We can understand the physical or etheric, the astral, the mental and the buddhic. Astral reflects emotions, mental is concerned with thoughts, and buddhic is concerned with our spirituality. The others are beyond our ability to comprehend. Besant and Leadbeater drew from their understanding of the science of their day to validate their occult beliefs. They likened the aura that surrounds us in all directions to energy emanating from a Leiden jar—a device that stores static electricity. They also linked the clairvoyant ability of visualizing thought to work done by Ernst Chladni, the German physicist sometimes called the father of acoustics (Besant and Leadbeater, *Thought Forms*, 28). In 1787 Chladni demonstrated the patterns sand makes when tossed onto a glass or metal plate that is vibrated by different frequencies of sound. Besant and Leadbeater explained that like sound, the mental activity of thoughts and desires caused vibrations in the surrounding atmosphere, and that these could be detected by clairvoyants. Clear thoughts exist as defined shapes. Vague thoughts exist as mist or clouds. To the authors, colors, vibrations and shooting bolts of energy could all be seen by clairvoyants, just as a scientist sees patterns of sand on a Chladni sound plate or lines formed when sand is released from a moving pendulum. This overlapping of the senses is called synesthesia. It is the ability to sense a stimulus with more than one of our senses. Possessing this ability was believed by Steiner and the Theosophists to be a sign of spiritual advancement.

According to Besan and Leadbeater, the description of color, surrounding and emitted by humans in their auras and by their thoughts gets more complicated. For example, when a person feels a strong emotion, the color of his or her aura is obscured and may appear as carmine, blue or scarlet depending on the rate of vibration of the emotion. In addition, thoughts are not simple, and each complexity will have a different vibration resulting in different effects.

The book also summarizes information about the meaning of colors. Black means hatred and malice, red means anger, burnt sienna signifies avarice, green stands for adaptability, deep orange for pride and ambition (Besant, *Thought Forms*, 32–33). The devotional thought of an unselfish heart is the lovely deep blue of a summer's sky (40–45). The book also contains colored pictures of auras and thought-forms that members of the society claimed to have seen. These appear as blobs of color and geometric and organic shapes denoting emotions such as anger, watchful jealousy, sympathy, fear, and selfish greed. The authors get even more specific, showing the thought forms we emit during different scenarios such as a shipwreck, being an actor on the first night of a play, being a gambler, having a street accident, attending a funeral, or when meditating.

Man Visible and Invisible is illustrated with full color pictures of astral bodies, mental bodies and causal bodies. The author, Leadbeater, asserts that there is overwhelming evidence in favor of the existence of clairvoyance. He also explains that the world consists of the realm of nature, the astral world and the mental realm. These exist at the same time, with all parts belonging to a large and stupendous whole, filling the same space and interpenetrating each other. This book delves more specifically into the meaning of colors. For example, black clouds floating in an aura like poisonous smoke signify a passionate fit of anger. Greenish-brown will be lit up by deep red or scarlet flashes to show jealousy. Yellow (the favorite color of Vincent van Gogh) is a very good color in the opinion of the author. Yellow will become brilliantly golden and gradually rise to a clear luminous lemon to show the possession of unselfish intellect.

One of the founders of abstract art was František Kupka (1871–1957), who was very aware of the ideas of Besant and Leadbeater and who regularly communicated with spirits of the dead. As a child, Kupka was a "sensitive." He had developed mediumistic powers enabling him to lead séances. Born in a poverty-stricken part of Bohemia (now located in the Czech Republic), he was not able to attend secondary school. Instead, he was apprenticed to a saddle-maker who belonged to a secret society that regularly communicated with the dead (Tuchman, 35). Kupka soon became a medium, a practice that he continued throughout his life, especially when he was short of cash. The saddle-maker helped Kupka attend a crafts school, which led to his entrance into the Academy of Painters in Prague. Perhaps because Kupka was coming from the perspective of a craftsman, his art training was unusual. Kupka learned how to draw, but his education also focused on pattern making and the study of ornamental Islamic art. The young man continued his art training in Vienna, where he became friends with German and Austrian Theosophists such as the painter Karl Diefenbach. Diefenbach invited Kupka to live in the Himmelhof Commune, which he had established for artists and musicians based on nudism, free love, and Theosophical ideas.

In 1896 Kupka settled in Paris and attended the Académie Julian, home of the cult-like Nabis group of artists who revered Paul Gauguin. He then studied at the Ecole des Beaux-Arts. Because of his mediumistic abilities and his theosophical conviction that he was a clairvoyant, Kupka believed that he could see things others couldn't see. He illustrated ideas of Spiritualism and Theosophy in representational work such as *The Beginning of Life* (1900), which depicts a fetus suspended over lily pads near a bright yellow form similar to Leadbeater's aura of enlightenment. Another one of his works is *The Way of Silence* (1903), in which statues of pharaohs cut the sacred geometric figure of the triangle into a star-studded sky. Kupka moved to creating purely non-representational work such as *The First Step* (1909), *Disks of Newton* (1911), *Amorpha: Fugue in Two Colors* (1912) and *The Position of Mobile Graphic* (1912–13). In these works, the artist focused on the sacred geometry mentioned in Blavatsky's *The Secret Doctrine* as well as the color theory of Leadbeater and Besant.

Kupka was a mystic and devout Theosophist his entire life (Swartz, 342). In his mature work he explored the Theosophists' fourth dimension—multidimensional realities, sensed by those with an elevated consciousness, that linked the spirit world with the physical world including astral planes (Long, 206). He exhibited his non-representational paintings in 1912 with a group of artists known as the Section d'Or. The poet and art critic Guillaume Apollinaire pointed to Kupka's works as perfect examples of pure painting, meaning that the work was not tied to the observable world but existed on its own as an art form, much as music differs from linguistic communication. Apollinaire named this new style of painting "Orphism" and hailed Kupka for being the leader of a new movement. Instead of being pleased, however, Kupka took offense. He denied that his work was part of any movement and believed that the other artists were merely copying him.

The artist who is credited with being the father of abstract art is Wassily Kandinsky (1866–1944). His mother was Russian, his grandmother German, but his father was born in Kyakhta, Siberia, a small town near the Chinese border. His father was a successful tea merchant who had to travel a lot, and he took his family with him. These trips exposed the boy to people with different practices and ideas. As a university student, Kandinsky studied law and economics and became a professor. He gave up this career at the age of thirty in 1896 to devote all his efforts to art. One of his early works, an untitled watercolor painted in 1910, is considered by art historians to be the first abstract painting ever to be made. It is now in the collection of the Musée National d'Art Moderne, in Paris, France.

Kandinsky was influenced by the Symbolist and Fauve artists but became interested in Theosophy and practiced meditation and visualization techniques. He also read Theosophical books such as *Thought Forms* and *Man Visible and Invisible,* and placed them in his library. Living in Munich, Kandinsky was also influenced by Rudolph Steiner. Steiner's book *Theosophy: An Introduction to the Spiritual Processes in Human Life and in the Cosmos* and several transcripts of the man's lectures given in Munich and Berlin were also found among Kandinsky's effects after his death (Ringbom, "Transcending the Visible," 147). Steiner believed that there are three levels of being, the physical, spiritual and the soul. Steiner's book *Theosophy* contains chapters with names such as "The Soul World," "The Soul in the Soul World After Death," "The Country of Spirits," "The Country of Spirits After Death," and "The Physical World and Its Connection to the Worlds of Soul and Spirits." The final chapter of Steiner's work is on human auras and thought forms. To Steiner, and subsequently Kandinsky, one does not have to die to become a spirit. One already exists as body, spirit and soul when alive. After death, our continuing spirit takes on a new physical body when reincarnated. We see our physical bodies with our eyes and brain, but in order to see spirits or the auras they manifest, one must develop clairvoyant abilities. Steiner (58) wrote: "Thus we each take part in three worlds—the physical, soul, and spiritual worlds. We are rooted in the physical world through the material-physical body, ether body and soul body; we come to flower in the spiritual world through the spirit self, life spirit, and spirit body. But the stem, which roots at one end and flowers at the other, is the soul itself."

Steiner echoed the Theosophical belief that humans were made up of several "bodies": the physical, the astral, the mental, the buddhic, the etheric, and others we can't comprehend. It was also his belief that these spirits continue to exist after our death.

Kandinsky disliked the often tedious theorizing of the Theosophical Society and published his own book in 1910, *Über das Geistige in der Kunst* (*Concerning the Spiritual in Art*). Parts of this book were immediately translated into English and published by Alfred Stieglitz in his *Camera Works* magazine. By 1911, the entire work had been translated and made available for purchase in the United States. This book, and Kandinsky's ideas, became one of the most important influences on art of the 20th century.

In his book, Kandinsky expressed his belief that art belonged to the spiritual life; therefore, art must be more than the representation of observable things. A connoisseur might recognize the skill and admire the quality of realistic painting, but it is merely an echo of contemporary feelings and adds nothing to them. A true work of art must raise the spiritual level of the viewer. Representational art is "art for art's sake." It leaves the soul of the viewer still hungry (Kandinsky, 12). Artists must offer "spiritual food" because when there is no artistic champion, true spiritual food is lacking. Kandinsky declared that humans live not only in the physical world but also in a spiritual city. He accepted the Theosophical insistence that artists possess the prerequisite for spiritual abilities. Artists were guides to the spiritual. Art expressed the internal truth. Kandinsky echoed Blavatsky's belief that humans were evolving in a new age and that artists would lead society away from materialism to more spiritual concerns. Kandinsky insisted that it was up to artists to lead the world in the new century.

Kandinsky's own art moved from representation of the material world, to representation with references to the spiritual, to spiritual representations with occasional references to the material world. He eliminated depth, painted auras and created abstract glyphs in an attempt to communicate deep themes and emotions on a spiritual level. In his review of the Kandinsky exhibition held at the National Gallery of Art, the art critic Hilton Kramer wrote, "Kandinsky's ideas—and sometimes the very shapes used to represent them on the canvas—were drawn from a wide range of literary and religious writings on the occult" (*New York Times*, May 10, 1981).

Theosophical thought, sometimes confused with spiritualism, was very influential in Kandinsky's earliest abstract work. For example, in his 1912 painting *Woman in Moscow*, space is flattened, de-emphasizing the material world. A bluish-green aura surrounds the main figure—a woman. In *Thought Forms* we are told that green denotes adaptability and blue represents "the devotional thought of an unselfish heart" (Besant, 34). On the right of the figure is a fully formed cloud shape of pink and orange that might have been directly copied from Leadbeater's illustration of "Vague Pure Affection" (Besant, 40). Floating above this aura shape is a hard, black oval, which in Leadbeater's vocabulary of clairvoyant sight meant malice or anger. This is topped with a smaller oval of orange, brown and yellow that looks like the aura Leadbeater and Besant depicted denoting intellect mixed with savagery. Understanding these references gives the viewer an entirely new perspective on this painting. But Kandinsky did not want his viewers to have to study any text. Instead, he hoped that these colors and shapes would immediately be recognized by our own spirits.

In the United States, the photographer and gallery owner Alfred Stieglitz (1864–1946) was so impressed with Kandinsky's book and artwork that he helped raise money to send the American artist Marsden Hartley to Berlin to meet with him. Unfortunately, Hartley didn't speak German or Russian and so was not able to communicate well with the man. Nevertheless, when he returned, Hartley, Arthur Dove and Georgia O'Keefe began to paint abstract work with an American Transcendentalist slant. While they continued to be steeped in landscape and material objects, these artists tried to transcend them by simplifying objects into shapes and distorting space and color in an attempt to depict the inner spirit of things. Their work was eagerly exhibited by Stieglitz in his Gallery 291, but the artists themselves were not enthused to work in this style. Having read *On the Spiritual in Art* on the recommendation of her teacher, Alon Bement, Georgia O'Keefe wrote, "I have a curious sort of feeling about some of my things—I hate to show them—I am perfectly inconsistent about it—I'm afraid people won't understand—and I hope that they won't—and am afraid they will" (Eldredge, 118). On the advent of World War I, O'Keeffe and the others went back to painting landscapes in their representational styles.

European abstract art was exhibited in New York for the first time in the International Exhibition of Modern Art held at the New York City Armory in 1913. "The Armory Show" displayed 1,400 works. One third of these were by European artists and many of these were abstract. Not understanding the concept behind the abstract style, most viewers were shocked and horrified, believing that the art work represented a backward step in civilization. A show-stopper was the Cubist painting by Marcel Duchamp (1887–1968) called *Nude Descending a Staircase*, painted in 1912. Duchamp was influenced by another founder of abstract art, Piet Mondrian (1887–1966), who had read *The Secret Doctrine* and had joined the Theosophical Society in the Netherlands in 1908. Mondrian had been interested in communication with the dead since at least 1898 but had been too frightened to attend a séance. After joining the society, he became interested in how theories of mathematics could be used to demonstrate the cosmic order. When he moved to Paris in 1912, he lived in the Theosophical Society building before finding a place of his own.

His published articles on art sound like those of many others in the society in that he believed in an evolution where artists and non-artists will become fully human beings imbued with beauty so that they no longer needed art. As an artist, he reduced line to essentials, contrasted the horizontal to the vertical, and used the three primary colors. This minimalism was to show the unity that was the human destiny, "the unity that would resolve harmoniously all antitheses between male and female, static and dynamic, spirit and matter" (Blotkamp, 96).

In 1907 Leadbeater was asked to resign from the Theosophical Society for helping young men to masturbate to relieve their homosexual tensions (Washington, 121–123). He was reinstated the same year after Olcott's death and raised to a high position in the society by Besant, much to the dismay of many of its members. Complaints of sexual misconduct continued until his death. When Besant and Leadbeater declared in 1912 that the teenager Jiddu Krishnamurti was the Maitreya, or personification of Christ, that Blavatsky had predicted, thousands of members dropped out of the society. Steiner was so incensed with the deification of Krishnamurti that he forbade anyone under his leadership to believe that Christ had returned. Today, the Theosophical Society still exists, but without the influence and membership it once had. Still, 20th century artists continued to be fascinated by death. And while contemporary artists may not be aware of it, they have been inspired by the work of artists who had studied and believed in Theosophy, spiritualism and the occult ideas of continued human existence after dead.

4

Mourning Garb

Mourning Franklin, Hancock and Washington

Fine artists, mediums and performers could glorify, dramatize, mourn and try to defeat death with their manifestos and their art. They could express their feelings and heal themselves and their viewers from the deep sadness they felt through their creativity. But with life being so uncertain, and death hovering around every corner, ordinary people also needed a way to feel more in control. They needed a way to deal with the deep sorrow death caused, and because of this, they thrust themselves into the mourning process by ritualizing their response to death and by draping their bodies in special clothing. Nineteenth century Americans and Europeans were not ashamed to mourn the death of a loved one. Quite the contrary, they were required to advertise their losses and overwhelming grief, making walking billboards out of their bodies, the bodies of their children, and in some cases the bodies of their servants or slaves. Men wore these items of clothing, making artistic choices about what to wear for each death. Women, on the other hand, designed the clothing, sewed the clothing, decided on and fabricated their accessories. Retail clothing stores did not exist until the end of the century. Wealthy women might have conferred with their dressmakers, but all women played a large part in creating their own mourning "look." They were the canvas, and fabric was their medium. The message of the work they created was loss, grief, and death—a message sent loud and clear, and easily identifiable to all in their community.

While religious leaders advised that mourning clothing be simple, superstitions sprang up discouraging wearing the same mourning clothes for different deaths, and powerful societal pressures insisted that all clothing be fashionable. Nineteenth century styles changed constantly in response to the technological breakthroughs of the Industrial Revolution and couturiers who made clothing for the elite. Some of these designers became powerful people who mingled with political leaders, the aristocracy, and the wealthy bourgeoisie. Fashion illustrators kept the public informed of these latest trends. Published in lady's magazines, these drawings made certain that some illustrations were colored in black to demonstrate how easily these styles could be adapted for one who mourned.

Religion and politics provided blueprints for mourning. One of the first books to be published in the fifteenth century after the invention of moveable type was the *Ars Moriendi*, translated into English as *The Art of Dying*. Written in Latin by a Dominican brother devastated by the scourge of the Black Plague, the book explains the proper

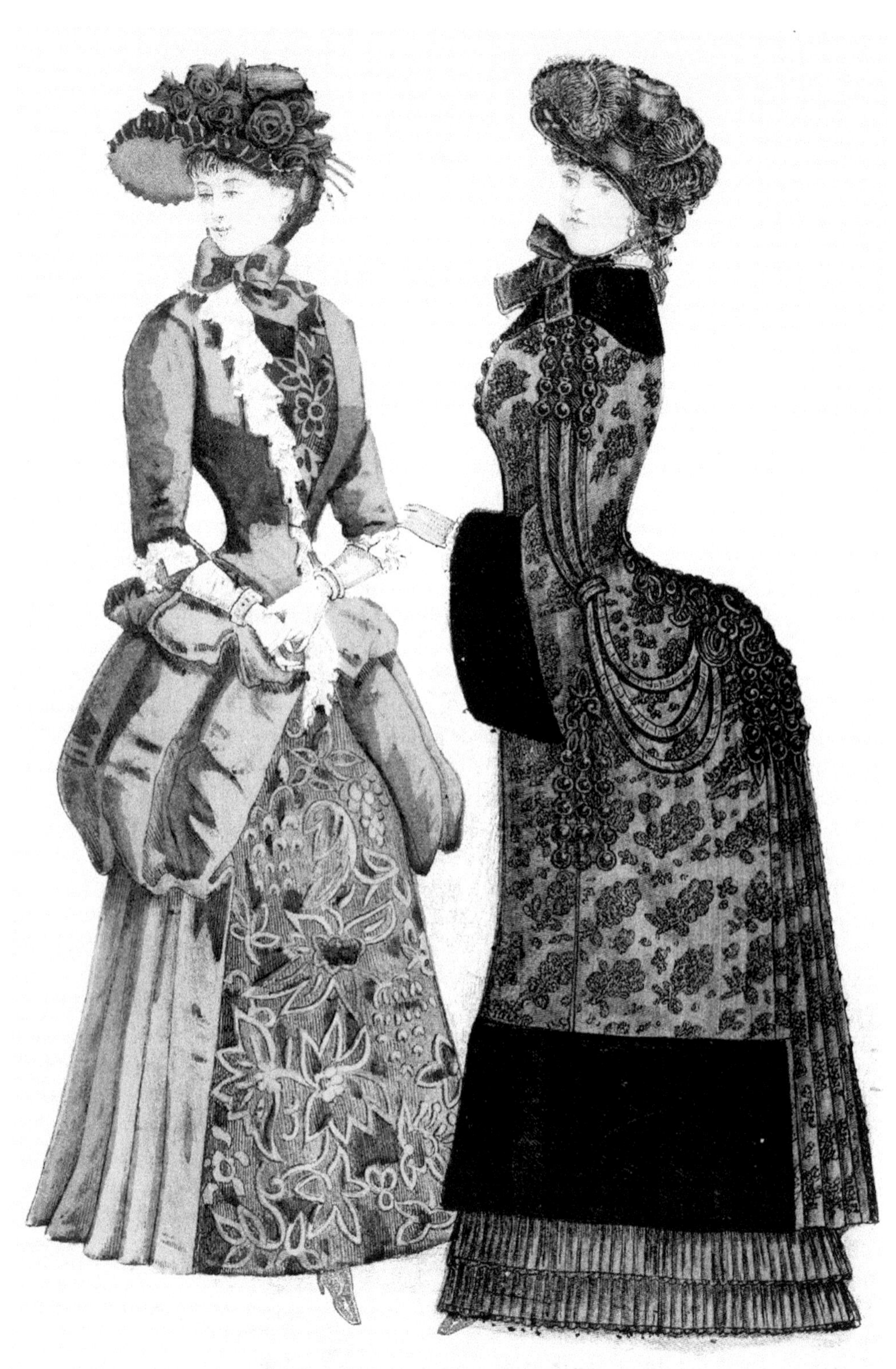

GODEYS FASHIONS.

approach to death for followers of Jesus Christ. This work was reinterpreted by the Anglican cleric Jeremy Taylor (1613–1667) to fit the tenets of the Church of England. His book, *The Rule and Exercises of Holy Dying*, was written in 1651 but was reprinted several times, including once in 1850 by Charles Wittingham of Chiswick. Written for the edification of the "Right Honourable and Noblest Lord, Richard, Earl of Carbery" (Taylor, 2b), the work instructs readers on how to prepare their souls for the inevitable time when their bodies will mingle with that beloved dust. The book also prepares survivors for the death of a loved one and gives instructions on how to visit the sick and what prayers should be said by survivors (Taylor, xxiv). When writing about the treatment of our "dear friends after death" Taylor references a book called *All-Virtuous Wisdom of Joshua ben Sira*, known as the *Wisdom of Sirach* or the *Book of Ecclesiasticus*. This is a compilation of ethical teachings dating from 200 to 175 BCE that is included as part of the biblical canon of the Catholic and Lutheran churches. The passage says: "Weep bitterly and make great moan, and make lamentation, as he is worthy, and that a day or two, lest thou be evil spoken of, and then comfort thyself for thy heaviness. But take no grief to heart; for there is no turning again; thou shalt not do him good, but hurt thyself" (Eccles. 38:17, quoted in Taylor, 249).

Taylor firmly believed in the immortality of the soul. He wrote that if a man has died in the grace of the Lord, it is a cause for joy. If, however, he perished in sin, there is no hope of redemption and grief is a useless exercise. Some shedding of tears at a funeral is always required, but excessive mourning was seen as a self-love that bordered on the sin of pride. In Taylor's view the dead, even children, gave up the life of turmoil and pain seen on their deathbeds, to rise up to heaven and a peaceful existence. Therefore, death should not be a time for grief. Excessive grief was ill-placed and even indecent. But this viewpoint was not the case for royals, or for political figures in the United States. Death, as in the case of Benjamin Franklin in 1790, John Hancock in 1793, and George Washington in December of 1799, brought people together. Death demonstrated the federal government's military might and was a useful political tool to unite the collection of disparate states into a unified country.

Benjamin Franklin died in Philadelphia, Pennsylvania, when it was the acting capital of the new country. To honor the man and his passing, James Madison, a congressman at the time, was able to get his colleagues in the House of Representatives to agree to wear symbols of mourning for one month after the statesman's death. The Senate, however, did not follow suit, possibly because John Adams, who was presiding over that body, had not liked Franklin. Thomas Jefferson urged President George Washington to order members of the executive branch of the government to wear mourning for Franklin, but Washington declined. Washington thought this act would be too similar to what was done for European royalty. Washington stayed true to his republican ideals of not creating an aristocracy in the new nation, but citizens responded to the loss. It is estimated that 20,000 people attended the funeral of Benjamin Franklin, which was remarkable when considering that the population of the city at the time was only 28,000 in total (Davey, 91).

John Hancock was the governor of the state of Massachusetts when he died in his mansion on Boston's Beacon Hill. The day of his funeral was declared a state holiday by

Opposite: **Fashion plate from Antique Archives,** *Godey's Ladies' Book*, **May 5, 1860 (Accessible Archives Collection, www.accessible-archives.com).**

the acting governor, Samuel Adams. Hancock's funeral procession included Vice President John Adams, members of the U.S. Congress, foreign ministers, judges and secretaries of the United States. Also included was his wife, Dorothy Quincy Hancock (Dolly) (1747–1830), who was no stranger to death. In 1777 her first child, Lydia, died when she was only ten months old, and Dolly's son, John George Washington Hancock, born in 1778, died from a skating accident in 1787 at the age of nine.

George Washington's death at 67 years of age on December 14, 1799, only two years after stepping down as president, was seen by some to be a bad omen for the new century and the new nation. But for others, such as Alexander Hamilton and the Federalists, it was an opportunity to encourage a sense of national identity in the citizenry while demonstrating the importance of a centralized military and a strong government. When the news of the death of the former president was announced in Congress, Congress immediately adjourned. Members of the House of Representatives shrouded the Speaker's chair in black cloth, and the government declared a 69-day period of mourning, which was to end in the new century on the day of Washington's birth, February 22. Members of both houses of Congress wore black clothing for the remainder of the session, and President John Adams issued a presidential proclamation that citizens wear black crepe armbands on their left arms for thirty days to demonstrate the nation's grief ("Death of George Washington").

Fearing that he would be buried alive, President Washington had asked not to be buried for 3 days after he was declared dead. When he was finally laid to rest in his vault facing the Potomac River at his home in Mount Vernon, Virginia, it was in a private ceremony held on December 17. Soon after, however, a joint session of Congress drafted a resolution declaring December 26, 1799, the national day of funeral and mourning for the great man. This day included an elaborate procession through Philadelphia—still the temporary capital of the nation. A bier draped in black carried a coffin containing Washington's hat and sword. Accompanying it was a parade of senators, congressmen, judges, other officials and clergy. Ceremoniously, the band of mourners wound its way down city streets accompanied by uniformed soldiers, cavalry carrying mourning flags, and two Marines wearing black scarfs leading a single, riderless, white horse draped in black gauze with white and black plumes on its head. In the tradition of ancient fallen leaders and European royalty, Washington's boots were placed in the stirrups facing backwards. After Washington's funeral, his wife, Martha, appeared in public wearing mourning clothes including a black lace shawl, black gloves, and black kid shoes. She also wore a mourning locket or ring containing a lock of the president's hair. Mrs. Washington was 68 years old at the time of her husband's death. She lived only 2 ½ years more ("The Twilight Years").

Etiquette

As a former part of the United Kingdom, early Americans followed English social etiquette, which heavily relied on the customs of the French. Strict laws and protocol had evolved in those countries for honoring royalty and members of high social status. In England, mourning procedures for the court were regulated by the Lord Chamberlain and the Duke of Norfolk, also known as the Earl Marshal—both hereditary positions. The Earl Marshal decided the length of time for an individual stage of mourning for each royal death, and the Lord Chamberlain, the senior officer of the royal household, set the standards for mourning dress for members of the court and all visitors, including any foreign diplomats (Davey, 99). Black dye, once very expensive, was used to color cloth that was made into clothing worn to mourn members of the royal family. After the death of a royal, members and visitors to the court were also required to wear black clothing in public as well as to formal court events for a specific period of time.

Wearing black clothes to show bereavement can be traced back to Roman times in Europe and the British Isles. Black was seen as the absence of color. It stood, and still stands for, the extinguishing of light and the absence of life: "The midnight gloom of sorrow for the loss sustained" (Davey, 104). The practice of wearing black was revived again from the mid–1300s to the 1600s when the Black Death, bubonic plague, killed 25 percent of Europe's population. Since so little was known about the causes of and the cures for disease, there was a belief among the European population, backed by observation, that death could claim the relatives of the deceased. Since germs were unknown, the belief was that spirits of the dead returned and persuaded the living to join them in the afterlife. It was hoped that wearing black would make the mourner invisible to these spirits and protect them. But for commoners, wearing black was not always allowed. In medieval times European and British countries placed prohibitions against ordinary people wearing black, to prevent them from copying their "betters." Their mourning garb might have been nothing more than the wearing of a dark cloak with a hood over their regular clothes. Under these cloaks, widows were discouraged from wearing bright colors. Even if it had not been forbidden, black dye was expensive and affordable only by the rich. Commoners took to wearing "brunette"—dark brown cloth—as a symbol of their grief. By the 1400s European and British women no longer wore a wimple, a cloth headdress that covered their heads, necks and sides of their faces, but it became a tradition for widows to wear a veil (Tortora, 172). Veiled and clothed in dark, non-reflective cloth, these mourners hoped to be invisible to spirits and that their mourning garb might safeguard them from death's call (Brett, 134).

To show distain for the aristocracy, the French anti-royalists outlawed the wearing of mourning black once they gained power after their first revolution in 1789, referred to now as the Reign of Terror. This decree was not followed by the infamous queen of France, Marie Antoinette. When she learned that her husband, King Louis XVI, had been executed in 1793, she had her dressmaker, Rose Bertin, make black mourning clothes for her and her four children even though they were in prison. The deposed queen wore her black dress and widow's coif (a close-fitting cap) for months while she awaited her trial and execution. However, on the day of her death, Marie Antoinette was ordered to change into a simple white dress and cap so that that she wouldn't remind the crowd of her royal standing or evoke their sympathy for being a widow (Stuart, 337). The French Revolution and the French Republic ended in 1799 with a military coup, the rise of Napoleon Bonaparte and the First Empire, which reestablished a French court and allowed black mourning clothes once more.

The English rebellions against their royals were not successful. British society was seen as a grand machine. The anonymous author of the book *The Mirror of the Graces: or the English Lady's Costume*, published in 1830, wrote that the "Laws of Precedence," unwritten rules of English society passed down from the middle ages, maintained that there was a "harmonious order amongst civilized men and women as the laws of attraction keep heavenly bodies in their orbits" (*Mirror of the Graces*, 162). This book justified the divisions between the social classes, saying, "As one star differs from another in magnitude and splendor, in proportion to the destiny it hath to fulfil; so do the talents and degree of men vary according to the duties they have to perform" (*ibid.*). British culture supported the "divine right of kings." The monarch's position was given to him or her by God. Just so, the Laws of Precedence declared that each person's rank was given to him or her by God, and that each individual had his or her proper place. British women had a long tradition of following social mores. Their position in society was practically frozen by the circumstances of their birth.

At the beginning of the 18th century, when the monarchy was powerful, a man's or a woman's social standing came from his or her relationship to the ruler and the aristocracy. Strict standards of behavior set the aristocracy apart from the lower classes, and there was no social mobility. The lower classes could never aspire to be royalty or part of the aristocracy. But all this changed by the end of the 18th century and the beginning of the next, when the emerging European and British merchant classes gained economic power. Lord Chesterfield, the British statesman, noted this in a letter he published in 1774 when he coined the word "etiquette" and used it to refer to coherent moral principles (Arditi, 417). As the 19th century progressed, Queen Victoria's powers lessened and Britain became more of a true constitutional monarchy. France finally rid itself of its monarch with the Revolution of 1848. They did this only after twice restoring the Bourbon dynasty and then crowning a cousin, Louis-Phillipe d'Orléans, king. American rulers decided against establishing an aristocracy. These countries became class-based, meaning that the merchant class, the bourgeoisie, and the middle class could attain new respectability and were able to reach new societal heights. Etiquette became very important. Manners and ethics gave the bourgeoisie their position in society and identified those who had them as the dominant group. The merchant and the middle classes were able to afford expensive items and fashions. To ensure their position in society, they established rituals, including mourning rituals, patterned after royal behavior. These rituals were strictly followed by these newly empowered folk, commoners nonetheless. Knowing and demonstrating this proper etiquette grew to be extremely important. Not being born to a high station, behavior had to set a person apart from the masses. Correct behavior allowed entrée to higher strata of society. The behavior, manners and the etiquette people followed made them accepted and gave them power.

Copying the aristocracy, the bourgeoisie of England and France incorporated royal etiquette into their lives and adopted the practice of wearing black mourning dress. Unfortunately, there were plenty of royal deaths to inspire the commoners. In England, King George III's son Octavius died in 1783 at 4 years of age. His brother, Alfred, died in August 1782 without even reaching the age of 2. Amelia, the youngest and favorite child of King George III and his queen, Charlotte, was born in 1783 but died in 1810. Before her the Duke of Gloucester, brother of the king, died in 1805, followed in 1806 by the Duke of Brunswick, the king's brother-in-law. In 1813 the king's sister, the Duchess of Brunswick and Princess Royale of England, passed away. Then, on November 6, 1817, Princess Charlotte, the only grandchild of King George III, and heir to the British throne, died in childbirth, along with her stillborn son. Once again, the Lord Chamberlain and the Earl Marshal set the rules for mourning dress and established the length of time for mourning for the royal court and diplomatic visitors. The royal deaths did not stop with the princess. A year later Queen Charlotte, wife of George III and the princess's grandmother, died. Two years later the Duke of Kent, the youngest son of King George III, passed away. Happily, he had hastily married after the death of Princess Charlotte and sired a daughter. This baby eventually grew up to become Queen Victoria. Finally, in 1820, the tormented King George III breathed his last.

Mourning Princess Charlotte

Of all of these deaths, the death of Princess Charlotte was the most tragic. The British people had followed her life, marriage and pregnancy with great interest because with her lay the continuation of their monarchy. And she was young—just 21 years old. Charlotte had exhibited an indomitable spirit by breaking her engagement to the Prince of Orange and had only married Prince Leopold, the Prince of Coburg, the year before. It was also hoped that her reign would restore respectability to the realm. The British people had suffered indignities and losses because of their recent kings. Charlotte's grandfather, King George III, had completely lapsed into madness in 1810 after the death of his daughter, Amelia. Some think he was bipolar and that the death of his favorite child caused him to lose his grasp on reality, while others believe his insanity was caused by a condition known as porphyria, a genetic blood disorder. The king lived until 1820, but from 1811 on, all royal duties were performed by his eldest son, also named George. Called the Prince Regent during this time, the younger George ruled in place of his father, but his scandalous treatment of his wife, Caroline, his affair with his mistress Maria Fitzherbert, and his extravagancies shocked his subjects, if not the world. When King George III finally died, he became King George IV, but only lived ten more years.

Charlotte, George IV's daughter, was the only legitimate heir to his throne. Her death was a considerable blow, throwing the country into a panic and into deep mourning. The government shut down, and everyone who could afford it wore black clothing or black arm bands until there was no more black fabric left to buy. To honor Princess Charlotte, shops closed for weeks, and mourning dress was worn by all commoners who could afford it, and even by some who could not (Taylor, 94). The Western World was in the middle of the Industrial Revolution. The urban working population lived under appalling conditions and most could never hope to afford mourning clothes of their own, but burial and friends' societies sprang up, which allowed people to borrow or rent mourning garb.

The Lord Chamberlain determined that there would be three stages of mourning for Princess Charlotte: full or deep mourning, followed by second mourning, followed by half mourning. Each stage was demonstrated by the wearing of approved clothing. As each stage passed, restrictions concerning dress eased slightly, but strict adherence was required by the entire court.

The Earl Marshal decided the length of mourning for each stage. According to Richard Davey, the author of *A History of Mourning* (1890), the registry at the Lord Chamberlain's office in England decreed that full mourning for a sovereign would last eight weeks for relatives and royals of the court. Mourning would last two weeks, and half mourning would also last two weeks. In total, mourning for a king or queen for the royal court lasted only three months. If the son or daughter of a sovereign died, full mourning lasted four weeks, mourning lasted one week and half, and half mourning an additional week. The brother or sister of the sovereign was mourned for three weeks: two weeks of full mourning, four days of mourning and two days of half mourning. A nephew, niece or uncle was mourned for only two weeks: one week being full mourning, a half week for mourning and the rest of the week for half mourning (Davey, 103). Because there had been so many royal deaths, the Earl Marshal was petitioned by merchants to shorten the length of mourning for Charlotte for fear that they would go bankrupt if the stages were too long.

For full or deep mourning, ladies were to wear dresses made of black muslin or bombazine (a fabric with diagonal ridges made of wool and silk). They could also choose to wear a long lawn hood made of crepe—a crisp fabric made of either silk or wool). Both bombazine and crepe were dull materials that did not reflect any light. Crepe was also scratchy, with a crinkled appearance. The Lord Chamberlain decreed that the ladies were to wear "Shamoy" shoes, which were probably made of dull chamois leather, and gloves and crepe fans. When at home or in casual situations, the Lord Chamberlain decreed that dresses should be made of dark Norwich crepe, a fabric made by Grout and Company in Norwich, England. Gentlemen were ordered to wear black cloth clothing without buttons on the sleeves or pockets, plain muslin or long lawn cravats (a long piece of fabric tied around the neck in a knot) and weepers (a black mourner's veil). Men also wore shamoy shoes and gloves, crepe hatbands, and black swords and buckles. Casual dress for men was a dark gray frock coat—a coat with a knee-length skirt. This stage of mourning was to last two months (Davey, 100).

For what was called the "second mourning," clothing for women could be made of black silk, fringed or plain linen, white gloves, black shoes, fans and tippets (a woman's long scarf, usually made of fur). At this stage they were allowed to wear white necklaces and earrings, because the combination of black and white expressed sorrow, but also hope. Casual dress, or "undress," for ladies consisted of white or gray lustrings (a glossy silk or satin fabric), tabbies (plainly woven fabric), or damasks (a fabric woven with a reversible pattern). Men were to continue to dress in black, full trimmed, fringed or plain linen, black swords and buckles. Men's undress was to be a gray coat (Davey, 100).

With the passage of time, mourners entered the half mourning stage. For this, the Lord Chamberlain decreed that women's dresses could now include black silk or velvet, colored ribbons, fans and tippets, or plain white, white and gold, or white and silver stuffs (meaning any type of fabric), with black ribbons. Men could wear black coats, with black or plain white, or white and gold, or white and silver stuffed waistcoats, colored waistcoats and buckles (Davey, 100).

We must remember that wealthy mourners did not wear mourning garb just for the funeral or for formal wear. Mourning garb was to be worn throughout the day for the designated period of time, no matter what the mourner was doing. This meant that mourners had to have several outfits for each task they performed during their day such as walking, visiting, dining, or riding in carriages. Every outfit had to fit the requirements of the Lord Chamberlain for the period of mourning as well as be fashionable as befitting the social standing of the one wearing the clothes.

Interest in Princess Charlotte's death, and royalty's reaction to it, was so high that fashion magazines began running images of the mourning clothing the royals wore. These illustrations, called fashion plates (detailed prints made from drawings of the fashionable elite), began appearing in periodicals such as the British magazine *Ladies' Magazine or Entertaining Companion for the Fair Sex: Appropriated Solely to Their Use and Amusement*, and *Ackerman's Repository of the Arts*. This illustrated British periodical was published from 1809 to 1829 before changing its name to *The Repository of Fashion*; which merged with *La Belle Assemblée*. Along with images of stylish black evening gowns, these magazines also featured fashion plates of casual apparel such as walking attire and carriage outfits. For the price of 4 shillings (or about $20 in today's money), anyone who could afford one of these journals could get glimpses of the clothing worn by the rich and famous of their times. In response, middle class and society ladies altered their clothing accordingly and dressed in mourning for the important princess. If you were clever with a needle and had the money to buy fabric, you, with the help of your daughters or your servants, could make the clothing yourself. If you were a member of a wealthier class, you could bring the journal page to your dressmaker and have her or him fabricate clothing for you in the most elegant and socially acceptable style of the day. For mourning Princess Charlotte this meant the neo-classical style, which including padded hems, sleeve puffs (or "jockies"), and neo–Gothic decorations.

The neoclassical style became popular in the early 1800s in Paris following the military victories of Napoleon Bonaparte in Austria and Italy and other victories against the British and Turks in Egypt. After the failure of the French Revolution, the French established a government of five committee members called the *Directoire* ("Directory"). This group gave Napoleon command of the army. As a result of Napoleon's successful military campaigns, captured territories were forced to send money to a bankrupted France, replenishing funds given by the French king to the Americans during their revolution against the British. These defeated nations were also made to send art to fill the newly established museum in the Louvre palace in Paris. Napoleon eventually staged a coup and overthrew the Directory in 1799. He gave himself dictatorial powers and the title of emperor of the French. The skirt of women's dresses of this time, called the "empire dress" for Napoleon's empire, no longer had side pannier frameworks. They fell directly from a high waist to the floor and often had short sleeves. Because of this, they were worn with an Indian cashmere, Japanese silk, or muslin shawl, mantle (cloak), or mantelet (a short cape) purchased from milliners who sold hats and also fabric. Since these items were imported, they could be very expensive.

Marie Antoinette and Rose Bertin

This style of dress actually originated with Marie Antoinette (1755–1792), famous for the elaborate wardrobe that she created with the help of her dress designer and couturier, Rose Bertin. Bertin designed the dress Marie Antoinette wore as a teenager when she attended the coronation of her husband, Louis-Auguste, a year after King Louis XV, his grandfather, died after reigning for 60 years. The prince's own father had died in 1765. At the time, it was French custom for royalty to mourn for four and a half months for a grandparent and to wear black. The coronation of Louis XVI was not until a year later on June 19, 1775. Portraits of the new king show him wearing white pantaloons and white stockings and shirt, covered with a purple and gold robe with ermine trim. Portraits of the new queen show her dressed in a formal gown made from diaphanous white fabric, trimmed in gold with a very long train. Under the dress were side panels, called "panniers," which were baskets worn underneath the skirt at each hip. The panniers made the dress jut out several feet on either side, making the queen appear much larger than her male companions. Bertin became the personal designer to the queen and consulted with her every day to discuss what she wanted to wear. After making a costume for the queen, Bertin would make similar gowns for other aristocratic ladies of the court. Bertin also introduced the young queen to the heavily powdered "pouf" hairstyle. For this, she worked with the famous hairdresser Léonard Autié to create the queen's elaborate ensembles that often went along with the theme of each theatrical ball given at the palace of Versailles.

But Marie Antoinette didn't always dress in such elaborate clothing. When alone, or in the privacy of her retreat, the "Petite Trianon," she was said to have worn thin white muslin chemises with sashes in a style called the *chemise a la reine*. Chlorine bleach had recently been invented in 1774, and for the first time, dressmakers were able to purchase really white fabric. But the unfortunate queen was vilified by the French people and the French court for dressing like this. Marie Antoinette was not liked at court. She did not produce an heir for several years after her marriage; she gambled; and she broke fashion laws. She also did not want to be dressed by the court ladies as was the tradition in France. She was impatient with formality and was said to wear breeches in the saddle and ride a horse astride, like a man. After the revolution and her execution, her casual style was embraced and morphed into the neoclassical look. The fabric of the dresses was sheer and white, in mimicry of the newly arrived ancient Greek and Roman statues that had been carved in white marble. Sewn in black, this was the same style of mourning dress women wore for Princess Charlotte's funeral.

During the Renaissance, clothing fashion for the elite was set by Italian designers and later by Parisian couturiers. In the eighteenth and early nineteenth centuries, fashion designers such as Rose Bertin dressed dolls—called Pandoras, *poupées de modes*, or Queen Anne Dolls (depending on the language you spoke)—in their latest designs, and shipped them to royalty all around the world, setting fashion trends among the elite. These dolls were made of wood or plaster with painted faces, glass eyes and fashionable hair, styled from flax or wool. By the time Marie Antoinette arrived on the scene, magazine articles illustrating and describing what she wore appeared in publications such as *Le Journal des Dames*. Although Marie Antoinette was accused of bankrupting her adopted country with gowns made of yards and yards of expensive textiles, heavily decorated with gemstones, and silver and gold thread embroidery, the public was nevertheless fascinated with her clothing. But Marie Antoinette was not the only trendsetter from Paris. A generation before her, King Louis XV's mistress, Jeanne Antoinette Poisson, otherwise known as Madame de Pompadour, established the Parisian Rococo fashion style. Coinciding with the Age of Enlightenment and the emergence of the new print medium of magazines, the Rococo style of dress captured the attention not only of royalty and the well to do, but also that of the lower classes, who were able to see illustrations and read about what was fashionable among the elite. Members of the merchant and emerging middle classes coveted Pompadour's pastel colors, side panniers, tightly corseted waists, plunging necklines and elaborate sleeves.

Members of the royal family, wealthy clergy, and others in high positions left France at the onset of the revolution in 1794 to escape the guillotine. Many settled in England and lived as émigrés, such as the Comte d'Artois, the brother of Louis XVI, who settled in London. He would eventually return to France to be crowned King Charles X. Marie-Jeanne (Rose) Bertin stayed in Paris and remained faithful to the fallen queen. The dressmaker continued to make clothing for Marie Antoinette even while she was in prison, including the queen's notorious mourning clothes. As soon as Marie Antoinette was executed, Bertin escaped to London and set up shop, creating clothing for the French émigrés

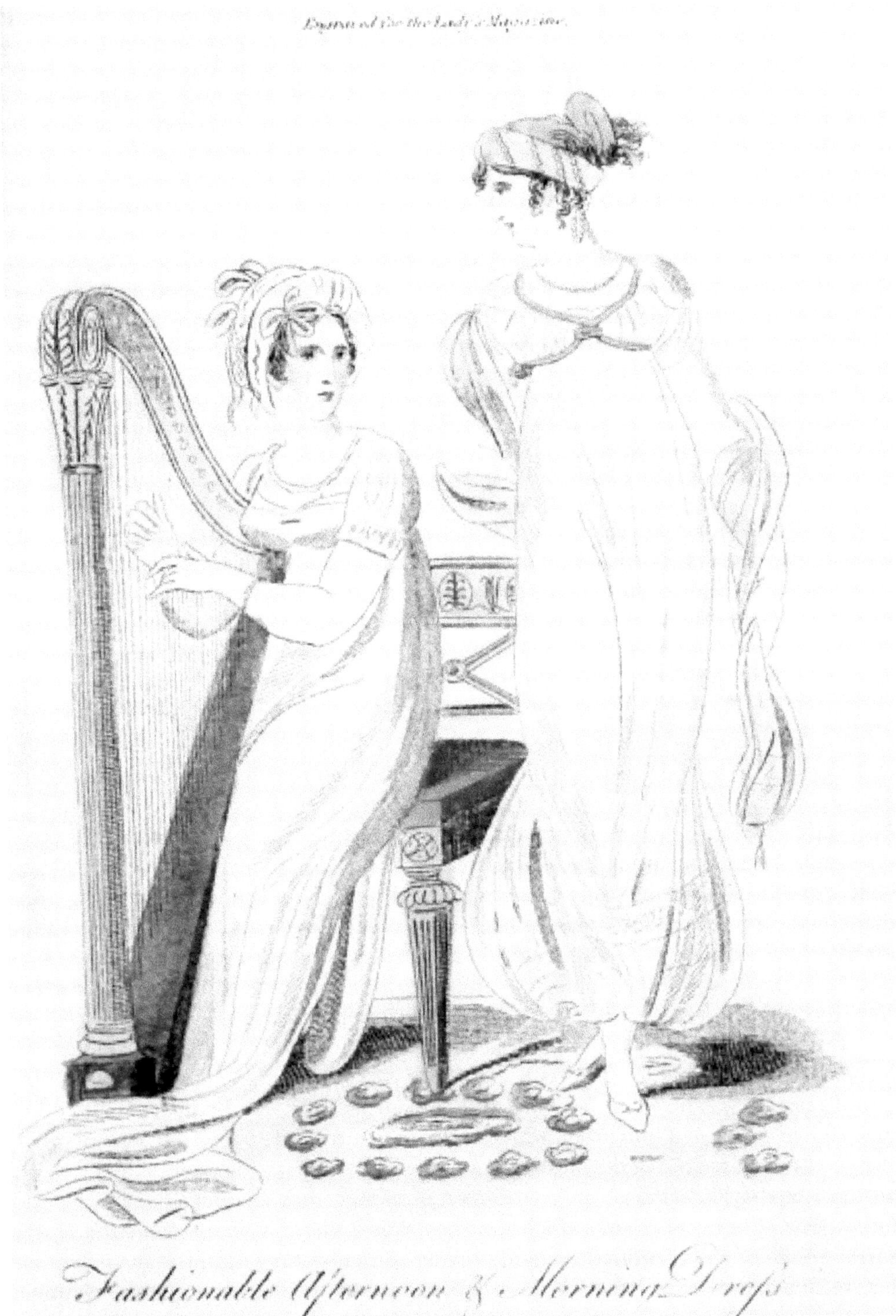

Empire dress fashion plate, 1807. *Ladies' Magazine or Entertaining Companion for the Fair Sex: appropriated Solely to Their Use and Amusement, London, Printed for G. Robinson, no. Paternoster-Row* (Accessible Archives Collection, www.accessible-archives.com).

who had settled there. From London, she even continued to send her dolls to foreign royalty. After the Reign of Terror, Bertin moved back to France but retired, giving her business to her nephews. She died in 1813. None of the queen's clothing has survived. During the revolution, everything she owned was either ransacked or destroyed.

Emerging Magazines

Continentals, the British, and Americans were able to keep up with the latest fashion trends because illustrations of what the elite wore were published in magazines—the revolutionary communication technology of this age. Johannes Gutenberg (1398–1468), originally a goldsmith, had invented moveable type around 1439 and used his invention to print a Bible that rivaled, in appearance, those that monks labored over for years by hand. Breakthroughs in print technology proceeded at a steady rate until the eighteenth century, when technology really took off. In 1712, Count Carl Hildebrand von Canstein (1667–1719) got the idea of copying an entire typeset page and printing from that. Called a "stereotype," the process was further refined by Scottish goldsmith William Ged (1699–1749) in 1725. British statesman and scientist Charles Stanhope (1753–1816) created the first printing press made entirely of iron in 1800. This greatly reduced press maintenance and improved the durability of the press. Two men using a stereotype working on an iron press could print around 250 sheets of paper an hour on both sides, and this press could last up to 70 years or more. But the real breakthrough came in 1814 when German inventor Friedrich Koenig (1774–1833) and watchmaker Andreas Friedrich Bauer (1784–1860) did away with the men. They were granted an English patent for a high-speed, steam-driven printing press that used stereotypes and could print over a thousand copies in an hour. R. Hoe and Company in New York had been making their own iron Acorn presses in 1822 (this type of press was used to print the 1830 Book of Mormon). But Hoe made an even more ingenious improvement to the printing process. Hoe made the stereotype mold of the page using papier-mâché. He filled the mold with molten metal and bent it around a form to create a steam-powered, revolving, cylindrical printing press that could print over 5,000 pages an hour. Hoe added more and more cylinders to the machine and called it "The Lightening." This press was bought by newspapers such as *The Public Ledger* of Philadelphia, *The Sun* of Baltimore, *The New York Times* and *The New York Herald* of New York City (American Printing History Association).

Of course, these printing presses needed paper, and thanks to French soldier and mechanical engineer Louis-Nicolas Robert (1761–1828), a machine that produced "continuous paper" was invented. The machine took a slurry of wood pulp, rags and other materials and turned it into mash, which was then poured onto a forming table of mesh. Water was squeezed out of the mash by a series of rollers operating under high pressure. Steam-heated cylinders dried and removed more water from the rough paper. This was followed by a coating of gelatin, which acted as sizing. Rollers finally smoothed the paper's surface. Robert, an indentured servant in a Parisian publishing firm, lost the patent for his creation to his bosses. When the French Papermaker's Guild objected to his invention, fearing that it would replace them, the machine was sent to England to avoid restraints. In London, it luckily escaped being trashed in the French Revolution. The machine was refined and was renamed the Fourdrinier machine, after Henry Fourdrinier, a London-based stationery wholesaler. Soon, steam printing presses pushed paper from continuous rolls measuring five miles in length through the cylindrical stereotypes at the rate of 800 feet a minute. The printed paper then passed over a knife that cut the pages apart. Another apparatus folded them. These combined technologies revolutionized communication by making newspapers and journals easy to produce. As more and more printed material became available, more and more people desired access to the knowledge contained in it. In the United States of America, public education was legislated during this time. An educated populace was seen as essential to the new democracy, and more and more people learned how to read ("Louis-Nicolas Robert").

One of the first journals to benefit from the breakthroughs in printing was *The Lady's Magazine,* which appeared in England in 1770 with the goal of entertaining and educating its readers. The first magazine for women, it contained fiction from major literary figures and articles about foreign and domestic events. It printed recipes, instructions for do-it-yourself projects, and cures for common ailments, sprinkled among advice columns on proper child-rearing methods and proper conduct. The magazine also contained fashion plates along with descriptions of the latest fashion styles from London and Paris. This magazine was successful, with estimated monthly sales of 15,000 copies. It spawned numerous imitations such as the *New Lady's Magazine,* published from 1786 to 1795, and *La Belle Assemblée,* published in England from 1806 to 1837 ("Fashion Plate Collection").

Even before these magazines, illustrations of fashions worn in Versailles could be purchased in France. They were published in *La Galerie des Modes et Costumes Français,* a series of engraved prints issued by merchants Esnault and Rapilly around 1778 during the reign of Louis XVI and Marie Antoinette. These plates could be purchased at their shop either hand-colored or left black and white. Artist Claude-Louis Desrais designed the first 68 plates. Other artists were Pierre-Thomas Leclère, François-Louis-Joseph Watteau (son of the famous painter), and designer Augustin de Sant-Aubin. Interestingly, in France, making fashion plates was an acceptable occupation for women when most other occupations were closed to them. The Colin sisters, Héloïse Suzanne (1819–1873), Adèle-Anaïs Toudouze (1822–1899), and Laure Noël-Colin (1827–1878), learned the trade from their father, Alexandre-Marie Colin. Toudouze's daughter, Isabell (1850–1907) took over for her mother and continued making fashion plates. The sisters and Isabell are considered among the greatest fashion illustrators of their times, selling plates to at least 20 different publications (Calahan, 176). When a journal was finished with an etched or engraved printing plate, the owners would sell it to another magazine to print. Plates made in France and Britain were sold to magazines in America, Spain and Italy, and the Colin sisters' work was seen around the world. Fashion plates also inspired painters such as Claude Monet, who copied a pose he saw in an illustration in his work *Women in the Garden* of 1866–67. Paul Cézanne's *La Promenade* shows that he copied directly from a fashion plate that appeared in *La Mode Illustrée* magazine in 1870–71.

Napoleon Bonaparte and Fashion Designer Hippolyte Leroy

Under Napoleon, Paris once more became the center of fashion for the world. Napoleon established the "First Empire," complete with its own court. The new elite were members of the military, army contractors and returned émigrés. Napoleon recognized that luxury was good for his country, and he encouraged it. The luxury trade and conspicuous consumption (enhancing one's prestige by purchasing and using luxury items) were important to the economy of France and good for French public morale. He made formal dress mandatory at his palace in the Tuileries, and the clothing for the courtiers, himself and his empress, Josephine, had elaborate embroidery at his coronation in 1804.

Napoleon, as the new emperor, saw France returning to the ideals and glory of ancient Greece and Rome. He restricted the importation of fabric and strove to restore France's textile industry, which had been destroyed in the Siege of Lyon in 1793 by Republicans when they demolished the city in an attempt to create a new revolutionary capital. Napoleon made a concerted effort to bring back silk manufacturing, along with tulle, French cotton and lace. Napoleon used fashion as propaganda. For his coronation his empress, Josephine, wore a white satin dress with puffed sleeves and a floral motif decorated with real gold and real diamonds. Napoleon himself wore a white satin tunic, with embroidery done in gold thread. On his shoulders was a red velvet cloak lined with ermine and embroidered with designs of bees, olive, oak and laurel leaves (Watt).

During Napoleon's reign, the conspicuous consumption of Louis XVI and Marie Antoinette's court was once more embraced (Stuart, 336). The habit of showing that one had a great deal of money and could afford luxury items continued after Napoleon's abdication in the restored Bourbon courts of Louis XVIII in 1814 and Charles X in 1824. This idea was driven by Parisian milliners and couturiers, who encouraged their clients to move from having necessities to desiring luxurious things. These ambitious entrepreneurs also encouraged their clients to embrace the idea of obsolescence of fashion and style, which encouraged everyone to continue to purchase more and more, and this included mourning clothes.

One fashion designer who survived the Revolution was Louis Hippolyte Leroy (1763–1829), the favorite couturier to Napoleon's wife, his beloved empress Josephine de Beauharnais. A widow, her first husband having been guillotined during the Reign of Terror, Josephine was six years older than Napoleon. Napoleon eventually divorced Josephine in 1810 because she could not bear him any children. He married Marie Louise, Duchess of Parma, but was said to have continued loving Josephine until he died. Josephine's daughter from her first marriage, Hortense, married Napoleon's brother, and their son became Emperor Napoleon III of France.

Leroy was the most celebrated milliner (hat maker) in Paris in the first quarter of the 19th century. To keep in business, he and other milliners encouraged the move from necessities, embracing the consumption of luxury items and fashion accessories. Leroy began his career as a perruquier, or wig maker. He was also a dresser to members of Marie Antoinette's notorious court. After the Revolution, he expanded his business, creating a wider range of merchandise including court dress, coiffures, laces and trim, cherubesques (fan-shaped collars), gloves, fans and bouquets of flowers. When Napoleon came into power, Leroy became Josephine's hat maker or milliner, dressmaker and *marchande de modes* (stylist). Using designs from the artist Jean-Baptists Isabey, he fashioned the coronation dress for Emperor Napoleon and Empress Josephine. Leroy also created dresses based on drawings from artists Louis-Philibert Debucourt and Auguste Garneray (Berg, 183).

Empress Josephine was said to prefer to dress simply (Stuart, 336), but she understood that she was "Empress of the French" and her appearance had to add credibility to the new regime. She also understood that what she wore had to promote her country's luxury trades, and rumor has it that she loved to shop. An 1809 inventory noted that Josephine had 49 grand court dresses, 676 other dresses, 60 cashmere shawls, 496 other shawls and scarves, 498 blouses, 413 pairs of gloves and over 200 pairs of silk stockings. She also possessed more jewelry than Marie Antoinette had ever owned (337).

Leroy became a very important man in Josephine's life. His sumptuous designs "showed Josephine off to the best possible advantage" (Stuart, 336). Because of this alliance, Leroy became a famous designer and a celebrity in his own right, attracting new and important clients among the European elites from all areas conquered by Napoleon, as well as monarchs and aristocrats from all over the continent. Women flocked to his establishment on rue de Richelieu in Paris. Once there, they were waited on by servants wearing blue livery decorated with black velvet. Footmen stood guard at the front entrance of the store. Having been a participant in the luxury of the old French regime, Leroy blended its luxuriousness with the new Greek style of the *Directoire*, decorating his empire gowns with silver and gold thread embroidery. The added detail made them so expensive that Napoleon had to pass a law to save his courtiers money. Embroidery was to measure only 4 inches high along the hem of a gown, unless the lady was a princess (Berg, 186).

Leroy advertised his business in the Paris trade directories, saying that he was milliner to the empress and supplied all kinds of the highest quality lace and embroideries as well as court and presentation dress. When Napoleon abdicated, Leroy continued to create costumes for the court of Louis XVIII. Historians are certain that he made mourning clothes for his clientele. Magazines from this time contained fashion plates based on what was worn by the rich and famous, and it is probable that his designs were sketched by artists and published, with detailed descriptive text, for everyone to see. Unfortunately, the magazines didn't mention the names of the designers, so we are not certain which specific designs were his.

American Ladies' Journals

As improvements in print technology reached the United States of America, and as the ability of the U.S. Postal Service to deliver mail improved, magazines started to be published here, too. The first American magazine for women was *The Ladies' Magazine*, founded by the Bostonian Congregational minister the Reverend John Lauris Blake in 1828. Blake hired Sarah Josepha Hale (1788–1879), an American writer and author of "Mary Had a Little Lamb," as editor. Blake's and Hale's goals for the magazine were to lift up the moral and intellectual character of the American woman. Drawings of fashions were the furthest things from their minds. Soon after, in 1830, Louis Godey, editor of Philadelphia's *Daily Chronicle*, decided to come out with a different magazine geared for American women called the *Lady's Book*. Godey's heritage was French, and he modeled his new journal after successful French fashion plates and English magazines, even republishing their articles and illustrations. With a small readership of only 10,000 subscribers, Godey urged that the two magazines merge in 1834. Hale became editor of the hybrid named *Godey's Lady's Book and Magazine* in 1837. She remained at this post until 1877, becoming one of America's most influential voices; she is also credited with having President Abraham Lincoln designate Thanksgiving Day as a federal holiday. Expensive, at $3 a year (most magazines cost only $2 dollars), it was not for working women or immigrants. Still, the magazine, published once a month in Philadelphia, became the most popular one of its time, numbering 150,000 subscribers by 1860. Read by men and women alike, and shared with other family members and friends, the estimated readership for each issue was a million or more. Hale's and Blake's magazine did not contain fashion plates, and Hale continued to think that they were frivolous. But Godey's magazine, following the successful English and European model, did. Godey insisted that fashion plates be included in the new combined journal, and they were. Positioned at the beginning of each issue, they became the most liked part. For Godey's, 150 women were hired to paint the prints with watercolor paints, and it is estimated that the colored illustrations cost the publishers $8,000 a year to produce. *Godey's Lady's Book and Magazine* couldn't afford to provide the workers with paint, so the color of the fashion was left up to each artist's discretion. When asked about the difference in color of the fashions from one magazine to the next, the editor explained that women could share magazines and compare the plates to see how a dress or outfit would look made from different fabric.

In 1842 the owners of the *Saturday Evening Post* decided to create a woman's journal to compete with Godey's. Costing a dollar less, at $2 a subscription, the magazine was called *Ladies' National Magazine*; Charles Jacobs Peterson was in charge. By 1848 the name was changed to *Peterson's Ladies' National Magazine*. It was eventually just called *Peterson's Magazine* from 1855 to 1898. Following the tradition set by the pioneering European women's magazines, the magazine contained short stories or novellas, sewing patterns, craft ideas, recipes, advice on domestic duties, and both colored and black-and-white fashion plates. Peterson is noted for modifying European fashions to suit a more modest American style. Ann S. Stephens was the nominal editor and early contributor, but the very successful magazine was really run by Peterson himself (Blanco, 143).

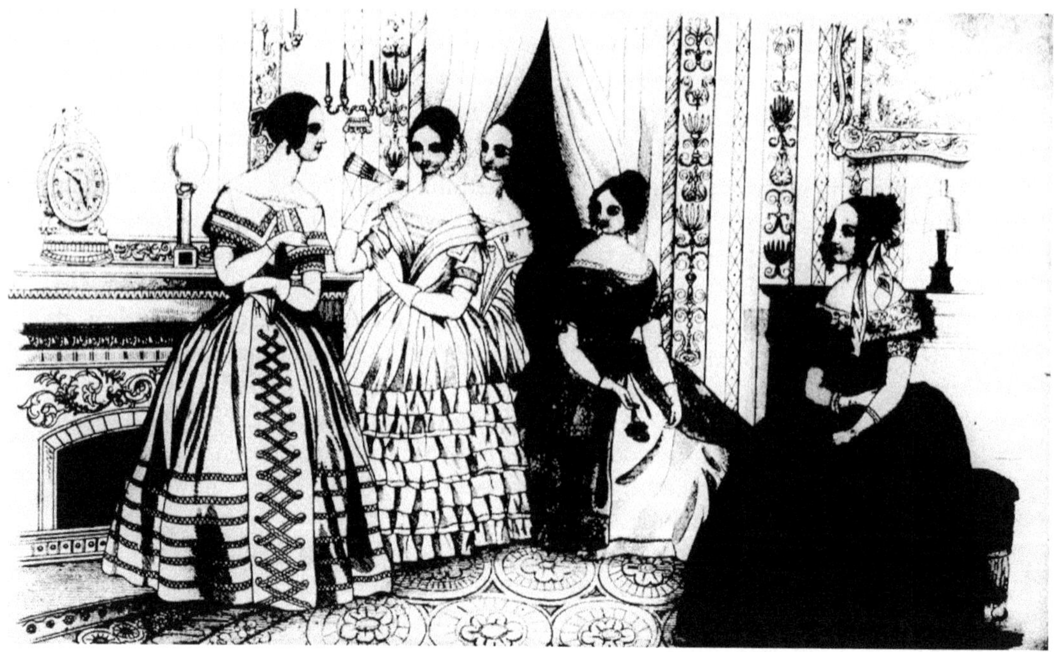

Illustration from *Godey's Ladies' Book*, 1843 (Accessible Archives Collection, www.accessible-archives.com).

Frank Leslie (1821–1880) founded *Leslie's Illustrated Newspaper* in 1852, modelled on those found in England. Leslie was born and educated in England but moved to the United States in 1848 as a young man. He began making wood engravings when he was just 13 years old and became such an expert in the process that he was able to land a job in America in 1852 working for *Gleason's Pictorial Drawing-Room Companion,* an illustrated American newspaper out of Boston. He quickly left that position and took a job with P. T. Barnum's short-lived New York City *Illustrated News.* When that newspaper failed, Leslie decided to publish several newspapers and magazines of his own. One was named *Frank Leslie's Ladies' Gazette of Fashion and Fancy Needlework,* and another became known as *Leslie's Weekly.* This continued publication until 1922 despite the fact that Leslie himself went bankrupt in 1878 and died in 1880 (Mott, 437).

The American magazine business flourished when, in 1852, Congress passed a new Post Office act reducing rates for the consumer and transferring "postage charges from subscriber to publisher" (Mott, 3). Leslie discovered that the most lucrative magazines were the ones that contained fashion plates. He deduced that American women wanted information about the latest fashions, especially from Paris, and the artwork in his magazine was stellar. William H. Thwaites was listed as being the chief artist for the fashion plates. His prints of Paris (and to a lesser degree London and New York) fashions made up for the criticism that the literary work in the journal often appeared to be substandard when compared to other magazines. *The Ladies' Gazette* sold for only 25 cents a copy. Each issue included a large, hand-colored fashion plate, much larger than the ones found in *Godey's,* containing up to 29 figures, including large crinolines, on one page. The magazine also came with a dress pattern and an embroidery pattern folded into the middle. American women could not only see the latest fashions from Paris, London and New York, but could also make one of them to wear. Leslie bought his own steam press and expanded his journal in 1857, raising the cost of each issue by 5 cents. The new journal, *Frank Leslie's New Family Magazine,* contained a chess department, sheet music, short stories, book reviews, notices of opera, theater and art galleries, and advertisements. In time, the magazine also covered society news from America and abroad. Leslie's fashion gazette became a 16-page supplement added to the new version. In 1862 the magazine had 14 pages about fashion, plus one fashion plate, out of a 96-page total. In explaining the goal of the magazine, the editor wrote: "We design to carry the influence of our work into social life, manners, household habits, and the thousand elegant and useful trifles which make up the entire life of an intelligent and refined social system" (Mott, 437).

Popular magazines had as much influence in the 1800s as all media has today, and the writers didn't hesitate to comment on mourning dress and mourning etiquette. In the fashion section of the March 1855 issue of *Godey's Lady's Book* the editors got quite explicit. For example, ladies were told that "for a daughter," the mourning dress should be made "of parametta cloth (a black, woolen cloth), trimmed with trains of crepe; small crepe collar with cuffs." Walking dresses should be made of "black silk and an over skirt of crepe; crepe collar and sleeves, crepe and silk bonnet with fall, entirely black inside; black parasol; jet brooch and chin; black kid gloves." The article went on to suggest that the aunt of a deceased child should wear a black poplin dress with white around the collar and sleeves for the street, with a black velvet bonnet and black cloth mantle. For evening dress while still in mourning, the aunt's gown should have lace or silk flounces "with little, but rich embroidery." She should also wear white kid gloves (Bell, 16).

Godey Lady's Magazine of December 1850 stated that widowers could go to work while mourning. Following British royal tradition, they were to dress in mourning clothes for three months. Men in mourning were advised to wear a mourning cloak and hat with trailing weepers (a black crepe hatband with streamers attached to it). Their gloves were to be black, as were their neckties, and they should carry a special black walking stick. At funerals, men could choose to wear black stoles or sashes. While men did not have to wear mourning as long as women did, according to the magazine, "proper male mourning attire was a sign of good breeding and also a symbol of social status" (quoted in Blanco, 191). Some references advised that a baby whose mother died giving it birth should be dressed in black. But it was *Godey's* opinion that children of the deceased were always to be dressed in white with a black sash. Children in mourning under the age of 12 were to wear white in summer and gray in winter, trimmed with black buttons. Their bonnets were to be trimmed with black ribbons or braids. Older children were to dress in black as did the adults, or dress in half mourning. Servants or slaves were required to wear mourning garb when a family member died. Female servants were to be provided with black dresses, shawls and bonnets, which they wore with white cuffs, collars and aprons. House slaves and drivers were to dress as the servants did.

Books on Etiquette

The revolution in print technology not only gave birth to the magazine and journal industry, it also made books easier to publish and print. In the early part of the 1800s American women continued to follow British rules of etiquette concerning mourning dress and seclusion practices. Books about proper etiquette came from England and were primarily written by men. Loosely basing their etiquette on rules set by the Lord Chamberlain and the Earl Marshal, they encouraged widowers to remarry within months of the death of their wife, especially if they had children, but recommended that the period of mourning for widows who were not aristocrats increase dramatically to two, or two and a half years. In both countries these books were purchased by an eager population who saw them to be important tools for social advancement. A popular book entitled *The Book of Manners and Rules of Good Society: or Solecisms to be Avoided, by a Member of the Aristocracy*, was first published in either 1871 or 1872. The book originated in England but was published in London and New York. Clothing for widows is described in this book; it explained that the grieving widow must be in full, or deep, mourning and wear black crepe and a mourning cap for a year and a day. The same was true for a mother who had lost a child. During this time, restrictions were also placed on what jewelry was allowed. The complete outfit was often called "widow's weeds," with the word "weeds" coming from the old English word "waed" meaning garment (*Manners and Rules of Good Society*, 243).

The author of *The Illustrated Book of Manners* called the nine months following the "deep mourning period" the "mourning period." During this time, women were allowed to wear jet trim on their black crepe clothes, and there were more choices as to fabric. During the last three months of mourning, considered the "half mourning period," the widow or mother no longer needed to wear crepe, but still needed to dress in black or other somber colors like gray, lilac or mauve. Widowers or fathers were also advised to wear special mourning black for two years unless they were required to enter back into society sooner because of work, or if remarriage was needed to take care of infant children.

Convention stated that the wearing of mourning clothes and jewelry might be halved for parents mourning infants or very young children.

Broadening the decrees made for royalty by the Lord Chamberlain's office, these books developed rules of dress for other relatives such as stepmothers, siblings, in-laws, grandparents, uncles or aunts, nieces or nephews. For example: if the parents of one's first wife died, the second wife was expected to dress in mourning for three months. For the parents of a son-in-law or a daughter-in-law, mourning clothes without the crepe were worn for one month. For a friend, one wore mourning clothes for one to three weeks depending on "the degree of intimacy existing" (de Valcourt, 226). Servants or slaves were also given mourning garb at the death of a master, which they wore while the family mourned.

Times of seclusion after a death for commoners were also explained in these books. Widows were not to accept or extend invitations for a period of twelve months. Daughters remained at home for two months and could not attend balls or dances while wearing crepe. Also, these books dictated men's dress by saying that in addition to wearing black, men attending funerals needed sashes over their coats, and were to carry wands covered in black cloth. As the century progressed, the large sashes shrank to black silk hatbands or armbands, and these bands were white if the funeral was for a young girl. If the funeral took place before 2 p.m. the family of the deceased was required to provide lunch for the attendees. According to the *Book of Manners*, if the funeral occurred after 2 p.m., friends were invited to the house of the deceased for light refreshments or tea. After the funeral, it was suggested that concerned members of the family remain to hear the reading of the will.

The Illustrated Book of Manners reflected changes in mourning made possible by the Industrial Revolution, which had begun in the eighteenth century and accelerated in the nineteenth century, making this period a time of great change. Inventions had a great effect on clothing, fashion styles, and textiles. The cotton gin, invented in 1794, had an enormous impact on cotton production in America. Imported textiles from India declined as steam was used to power American and European textile manufacturing. By 1840 textiles were mass produced, lowering the cost of fabric. The opening of Japan to American and then to British, Russian and Dutch trade greatly increased the availability of silk. As Japan adopted Western industrial techniques on a large scale, more uniform and superior silk thread was produced.

In 1856 an eighteen-year-old English student, William Henry Perkin (1838–1907), attempted to synthesize the anti-malaria drug quinine over his Easter vacation. Using aniline, a component of coal tar, he accidentally invented the first chemical dye. The color of this dye was called "mauve" after the French word for the purple Mallow flower. Before the invention of this synthetic process, dyes were derived from plants, shellfish or insects. The extraction of enough material to make a natural dye was labor intensive, greatly increasing the cost of fabric and clothing. The coal tar Perkin used was a byproduct of gas production from coal. It was thought to be useless and a nuisance, and so was readily available. Perkin developed the process of applying the dye to cotton. He patented his ideas and immediately started manufacturing it. (A German physician, Paul Ehrlich, discovered that the yellow dye he used for staining his microscope slides, called "falvine," killed bacteria responsible for abscesses. Many useful drugs are derived from chemicals found in coal tar. Germany dominated the synthetic dyestuff and drug industry with companies like AGFA and BASF Bayer and Hoechst.)

The textile industry was revolutionized by technology and so was decorative trim. As early as 1804 John Duncan created a machine that could do embroidery. By the 1840s machines had been invented to make lace in both narrow and wide widths. There was also the development of a knitting frame that made seamless hosiery, and there were new techniques for printing patterns on textiles. The prices for fabric dropped, making it available in great quantities, which influenced the size of ladies' skirts.

As with all fashion during this time, the style of mourning dress was created in France, imported to England, and then to America. The customs for mourning were followed first by the nobility, then by the wealthy, then by the middle class and finally by the poor, with the lower classes emulating the class above them. What a woman wore depended on what she could afford, and also what was expected of her by family and community. But as more free public schooling was offered in the United States, and more people learned how to read, more books on etiquette were written in the United States with Americans in mind. In the 1830s, 28 books on etiquette had been published in the United States, with many of them originating in the Northeast. By the 1850s there were 38 new titles published in America on proper etiquette, and by the 1890s published books on etiquette numbered 50 per decade (Arditi, 417). The writers of these books instructing decorum were ministers, teachers, and popular icons of society. Their advice was a complex code of behavior, seen first as rules to follow, and then, by some, as strict social laws. American authors made it a point to write that these laws of behavior applied to everyone, in all social classes, and not just the very rich. But the United States was a vast territory with the different states in various levels of development, and these books reflected this.

Several American authors of books on etiquette were women. Being a writer was seen as one of the few acceptable professions a woman could have in the patriarchal American society of the Victorian age. Between 1840 and 1880 close to ⅓ of American etiquette manuals and advice books were written by American women. By the 1880s these books were called "manuals on behavior" and reflected the differences one found in the country (Plante, 103). Florence Hartley's *The Ladies' Book of Etiquette, and Manual of Politeness* was published in 1869 and was meant for a predominantly American audience. Her book does not have a special section dealing with mourning. She folded this advice into other chapters, making death just another part of a woman's busy life. For example, she explained how to visit a family in mourning, and gave advice in the event that "death comes while you are with your friend" (Hartley, 73). The author also explained, rather matter-of-factly, that no offense would be taken if you decline to see visitors between the death of a family member and their funeral.

Hartley informed the reader that there was little uniformity when observing mourning rituals in America. She admitted that in the United States there was even a wide variety of opinions regarding the wearing of proper mourning clothes. Some women wore what she called "close black" for a long period of time for a distant relative, while others wore "dressy mourning" for immediate family (Hartley, 32). The length of time for the various mourning stages also varied widely. In fact, Hartley refused to assign a number of weeks for any of the different mourning stages. Instead, she chose only to describe the proper clothing to wear for each stage. In her opinion, for the first stage of mourning, which she called "deep mourning," the dress of the grieving women should be made of "bombazine, Parramatta cloth, delaine (a light weight wool and cotton blend), barege (a fabric made of wool resembling gauze), or merino (wool made from sheep), made up over black lining. The only appropriate trimming is a deep fold, either of the same material or of crape" (Hartley, 31).

Hartley advised that a mourning woman also needed to wear a plain black shawl or

SPRING DRESS.

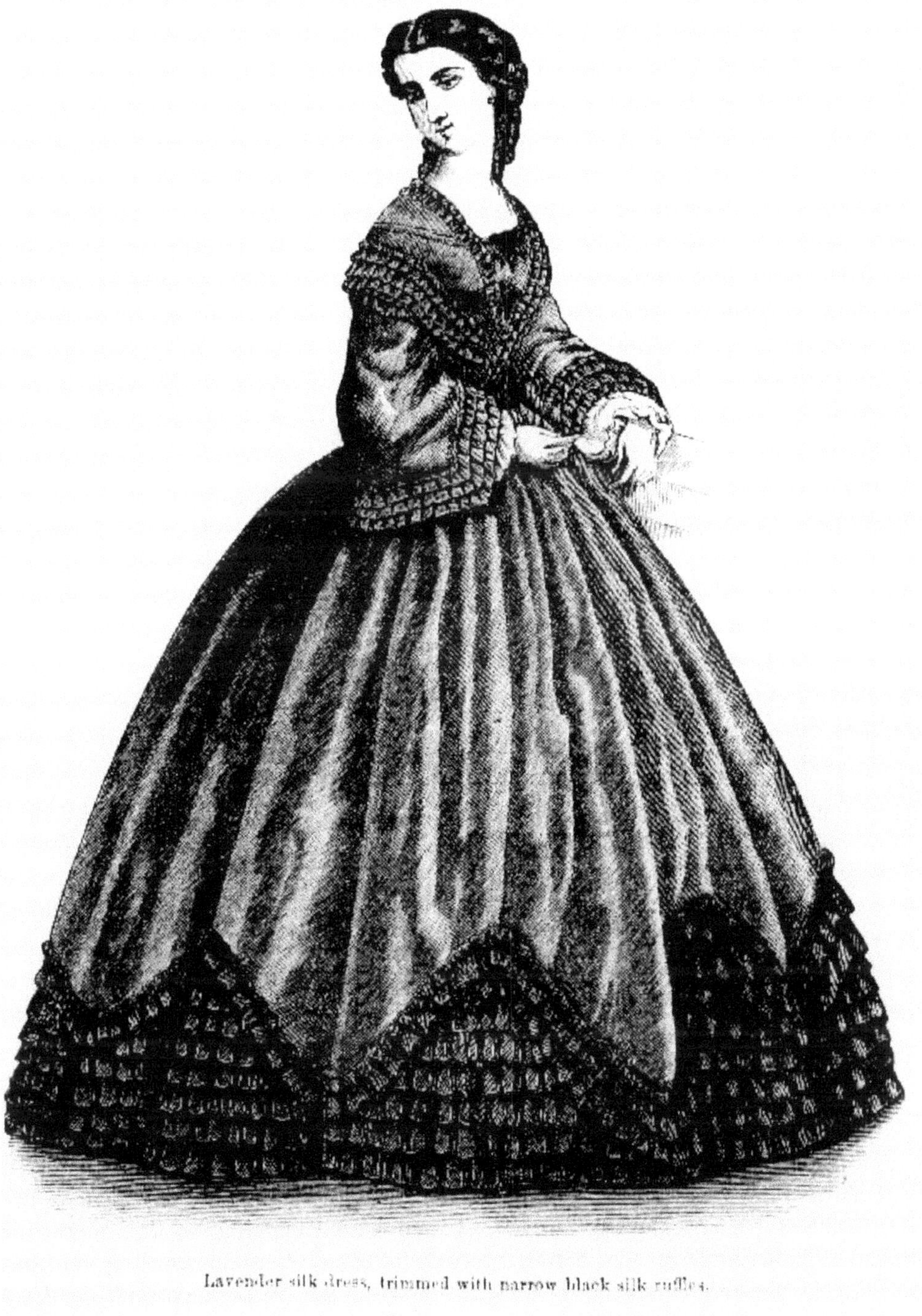

Lavender silk dress, trimmed with narrow black silk ruffles.

328

Illustration from *Godey's Ladies' Book* (Accessible Archives Collection, www.accessible-archives.com).

a cloak, without a border unless the border was made of crepe (the modern spelling of "crape"). Her bonnet needed to be plain and made of crepe; or she could wear a widow's cap. The widow was expected to cover her face and bonnet with a deep crepe veil. Crepe was also used for the collar and the sleeves of the dress, and the widow was to wear black boots and gloves.

For the next stage of mourning, which Hartley did not name, a white collar and white sleeves could be added to the black dress, and a crepe bow could be added to the lady's bonnet, which could be lined with plain white lace facing. The mourner no longer had to cover her face with a heavy crepe veil, and instead could wear one made of plain black net.

After a short passage of time, but still in the second stage of mourning, a mourner's dress could be made of black silk as long as the fabric was dull and without any gloss. This dress could be trimmed with crepe, delaine or bombazine, "with a trimming of broad, plain ribbon, or a bias fold of silk" (Hartley, 32). Hartley seemed to be describing four stages of mourning, because she went on to describe one stage where the mourner could exchange the crepe bonnet for one made of silk. Of course, the cap of the bonnet needed to be trimmed with crepe. In the last stage of mourning, dresses no longer needed to be black, but could be lead gray, dark purple, or black with white figures on it. She called the last stage of mourning the "second stage." This was when the grieving woman could wear a straw bonnet as long as it was trimmed with black ribbon or crepe flowers, or a silk bonnet with black flowers on the outside, and "white ones in the face. She also could wear a black silk dress, and gray shawl or cloak" (Hartley, 33). As time passed in the second mourning phase, wearing a white bonnet and shawl was permissible and one could gradually lighten the color of one's dresses. Recommended colors were light purple or lavender.

Hartley offered her readers this advice: "It is especially to be recommended to buy always the best materials when making up mourning. Crape and woolen goods of the finest quality are very expensive, but a cheaper article will wear miserably; there is no greater error in economy than purchasing cheap mourning, for no goods are so inferior, or wear out and grow rusty so soon" (Hartley, 33).

Creation of Patterns, Empress Eugénie and Charles Frederick Worth

With the discovery of synthetic dyes, the price of black dye also came down in the 19th century, and black fabric was not used to create only mourning wear. The American children's book writer Laura Ingalls Wilder (1867–1957) was married in a black cashmere dress in 1885. For ordinary people, the cost of making a dress was still quite high, and a woman's wedding dress was often the best dress she owned, and the one that she wore for a variety of special occasions. Wilder explained that the material, woven from the fur of goats from Kashmir, an area between today's India and Pakistan, was luxurious but also durable. She and her mother fashioned and sewed her clothes themselves, and the black cashmere dress was the only one they could finish in time to thwart her mother-in-law's plans for the couple to waste money on an expensive ceremony. Wilder still considered this gown to be the best dress she owned when she moved to Missouri in 1894 (Wilder, 320). At the time, white had not become the standard color for wedding gowns in South Dakota, where she had lived, but still, a black wedding gown was considered unusual. After the Civil War, some brides wore gray or black gowns to honor those who had fought and died, but by the time Mrs. Wilder was married, a bride only wore black if she was marrying a widower. Almanzo Wilder was ten years older than Laura, and at 28, it is possible that he had previously had a wife who had passed; but Laura never mentioned this in any of her work.

When the future Mrs. Wilder and her mother were sewing her wedding gown she was probably taking advantage of dress patterns created with the help of Ellen Louise (Curtis) Demorest's (1824–1898) invention of what she called the "Excelsior Dress Model Drafting System." Curtis' fiancé and future husband, William, was a widower who owned "Madame Demorest's Emporium" in upstate New York. Ellen married him and helped expand the business by developing a method of making patterns for clothing. The couple mass-produced her patterns and advertised them in popular magazines such as *Frank Leslie's Ladies Gazette* as early as 1854, first testing the market with patterns for children's clothing before moving on to women's fashions. In 1864 the couple published their own quarterly designs under the name of *Madame Demorest's Mirror of Fashions,* with a paper pattern stapled inside. By 1870 the Demorests were selling sized patterns. In 1876 they sold over 3 million paper patterns to customers in Europe as well as in America. Their journal underwent minor name changes and was published monthly, reaching over 100,000 people a year from 1877 to 1884.

The couple also opened shops where one could buy patterns. Dressmaking services were provided for those who could afford to pay. In the mid–1870s there were 300 Demorest shops employing 1,500 female sales agents, many of whom were African Americans. The Demorests exhibited examples of their clothing in London and Paris exhibitions. They also created a large display for the Philadelphia Centennial Exhibition held in 1876. Unfortunately, Madame Demorest never filed a patent on her process or her patterns. This was done by Ebenezar Butterick, a tailor, in 1863. The innovation he made to paper clothing patterns was to have them be graded so that one pattern could be used for different-sized people without it needing to be redrafted. He also printed his patterns on thin tissue paper. Butterick's graded patterns became very popular for home sewers, making modern fashions and styles accessible to the lower and expanding middle classes who could not afford to go to a dressmaker, but still wanted to dress stylishly. Butterick patterns cost 25 to 75 cents each. Working class people earned $1 to $2 dollars a day, so this price was affordable. Butterick started his business in his home in Massachusetts selling patterns for boys' and men's clothing only. Within a year he moved to New York City and started a factory. In 1866 he began making patterns for women's clothing. He also published *The Ladies' Quarterly of Broadway Fashions* magazine to promote his patterns and make it easier to order them by mail. In 1868 his monthly *Metropolitan* magazine offered fashion news, and in 1873 his publication *The Delineator* became the premiere women's fashion magazine of the times. Butterick also grew to have 100 branch offices and 1,000 agencies in the U.S. and Canada.

Toward the middle of the nineteenth century, designing dresses for the very rich, including mourning garb, became less the domain of the individual dressmaker and more of an enterprise. Men seized on the opportunity. These male fashion designers considered themselves to be great artists, such as the Parisian designer Paul Poiret, (1879–1944) who much later in the century became known in the United States as "the King of Fashion." Poiret wrote: "Am I a fool when I dream of putting art into my dresses, a fool when I say

Fig. 2.

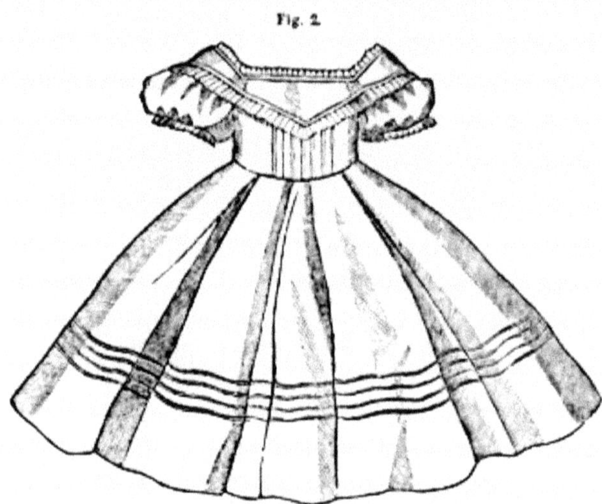

Zouave jacket is cut in large scallops, and trimmed with six rows of plain braid. The seventh row is put on in a little design, and the edge of the scallops is finished with tat- ting. The skirt is made in the tablier style, and trimmed to match. The Garibaldi shirt is formed of fine tucks, and one row of tatting down the front.

Fig. 3.

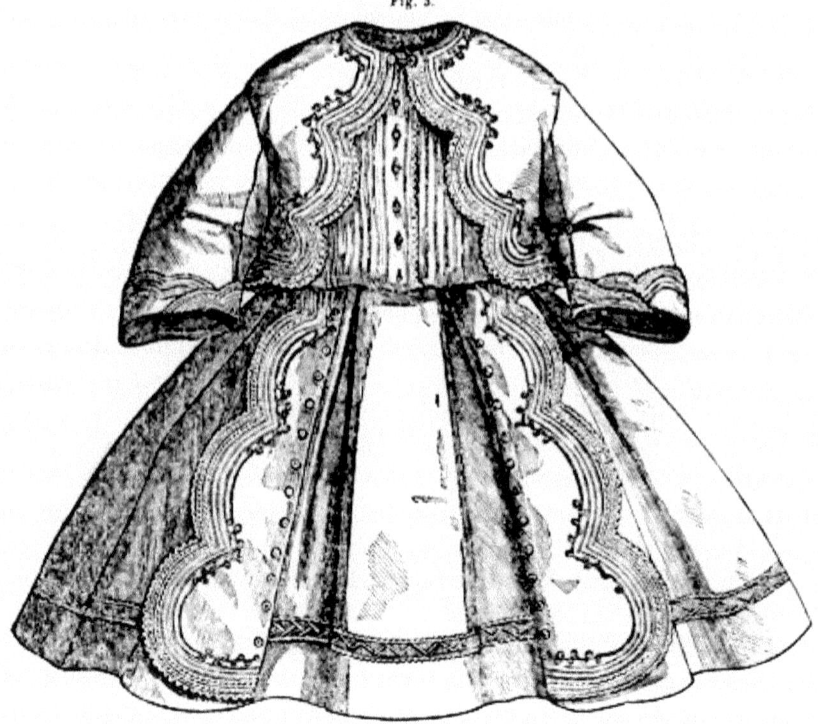

Illustration from *Godey's Ladies' Book* (Accessible Archives Collection, www.accessible-archives.com).

dressmaking is an art? For I have always loved painters and felt on an equal footing with them. It seems to me that we practice the same craft and that they are my fellow workers" (Koda, 1904). Poiret became known for the "uncorseted" style. He began liberating the body first from corsets and then petticoats in 1903.

The most famous French designer of the Victorian era, and founder of Parisian haute couture, was actually an Englishman named Charles Frederick Worth (1825–1895). Worth's father mismanaged the family's money, and the child was apprenticed to George Swan's and William Edgar's sewing supply and fabric business in London when he was 12 years old. Here, he helped supply dressmakers with cloth and trim and learned about the tastes of the rich and privileged. In his spare time, he went to the National Gallery and studied historical portraits to see what important people had worn. When older, Worth found a job at Lewis and Allenby's silk merchants, a London shop that sold more expensive merchandise to an even wealthier clientele. Worth stayed in this position until 1845, when he decided to move to Paris, the capital of high fashion. Here he was hired by Maision Gagelin, a high-end shop that sold fabric, coats and shawls that were very expensive and still an essential part of a lady's wardrobe. The business in shawls was so important that Gagelin's employed young women to model them. Worth fell in love with a model named Marie Vernet. They married, and he began designing dresses for her to wear to work. Customers, seeing her gowns, asked him to design dresses for them, too. Worth became so successful at designing gowns and dresses that he was allowed to set up a small dress department in the store (Thieme, 18).

Meanwhile, back in London, Prince Albert was instrumental in organizing the Great International Exposition of 1851. More than 14,000 exhibitors participated in the event, envisioned to be a celebration of the arts and industry of humankind, and several individual countries had displays. Dubbed "The Crystal Palace Exhibition," after the glass building that housed it, an average man or woman could pay a small fee and see sights normally reserved for royalty (Bell, 11). Worth submitted his dresses to the great event and came back having won prizes for his clothing designs. His fashions won again when he exhibited them in Paris in 1855 at the Exposition Universelle. Worth exhibited his dresses in Gagelin's shop and gained a reputation for his ability. Women flocked to his dress department to see his latest creations. Some bought them off the rack, which was an entirely new phenomenon; previously women had sewn their own or hired a dressmaker to sew them. More often than not, the dressmaker came to the woman's house. This was especially true if the lady was in mourning and was in seclusion. Purchasing garments that were already made was unheard of, but a great idea whose time had come.

Business in Gagelin's dress department was so brisk that Worth asked for a partnership in the store. When he was denied, he left to open his own firm in 1858 in a posh location near where the new Parisian opera house would be built. The timing for his move couldn't have been better because it shortly followed the establishment of the Second Empire in France, led by Napoleon III, nephew of Napoleon Bonaparte, who was declared emperor in 1852. Once more he and his wife, Empress Eugénie, made Paris an imperial capital, complete with a multitude of formal affairs and a renewed need for luxury goods and clothing.

Worth proved to be an excellent promoter of his merchandise. In 1860 he gave his wife an album of his dress designs and sent her to meet Princess Pauline de Metternich at the Austrian Embassy. The princess saw his caged crinolines made of wire and immediately sensed that Worth was a great artist and designer. Worth sold her two dresses for a very reasonable price in exchange for her wearing one of the gowns to the next court ball. She, the caged crinoline and Worth's gown, were noticed by Empress Eugénie, who interviewed the designer the very next day. The empress ordered some pieces from him and liked what she received. Soon, all of the empress's clothing came from Worth and he became court couturier by 1864 (Kellogg, 319). As couturier to the empress, his fame quickly spread. By 1865 Worth was so well known in America that *Peterson's Magazine* published a story about a woman who bought four new Worth outfits in an attempt to gain the love of someone she wished to be her spouse. Unfortunately, her fancy clothing did not work, and the man continued to love another.

Empress Eugénie, a Spanish countess, was much younger than Napoleon III. On the rare days she was at home, it was said that she wore a simple black dress because, like her predecessors, she was really not that interested in fashion. However, she dressed lavishly for state functions and could not wear the same gown twice. Following the norm for members of the French aristocracy, she was expected to change outfits several times a day. The empress worked well with Worth. She had four dressmaker forms fabricated in her exact measurements, which allowed her the luxury of not having to try on items of clothing as they were being made (Tortora, 354).

The House of Worth grew famous. In the 1860s Worth employed hundreds of people and made several innovations. For one, he put labels in his fashions. For another, his dressmakers used sewing machines to speed up production. He also used machine-made trims, loaned clothing to important people, and showed entire collections in advance, using young women as models for his outfits, creating the first "fashion shows."

Worth became even more innovative. The hoop, with its various undergarments, had been popular for a long time, and, in 1868, the empress enlisted Worth to revolutionize lady's fashion. He is credited with creating the half-crinoline, making the front of a skirt straight and narrow and pushing the fullness of the fabric to the rear, eventually becoming what is known as a bustle. Princess Pauline de Metternich wrote in her memoires that she was the first to discard the crinoline, and that she acted as the inspiration for the great Worth (Metternich, 32). Years later, American girls like Laura Ingalls embraced the new style and described the new undergarment:

> Hoops had been improved. There were now tapes across the front almost to the knees, letting the dress lie close in front. There was a wire bustle attached at the back and a tape fastened to it by one end at each side. If a bustle was wanted, these tapes were buckled together at the back underneath the bustle, the size of the bustle being regulated by how tightly the tapes were drawn [Wilder, 299].

If a woman wanted to, she could buckle the tapes in the front to make the bustle lie flat. Still the girl thought they were "a great nuisance, though Ma said they were not nearly so large as the ones she used to wear" (Wilder, 299).

All of Worth's designs were sewn first in black fabric and then in white muslin. Manufacturers sent him samples of their latest fabrics. He used what he liked to make his finished work and used the sample dresses for another function. Each part of a Worth outfit could be adapted to fit any other. Each sleeve fit any bodice and each bodice could fit any skirt (Tortora, 354). Clients could choose from the various pieces and create their own original outfits. In one room of the House of Worth, clients could request models to wear the sample clothing. In another room, clients could try on the ensembles themselves. At the end of the season, Worth sold these ready-made costumes to buyers who copied them. By the 1860s his clothing had reached the American market.

Fashion magazines around the world covered Empress Eugénie's fashions. When Worth created "the walking dress" by shortening the hem of her skirt to show her feet and allow the dress to clear the street and not drag on it, the Austrian press went crazy with comments. *Godey's Lady's Book* had a "Chitchat on Fashions" column, which covered everything the empress wore. Fashion plates of Worth's clothing were in every magazine. Some even included patterns so women could make their own designer gowns. Dressmakers used these to create mourning clothes for their clients. Others used them to sew their own mourning clothes.

In 1870 the Second Empire fell and Empress Eugénie fled to England where she lived in exile. In 1871 France surrendered to the Prussian army, and again French symbols of aristocracy were destroyed. After a French government was restored, Worth once again opened his doors. The ladies of the French court had departed, but now his clients were fashionable women from Britain, America, Sweden, Italy and Russia. By 1871 he was employing 1,200 people. The House of Worth became the epicenter of elegance in fashion. After the exile of the French court, famous and wealthy Americans such as the Vanderbilts, the Astors, the Carnegies and Rockefellers became his best clients. He designed 6,000 gowns a year and 4,000 outer garments, with some of his clients spent $10,000 on a single dress. Worth revolutionized the clothing industry. He sold his original dresses to foreign buyers and gave them the rights to copy and sell them in newly emerging department stores. Buyers from America made trips to Paris and brought back the latest fashions. These were illustrated and published in American magazines. The House of Worth created mourning clothes in the latest fashion for its regular customers as well as designer mourning clothing containing embellishments such as ruching, rosettes and swags.

Changing Fashion Styles in the Victorian Era

Throughout the nineteenth century and into the next, fashion designers and couturiers such as Bertin, Leroy and Worth changed dress styles constantly in response to the changing society. They also changed styles to encourage more frequent sales. After Napoleon's abdication, skirts flared out rather than falling straight down, and the Romantic style of dress came into fashion. Waistlines dropped, skirts became fuller, and sleeves grew very large. In 1837 when Queen Victoria ascended the throne, puffy, leg-of-mutton sleeves were popular. These were quickly replaced in the early 1840s by tight sleeves fitted low on the shoulder that made it impossible for a woman to raise her arms. By the end of the 1840s, skirts ballooned out in a wide circle supported by multiple starched petticoats stiffened by whalebone, cane or horsehair. The whalebone corset was required to make the waist as small as possible under so many layers of petticoats and skirt. In 1856 the cage crinoline came into fashion, made of concentric rows of thin, flexible, spring-steel bands held together by vertical cloth tapes. With this invention, skirts reached their greatest diameter and dressmakers had to figure out how to reduce so many yards of fabric at the hem to fit a tiny waist (Cunningham, 3). During the Civil War the size of the cage crinoline diminished, reflecting economic austerity, but by the end of the decade the fullness returned. This time, copying the styles from the House of Worth reflected in English magazines such as *The Queen* and *The Englishwoman's Domestic Magazine,* American women moved fabric to the rear and held it up and formed it with a wire bustle. Skirts were pulled tightly in the front and full in the back, sometimes drawn together to form a train. Dresses were heavily decorated with flounces, ribbons, drapery, pleated bands and fringes (Thieme, 18).

The French Revolution and its Reign of Terror had a great and lasting effect on American and European men's fashion. The court of Louis XVI and his queen at Versailles was known for the luxurious dress of its male courtiers despite the economic hardships of the times. To make matters worse, a famine ravaged the country. The nobles and clergy refused to pay higher taxes and resolved to get money from the working class and peasantry, who had nothing left to give and so rebelled. French culture was regarded as a model for the elites of other Western nations. The failure of their system, and the execution of their king and queen, were warnings to the aristocrats and rich of other lands that luxury was no longer tolerated, especially in men's clothing.

Before the French Revolution, clothing separated well-to-do men from the rest. The rich wore ostentatiously colorful and elaborate embroidered brocade satin suits, waistcoats and breeches, which ended at the knee. White stockings, high-heeled shoes and powered wigs made their outfits complete. Poor men wore loose, floppy trousers instead of breeches, shirts made of linen with attached collars, and a cravat tied at the throat. After the revolution, all men adopted these simple and somber suits, jackets, vests, and trousers to demonstrate republican austerity (Tortora, 307). Napoleon, and then King Louis XVIII, who ruled France from 1814 to 1824, tried to revive the luxurious dress of Versailles's royal court. Once crowned, King Charles X went further and attempted to restore the absolute power of the monarchy. This led to another revolution in 1830, after which men adopted the fashion of wearing working class clothing for good.

To differentiate the wealthy from the rest in England, great emphasis was placed on excellent tailoring and the fit of the suit. As the variety of choices for men's dress diminished, "good taste" became more important than luxurious clothes. During the Regency period in England (the period after King George III was deemed incapable of ruling), George "Beau" Brummell (1778–1840), friend of the future King George IV of England, introduced the men's modern suit and necktie to high society. Following his lead, men abandoned their breeches and instead wore light colored trousers during the day and dark colored ones in the evening with high boots. Abhorring wrinkled clothing and bragging that his trousers fit like skin (Lavar, 158), Brummell urged upper class men to employ the best British tailors to create beautifully fitted pants, coats, shirts and elaborate neckwear. Brummell also made improvements to men's hygiene. He advocated the importance of wearing clean clothes and brushing one's teeth. He also went wigless and cut his hair short in the fashion of ancient Rome, reportedly spending hours tidying his hair and his beard. Finding himself deeply in debt, Brummell escaped to France in 1816, where he continued to influence men's fashion. He eventually fell out of favor with the king and died penniless and in disarray. Still, his reputation as a "dandy" or a meticulously fashionable man survived intact. After his death, in the mid–1800s, several books and articles appeared about him both in England and France as well as in America.

Retail Mourning Clothes

Victorian rules for the seclusion of mourners, and especially widows, were strict. Grief-stricken relatives were never to be seen going to a dressmaker or shopping for fabric. Instead, aristocrats were advised to always travel with sets of mourning clothes just in case somebody died (Taylor, 132). Much of Europe's royalty were related to each other, and with the death rate so high, one could never tell when someone would breathe his or her last. Aristocrats were required by protocol to dress in mourning. If they were in the deceased's country, they had to attend the funeral and pay mourning visits to the family. Their mourning clothes were made by famous dressmakers who usually came to the royal's residences and fitted the clothing on them. When the great clothing salons opened, such as Leroy's or the House of Worth, aristocrats went to the shops if a death was imminent, picked their design and had the clothing fitted there. Relatives of deceased commoners would have a servant summon the dressmaker to come to the house and fashion mourning clothes for the family. The poor would have someone, perhaps a child, go to the draper and purchase black fabric, which was then sewn into mourning clothes by hand at home. Some grieving women found sewing a consolation and a distraction from their grief. Sewing their mourning clothes was a way to keep their hands busy and the memory of the deceased alive. But others were too distraught to concentrate on fabric and thread, or just not capable of making so many clothes in so short a time. The very poorest were often traumatized by the requirements of wearing special mourning clothing. They needed help, and in response, trade organizations sprang up where they could rent mourning clothing. Merchants saw this and seized on the opportunity to expand their establishments.

By the 1850 large warehouses specializing in mourning goods appeared in major cities in Europe and America. These mourning warehouses, or mourning "emporiums," supplied everything one needed for a socially correct funeral including the hearse, horses, and the necessary fabric to make mourning clothes and accessories. Warehouses advertised in fashion magazines that they could send representatives to the homes of the bereaved who would offer advice about what was needed during the laying in of the corpse, the funeral, and afterwards. An advertisement for Peter Robinson's Family and General Mourning Warehouse, located on 103 Oxford Street in London, appeared on the back of a children's Christmas book dated 1859: "Mourning kept made up ready for immediate use; it being needful only to send Dresses or Bodies for pattern, with a note, descriptive of the Mourning required, to ensure its being carefully prepared and sent forthwith" (Martin).

Messrs. Jay of Regent Street, in London, established their business in 1841. They advertised that they had experienced dressmakers and milliners who would travel, and in the event of immediate death, "one [could] be dispatched to any part of the kingdom on receipt of letter or telegram without expense to the purchaser" (advertisement in *Grace's Guide*). Once summoned, salespeople from mourning warehouses arrived with patterns and took measurements of family and servants, with a guarantee that the clothing would be ready in a short amount of time. Jay's London General Mourning Warehouse, located on Regent Street, sold everything for mourning, but also dresses for general use in colors confined to those worn for either full or half mourning. Black silks were a specialty of the house, and the owners assured customers that they sold textiles, taking only the "slightest profit." According to their literature the material for mourning costumes "must always virtually, remain unchangeable, and few additions can be made to the list of silks, crapes, paramattas, cashmeres, grenadines, and tulles as fabrics." But they warned, "Fashion in design changed with the times. Fashion in design, construction, and embellishment may be said to change, not only every month, but well-nigh every week" (Davey, 95; Davey was commissioned by Jay's London General Mourning Warehouse to write it).

Advice books such as Davey's offered information but also encouraged grief-stricken mourners to buy the latest fashions, which they might not be able to afford. The author went on to describe the funeral of Albert, the prince consort, in fine detail and promoted upper class ideas of mourning, hoping to appeal to the socially pretentious middle class.

While it does not appear that they sold off the rack mourning clothes, a mourning warehouse named Priestley and Dodge's evoked the name of Queen Victoria and her daughter when advertising in the United States, in hopes that their names would encourage Americans to purchase Marie Stuart caps and long veils made of crepe. Davey had described the cap that Empress Frederick of the imperial house of Germany wore during her twelve months of widowhood, saying that her black crepe veil fell like a mantle behind her to the ground. She also wore a white batiste collar with two narrow white bands falling from her head to her feet (Davey, 88). American mourning warehouses sold fabric for mourning clothes and also items such as ribbons, hats, rings, gloves, handbags, shoes, flowers, and black drapery for the house. In Nashville, Tennessee, the firm of Stevenson and White placed an ad in the *Republican Banner and Nashville Whig* on January 21, 1853, which read, "We have a beautiful assortment, such as Alpacas, DeLaines, Canton Cloths, black English Crape, Italian do, Bombazines, Silks and Ribbons, Crape Veils, Mourning Handkerchiefs, Hosiery, Collars and Sleeves, Gloves &c." On the same day, the paper posted an ad from McNairy and Furman, located on College Street, saying that they had the same merchandise, but: "Our friends may rely upon finding our stock as beautiful as ever before offered and by far the largest and most complete, and at prices none can object to; and we most respectfully invite each and every one to call, and we will take great pleasure in trying to please them." Besson & Son mourning warehouse in Philadelphia, Pennsylvania, advertised that they offered the perfect shade of black and none of their textiles were dyed over another color.

By the last quarter of the century, Americans could order mourning clothes in the mail from companies such as Montgomery Ward. Aaron Montgomery Ward (1844–1913) started the first mail-order company in 1872. By 1884 Ward had a catalog 240 pages thick, filled with illustrations of merchandise. Richard Warren Sears, originally a watchmaker, saw mail order as a new strategy for marketing apparel. By 1895 he was producing a 532-page catalog with a rapidly growing circulation. The Bloomingdale Brothers of New York City issued a catalog in 1886. Their Manhattan shop originally sold hoops, crinolines and ladies' notions. When the hoop skirt went out of style, they started selling a variety of ladies' garments, gentlemen's clothing and European fashions. The department store Jordan Marsh, from Boston, advertised that mourning clothes were always stocked for immediate delivery. Their mourning dress "number 7" was described as being a "very pretty all wool French cashmere costume, waist trimmed with handsome lace effect bolero, crushed collar and belt, finished with mourning silk ribbon, skirt cut in Parisian style." They guaranteed: "Dresses can be made to order from any measurements in two days."

Mourning clothes were expensive. Styles continued to change and literature from mourning warehouses made it seem essential to purchase new mourning garb for each new death. The *1883 Collier's Encyclopedia of Social and Commercial Information* noted: "Mourning has generally to be purchased hurriedly, and too often a dressmaker gets carte blanche almost to furnish the mourning. No wonder mourning is considered expensive" (Plante, 199).

* * *

By the 1880s the periods for mourning shortened, and restrictions concerning mourning clothing eased. The demand for crepe fabric decreased in America. It became socially acceptable to wear any style dress as long as it was black. This was partly in response to the high cost of mourning clothes, and partly due to the growing criticism of women's fashion by many, including English artists who founded the Aesthetic Movement in art that found corsets unappealing. Doctors and feminists also disapproved of women's dress fashion because of health concerns. Widow's weeds didn't fit with the Gay Nineties' outlook on life. Feminists and suffragettes criticized widow's weeds as being "a survival of the outward expression of the inferiority of women" (Gilmartin, 149). After World War I, women still wore black and some even continued to wear black for the rest of their lives, but most women wore any black clothing they already owned to mourn, and some only wore black on the day of the funeral.

The Role of Widows and Charles Dana Gibson

In the 19th century, America girls were taught from birth that they were to be wives. It was believed that not being married was an unnatural state and might even result in disease (Rosenberg, 135). Marriage was the end goal. It was believed that marriage would fulfill the woman and give her higher purpose. The same was true for the British woman, whose goal was to be a virtuous wife and mother (Tortora, 354). 19th century novels and advice manuals portrayed the home as a "kingdom" where the wife was the queen. Her job was to be cheerful and beautiful. Above all, she was to make her husband a happy environment. Wives were to be dutiful, virtuous and complacent; they were to avoid arguments at all cost. Working outside the home for money was not allowed. A woman's place was in the home. An advice book printed in the 1830s said "woman was made to be the helpmate of man—that, by rendering herself pleasing in his sight, she is the assuager of his pains, the solacer of his woe, the sharer of his joys, the chief agent in the communication of his sublunary bliss" (*The Mirror of the Graces*, 8).

But where was the place for a widow?

Many ancient civilizations didn't know what to do with widows. Some were killed or ordered to commit suicide when their husbands died. This tradition survived almost to Victorian times, forcing the British, in 1829, to outlaw the practice of "Sati," the funeral custom where a Hindu woman leapt onto the flames of her husband's funeral pyre (Gilmartin, 149). It was thought in India that a widow might have caused her husband's death, so widows were feared. There was also the belief that death was contagious. A widow had intimate contact with death and might even be a witch. In societies where a widow was allowed to live, there was usually a period of time when she had to be isolated and purified before she could be trusted to return to the community.

In European societies of the Middle Ages, widows were required to mourn for a year. They were isolated in their homes, and their rooms were hung with dark, nonreflecting cloth. The period of this isolation probably had to do with inheritance and the paternity of any children born after a husband's death. In Britain, women were not allowed to inherit or own any goods or land until the passage of the Married Women's Property Act of 1882. A deceased husband's property was inherited by his male relatives, and hopefully his sons, including any who were to be born. While a pregnancy lasted approximately forty weeks, an extra twelve weeks were added to the mourning period in case of unusual circumstances.

Remarriage for widows was allowed after the period of mourning was completed; however, great respect was given to a woman who remained chaste. Before the establishment of the Church of England, some wealthy women even chose to enter a convent on the death of a spouse, insuring that their sexuality belonged to their husbands alone. This was very difficult to do in Victorian times. Nunneries were part of the Catholic religion, and although there were a few Anglican nuns in Britain during the Victorian Era, their numbers were small. In America, nuns from Quebec and the former Spanish territories tried to establish religious orders for women in the United States during Victorian times, but these were relatively unsuccessful.

How exactly did a widow fit into 19th century society? According to Congregational minister George Washington Burnap (1802–1859), lecturing in 1848, a widow must endure this life, and "finish the journey of life alone" (Burnap, 123). She must renounce wide and boundless expectations of happiness, and live for her children, gaining wisdom and strength. Her clothing, her widow's weeds, were supposed to distance the wearer from those around her. In the English tradition, a widow removed herself physically from society as well, or wore a thick veil to hide herself from view as if her presence was a burden on others or, possibly, bad luck. This was a dreary outlook for women, especially young widows, who were seen by Pastor Burnap as having outlived their usefulness. Their situation was made worse by the deep financial hardships widows often faced.

Abel Boyer (1667?–1729), a French and English journalist, noted the trend for excessive female mourning and thought it was a dismal and troublesome vanity. To Boyer, the women were insincere, and the practice was "most prevailing with ambitious women; for their sex rendering them unable to advance themselves by eminent virtues, they strive to signalize their reputation by the pageantry of an inconsolable sorrow" (quoted in Trumbach, 40). Exaggerated mourning became a way for a woman to earn respect and demonstrate her worth. Despite having female queens, British women did not have basic rights until quite late in Victorian times. They did not have the vote until 1928, they could not hold elected office, and they could not earn college degrees. Married women could not inherit or own property. They could not even keep the wages they earned until the Married Woman's Property Act of 1870 and 1882. (The struggle of British women to obtain the vote was a difficult one. They began forming societies urging that they be given the vote in 1867, but it was only in 1918 that British women over 30 were finally granted the right, and women did not gain equal voting rights with men for another 10 years.) American women fared slightly better once the colonies won their independence from Great Britain. Separate states enacted married women's property acts and married women's earning acts, such as Mississippi in 1839, Maryland in 1843 and Michigan in 1844. As an independent country, Texas enacted laws allowing a married woman to write a will, enter into contracts, sue for divorce, and keep her homestead; and in 1845 the State of New York passed legislation allowing a woman to keep the earnings from an invention she had patented; but protection was not uniform throughout the nation. At the end of the 1880s fully one-third of American states still did not have laws allowing women to keep and control their earnings. As to higher education, American women could earn college degrees at a few universities such as Oberlin College, founded in Ohio in 1833; the all-female colleges Mount Holyoke, founded in Massachusetts in 1837; and Queens College of Charlotte, North Carolina, founded in 1857; but most universities were closed to them. Those who did work were paid less than men for the same jobs.

Without the same legal protection as men, women worked longer hours. As to the vote, Wyoming granted it to women in 1890, but it wasn't until the 19th Amendment passed, in 1920, that women in all states could cast their ballots for elected officials.

In the United States, the 19th century was the time of the awakening of the women's movement as more and more women marched for the right to vote, fought for participation in the work force and the right to keep their earnings, and demanded information on birth control. During the Civil War, women had been called upon to fill jobs once held by men. This gave even more of them the confidence they needed to advocate for more rights.

American widows were at least able to inherit money, if not property, and many found that they had more independence than they ever had living with their fathers or as wives. Some widows, like Miriam Florence Leslie, were able to keep and run a successful business after their husband's death. Mrs. Leslie continued to own and run *Frank Leslie's Illustrated Newspaper,* and she became a campaigner for women's right to vote, but she was the exception and not the rule.

As early as the 1848 September issue of *Godey's Lady's Book,* Sarah Hale, also a moderate advocate for women's rights, recognized the circumstances widows faced and noted in its instructions for making a lady's netted mourning cap that "a widow might appear quite fashionable despite the subdued color of her dress." Later on, Hale fought for higher wages for women, and their ability to retain property rights. In time, tastes changed. In 1876, an article appeared in the English journal *The English Woman's Domestic Magazine,* noting that black clothing was no longer for mourning alone. By this time black dye had come down in price so much that the color had become correct for evening and visiting clothes, especially for older women.

Black continued to be the color of widow's weeds, but these clothes were often ornate depending on the age, money and community of the mourner. Despite advice from books on etiquette urging 19th century Americans that mourning clothes were to be simple so as not to appear insincere, this guideline was not always followed. The Smithsonian Museum owns a black evening dress worn by First Lady Jane Appleton Pierce in 1853. Described as having a fashionable V-shaped waistline and a fully gathered skirt made from black taffeta, the dress has an overskirt of black tulle, embroidered with silver dots. The First Lady wore it with a black lace net and velvet headdress trimmed with dull jet and gold. Mrs. Pierce was not a widow but a grieving mother. Two of her sons had died in 1842. Her one surviving son, a boy of twelve, had been killed in a railway accident the year she wore the dress.

As mourning dress became more fashionable, one couldn't help but notice that black could also be alluring and draw attention to the widow, who was an enigma of her times—no longer a virgin but also not a courtesan. The role of a widow was explored in a series of drawings done by Charles Dana Gibson (1867–1944), the American graphic artist, whose work was published in *Life, Harper's Weekly,* and *Scribner's and Collier's* magazines. In 1890 Gibson developed the "Gibson Girl" series about the lives of modern young women, using his wife and her sisters as inspiration. One of the sisters had married an English lord and had become the Lady Nancy Astor. She would go on to be the first woman to serve as a member of Parliament in the British House of Commons in 1919. The drawings for his series entitled *A Widow and Her Friends* are comic and satirical. One picture shows a beautiful young widow, dressed in black, surrounded by a crowd of interested men, while the rest of the women sit alone in a corner of the room. Gibson's young widow was vulnerable but also seductive. In Victorian times, a decent woman could be either nonsexual or a wife. But a widow was neither, and as such was a destabilizing force in society. Robert De Valcourt noted in 1855, "Black is becoming; and young widows, fair, plump, and smiling, with their roguish eyes sparkling under their black veils, are very seducing" (De Valcourt, 157).

5

Illustrious Widows' Influence on Art and Design

Mourning Clothes

When choosing a wardrobe, people make artistic choices. They apply clothing to their bodies as a painter applies paint to a canvas. Their clothing is then seen by the public, who interpret them and use them to deduce a person's character. This is reflected in the old saying, translated from the Greek, "Clothes make the man," which was repeated in the 1500s by Dutch priest and social critic Erasmus. The emerging women's journal industry kept people informed of what the elite were wearing in the late 18th and early 19th centuries and informed the public as to what styles were fashionable. But as time went by, their illustrations became more personal and were done of popular figures. Two of the most popular women of the time were Mary Todd Lincoln and Queen Victoria.

Illustrations of Mary Todd Lincoln and her children appeared on the cover of journals such as the December 15, 1860, issue of *Frank Leslie's Illustrated*. Numerous illustrations of Queen Victoria appeared in newspapers, journals and books published in the United Kingdom and in France. Once widowed, these two served as role models for grieving women of the 19th century. Both of these women were highly visible and closely followed by the media. Both performed the grand part of the dutiful and grieving widow. After the deaths of their spouses, both made the artistic choice of draping themselves in mourning clothes for the rest of their lives. With these clothes, they meant to elicit emotions from the public and those in power with various degrees of success.

These women were not unique. Many widows made the choice to wear black for the rest of their lives. Queen Victoria and former First Lady Mary Lincoln knew that by wearing these clothes they would be making a statement, but what were they saying? Did they want their clothing to show respect for their dead husbands? Mrs. Lincoln was a spiritualist. She began attending séances when her eleven-year-old son Willie died in 1862, and continued to attend them, often in disguise, for the rest of her life. She even had a photograph of herself with the ghost of her deceased husband taken by William H. Mumler, the famous spiritualist photographer. It is believed that Queen Victoria also attended séances performed in private by her servant and constant companion, John Brown. Did these two illustrious women really believe that the spirits of their husbands watched them from beyond death's door and appreciated their sartorial choices? Did they hope that their dead husbands appreciated the respect that their widow's weeds gave them? Or did these powerful women decide that fashion no longer interested them? Had

99

they withdrawn from the world of fashion? Did the black clothing give them freedom from the ever-changing styles and expectations they no longer wanted to fulfill?

In her younger years, Queen Victoria had a keen interest in fashion. Her journals and letters dating from the time before her husband's death contained meticulous notes about what the women of her court wore. She carefully picked out trousseau dresses for Vicky, her eldest daughter, when she married the Prussian prince Frederick in 1858. Victoria knew that clothes were important, and she hoped that her daughter's marriage would help form a great alliance between Britain and that part of Germany. The public came to assume that the queen wasn't interested in clothing because, once a widow, she appeared to be so dowdy, but as late as 1897, she wore a dress with a fashionable off-the-shoulder bodice for her diamond jubilee (Munich, 65).

Mary Lincoln claimed that she had limited funds. Those that didn't believe her felt that the former First Lady dressed in black only to gain sympathy. When she was the First Lady everything about her, including her fashion sense, had been criticized by the Washington elite. After her husband's death, her attempt to sell her clothing to raise money was a powerful symbol that she would never wear these ensembles again. She turned her back on fashion, and no longer cared what people said about her.

Queen Victoria—Fashion Trendsetter

It is interesting to note that Queen Victoria (1819–1901) was born only thirty years after the French Revolution and almost wasn't born at all. At the death of George III's only grandchild, Princess Charlotte, his son Edward, Duke of Kent (1767–1820), the king's fifth child and fourth son, saw that there would be no one left to inherit the British throne. He quickly got married in 1818 and sired his only child, Victoria, before passing away in 1820. Victoria was a teenager, only 18, when her uncle, King William IV, died, and she was crowned queen in 1837. William had been 62 at his coronation. He inherited the throne from his brother, King George IV. Victoria married her cousin Albert (Francis Charles Augustus Albert Emmanuel) and had nine children in seventeen years. There were at least half a dozen attempts on her life. After her husband's death, she retreated from regal duties, yet during her reign ten prime ministers and ten lord chancellors came and went while she remained a constant in a rapidly changing world.

Victoria was only 4'10" tall, which was short even for those times. Experiencing trepidation over having a young, female sovereign, there was, at first, a concerted effort to downplay her position as queen and promote her femininity. Artists painted portraits of the young lady, and poets extolled her good qualities. Victoria was often portrayed as "beauty personified" (Plunkett, 79). Unfortunately she looked a lot like her uncle, the scandalous George IV, who was considered to have had vile taste, and who was also criticized as being "elaborate in dress and lax in morals" (Munich, 59). After Victoria's marriage, she wore increasingly unfashionable garments in an attempt to distinguish herself from her uncle. In this way she strove to "refashion" her monarchy and distinguish it from the garishness of the Regency era.

Queen Victoria dressed down, attempting to look more like her people. Her unstylish clothes stood for her democratic and earnest religious beliefs. They told much about her character, or about the character she wished people to know her by. Like most women of her time and status, her clothes were made by dressmakers, but it is believed that Prince

Albert, her husband, had a heavy hand in designing them. Victoria's dressmakers were Sarah Ann Unitt and Elizabeth Gieve, who was the sister of James Watson Gieve, the owner of Gieves and Hawkes, which catered to the British Army and Royal Navy. Gieve held Queen Victoria's Royal Warrant and was her dressmaker and milliner from 1852 to 1889. Eventually it was Martha Dudley who designed mourning clothing for the queen.

Victoria was the first royal superstar. She was crowned queen only a short while before the invention of photography. The first British monarch to be photographed, her face was recognized by all. Even before she was photographed, the British printing company Hodgson and Graves produced exclusive sets of coronation and royal wedding prints of the queen. Priced at the enormous price of 10 to 12 shillings (about the average weekly wage) they were marketed to the bourgeoisie, and although pricey, were often given as special gifts (Plunkett, 79). Stories about the queen and her family appeared regularly in heavily illustrated British newspapers and journals like the *Lady's Newspaper and Pictorial Times* and *Queen*. These sold for 6 pennies an issue and were geared to the middle class (Plunkett, 78).

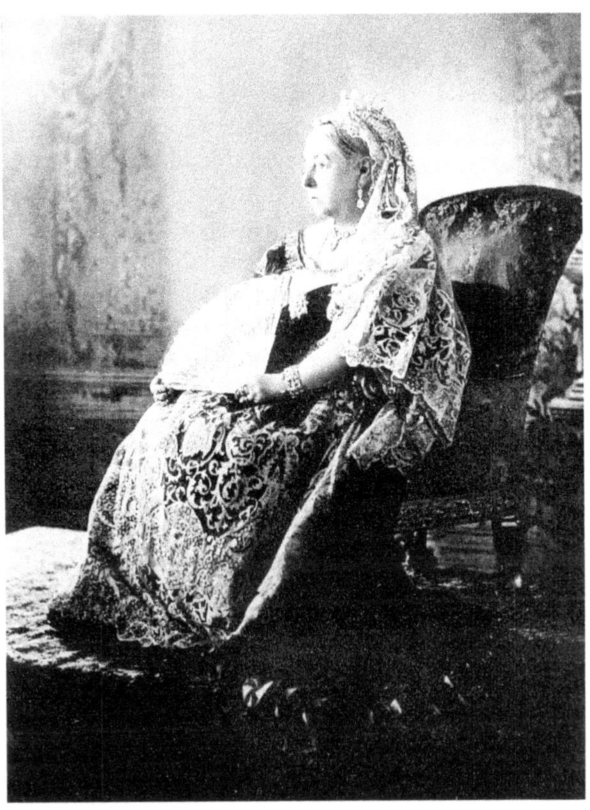

Photograph of Queen Victoria taken at the wedding of Prince George, Duke of York, in 1893 but used to mark her Diamond Jubilee of 1897 (Wikimedia Commons).

The queen was popular in America, too. Sara Hale, the editor of *Godey's* magazine, held Victoria in high esteem and saw her as the role model for all women. *Godey's Lady's* magazine published article after article about the queen, the queen and her children, and the queen and her family, and the words and illustrations influenced American women. For example, copying the description of Queen Victoria's wedding gown, more and more American brides decided to wear white, and Christmas trees became a customary part of the American Christmas celebration in response to *Godey's* reprinting of an illustration and story that appeared in the *Illustrated London News* depicting the royal family with a tree, complete with decorations, candles and toys.

Queen Victoria also contributed to her popularity by writing two bestselling books. The first one contained extracts from her personal diary and was called *Leaves from the Journal of Our Life in the Highlands*. This book immediately sold 20,000 copies. It was reprinted several times, selling better than the novel *Little Women*, which was published the same year. *Leaves from the Journal of Our Life in the Highlands* was published seven years after the death of Prince Albert during the queen's self-imposed seclusion. People all over the world were interested in what had happened to her, and her book showed her subjects that she was flesh and blood like them. With it, she invited all into her life as if they were part of the royal family (Rennell, 28). This book was followed years later, in 1884, by a sequel, *More Leaves from the Journal of Our Life in the Highlands.* By this time her sons and daughters were old enough to raise objections, but the queen insisted on making the book available for sale. Her reason was that she wanted to ensure that biographies of her did not contain false information (Rennell, 29).

In the early part of her reign, clothes were a big deal for Queen Victoria. If she dressed too fashionably, she could be dismissed as a frivolous woman instead of respected as monarch. If she dressed too stylishly, she would be criticized for following the fashions of France and slighting British clothing designers and manufacturers. Worse still, from the start of her reign, she had been made fun of for wearing the pants in the family instead of her husband. Women's clothing of the mid–19th century was restrictive and denoted a woman's limited role in society and inferior political position. To hold up their breasts, women wore corsets or "stays," from the French word *"ester"* or *"estayer"*—which means "to support." These were made of coarse material boned in both the front and the back and laced up tightly, unless the woman was very fat or pregnant. As women attempted to look like the illustrated fashion plates published in magazines, they laced their corsets tighter, trying to make their waists as small as possible in the belief that a tight corset implied a refined lifestyle. Unfortunately, tight corsets restricted movement so much that it made completing household chores impossible. By midcentury some women pulled their corsets so tightly that they restricted breathing and caused their ribs to overlap. In response there was a movement for dress reform. Amelia Bloomer (1818–1894), the American feminist, began wearing trousers in 1851, based on the Turkish style of women's clothing. Many people in Europe, Britain and America saw this as "usurpation of the rights of man" (Cunningham, 3). Victoria had to be careful with her dress to avoid similar disapproval.

The year 1861 was a difficult one for the middle-aged queen. In March, Queen Victoria's mother died. She wore a black moiré silk mourning dress to the funeral. Nine months later, on December 14th, her beloved husband Albert passed away. He had been chronically ill for the past two years but died from what was described as typhoid fever. Victoria was so grief stricken over the death of her husband that people feared she would go mad (Munich, 81).

Writing several years later, in 1890, author Richard Davey described Prince Albert's funeral:

> The day was observed throughout the realm as one of mourning. The bells of all the churches were tolled, and in many of them special services were held. In the towns the shops were closed, and the window blinds of private residences were drawn down. No respectable people appeared abroad except in mourning, and in seaport towns the flags were hoisted half-mast high [Davey, 88].

Davey, writing for a warehouse that sold mourning clothes and accessories, noted that Queen Victoria dressed in traditional black but modified the mourning cap by "indenting it over the forehead a la Marie Stuart, there by imparting to it a certain picturesqueness which was quite lacking in the former head-dress. This coiffure has been not only adopted by her subjects, but also by royal widows abroad" (88).

Victoria was only 42 when Albert died. She was the same age as Albert had been. His birthday was in August and hers was in May. There were hopes that she'd remarry, but she retreated, wearing black mourning clothes including the widow's headdress, for the rest of her life. She refused to take off her mourning clothes for the wedding of her daughter, Princess Alice, in July of the next year. This was not unusual, because the court might still have been in mourning for the prince. But when her son Albert (known as Bertie, and later King Edward VII) married almost two years later in March of 1863, she continued to wear black and took no part in the service. Instead, she sat apart from everyone in a separate gallery.

It was customary for the sovereign of Britain, as head of state, to formally open each new session of Parliament by giving a speech in the House of Lords. Queen Victoria did not do this from 1862 to 1865, the years following prince Albert's death. Until the end of her reign, she only attended the opening of Parliament seven more times. In a letter to Prime Minister Lord John Russell, she wrote that she was a "poor, brokenhearted widow, nervous and shrinking, dragged in deep mourning, alone in State as a Show, where she used to go supported by her husband, to be gazed at without delicacy of feeling" (Munich, 81).

Victoria became known as the "Widow of Windsor." At first, she was very unpopular. England had never had a widow queen before, and Victoria had no rules of behavior to follow. She celebrated the first anniversary of her husband's death as if it was a "birthday in a new world" (Munich, 87). Dressed in mourning for the remainder of her life, she hid behind the closed doors of Balmoral Castle in the Highlands of Scotland, which she purchased in happier times, in 1848, as a summer home. She made her husband's former hunting attendant, John Brown, controller of her household. Brown, who possibly acted as a medium and led séances, was constantly at her side, also serving her in her other residences at Osborne and Windsor. Rumors spread that she had married John Brown, and secret in-structions she gave about her death asked that she be buried wearing a ring he had given her (Rennell, 294).

The queen came out of seclusion to open Parliament in 1866. In 1872, when her son and heir to the throne recovered from a life-threatening case of typhoid fever, she held a parade and a service of thanksgiving. Having transitioned from full mourning to second mourning, she wore less crepe and more silk, but continued to refuse to wear a crown, wearing the symbolic widow's bonnet instead. Pictures of her at this time show a stout woman dressed in black with touches of white and a white widow's cap. From 1880 on, she wore clothes appropriate for the third stage of mourning. Ribbon and trim might be of different fabrics than crepe. Her dresses and gowns could be trimmed with black beads or embroidered or bordered with lace. In photographs she appeared with shawls and mantles.

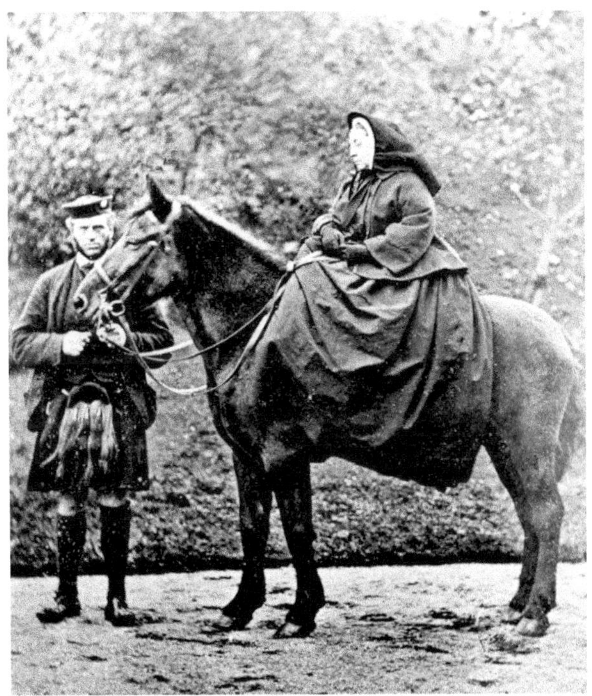

Queen Victoria on "Fyvie" with John Brown at Balmoral. Medium carte de visite (gift of Mrs. Riddell in memory of Peter Fletcher Riddle, 1985, National Galleries of Scotland Commons).

Dressed in mourning, the queen appeared more regal to her people than ever before, and they united behind her (Munich, 72). In 1897, a children's book written about the queen titled *The Fairies Favourite* asked the question: why was Queen Victoria the worst dressed person in the world when she could easily have bought beautiful dresses for very little money? It answered that she had been dressed by the fairies, who pulled her clothing out of their "rag-bag." The book went on to explain: "her natural majesty, and with such unaffected dignity, withal the simplicity and modesty that became her so well, that the people, having loyal hearts and loving her so dearly, knew her well for their Queen" (Munich, 76).

The book implied that Victoria did not need to wear fancy clothing or precious jewels to show her imperial power. Her plain black widow's weeds distinguished her from other European royalty. She loved the dress the fairies made her and became a fairytale queen. To adults, she was a republican leader. She was one of them. The poorest widow in the realm could wear the same widow's weeds as the queen. Her mourning clothing gave her distinction. Her lack of sartorial taste showed her spiritual and monarchial worth. She conquered her people, and her plain appearance denied her growing wealth and power.

In addition, Queen Victoria took advantage of her widow's weeds to dress comfortably. At a time when fashion changed from year to year, it must have been a great relief for Victoria not to have to worry about what she wore. Women's clothing was at best impractical and at worst dangerous. Some American and European religious movements banned the current fashion trends and developed styles of their own. In the United States, feminists such as Amelia Bloomer and Elizabeth Cady Stanton also rebelled, noting, "Tight waists and trailing skirts deprived [women] of their freedom" (Fashion, 3). Long skirts were difficult to wear outside, and so they kept women at home, making women seem not as intellectually curious as men. The crinoline hindered and limited women's movements at a time when women were demanding more rights and more independence. Suffragettes even believed that the crinoline and then the bustle were approved of and designed by men because it made it more difficult for women to move into a man's world.

Bloomer (1818–1894) became owner and editor of the first newspaper geared for women, called *The Lily*, which was published from 1849 to 1853. In it, she advocated a new style of clothing for women that was brought to the public's eye by the British actress Fanny Kemble. The outfit consisted of a dress with a shortened skirt worn over trousers, called pantalets—a style inspired by women's clothing from the Middle East. The new style influenced women's sportswear and children's clothing, but aside from that, women who wore the new outfits were harassed and criticized. In 19th century America and Britain, all women wore skirts and all men wore trousers. After only a brief experiment wearing the new design, Bloomer herself went back to wearing "fashionable" clothing, conceding that the new wire hoops were an improvement and were light and pleasant to wear (Snodgrass, 3).

Another attempt to reform women's clothing came from English artists such as William Holman Hunt, Dante Gabriel Rossetti and John Everett Mallais, who were inspired by an ancient statue called the *Venus de Milo,* which had been discovered in 1820 and brought to France. These artists saw the ancient work as being the personification of female beauty and proportion. In contrast, the tight corseted waists, tight sleeves and full hooped skirts made women seem artificial. These artists established the Pre-Raphaelite Brotherhood in 1848 while they were students at the Royal Academy in London. They encouraged the women in their lives (their wives and models) to dress in simple, loose and full-skirted clothing, without hoops or corsets. They also portrayed women dressed this way in their art. Known as the "Aesthetic Style," this type of clothing gained some support from other artists and actresses (Snodgrass, 10). In the 1860s intellectuals rejected the highly structured and heavily trimmed fashions of their times, but most women were not freed from corsets until much later.

The queen may have been influenced by this movement when she took to wearing mourning clothes in 1861. But in time, Queen Victoria grew fat. An outfit of hers that was auctioned in 2013 had a waist measuring 45 inches wide ("Pants? Queen Victoria's Underwear"). A pair of her underpants that were auctioned in 2008 measured 50 inches around the waist ("Queen Victoria's Bloomers"). For the last ten years of her life, her dressmaker, Mrs. Dudley, used a master pattern that varied little except for beading and embroidery. The queen's large-waisted black dresses were worn without stays or a corset. They were easy to put on and easy to take off. They even had pockets in which she kept her watch, keys and glasses.

Mary Todd Lincoln—Fashion Designer

It is odd that we refer to the wife of the slain president as Mary Todd Lincoln (1818–1882), when she herself distained her maiden name. It is also odd that the widow of the much-esteemed Lincoln did not have the support or sympathy of the American people. Congress even refused to grant her a pension after her husband's death. Instead they gave her $20,000, which was the remainder of Lincoln's salary for the year. The senator from her home state of Illinois, David Davis, who became an associate justice of the Supreme Court, estimated that the slain president's estate was worth $110,000. But inheritance laws were decided by each a state. As a wife, Mrs. Lincoln did not own anything. Her husband was the legal head of the family. As a wife she could not buy or own real estate or personal property. As a widow Mrs. Lincoln was entitled to only ⅓ of her husband's estate, but according to the laws of inheritance of 1865, she would be given money only; she would not be given any property, including the family house. As a widow, she had many more rights than she had as a wife, but unfortunately, she was also responsible for her debts.

In Illinois, Mrs. Lincoln had the reputation of being a frugal and even a stingy wife (Williams and Burkhimer, 66). As the First Lady, her reputation was completely reversed and she became a known as a terrible shopper who had no idea how to keep within a budget. During her husband's first administration, she overspent the $20,000 allowance Congress had allocated to her by $7,000 when redecorating the White House (Keckley, 149). She purchased French satins, plush brocatelles (upholstery fabric), and 508 yards of blue and white duck canvas that the Marines used to shade their band during the free concerts they gave every Wednesday and Saturday on the White House lawn. Quickly she was seen as an embarrassment. Even her husband chastised her and said that her spending was inappropriate when soldiers fighting for Union causes did not have enough decent blankets to cover them.

Mrs. Lincoln also came home with lavish items for herself. This might have been because she had been schooled by Monsieur and Madame Mentelle, former members of the French court (Sandberg, 22). It is possible that they gave the young girl in their care the false impression that stores like A. T. Stewarts in New York City would give her gifts, as European stores customarily did for their aristocracy. The usually thrifty First Lady returned from her shopping sprees with costly furs, silks, laces, and jewelry. For example, in 1860 she paid $3,000 for earrings and a pin, and $5,000 for a shawl (Keckley, 149). Sadly, it turned out that these were not gifts. Instead she discovered that the stores were giving her open lines of credit. After her husband's death, she was expected to pay for everything.

At the start of Lincoln's second term the First Lady had been stocking up on items that the family would need for the next four years, such as white kid gloves, used to greet visitors at weekly White House public receptions the Lincolns held, called "levees" by Lizzie Keckley. The tradition of having a weekly "levee" making the president accessible to the public began with George Washington and his wife, Martha, who patterned these receptions after the tradition of French and British monarchs. Thomas Jefferson broke with the tradition of receiving visitors on a weekly basis, but the Lincolns revived it, whenever possible, during his presidency. When the president was assassinated, shortly after his second inauguration, his wife owned 200 pairs of gloves, which might make her seem insane if one did not understand that she and the president shook so many hands that they went through 4 pairs each for a single event. The amount Mrs. Lincoln owed shopkeepers at the time of his death was $70,000, the equivalent of approximately one million dollars in 2015 (Keckley, 202). Mrs. Lincoln's portion of the inheritance, approximately $33,000, didn't cover this much. To make matters worse, the family's house in Springfield had become a shrine for mourners. Even if she had wanted to return there to live, she would have been hounded by curious tourists. Once she moved out of the White House, the former First Lady found herself homeless; she had nowhere to go.

Mary Todd was born into one of the founding families of Lexington, Kentucky, a town in a slave state that prided itself on being the "Athens of the West." Her father, Robert Smith Todd, was trained as a lawyer but became successful in commerce and land speculation. He was a member of the Whig political party and a member of the Kentucky legislature. At an early age, Mary was introduced to politicians such as Henry Clay and General Andrew Jackson, who went on to become president, and whose policy of Indian removal was one that the Whigs objected to. Although he objected to slavery, Robert Todd owned several slaves but was a member of the Kentucky Colonization Society, a group that sent free black Americans back to Africa. Across from the Todd house the family could see the long chain of slaves going to the public square to be sold. Across from this was the whipping post where slaves were routinely punished (Sandberg, 22).

Mary's mother, Eliza Ann Parker, died when the child was only six years old. A widower with six children, her father remarried after only six months, much to the chagrin of the Parker family, who were also relatives of the Todds, Mary's step-mother, Elizabeth (Betsy) Humphreys, immediately became pregnant. Sadly, the baby died in infancy. Betsy got pregnant again soon after and continued to have eight more children in the next fifteen years. The household was chaotic, and a chasm developed between Betsy and her step-children. As soon as Mary was old enough, she was sent to boarding school, where she excelled. After graduation, at the age of 14, Mary continued her education at Madame Mentelle's Boarding School for Young Ladies, run by Madame Victoire Charlotte LeClere Mentelle and her husband, Monsieur August Mentelle. Monsieur Montelle had served the French royals and possibly King Louis XVI during his reign. After the king's execution, the couple fled the revolution and arrived in America. Their knowledge of French court procedures and fashion may have had a great influence on the impressionable young girl.

Mary grew up at a time when a married woman sewed at home and was expected to create clothing for herself, her family and the family's slaves (if she was from a slave state). Wives also sewed linens, curtains, and the like for the house. Daughters were required to help with the task, and the Todd girls were taught to sew and embroider, working along with their mother or step-mother and, perhaps, a sewing woman, who was probably a slave. After school work, at night, Mary even knitted socks. Mary was the only one of the siblings who developed skill with a needle. It is reported that at 10 years of age, she sewed willow branches into the hem of her skirts to make them look like the popular style of the day (Williams, 190)

Coinciding with the new availability of fabric, women's skirts grew wider and more voluminous. Some even had a train that dragged on the floor, bringing dirt and vermin into the house. Eventually skirts were lifted off the ground by heavy crinolines made of horse hair or other stiff material. Later on, these were fabricated with wire. Crinolines lifted the bottoms of the skirts, but the width of them made it difficult to see one's feet. Women often fell when climbing stairs or maneuvering a curb. Sometimes this caused the rigid hoop to lift the skirt up, exposing the woman's underwear. Worse still, the size of the hoop and skirt made it difficult to maneuver around fireplaces, and it was not uncommon for a woman to catch fire and be burned alive (Williams and Burkhimer, 195).

Mary and her family sewed by hand. The first sewing machine had been invented in Germany in 1755, but it was complicated and not constructed for home use. Over the next hundred years, the mechanism was continually refined by several inventors including Elias Howe, but it wasn't until the American inventor Isaac Merritt Singer (1811–1875) came along that it became an indispensable American home appliance. Singer was granted an American patent for his machine for home use in 1851, which was contested by Howe in court. Howe won and Singer paid him a sum for his invention, and continued to pay him a royalty on each machine sold. Singer ingeniously allowed women to purchase the expensive machines on the installment plan. For only $5 down and a small monthly payment, American women were able to rapidly create their own clothing using the machine. Improvements in the textile industry meant that fabric, trim and lace were affordable and at record low prices. In response, dress skirts got bigger and bigger. Fashion was no longer the domain of the wealthy. It became "equally important to both upper and middle-class women no matter where they lived" (Williams and Burkhimer, 191).

It does not appear that Mary Lincoln owned a sewing machine as a young wife in Springfield, Illinois. Instead she reportedly gathered with other women to use one that belonged to a neighbor. When she moved into the White House, one was given to her by the Wheeler and Wilson Sewing Machine Company of Chicago. This was mounted in a solid rosewood cabinet and richly ornamented with silver plating, enamel and inlaid pearl. It's doubtful that she had much time to use it (Williams and Burkhimer, 190).

Mrs. Lincoln had spilled coffee on the dress she was to wear to the reception after Lincoln's inauguration. She needed a new dress, and was introduced to Elizabeth (Lizzie) Keckley, a former slave and seamstress, who had made dresses for the wife of Jefferson Davis and the wife of General Robert E. Lee. Mrs. Davis, Varina, even urged Keckley to go south with her, warning her that northerners would see the black people as the cause of the coming Civil War and treat them harshly. But having bought her own freedom from slavery, the dressmaker stayed in Washington, D.C., and was delighted to help Mary Lincoln out of her predicament. Keckley had to promise Mrs. Lincoln that she would not charge her too much for the new dress. She took Mrs. Lincoln's measurements and went back to her shop, where she refashioned a rose-colored moiré dress for the First Lady, whom she described as being 40 years old, measuring 5 feet, two inches, and inclined to be stout (Keckley, 78). By the time the dressmaker finished and returned to the White House it was late in the day. Fearing that she had nothing to wear, Mrs. Lincoln decided she wouldn't go to the reception, but the dressmaker did return. Keckley dressed the First Lady and arranged her hair, allowing her to attend this important event. Both women were delighted when President Lincoln said that he was pleased with the results.

Lizzie Keckley, the former slave, became Mrs. Lincoln's personal stylist, dresser and confidant, much to the chagrin of the Washington elite, who may have been against slavery but were shocked that their First Lady would allow a black woman into the private rooms of the White House. Keckley went on to write a book about the Lincolns called *Behind the Scenes: or Thirty Years a Slave and Four Years in the White House,* which gives readers her inside look at the president and his wife.

Mary Todd married Abraham Lincoln in 1842 when she was 23 years old and he was 33. For the first two years they lived at the Globe Tavern in Springfield, Illinois, but then moved into their own home shortly after their first son, Robert, was born. Abraham was on his way to becoming a successful lawyer. His clothing greatly improved after his marriage and was probably tailor made, as was the norm for professional men of his time. Even as early as 1827, T. S. Whitmarsh of Boston advertised that their establishment sold every article of clothing for a man (Tortora, 314). Still, Mary probably made his underwear, nightwear and the rest of the clothing for herself and her family. It is unknown if she copied ideas from fashion plates in magazines or if she designed her dresses herself. Store receipts from the time showed that she bought whalebone, corset lace, and the cambric used to make her underwear and her petticoats. She also bought muslin, used for making nightshirts, undershirts and chemises for her and her family. In the 1840s Abraham Lincoln's niece hinted that Mrs. Lincoln was "stingy." Neighbors of the Lincolns reported that Mary regularly wore inexpensive calico dresses and a sun bonnet to church. They described her as being someone who traded dresses with her neighbors and someone who was "very plain in her ways" (Williams, 66).

An early photograph taken of Mrs. Lincoln in 1846, before her husband served in Congress, and when she was probably sewing her clothing herself, shows she had a tendency to be unconventional by not wear a mantel or shawl to cover her dress, nor a cap, which was a required item for a wife and a mother of her times. But in other respects, her outfit is conventional. For example, in the photograph, her chemise peeks out of the neckline of her bodice, which is hidden under an elbow-length, sheer lace bertha (a collar worn to hide a woman's cleavage). This was pulled at the neck and fastened with a brooch. Wearing the chemise this way saved on the wear and tear of Mrs. Lincoln's expensive bodice in the areas that rubbed on her skin. The ruffles of white fabric at Mrs. Lincoln's wrists would also be washed or changed, while her dress, made from expensive cloth, would never be washed.

The young wife may have used 6 yards of fabric or more to make her skirt, as was common for women's clothing in the 1840s. It would have been full, sticking out and away from her body, supported by layers of petticoats underneath. The first petticoat, called a crinoline, was knee-length and of a stiff material, usually made with a horsehair warp and wool weft. On top of it she wore four to six petticoats to add bulk, made of muslin in summer or of flannel in winter to keep her warm. Topping these was a final petticoat made of fine cambric (lightweight linen or cotton), which might be embroidered or trimmed with lace. Reaching down to Mrs. Lincoln's feet, the skirt would be lifted when needed, as when dancing. In Mary's photo there are rows of large ornamental buttons on her skirt. These probably went all the way down in rows. Her bodice had a wide neckline to balance the width of the skirt, and probably had a hook-and-eye closure in the back. Mrs. Lincoln followed fashion trends when designing her dress. Like dresses worn by Queen Victoria, it had a dropped shoulder line and tight sleeves. Her dress was pointed at the waist and was tied with a ribbon cincture. This outfit was probably hot, tight, and uncomfortable as well as being difficult to move in and dangerous.

As the century progressed, an influx of immigrants to America made hired domestic help part of every respectable household, including the middle class, to which Mrs. Lincoln belonged when she wore the dress for this photograph. A woman's task was to supervise the family servants, or the family's slaves. Servants or slaves did the laundry, cleaned the house, took care of children and prepared everyday meals. The wife might still do some of the baking. She might cook spe-

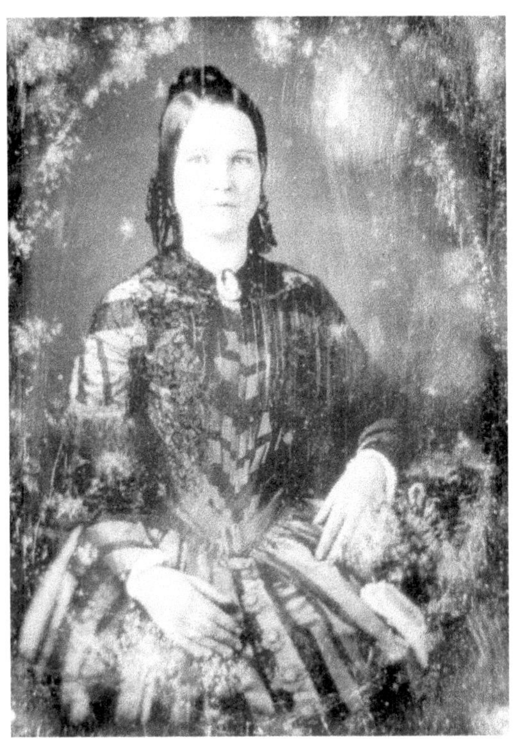

Mary Todd Lincoln, wife of Abraham Lincoln, three-quarter-length portrait, seated, facing front (Library of Congress, Prints and Photographs Division).

cial things. She might also sew, embroider, or do arts and crafts. The same was true in Britain and in France. To reflect the new position of women, Parisian designers created sleeves constructed to pull the shoulders down and pull the arms nearer to their torsos. Tight sleeves set low on the shoulders restricted a woman so that she could not completely raise her arms. This made the clothing less practical, as if to demonstrate that a woman need not lift her arms when she had servants to do all the work (Williams and Burkhimer, 195). Americans, even those of the middle class to which Mrs. Lincoln now belonged, continued to copy the fashions of Paris, which they saw in the fashion plates in lady's magazines.

Abraham Lincoln was elected to a two-year term in Congress. While he served, Mary Lincoln broke with tradition and took her children to Washington, D.C., to be with him. For two three-month periods, she joined her husband in living in Mrs. Sprigg's Boarding House, an establishment frequented by Whig abolitionists. She was even seen sitting in the gallery of the House of Representatives, listening whenever her husband made a speech. During her stay in the country's capital, she attended a reception at the White House, which must have prepared her for what lay in store (Sandberg, 22).

Lincoln was offered the appointment of governor of Oregon by newly elected President Zachary Taylor, but he declined and returned to Springfield, Illinois. Sadly, the couple's second son, Eddie, died on February 1, 1850, before he was 4 years old. Their third child, William (Willie), was born in December of that year, and Thomas (Tad), their last child, was born in 1853. Tad was born with a clef lip and palate (Sandberg, 64).

While today this condition is repairable, no such procedure existed at that time, and the boy suffered with a condition that made it difficult for him to speak and even eat. By the mid–1850s Mary had maids to help with the housework, but she was still making her own clothing and clothing for her sons. Prices for material and notions were so affordable that the English author Robert S. Surtees in his book *Ask Mamma* (1853) wrote that servants were better dressed than their masters had been twenty years earlier wearing their Sunday best (Laver, 177). It was becoming more difficult to tell working class people from the upper classes based on what they wore.

In the mid–1850s petticoats were replaced with a "cage" crinoline, or "hoop" petticoat, contraptions that made the skirt look like a balloon swaying side to side. Flexible steel hoops were suspended by tapes from the waist or sewn into a petticoat to hold the dress away from the body, making a woman "a majestic ship, sailing proudly ahead, while a small tender—her male escort—sailed along behind" (Laver, 177). A major drawback to this style was that the wind sometimes caught the hoops and blew the skirt up, exposing the woman's legs and even her underpants. To counter this, women wore long linen pantaloons edged in decoration, or boots that laced halfway up their calves. Laura Ingalls Wilder (1867–1957) described wearing dresses with a tight waist and full skirts over hoops to school when she lived in De Smet, South Dakota:

> Walking to school in the wind, the wires would creep up and up until they would all be bulging in a circle above our knees, taking our skirts with them. That would never do and we learned to walk a little way, then whirl around and around like a top to let them fall down. So on our way to school we would walk a little way and then twirl, walk and twirl, all the way [Wilder, 290].

The full hoops were even more of a problem when riding in a horse-drawn buggy. When a neighbor, Fred Gilbert, offered to drive Wilder and her friend to a school presentation, he wondered where he was supposed to sit. Wilder describes: "Our bulging hoops touched each other and filled the buggy full…. We crowded the hoops to the sides until he could sit down between us, but when he did, nothing of his feet or legs from the knee down could be seen" (Wilder, 298).

James Laver, once a curator at the Victoria and Albert Museum, wrote in his book *Costume and Fashion* that the 19th century was a period when the clothing of the two sexes was as different as possible. The crinoline symbolized female fertility by expanding the size of a woman's hips. The crinoline was also a symbol of the unapproachability of women and was a response to the extravagances of Napoleon III and his Second Empire, and of Empress Eugénie who was called the "Queen of Crinolines" (Laver, 184).

Receipts show that at this time Mrs. Lincoln dressed more elegantly. The material she bought was more expensive, and she followed fashions designs from France. Mary was now the wife of a successful lawyer and politician (Williams, 191). Helping to further her husband's political ambitions, she hosted several social events and was always concerned with what society said about her. Mary's older sister, Elizabeth Edwards, who also lived in Springfield, Illinois, constantly reminded her that she was a Todd. She was part of an important Kentucky family, and she had standards to maintain. Coming from the South, clothing and fashion were very important. One fashion mistake could lead to ostracism. In Victorian times, a "nicer wardrobe indicated a higher level on the social plane, and one's social plane was extremely important to Victorians. To the Victorian eye, first appearance and the way one was dressed made a lasting impression" (Williams, 193). Making a positive first impression was very important to proper Victorian ladies.

Mary became a public figure in Illinois when Abraham Lincoln ran for the Senate (but lost) in 1855. In 1858 he ran again, against Stephen Douglas, and lost once more. When he was nominated for president, his wife became even more visible. When he won and she became the First Lady, Mrs. Lincoln felt that everyone was looking at her and scrutinizing what she wore. She was right. She was being watched. Reporters even followed her when she and her children went on a vacation to Long Branch, New Jersey, at the end of August 1861. Illustrations and descriptions of Mrs. Lincoln's gowns and her comportment were published in newspapers. Some of these even made the front page (Sandberg, 83). She and Abraham had been born in Kentucky. Washington, D.C., high society labeled as them country bumpkins coming from "the western frontier." The elites assumed that she would embarrass the country and hurled plenty of criticism at her for what they and the public thought were the too low necklines she wore. What was worse, her stepmother was a Southerner and still owned slaves. Her brother George and her half brothers Alexander, David and Samuel were fighting for the Confederate army. Although newspaper articles came out explaining that these relatives were not her "real" brothers, gossip spread that she was a spy. Because of these rumors, the president had to appear before a special committee to testify that his wife was loyal to the North (Sandberg, 83).

During the Civil War, England and France were being courted by the Southern states, and while Mrs. Lincoln believed that she had to look dignified, she also took fashion seriously and imagined that she was doing her part to keep the country unified by looking stylish. When Mrs. Lincoln gave a party in 1862, *Leslie's Weekly* gushed that it was a brilliant success. Although it was a public reception, or levee, Mrs. Lincoln had invited 500 of the brightest and most distinguished as her guests. A possible holdover from her boarding school days at Madame Mentelle's Boarding School for Young Ladies, Mrs. Lincoln called those visiting the White House "the Court." Newspapers complimented the White House decorations, saying that the North now rivaled the South in elegance. *Leslie's Weekly* described Mrs. Lincoln's dress: a white satin robe, with a train a yard long, trimmed with flounces of black Chantilly lace surmounted by white satin ribbon edged with narrow black lace. More specifically the reporter noted that the dress was décolleté with short sleeves to show off her perfectly molded shoulders and arms. Mrs. Lincoln's ornaments were pearls and she wore a headdress of black adorned with white crepe myrtle blossoms, causing her to be referred to, in the article, as the "Republican Queen," and comparing her "rare beauty" to that of Empress Eugénie of the French (Sandberg, 83).

February 1862 brought tragedy to the Lincolns when their two younger children took ill and twelve-year-old Willie died. Willie had been his parents' favorite, and they were both devastated by their loss. Dressmaker and stylist Elizabeth Keckley wrote that Mary took to her bed for three weeks. She did not attend the funeral and could not take care of her youngest son. The oldest sibling, Robert, was so alarmed by this that he wired his Aunt Elizabeth Edwards and had her come to the White House to help tend his little brother, Tad, who eventually recovered (Williams, 212).

In a letter to her daughter, it was Edwards who insisted that Mary begin wearing mourning clothes. These were made by Keckley, who described them in her book as being dull black dresses of crepe. Keckley also wrote that the First Lady's black crepe and straw bonnets were so heavily draped with weeping veils that she couldn't turn her head and looked like she was always facing forward. Keckley continued to say that Mrs. Lincoln also wore black jet jewelry and wrote on writing paper with black margins. The dressmaker was not sure when Mrs. Lincoln took off her mourning clothes. She thought she wore them continuously, and only "went out of them" for special occasions, like the White House's celebration of the marriage of performer Tom Thumb and his wife, Lavinia, on February 13, 1863 (Williams, 212). For this, Keckley remembered that Mrs. Lincoln wore a pink low-necked gown of rich silk, with flounces high on a hooped skirt and pink roses in her hair. That same year, *Leslie's Weekly* published, "She was superbly dressed." The reporter went on to write, "I think the features are not classical, but I forget them. It was a pleasant face to look on" (Sandberg, 83).

In 1863, Mrs. Lincoln entered half mourning, and she ordered new outfits from Keckley. The dressmaker wrote that Mrs. Lincoln could now wear lavender, gray and somber purple with a little white at the cuffs. However, in a photograph of Mary Lincoln made in 1864 it appears that she still continued to dress in black. The material of the dress was silk, not crepe, and the pleating on the sleeves and front of the bodice, and the thin braid trim at the top of the sleeve, were simple but fashionable. The dress was trimmed in jet. Even in her grief, the First Lady continued to follow fashion's trends, as was required by the social standards of her upbringing and her times.

One by one, Mary Lincoln's half-brothers were killed in the war as they fought for the Confederacy. Mrs. Lincoln did not mourn them, because she believed that they were her husband's enemies, who would have hanged him and her if they had the chance. But when her full brother, Levi, died fighting for the Union in 1865, she again wore black. To mourn a sibling in the United States it was expected that the sister be in deep mourning for three months, followed by two months in full mourning, and one month in half mourning. In a photograph of Mrs. Lincoln mourning for her brother she wears a dark silk dress with simple but fashionable trim. The dress had narrow white cuffs and a narrow white collar. A big bonnet, stuffed with flowers and covered with a veil was on her head. When she came out of mourning for her brother, Harrison Grimsley—the husband of her cousin Elizabeth—died. Elizabeth had traveled to Washington, D.C., with the Lincolns and stayed there for six months to help. Elizabeth's father, Dr. John Todd, died four days after Grimsley. Mary once again donned mourning clothes. It was believed that it was bad luck to wear the same clothes when mourning different people. New clothes had to be made for each new death.

Unfortunately, for Mary Lincoln, the worst was yet to come. On April 14, 1865, President Abraham Lincoln was shot. He died the next day. Her eldest son, Robert, accompanied Mrs. Lincoln back to the White House, and Keckley came to comfort her. Mary soon put on widow's weeds and wore black continuously for the rest of her life.

It took Mrs. Lincoln a month to pack her family's belongings and move from the White House to Chicago. Seeing the numerous packed crates, an angry public believed that she was stealing from the government. Lizzie Keckley accompanied the widow, but Mrs. Lincoln couldn't afford to pay her a salary. Keckley went back to her shop in Washington, D.C., and back to work. Like all married women of her time, Mrs. Lincoln had been dependent on her husband. She was 47 at the time of his assassination. Even if she had wanted to remarry, there was little chance that this would happen. She was old, and she was broke, two factors that made her very unattractive. In her day, widows sought to marry widowers, but widowers who did remarry found someone either young or rich. Mrs. Lincoln, although highly educated, had no job experience, and as the former First Lady, had no employment opportunities open to her. If she had been an unknown with a school-aged child with a disability to support, she might have opened her own dressmaking shop, as other widows did. She might have taken in laundry or sent her son out to earn what little wages he could. Another option for a destitute widow was to seek work in a factory, or seek employment as a domestic servant, perhaps a governess. But all these venues were closed to the former First Lady, and she was in dire pecuniary straits.

Shortly after Keckley returned to her shop, Mrs. Lincoln asked her to accompany her to New York City in a scheme to raise some much-needed funds, promising Keckley a share of the profits if she would act as her intermediary. Wearing widow's weeds and a heavy crepe veil that hid her features so she wasn't recognized, Mrs. Lincoln traveled under an assumed name to sell or put on display the clothing, jewelry and effects she had worn as First Lady and President Lincoln's wife. Earlier, Empress Eugénie in exile had done the same thing, and no one had thought ill of her, but in Mary Lincoln's case, it was another story. Few of her dresses sold, and they did not bring in enough money to cover the fee she owed the company handling the sale. What was worse, the exhibition she planned to open in Providence, Rhode Island, charging admission of a dollar a head to see her dresses, was cancelled. Perhaps the clothing she had worn when her husband was shot would have garnered more interest, but the black silk dress with a little white stripe was given to Mrs. William Slade, the wife of Lincoln's valet. Her earrings, bonnet and velvet cloak, covered in the president's blood, were given to Mrs. Eckley, another White House servant (Keckley, 307).

Mrs. Lincoln continued to order widow's caps from Keckley, and later asked her to travel to Chicago and stay with her for six weeks to make more mourning clothes. Believing that she didn't have long to live, Mrs. Lincoln wrote, "The probability is that I shall need few more clothes; my rest is near at hand" (Keckley, 366). Heavily in debt, Mrs. Lincoln moved to Europe, where she could live more cheaply, but she continually asked other people to petition the government to grant her a widow's pension. This was not unusual. Mary Anna Jackson, wife of the slain Confederate general Thomas Jefferson "Stonewall" Jackson, and Elizabeth Custer, widow of General George Armstrong Custer successfully petitioned for pensions after their husbands died and were granted them even though Stonewall Jackson had fought on the losing side. However, the act was unthinkable behavior for the widow of an American president, who was the Commander in Chief of the military but not an actual soldier in the field. Also, the proud Mrs. Lincoln didn't want to beg for money herself. Instead, she asked others to plead on her behalf, so she wasn't as effective. When

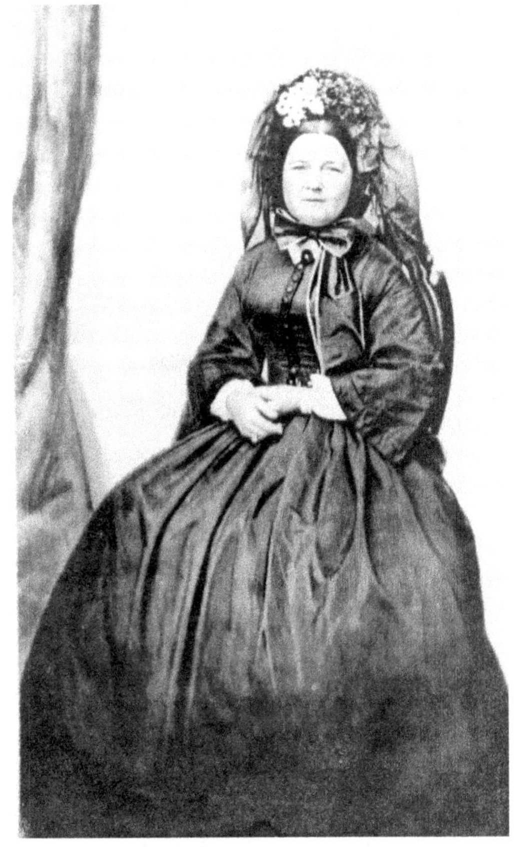

"Mary Lincoln in mourning attire," Joseph Ward, Ward & Son photographer, photographed between 1865 and 1882 (from the Lincoln Financial Collection, courtesy Allen Public Library and Indiana State Museum).

Congress finally granted her $3,000 a year in 1870, she complained that it was not enough and asked for $2,000 more, noting that Ulysses S. Grant and his wife Julia had been presented with gifts of three houses, and at the time there was talk of raising President Grant's salary to $100,000 a year.

Mrs. Lincoln wore black for the rest of her life and would not be consoled. Most citizens criticize her for not mourning with decorum. She did not accept that her suffering was part of God's plan as other woman of her times were expected to do. Instead, she was seen as the "diva of grief" and someone who perceived her grief to be worse than the grief of others. For this she was reviled (Williams, 30).

The former First Lady and her youngest son, a teenager, returned to America in 1871. Shortly after, he died. A believer in spiritualism, Mrs. Lincoln had been consulting with mediums since the death of her son Willie. After Tad's death, she started seeing ghosts, or, as most believed, she began hallucinating. She continued to ask for more money and became an embarrassment to the government and her one surviving son, Robert. Now an adult, Robert had her committed to an insane asylum in 1875. After a stay of a few months, she was declared sane by the courts. She quickly returned to Europe to live until, at 60 years of age, she fell from a stepladder, trying to straighten a picture hanging over a mantelpiece. She injured her spine and was partially crippled. Returning to America in 1880 on a ship called the *Amerique,* she slipped again and almost fell to her death. Fortunately, the former First Lady was saved by the famous actress Sarah Bernhardt (Ellison, 247). On reaching the United States, Mrs. Lincoln sought medical treatment in New York City and then went to live with her sister, Elizabeth, in Springfield, Illinois. She died in July of 1882. A year before her death Congress finally granted her the $5,000 pension she had asked for. This was the same amount they had granted the widow of slain president John Garfield the year before.

* * *

A black dress and veil are reminiscent of a nun's habit, and dressed this way, Queen Victoria assumed a holy air. In reality, she cleverly married her numerous children into royal families all across Europe, and after she emerged from seclusion in 1870, Victoria had more freedom than she had had as a wife. Young women had to be married, but as a widow, the queen could remain autonomous. Dressing in widow's weeds signaled that Victoria was sexually unavailable and also gained her the continued sympathy of her subjects.

The widow Mary Lincoln craved sympathy and a pension. She had suffered the death of her mother at an early age and then the deaths of her children later in her life but was viewed with suspicion during the time she spent in the White House. The guilt that she felt for attending a White House event when her son Willie was ill must have been unbearable when he eventually died, and the assassination of her husband so early in his second term of office left her deeply in debt, homeless and alone, and caring for a disabled child. Her black clothes and veil earned her little sympathy in America. Instead she was seen as indulgent and self-aggrandizing when the nation was trying to heal after the catastrophe of the Civil War.

6

Memorial Jewelry

Fashion design and jewelry are considered "decorative arts" or "crafts" rather than fine art because required steps must be performed when making clothing, necklaces, rings and the like. Technical skill must be learned, practiced and repeated for successful items to be made, and more often than not, the finished work has to stay within the parameters of the fashion of the day. In Victorian times and earlier, professionals were commissioned by their elite clients to create unique clothing for them. Those who sewed their own items could vary a design at will. But jewelry was different. The materials and tools for making jewelry were specific, and available to only a few. Special knowledge was needed to set gemstones or solder metal, for example. Special techniques were needed to engrave images on items or to carve cameos. Sometimes elite clients came up with a design and the jeweler executed it. Most often, ideas for jewelry designs sprang from the jeweler's creativity. But with technological advances, more and more of the production of jewelry became mechanized. With mass production, jewelry became affordable to virtually everyone, and a single piece, the creative idea of a jeweler, could be duplicated thousands of times.

Some jewelry has a function, such as the brooch Mary Lincoln put on to fasten the cloak she wore for her photograph in 1846. Jewelry may help to hold our clothing together or keep our hats on our heads, but most jewelry is worn to embellish or identify ourselves. It is in that act of selecting jewelry pieces to wear that we make artistic choices and use our creativity. In the case of mourning jewelry, Victorians chose to identify themselves as the ones who were left behind. Hopefully this jewelry helped them deal with the pain and grief of their losses.

Jewelry has been adorning our bodies for tens of thousands of years. Some ancient jewelry, made from rocks, shells, bones, feathers or other organic materials, kept our clothing from falling off, but some was worn just because it looked pretty. Jewelry was also worn in hopes that the material contained magical protective and healing properties. Some was worn because it held symbolic meaning. Another important job jewelry fulfilled was to show the wealth and social status of the person wearing it.

Excavations of the city of Ur in Mesopotamia reveal that royal women wore elaborate gold crowns, necklaces and earrings five thousand years ago (Tortora, 24). This jewelry was embellished with lapis lazuli and carnelian gems. Both ancient Greek men and women wore decorative pins called *fibulae* to keep their clothes from falling off (Tortora, 67). Greek women also wore hair pins, bracelets, necklaces, rings, and brooches (some made of gold). Roman women wore carved cameos, rings, bracelets, necklaces, armlets, earrings and diadems set with gemstones. Roman men wore rings, and their slaves wore bracelets to show who their owners were. In the Middle Ages only kings were allowed to wear jeweled gloves. Nobility wore crowns along with rings and decorative brooches. Jewelry is rarely depicted in paintings from this time, but literature describes rings, belts, and a pin called a *fermail* or an *afiche,* which fastened one's tunic or outer coat (Tortora, 158).

Commoners in England and France from the Middle Ages to the 1600s seldom wore jewelry unless it was a brooch used as a fastener, or a pin to hold their hats on their heads, and these could not contain any gems or stones. Sumptuary laws passed by the rulers of those days restricted what the middle and lower classes could wear so that their station in life could be easily identified. Anyone dressing above their class was punished (Taylor, 35). Even wedding rings, so much a part of today's ceremonies, were not allowed until sometime in the seventeenth century. Prior to that, medieval European brides and grooms took half of a coin that had been cut into two pieces to symbolize their bond.

After the sumptuary laws relaxed, the wealthy and esteemed still had to be careful when it came to giving jewelry as gifts. An example of this is recorded in the diaries of Samuel Pepys (1633–1703), a member of the English Parliament who rose to be Britain's chief secretary to the Admiralty during the reigns of King Charles II and King James II. At the end of his life, Pepys ordered jewelers to make 128 memorial rings, which were to be distributed to his family, servants, and closest friends at his funeral. According to Pepys's diaries, distributing great quantities of rings at a funeral was common practice among his peers. The rings were a demonstration of a family's wealth and increased its social status. One didn't even have to attend a funeral to be given a memorial ring. In July of 1661 Pepys wrote that his wife and her friend, Lady Batten, attended the burial of the daughter of Sir John Cawson, where they received "rings for themselves and their husbands" (quoted in Taylor, 228).

The practice of wearing jewelry in memory of a deceased individual became popular after the British executed their King Charles I in 1649. Charles was the second son of King James I of England and Wales, also known as King James VI of Scotland, who became ruler of both kingdoms after the death of Queen Elizabeth I. Married to a Catholic and at odds with the parliaments of both England and Scotland, King Charles I's kingdoms were plunged into a civil war. Charles was captured, tried for treason, and beheaded, and for a time the British Islands were a commonwealth, with Oliver Cromwell serving as lord protector. When Cromwell died in 1658 the islands were plunged into chaos. The son of the decapitated king was asked to return from exile and was crowned King Charles II in 1660. Prior to the restoration of the monarchy, those who sympathized with or fought alongside King Charles I were known as Royalists. These Royalists wore rings or brooches with a portrait of the king, or the letters "CR," engraved on them to mean "Charles Rex" (*rex* being the Latin word for king.) Named "dead head" rings, this jewelry was commemorative jewelry and served as a remembrance of the deceased. Sometimes the slogan "Prepared Be to Follow Me" was written on the rings as well (Taylor, 228).

Royalists or not, the upper classes watched how effective the rings were and decided that commemorative jewelry was a good idea. Those who could began setting aside money from their estates to make their own commemorative jewelry to distribute upon their deaths. Pepys noted in his diary that he spent over 100 pounds on his memorial rings, a total of $23,000 in today's currency (Llewellyn, 86). Pepys realized that mourning jewelry given at a funeral, or distributed after a death, needed to be carefully selected for the closeness of the relationship and the social status of the recipient. In order to enhance his social standing Pepys had jewelers make three different types of rings in three price ranges: 46 of these rings cost him 20 shillings each; 62 rings cost 15 shillings each; and 20 rings cost 10 shillings a piece (Taylor, 232).

Rings were the most common of this type of memorial items given at funerals, but in some instances, spoons were distributed instead. These would have inscriptions such as "Live to Die, Die to Live" written on them. While some people left instructions for the making of memorial items or jewelry in their wills, it was not uncommon for someone like Pepys to take an active role in their design before he passed. It is probable that his name and the date of his death were engraved or written in black enamel on the rings. Enamel is a glassy base fused to metal at a high temperature. It was even more probable that the type of rings handed out were of the *"memento mori"* style, meaning that they commemorated Pepys' passing but also served as a reminder to the recipient of the transient nature of life. *Memento mori* is a Latin term that means a reminder of death. *Memento mori* jewelry had been created since ancient times, and while it is still being produced and worn today, it became very fashionable from the 1500s until the early 1800s. Inscriptions written on black or white enamel were combined with symbols of death such as skulls, skeletons, crossed bones, gravedigger's tools, coffins, and worms. Other symbols from this time period were the serpent, the symbol of wisdom and eternity, and the hourglass, a reminder of the brevity of life. In time, inscriptions were left off and these symbols of death were made into pendants, charms and the like. This type of jewelry did not have to mourn a specific person and did not have to be given only at funerals. *Godey's Ladies' Magazine* described engravings on a watch given in 1569 by Mary Queen of Scots to her lady-in-waiting, Mary Seton, who served as maid of honor for the queen's wedding: "On the forehead of the skull is the figure of Death with the scythe and sandglass ... on the opposite is a representation of Time devouring all things." The article went on to say that next to Time was a serpent devouring its own tail, the symbol of eternity (*Godey's* quoted in Brett, 111).

Jewelry decorated with macabre reminders of death was given as gifts or handed out at funerals to portray and honor the deceased as a free and deep thinker. Wearing this type of jewelry at the time of Pepys' death showed that the deceased, and the recipients, acknowledged the inevitability of death—a profound, biological and philosophical truth. The image of a skull or a skeleton might well have been enameled onto Pepys' rings and set with diamonds for the eyes.

Memento Mori jewelry was commonly inscribed with the actual term, *Memento Mori,* or with another reflective saying such as; *Vita Fugitur,* life is fleeting; *Spes Lucis Aeternae,* meaning the hope of an eternal life; and *Incerta Hora* meaning the hour of death is uncertain. These rings reminded all that death was inevitable, life was short, and that it was best to live piously and make the most of each day, for each could be our last. Inscriptions like these also signaled that the wearer could read and understand some Latin—a clear indication that he or she was highly educated and probably wealthy to boot.

By the crowning of Britain's King George I in 1714, acceptance of the harsh reality of death softened, allowing sentimentality into the mourning process. This resulted in a change of memorial jewelry. Poets such as Edward Young (1683–1765), Robert Blair (1699–1746), Thomas Gray (1716–1771), and Samuel Richardson (1689–1761) wrote poems that were catalysts to these changing ideas about how to grieve death. Writers of this kind of work, named the "Graveyard School" of British poetry, believed in an afterlife and believed in God, but also looked at the effects of death on survivors. From Young's poem *Night Thoughts:*

> Life's little stage is a small eminence,
> Inch-high the grave above; that home of man,
> Where dwells the multitude: We gaze around;
> We read their monuments; we sigh; and while
> We sigh, we sink; and are what we deplor'd;
> Lamenting, or lamented, all our lot!

Along with poetry, sentimental literature became popular in mid–18th century England, influencing or reflecting a changing attitude about death that spread to other European countries and resulted in the Romantic era in the arts from 1800 to the 1850s. The literature from this time period was emotional and depicted death from the vantage point of the mourner. Artists introduced new symbols to represent sorrow, such as the rural graveyard, a tombstone, a Grecian urn, a beached anchor, the mourning widow, a weeping willow tree, and broken Roman columns. These became the new iconography of mourners' grief, supplanting the gruesome images of *memento mori* work. Miniatures with these new symbols were painted on ivory or milk glass, fitted with gold and made into jewelry. Grief-stricken family and friends wore these along with their mourning clothes. Called memorial or "In Memory Of" jewelry (IMO) by collectors, early rings even contained hair of the deceased incased in a crystal loop called a "collar." By 1775 mourners began commissioning jewelers to make memorial jewelry in the form of clasps, brooches and pendants. Elliptical in shape, the miniature paintings were rimmed with pearls, diamonds, amethysts or glass gems called "paste." Gone were blunt inscriptions, replaced by hopeful messages such as "Asleep with Jesus" or "Not lost, but gone before." These reinforced ideas soon to be embraced by the Spiritualists that death was not an end, but rebirth to spiritual eternity.

Princess Amelia, the 15th child of Britain's King George III and his wife, Queen Consort Charlotte, took these changes to heart in the winter of 1810 when she knew she was going to die. She had been born in 1783, shortly after the deaths of her two brothers, Alfred (1780–1782), who died before reaching the age of two, and Octavius (1779–1783), who had only been four years old. Tragically, the toddlers had died as the result of being vaccinated for smallpox. The royal house did not go into mourning for the boys because they had not reached the age of fourteen years old, the official age for mourning. Instead, the queen cut a lock of baby Alfred's hair from his corpse and sent it to Lady Charlotte Finch in acknowledgment of her affectionate attendance, and in hopes that the woman would wear it as a remembrance and a mark of the queen's esteem (Georgian papers, Royal Archive, quoted in the *Telegraph*). Amelia survived the inoculation but contracted tuberculosis as a teenager. By the time she was 27 her immune system was so compromised that she acquired a strep infection and died.

An exposé of the princess and her lover, General Charles FitzRoy, written by William S. Childe-Pemberton in 1910, may or may not be true. Nevertheless, in it, FitzRoy related that as death approached, the princess designed a ring that the royal jewelers hurried to complete so she could give it to her father before she passed. The ring, made of gold, contained a small lock of her hair enclosed in a crystal tablet set round with "a few sparks of diamonds" (Childe-Pemberton, 224). Amelia's design called for the jewelers to inscribe the ring with her name, "Amelia," and the words "Remember me." In Childe-Pemberton's tell-all, the ailing princess was said to have placed the ring on her father's finger, telling him that she hoped he would always remember her. George III took her death hard. Believing in the divine right of kings, and that he spoke directly to God, he didn't understand why he couldn't bring his daughter back to life as God had promised. Supposedly this drove him insane for the final time.

Albinia Cumberland wrote in her diary that shortly before Amelia died, the princess also gave a ring to her attendant, Mademoiselle Monmolin. The king heard about this and was fearful that his daughter would not leave a memento for her own mother as well (Cumberland quoted in Childe-Pemberton, 232). Queen Consort Charlotte had blocked her daughter from marrying General Charles FitzRoy, a descendant of the illegal son of King Charles I. Because of this, the relationship between Amelia and her mother had been strained. But Childe-Pemberton concluded that Amelia hadn't forgotten her mother after all. Close to her death, she forgave Queen Consort Charlotte and gave her a locket, which also contained a lock of her hair.

After Amelia's death, the insane King George III became too ill to rule the country. When his son, the future King George IV, became regent, he had the royal jewelers, Rundell, Bridge and Rundell, make 50 gold rings that he distributed to the family to honor Amelia in death. These rings were made of gold with a large central oval piece. The oval was edged with white enamel and the words "Remember me" written in gold. The hoop, or band, of the ring was also enameled in white. On this, written in gold, was the inscription "Pss. Amelia Died 2 Nov 1810 aged 27." The center of the oval was painted with black enamel and a red and gold crown. Under the crown, also in gold, was her initial, "A."

Even though Princess Ameila considered herself married to FitzRoy, and might even have borne him a child, the regent chose the white enamel because it symbolized purity and was a proper tribute to a young, unmarried woman. The black enamel in the center of the ring symbolized death. News of these rings spread among the aristocracy, and memorial rings became even more fashionable than before.

The United States was still a colony at the time of Pepys' death, and still under control of Britain's royalty. It was an independent nation at the time of the death of Princess Amelia but still owed much to British and European fashion tastes. The style of British antique jewelry is given the name of the British king or queen who reigned at the time the work was created. The period from 1714 to the crowning of Queen Victoria in 1837 is called the Georgian era, named for the descendants of Sophia of Hanover, a protestant and granddaughter King James I, who was declared, by the Act of Settlement of 1701, to be heir to the British throne. Sophia died before she was crowned, and her cousin, Anne, ruled in her stead. Queen Anne died leaving no heirs, so Sophia's son assumed the throne, becoming King George I; George II, George III and George IV ruled after him. Shortly before George I ascended the throne, England (which included Wales) united with Scotland, becoming the United Kingdom in 1707. In 1801 Great Britain united with Ireland, forming the United Kingdom of Great Britain and Ireland, now known as the United Kingdom of Great Britain and Northern Ireland after the south part of Ireland seceded in 1922.

Most historians and art appraisers describe jewelry made from 1714 to 1837 as Georgian; however, jewelry made after King George III went mad in 1810, up to the time of King William IV's death in 1837, may also be referred to as Regency style. This period begins with George IV taking over as regent and includes his official reign beginning in 1820. When he died, in 1830, the crown went to his younger brother, King William IV. William was well into his sixties at his coronation and did not live to enjoy the throne long. He died in 1837, leaving the responsibility and the realm to his 18-year-old niece,

Victoria. The Victorian age begins in 1837 when she was acknowledged to be queen and ends at her death in 1901. The Edwardian era follows, beginning in 1901 and ending in 1910 when her son, King Edward VII, passed away. However, some jewelry appraisers have the Edwardian Era continue until 1917, which was end of World War I.

Handcrafted jewelry of the Georgian period was made for the very wealthy and is highly valued. These were unique works of art imbued with symbolic meaning. Even the gemstones inserted into the precious metals were important. Diamonds stood for eternal love; pearls, especially little seed pearls, were the symbol of tears. Turquoise stood for remembrance, rubies symbolized regard and lapis lazuli represented love. In a time when few of the population could read, this symbolism was important. Symbols were also put into the work by the enameling process. Enameled forget-me-not flowers were the symbol for remembrance, and lilies-of-the-valley symbolized purity and also reunion with the departed in heaven.

Jewelry made in the Georgian period was expensive because it was crafted by hand. Because of this there is a lack of symmetry to it, and all gemstones have closed back settings. The best diamond cutters of this period came from the Netherlands or Belgium. Diamonds were round, cut and polished in what is known as the "rose cut" pattern of facets because they resembled the shape of a rose. This type of diamond is not that popular today because it does not sparkle as much as modern diamonds do. King Louis XV of France (1710–1774) commissioned a "marquise diamond" cut. This had twice as many facets as a rose cut diamond, and therefore better sparkle. It was also oval, supposedly to resemble the lips of his mistress, Madame de Pompadour. A marquis, a noble member of the French court, wore this cut of diamond on his ring finger to distinguish himself from a lowly count. Paste (rhinestone) jewelry was also invented at this time ("A History of Diamond Cutting"). Paste is glass infused with lead to give it more brilliance, an invention of the French-Alsatian jeweler George Frédéric Strass (1701–1773). The leaded jewelry was often worn instead of real jewels to discourage robberies.

Jewelers also use the names of the British royalty when dating jewelry made in America. Exceptions are made for the colonial period, which lasted until 1789. Neoclassical works created in the early days of the Republic are sometimes referred to as Federal style. Art movements such as Art Nouveau and the Arts and Crafts describe other jewelry made in the United States that was influenced by these styles. Art Nouveau jewelry was made from 1890 to 1910. Arts and Crafts jewelry could be made anywhere between 1880 and 1920.

Colonial Americans were not as wealthy as their European or British counterparts, and historians tell us that if colonists wore any jewelry at all it would have been a wedding ring, a watch, and perhaps a small locket containing the image or hair of a loved one. But different colonies owed their allegiance to different countries: the United Kingdom in the east, the Spanish in the West and Southeast, and France in the South. Charles O. Cornelius, a former associate curator of the Metropolitan Museum of Art in New York, wrote that American jewelers began creating jewelry around 1700. He described a pair of gold cufflinks engraved with a rosette design made by Paul Revere that was on display at the Metropolitan Museum of Art's first floor, along with knee buckles worn by John Hancock. Writing about colonial America he stated, "Much jewelry was worn by both men and women of the eighteenth century. Even in the seventeenth century, particularly about New York, there was more than a modicum of precious possessions of gold, set with stones" (Cornelius, 99).

From 1626 to 1664, New York was a Dutch colony called New Amsterdam. The settlers there had a much different outlook on life than the New England Puritans or the Spanish settlers living in St. Augustine.

Cornelius listed jewelry in an inventory compiled in 1682 by Dr. Jacob de Lange and his wife: one embroidered purse with silver bugle and chain to the girdle and silver hook and eye; one pair black pendants, gold hooks; one bold boat containing 13 diamonds and one white coral chain; one pair gold "stucks" or pendants each containing 10 diamonds; 2 diamond rings; one gold ring with a clasp beck; one gold ring or hoop bound round with diamonds. The couple also owned a gold child's whistle and coats with several silver buttons. Cornelius went on to say that the de Langes were merely well-to-do. Their wealthy neighbors from the same time period owned much more than this (Cornelius, 99). Dutch settlers in New York were noted for having a love of jewelry by Sarah Knight, who wrote in her diary in 1704 that the Dutch left their ears bare and "sett out with Jewells of a large size and many in number. And their fingers hoop't with Rings, some with large stones in them of many Coullers as were their pendants in their ears" (*ibid.*).

Early American colonists followed the fashion trends of their homelands, but as more written and illustrated material became available, they became influenced by the fashion plates in ladies' magazines and were made more aware of global fashion. Jewelers or silversmiths such as Paul Revere (1735–1818) made custom pieces for the wealthy. He also imported jewelry from England to sell to the elites. At the time of the American Revolution the London style was for wealthy women to wear several gold necklaces at once, with attached lockets, pendants or crosses. They also wore pendant earrings, hair ornaments, and layers of pearls on their neoclassical gowns. Some wore men's watch fobs, or watches on chains around their necks (Blanco, 164).

For a short while after the American War for Independence, and after the Reign of Terror in France, jewelry was out of fashion. Either American women had given their gold and precious gems to support the war effort and couldn't afford new items, or the spirit of democracy made women loath to show off their wealth. Portraits of our country's earliest first ladies show that they wore only small earrings, with either a small brooch or a few strands of pearls, and perhaps an ornament in their hair. The Reign of Terror influenced the amount of jewelry women from Europe and Britain wore, too, and only simple rings, necklaces, earrings, brooches and small watches attached to their garments were in style (Blanco, 164). In France, the royal jewels of Marie Antoinette were stolen by revolutionaries. Those recovered by the Directory were sold when it needed money in 1795. At that time, possession of jewels or gold belt buckles might condemn one to the guillotine. Many French aristocrats fled the country. Others patriotically donated their jewelry to support the republican cause. Donated jewelry items were broken down, precious metals melted, and gemstones sold separately. The gems actually flooded the market, lowering their price.

When Napoleon Bonaparte (1769–1821) became head of the First French Consulate in 1799 and then was crowned emperor of the French in 1804, he realized the importance style, clothing and jewelry had to the French economy. The same jewelers who had worked for the court of Louis XVI began making showy jewelry of gold and semi-precious gems. By 1803 the French elite were allowed to wear diamonds once more. Napoleon recovered all the royal jewelry he could find and bought much more for his empress, Josephine. By 1803 she had a new diamond parure (a set of jewelry designed to be worn together) consisting of a tiara, comb, earrings, pairs of bracelets, and a two-row riviere— a necklace of gems that increased in size as they reached the center. At the time of her divorce, the empress had more jewelry than Marie Antoinette had ever possessed, including a new laurel-wreath crown, long earrings and a necklace of immense gemstones, and she was able to keep her jewelry after the divorce in 1809 (Joan Evans, 170). Napoleon's backing quickly encouraged the wearing and creation of French luxury items, including the creation of cameos. French jewelry was so prized that in 1855 Prince Albert bought a suite of it while staying with Napoleon III and Empress Eugénie to attend the International Exhibition in Paris (Gere, 11). He kept the gift secret from his wife and gave it to her for her birthday the next year. The suite consisted of head ornaments, necklace, brooch, bracelet and earrings. Prince Albert loved to give jewelry as gifts and even designed some of it himself, like the Crimean brooch for Florence Nightingale.

As mentioned in a previous chapter, clothing worn by upper class men of France underwent a radical change after the Reign of Terror. Gone forever were lavish brocade jackets, knee breeches, powdered wigs, pins, rings, brooches and the jeweled shoe buckles men wore at the French court. Beau Brummell simplified style, emphasizing good tailoring rather than fancy gold buttons, diamond collar studs and jeweled belts and shoe buckles. Americans continued to follow the lead of England and France. The only American president to dress in colors was George Washington. After him, portraits of early presidents show men dressed in simple black coats, their one elaboration being the knot of the neckcloths tied at their throats.

In time, the Industrial Revolution created rapid changes in the fortunes of some lucky families in America and abroad. Not being able to wear much jewelry themselves, successful husbands loaded their wives up with silver, gold, pearls and gems to show off their newly gained wealth, and women acted as vehicles for exhibition of their family's affluence. One jewelry item that most 19th century American men did carry was a pocket watch. Those who could afford them continued to wear fancy buttons, studs and belt buckles. American soldiers began wearing lapel and hat pins during the Civil War to identify the number of their unit. The American military expanded this practice of handing out pins, now called "insignia," giving them for special awards or assignment designations. British military men of the Victorian era also wore medals and pins on their chests. Some pins attached to their shoulder braids and some were worn as necklaces, suspended around their necks by ribbons or chains. These medals might have identified a mission or had been given as an honor, but some had nothing to do with military service at all. When attending a royal funeral, men were often asked to wear their military uniforms, complete with this jewelry. To identify that they were in mourning, they tied a black band around their left arm. Civilian men from both continents were asked to wear only black buttons while mourning in addition to the black band they wore tied around their upper arm for a period of time.

Other necessary jewelry items for British men were swords and sword slings. Worn by the elite from the 1640s to present times, the swords have short, flexible and pointed blades that responded to the fencing techniques of Victorian times. Allegedly made and worn for self defense, swords also showed a man's status. By 1750 swords had elaborate gold and silver hilts made by jewelers who decorated them with fine metal, enameling and precious stones. Intricately decorated swords were also given as rewards for distinguished service. For funerals and while in mourning, men were required to exchange their decorated swords for plain black ones. Although Prince William and Prince Harry did not wear their swords to Prince William's marriage ceremony in 2011, they both wore gold sword slings (Peláez).

In Europe of the 16th century, men who were not allowed to wear swords carried heavy sticks for protection. In later centuries these sticks morphed into fashionable canes and became part of a well-dressed civilian man's attire. While American women sometimes carried them, a walking stick, or cane, was an essential item of American men's dress (Tortora, 281). The shaft might be made of exotic wood, but the knob or handle was jeweler's ware. Knobs might be made of precious metal or carved of ivory. Often they were decorated with enameling and encrusted with gems, which were covered with black fabric during the deep mourning stage. Rigid social codes of the Victorian era had men substitute their shiny buttons for black ones and carry black swords instead of ornate ones when mourning a death.

Early Victorians liked jewelry, and those who could afford it wore a lot of it with great exuberance. If something was good, a Victorian could not have enough of it, and there was little concern that wearing portable wealth in the form of jewelry might make the underprivileged resentful (Flower, 3). As did Napoleon, Queen Victoria encouraged her people to wear jewelry. Buying and selling jewelry helped British industries and the British economy. Queen Victoria gave jewelry as gifts and wore much of it herself. Portraits of the young queen always showed her wearing jewelry—several pieces at one time. These paintings were made into prints and bound inside popular magazines for commoners to frame and hang on the walls of their abodes. Constantly looking at the young leader of their country wearing jewelry must have had a profound effect on young British women. Everyone knew that Prince Albert had given Victoria a "smiling serpent" engagement ring in the form of a snake with its tail in its mouth. This snake signified eternity while the two emeralds for its eyes symbolized fertility (Blanco, 165). The public knew that Prince Albert had given Victoria a brooch containing a huge sapphire (the symbol of faithfulness) the day before they wed. Magazines also published reports about parties given by royalty and society's upper crust that included detailed descriptions of jewelry worn by the guests. Other articles gave accounts of jewelry given to wealthy brides by their grooms as wedding gifts. In the 19th century, it was customary for a French gentleman to give his fiancé a *"corbeille de mariage"* when she signed the marriage certificate. These were baskets or elegant trunks filled with gifts, which usually cost 10 percent of the dowry the bride's father gave to the groom.

Until late in the 19th century, jewelry was essential to a woman's dress. Experts on beauty and etiquette wrote books with titles such as *Female Beauty* (1837) and *The Young Lady's Friend* (1838). These gave advice concerning when and how to wear jewelry. For example, in 1837 Mrs. Walker in her work *Female Beauty* wrote that jewels were best for older women who were more intellectual (Flower, 5). Popular Victorian fiction was loaded with references to bracelets, necklaces, earrings and the like. But the richest source of information on jewelry came from the fashion magazines. Fashion plates depicted the aristocracy dressed for great events like balls and royal funerals. These were studied by wealthy women, who ordered jewelers to make them similar things. Poorer women could only wish for such luxuries, but as the century progressed, they were able to find inexpensive substitutes made of pinchbeck and paste. Pinchbeck, named after its inventor, Christopher Pinchbeck (1670–1732), is a gold-colored alloy that was developed in the 1720s but was not really popular until the 19th century. Made of 83 parts copper and 17 parts zinc, it was easily worked and molded and was much cheaper than gold (Brett, 128). Inventions during the Industrial Revolution also allowed jewelry to be mass produced. This made it less expensive to buy, and in time, it became available to all.

Prior to Princess Amelia's death, *Walker's Hibernian Magazine* (November 1786) said that it was acceptable to wear a brooch or ring set with a lock of the deceased's hair when in deep mourning; however, John Duke of Bedford described the clothing worn by the attendees at her funeral but failed to mention any jewelry. An article in *Ackermann's Repository of Arts,* from December 1810, described an appropriate mourning outfit for Princess Amelia that included "a neck-chain and convent cross of jet, with ear-rings and bracelets to correspond." Amelia died on November 27, 1810. Public mourning was to last through January 11, but Marie Joséphine of Savoy (the queen of France living in exile in London) died two weeks after Amelia, so the mourning period was extended for three more weeks. At this time, *Walker's Hibernian Magazine* advised that flashy jewelry and diamonds should be put away until mourning ceased.

When Princess Charlotte, the heir to the British throne, died in childbirth on November 7, 1817, the lord chamberlain decreed that the first stage of mourning, or "deep mourning," would begin on November 9th—a Sunday. Men associated with the royal court needed to swap out their colorful swords for black ones, remove all shiny buttons on their sleeves or pockets, and replace their gold or silver buckles with black ones. Once again women were to wear clothing of dull black fabric. Members of the court were in this stage of mourning for two months. Omitted in these directions again was any mention of women's jewelry. The deputy earl marshal, H. H. Molyneux Howard, issued orders for general mourning for the princess, decreeing that "it is expected, that upon the present, most melancholy occasion of the death of her late Royal Highness the Princess Charlotte Augusta ... all Persons do put themselves into decent Mourning" (Coote, 348). Descriptions accompanying fashion plates of suitable dresses for deep mourning for Charlotte in *Ackermann's Repository of Arts* explained that black jet buttons could be used to fasten the backs of bodices. The journal also noted that "all ornaments for the hair etc. at present are composed of jet" and explained that this clothing was "generally adopted by all persons of fashion, whether connected with the court or not" to show "every possible respect to the memory of our lamented Princess" (Coote, 362).

The death of the princess and her stillborn son was such a shock to the kingdom that everyone who could afford it went into mourning for the prescribed period of time. In contrast to the convention of commoners, mourning did not last a long time for royalty. Almost two months after the death of Princess Charlotte, on December 27, 1817, the lord chamberlain gave instructions for the second stage of court mourning. Along with clothing made of black silk, with white accessories, women were able to wear black jewelry or white necklaces and earrings. By this time commemorative brooches and pins for the princess were for sale that the middle class and some poor might have been to afford. Money earned from the sale of this jewelry went to fund Princess Charlotte's memorial. The third stage of mourning for the princess began on Sunday, January 28, and lasted until Sunday, February 1. In all, the total amount of time for mourning the future queen of the kingdom was less than three full months.

The fundamental rule for deep mourning of the court was that women were to wear no jewelry at all and men were to exchange their shiny accessories for dull black ones. If one was a commoner, different books on etiquette gave different advice. An important idea was that nothing was to reflect light. Mourning clothes were made from crepe, a very dull fabric that did not shine. Any mourning jewelry worn, including mourning rings, was made from non-reflective materials; at first pearls and ivory were used, and later jet. The reason for no reflections came from the ancient fear that the spirits of the dead hovered over the earth and tried to lure their living relatives into the afterlife. While we normally are unable to see spirits, it was thought that their images could be caught in a reflection. To safeguard yourself and your loved ones, no reflections were allowed. Some cultures and religions still ritualistically cover home mirrors after a death (Llewellyn, 90). Pearls and ivory were first used as mourning jewelry because they didn't reflect. Being white, they also signified virtue and purity. When pearls were unavailable, or virtue was in question, dull black beads sufficed. The 19th century was a wonderful time for black beads and black jewelry, for this was when an important discovery of jet was made on the Yorkshire coast of England. Individual pieces of jet were found along the seashore, but then seams of the stuff were discovered to be embedded in the cliffs and hillsides at Whitby. Jet had been cut and used as a gemstone for decoration and magic from prehistoric times, but the deposits of jet at Whitby were the largest in the world and made jet easily available to the British and Americans, becoming the prescribed material for mourning jewelry.

The source of jet was wood in Jurassic times that had been compressed for one hundred and eighty million years under layers of sediment to form a coal-like substance. As in coal, there are no growth rings on the material, and jet no longer resembles a plant. Unlike coal, jet is practically free of shrinkage cracks, and, like stone, is remarkably stable when exposed to air. There are two kinds of jet; the hardest, like that found at Whitby, is formed in salt water. This is the most valuable because it holds a fine edge when carved and can be polished if desired. There is also soft jet, like that found in parts of Spain, which was formed in fresh water and is found alongside amber in alluvial deposits. Soft jet cracks, shows damage, and doesn't hold up as well as hard jet. For that reason, it was primarily used for beads. All jet is lightweight and warm to the touch and will develop a static charge, enabling it to pick up small bits of paper when rubbed with wool or silk.

Around the turn of the nineteenth century, John Carter, a Whitby innkeeper, and Robert Jefferson, a painter, began making the first necklaces and crosses from local jet. The material had greater tenacity and elasticity than other jet, enabling them to carve pieces with files and knives. Captain Tremlett, a retired seaman, suggested to Carter that he use a lathe to turn the beads, which greatly increased production. Carter founded the first Whitby jet workshop in his own house sometime around 1808–10.

The French wore mourning jewelry made from jet to mourn Charles Ferdinand, Duc de Berry, the youngest son of the future King of France, Charles X, after his assassination in the Paris Opera House in 1822. Unpolished or "dead black" jet was also worn by the British court, including Princess Victoria, during the stages of mourning for King William IV when he died in 1837. Its popularity grew as a result of lives lost in the Crimean War (1853–56) and the Indian Mutiny of 1857. By 1853 there were fifty jet workshops in Whitby, amounting to an industry worth €20,000 annually. By 1873 the number of workshops rose to two hundred with an annual income of €84,000 (Flower, 22). By the end of the 19th century over 1,000 people were employed in the production of jet in Whitby, where jet was chopped, cut, turned, ground, milled, brushed and polished, powering by foot treadle machines (Traverse, 302). While not all jet jewelry was for mourning, Margaret Flower wrote in her book on Victorian jewelry: "Visitors to Whitby complained that the town had an excessively mournful aspect, as every window was filled with a somber display of jet jewellery" (*ibid.*). Today it is illegal to mine jet in Whitby. Jet is found in the seams of cliff walls, and disturbing these would endanger the town.

When Princess Augusta Sophia, Queen Victoria's aunt, passed away in 1840, the lord chamberlain ordered ladies of the court to wear black silk, fringed or plain linen mourning gowns, white gloves, and also "necklaces and ear-rings" along with their black or white shoes, fans and tippets. Men were to dress in their black, full-trimmed, fringed or plain linen, with black swords and buckles (Lord Chamberlain's Office, September 23, 1840). The same orders for dress were given when Prince Albert's maternal grandmother, the dowager duchess of Saxe-Gotha-Altenburg, passed away on March 1848 (*London Gazette* 20833, March 1, 1848). By this time jewelry made of jet could be purchased at English mourning warehouses. A brooch might be carved in the form of an oak spray with one empty acorn cup to signify a loss. Other designs carved to signify mourning included a bunch of lily-of-the-valley flowers, symbolizing reunion with the dead; forget-me-nots; weeping willow trees; crosses; anchors symbolizing hope; and funeral urns.

Little did Queen Victoria know when she accepted the suite of French jewelry that Prince Albert had bought in France for her birthday in 1856 that five years later her beloved husband would be dead. Although he had been ill for several years, upset about his teenage son's affair with the actress Nellie Clifden, and worried about a possible war with Union forces during the American Civil War, he continued to work until he was diagnosed with typhoid fever and died on December 14, 1861, at the age of 42 (Rennell, 32). Queen Victoria's mother had died that spring, on March 15, and only a month before, in November, the king of Portugal, beloved by Prince Albert, passed away. Albert's death was a terrible shock to the queen, who had borne a child almost every other year for the 22 years they had been married and had relied heavily on him. It was also a shock to the nation, which had believed that the worse of his illness had passed. Once more the lord chamberlain issued orders for royal mourning dress, and the country responded by wrapping their towns and themselves in black crepe. Business stopped, theatre performances and concerts were cancelled, and shops were closed.

Although the general mourning for the prince officially ended on February 10, 1862, reports from her diary say that Queen Victoria gave instructions that public mourning for the Prince Consort be "for the longest term in modern times" (*The Daily Mail*, Oct. 29, 2011). Members of her own royal household dressed in mourning for an entire year. Jay's London General Mourning Warehouse had such brisk business that it had to enlarge its establishment as "there was no let-up in what had become an almost incalculable demand for mourning goods" (*ibid.*). Newspapers reported that the queen would wear her widow's weeds at least until 1864, and many of the middle class followed her lead.

Directions for second mourning for Prince Albert were issued on December 31, 1861, allowing flack fans, feathers and "ornaments" (Taylor, 230). Once more ladies were allowed to wear jewelry and decorate their gowns, and men were permitted to change from black to silver buttons, buckles and swords. Orders went out that the third period of mourning for the prince, or the half-mourning period, would begin February 17 and last until March 10, 1862. Ladies of the court could wear muted colored clothing, and diamond, or plain gold and silver ornaments.

The ancient Greeks appreciated the hardness of a diamond. They named it *adamas*, meaning unconquerable, and wore the stone into battles in its uncut shape, which naturally comes to a point. Prior to the 1860s diamonds were found in streams in India, where they were cut and sold. Diamonds were discovered in Brazil in the early 18th century; however, they were still relatively rare and were only worn by the aristocracy. In 1866 Erasmus Jacobs discovered a small diamond on the banks of the Orange River in

Africa that ran near his father's farm. Others rushed to the site and discovered more diamonds, some of which sold for tens of thousands of British pounds. The land was named Kimberley and by 1871 miners had dug 2,722 kg of diamonds out of a hill, turning it into what is now called "the Big Hole." By 1873 Kimberley became the second largest city in South Africa, welcoming all immigrants to help run the diamond mines ("History of Diamond Mining"). The discovery of this new supply of diamonds allowed Parisian jewelers to gobble up the stones, helping to make them more fashionable and more available. Jewelers were able to use diamonds in fine pins, bracelets, earrings and rings. In the 1870s steam lathes and motorized saws allowed cutters to shape rounder and more brilliant stones. Charles Lewis Tiffany, nicknamed "the King of Diamonds," acquired the Tiffany Yellow Diamond, a huge 287-carat stone, from the Kimberley mine in 1877. Tiffany had his gemologist, George Frederick Kunz, study the gem for a year before cutting 90 facets into it and reducing it to its current 128.5 carat size. Tiffany also designed a six-prong setting for diamond solitaire rings. This cutting became the standard for American engagement rings up to modern times (Phillips, 2). Diamonds often surrounded cameos or the painted centers of lockets, pins, or brooches. They also surrounded woven hair, set in precious metal under crystal or glass. Americans decided that diamonds, the symbol of eternal love, were appropriate to wear for deep mourning as long as they were set in black. In later stages of mourning Americans used other stones, such as amethysts, the symbol for devotion, or emeralds, the symbol for hope.

Queen Victoria stayed in the deepest stage of mourning until 1870. This was the year she refused to wear her crown and had Garrand's make her a smaller one covered with diamonds that was light enough to be worn over her widow's cap.

The queen remained in practical seclusion until 1871 when her eldest son, Albert Edward (Bertie), recovered from a near-death bout of what was diagnosed as typhoid fever. In February 1872 a service of national thanksgiving was given in his honor at St. Paul's Cathedral, which the prince and Queen Victoria attended. Afterwards, the queen appeared on the balcony of Buckingham Palace to an admiring crowd. This was the beginning of her resumption of royal duties. To reflect that she was coming out of deepest mourning, Victoria wore simple jewelry of diamonds and pearls along with jet and hair. From 1880 on she wore clothing for the third stage of mourning, which allowed for dresses trimmed with black jet beads. The black of the gowns she wore for the rest of her life were always a good background for her diamonds and pearls.

As the country mourned Prince Albert, the trade in jet jewelry expanded. Whitby's jet jewelry industry blossomed as an eager populace bought strings of black jet beads to wear and to decorate their clothing. As the Romantic era progressed, people grew more and more interested in nature, and jet jewelers used the material to fashion jewelry in the shape of birds, insects, animals and floral designs. They also sold brooches, hair combs, headdresses and clasps for hats and bonnets made from jet. Because jet weighs so little, it was also used to make enormous beads, lockets, necklaces, brooches, and bracelets, which balanced the bulky, crinolined fashions of the mid–century.

Queen Victoria began her reign during the Romantic movement in arts and crafts, which nostalgically looked back to Gothic and then Renaissance styles for inspiration. Sir Walter Scott (1771–1832) and Alfred, Lord Tennyson (1809–1892) were popular writers for the English-speaking world while at the same time, those speaking French read works by Victor Hugo (1802–1885). Works such as Scott's *Lady of the Lake* (1810) and *Ivanhoe* (1820), Tennyson's *Lady of Shalott* (1833), and Hugo's *The Hunchback of Notre Dame* (1833)

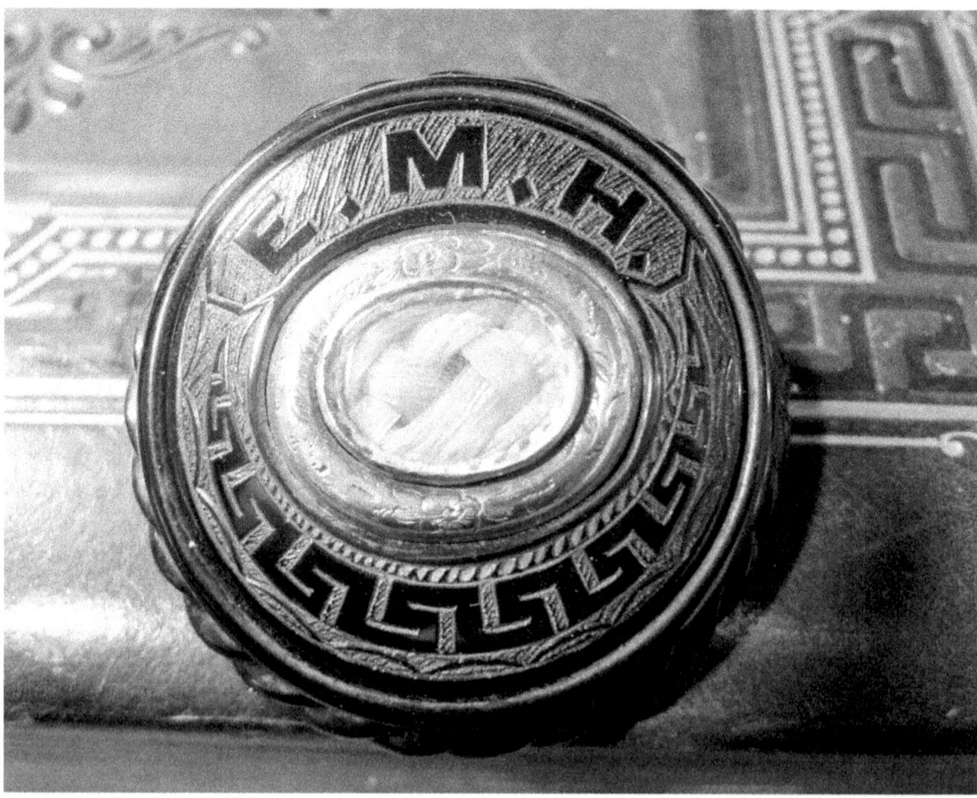

Whitby jet mourning brooch for E.M.H., circa 1860, Newbury, England (courtesy Ann Longmore-Etheridge collection).

encouraged interest in medieval costumes and jewelry. The noted Parisian goldsmith Françoise-Desiré Froment Meurice (1802–1855) is credited with the idea of blending medieval and Renaissance motifs to the jewelry of his time. His work, exhibited at international exhibitions in Paris and London, won prizes and was greatly admired by other jewelers such as Augusto Castellani (1829–1914) in Rome, Frédéric-Jules Rudolphi (1808?–1872), a Parisian jeweler originally from Copenhagen, and Robert Phillips (1810–1881), the most renowned of the English jewelry designers. Jet jewelry fit right into this craze because it had been popular in Europe's Middle Ages, when it had held a Christian significance. Known as *azabache* in Spanish, jet was believed to neutralize negative energy and to protect those who wear it against evil. From the tenth century to modern times, jet jewelry and souvenirs have been sold at Santiago de Compostela, one of the most important Christian pilgrimage sites in Europe, reached by traveling *el Camino de Santiago,* or in English, the Way of St. James. Visitors to the cathedral and the shrine of St. James, the patron saint of Spain, could buy crosses and rosaries made of jet. They could also pick up jet carvings of St. James, jet and silver pilgrim badges in the shape of scallop shells, and other jet articles in the shape of the crescent moon, boar's tusks, eyes, and open hands.

With the passing of time, designers at Whitby made larger and more doleful jet jewelry, which became very popular. As the queen continued to mourn, etiquette grew more exacting, extending the length of the mourning periods for British widows to more than two years. Not to be outdone, books of etiquette and magazine articles encouraged American widows enduring tragedies resulting from the Civil War to mourn for two and a half years. In the Romantic times of the 1860s to 1880s, Whitby jet was carved into every object of jewelry fashion dictated. Women in the Romantic era began wearing jewelry inspired by medieval times such as *ferronnières*—small, thin, headbands with a jewel in the front—and *cordelières*, long braided belts with knots at each end, which tied in the front. These were also made of silver and jet for mourning, as were chatelaines. A chatelaine is a large device made of some kind of precious metal that hooked either onto the *cordelières* or the waist of a woman's skirt. For mourning these were usually made of silver, or a dull metal like Berlin steel, and decorated with jet. Named after the French word that means *wife of the lord of the castle*, chatelaines were useful accessories for women at a time when pockets were bulky things worn over the chemise and under the first petticoat. A chatelaine consisted of a large central piece that hooked onto, or was pinned at, the waist. From this hung chains ending in specially fashioned cases that held household necessities such as the woman's spectacles, her scissors, needles, thimbles, coins, a knife, her watch and her keys.

The peak of the jet business was from 1870 to 1872, when 1,400 men and boys were employed in the industry at Whitby. As the best quality of the substance was mined, and the cliffs were deemed too fragile for further exploitation, prices sharply increased. The demand for jet mourning jewelry continued into the 1880s, resulting in a range of imitations in materials including ebonite and vulcanite, celluloid, dark tortoise shell, bog oak, gutta-percha and dyed horn. Popular from the mid–century on was "French jet." This was black glass cut into facets or blown into beads in European glass-producing countries such as Austria and Czechoslovakia. These beads were shipped to other countries including England and France to be made into jewelry or used to decorate ladies' gowns. "French jet" is easy to differentiate from real jet because it is cold to the touch, chips easily and is so much heavier that it could only be used for beads or small jewelry items. Its advantages were that it was much cheaper than polished jet and could be made into tiny beads. The English tried to come up with their own version of French jet, which they named Vauxhall Glass, but it had a slight reddish tinge so was not widely used.

Bog oak is found in Ireland in peat deposits and can be either pine, yew or oak. It was first used as structural timber for local houses, and also used for fuel, roofing, rope and fishing spears. The bog oak used for mourning jewelry came from oak trees. It is dark brown, almost black, and woody with growth lines in it. An opaque material, it is dull and never highly polished. Bog oak is easy to carve and was usually decorated with Irish or Celtic designs. This material was used for mourning and religious pieces by the Irish, who preferred it over English jet (Carnevali, 301). Gutta percha is a latex or plastic material made from the sap of various Malaysian trees. It appears to be black, but when held up to the light it is translucent and will appear brown or purple. Gutta percha was introduced in Paris in 1842. It was much less expensive than jet and was used for making more practical things than jewelry, such as buttons, boot soles and golf balls. With age and exposure to light and oxygen, items made from gutta percha turn brown. Jewelry made from this material was molded and not carved. Since it is a rubber-like material, it has a rubbery odor (Bell, 17). Ebonite is the brand name for a hard rubber invented by Charles Goodyear (1800–1860), the American chemist. Goodyear vulcanized natural rubber in the 1830s by adding sulfur to it, which made the material harder and less sticky. Now known as vulcanite, this type of jewelry is often confused with gutta percha. Jewelry made from vulcanite was also molded, but was mass produced in the thousands. It was considered cheap jewelry in its day and has turned brown or khaki color with age (Taylor, 237).

Another material used as a cheaper substitute for jet mourning jewelry was horn that had been dyed black. The material was first boiled in water and then lifted with a small pick, which left a small hole in it. Horn was a favorite material for buttons in Victorian times. It was soft enough to be molded with a portrait of the deceased, usually in profile, yet durable and inexpensive. Dyed black and molded, buttons made from horn were very popular for mourning from 1850 to 1889 (Brett, 122). Tortoise shells could also be molded and dyed black. The best tortoise shells came from the hawksbill turtle, a sea creature found in tropical coral reefs.

Instead of black jewelry, ivory continued to be used when mourning young children or chaste adults. The most expensive ivory came from African elephants because it retained its white color, but also used were hippopotamus teeth, sperm whale teeth, bones of other animals and seeds of some palm trees. Sometimes porcelain was used to make mourning jewelry. The favorite porcelain was Parian, a statuary porcelain, sometimes called Carreran. Flowers wrote that Mrs. Mary Brougham of Burselm was famous in her day for making this kind of work (Flower, 23). Porcelain resembled ivory but was ⅓ the cost. A major disadvantage of it was that it was fragile and could easily break. An advantage of the material was that it could be easily molded into intricate floral and bouquet designs. It could also be painted with either a mournful scene or a portrait of the deceased. These would be used as centerpieces for bracelets, clasps or brooches. Jet beads might surround them, or as an alternative, diamonds or seed pearls. Seed pearls often surrounded a lock of the deceased person's hair set under glass. Most etiquette books and articles deemed seed pearl jewelry appropriate to wear for all stages of mourning. Popular in Britain from the late 1700s to early Victorian times, seed pearls lost their cachet with the discovery of the jet deposits and the later cheap substitutes for jet.

In America, jewelry with a central focus of ivory bordered by seed pearls became popular during the Federal period of the new United States. Not all seed jewelry was for mourning, and pins or bracelets made from the material without painted sentimental scenes were often given to brides upon their weddings. Neoclassical jewelry was popular in America from the 1780s to 1810, and items containing a black onyx stone surrounded by seed pearls were valued and bought by upper- and middle-class families. While it had gone out of favor in Britain, seed pearl jewelry continued to be worn in antebellum America because it was a favorite of Mary Lincoln, the wife of the American president. Most seed pearls came from China or Madras, India, and were less than a quarter-grain in size. They had tiny holes drilled into them and were strung on white horsehair pulled from a living horse (Flower, 20). Since they were found in the ocean, in salt water, they symbolized tears, but they were also used as a symbol for beauty and so were perfect for sentimental and bridal jewelry as well as for mourning. The young Queen Victoria wore seed pearls in floral patterns or with feathers as ornaments for her hair.

In 1760, black onyx jewelry was allowed for the second stage of mourning for King George II, along with pearls and jet. Onyx is a banded silica mineral consisting of different crystals of quartz. Because of the different layers, onyx has been used since ancient times to make cameos, which were also used as mourning jewelry in Victoria's day. In America, black onyx could be worn for deep mourning and second stage mourning. It was also popular for a much longer time than it was in Britain. In their 1879–80 catalog, B. Altman's department store of New York City advertised an onyx bar pin or brooch for 95¢ in either a dull or bright finish—dull was used for the deep mourning stage. The Fowler brothers from Providence, Rhode Island, developed a unique process that really dulled the stone. In what they called the "English Crape Stone" process, workers took onyx and roughed it up with acid. Then they colored it, producing a product with a dull black finish that resembled the fabric. Made in Rhode Island, the brothers must have believed that adding "English" to the name would make the jewelry seem more traditional (Taylor, 239). An imitation onyx used to make mourning jewelry was made from glass roughened with acid and colored to create a similar effect. In its catalog dated 1886–7, B. Altman's department store advertised that this was the equal of mourning jewelry made in onyx. T. Granbery of Nassau Street, New York City, advertised that their July 16, 1878, patent for a locket made with double glasses in numerous shapes and sizes showed less gold and was lower in price "than any other onyx locket manufactured. Is especially designed for Ladies' and Gents' Mourning Wear" (Advertisement, *Jeweler's Circular and Horological Review*). In the same circular, G. & S. Owen & Co. advertised that they specialized in black onyx goods, "chair chain mountings, hooks and bars" (xxiii). In addition, they made lockets which could attach to hair jewelry, allowing mourners to place a photograph of departed loved ones inside.

* * *

In Great Britain, Birmingham became the center for the manufacturing of jewelry other than jet. Manufacturers produced patterns and had London retailers chose the ones they preferred. Unlike the United States, retailers kept the exclusive rights to the patterns they bought and did not have to give the Birmingham producers any credit (Flower, 34). In the United States, jewelry plants sprang up in Newark, New Jersey; New York City; and Attleboro, Massachusetts; but it was in Providence, Rhode Island, that Seril Dodge (1759–1802) and his brother Nehemiah became pioneers in costume jewelry production, having invented a process of gold-plating metal. Dodge had been a clock-maker in Connecticut, but he settled in the city of Providence, making that city the leading site for the America's jewelry industry. By 1820 the industry in Providence had grown so that there were 300 jewelry workers in that city. By 1860 the city had 75 jewelers employing 1,750 workers. These companies manufactured 2.2 million dollars of jewelry, which was 22 percent of the national production of the entire United States at the time (Carnevali, 302). Base metal gilded with mercury or electro-gilded jewelry was on display in the Paris Exhibition of 1844. This breakthrough eventually brought down the cost of jewelry. American workshops began making identical jewelry items in gold and in gold plate, and while the upper classes considered plated jewelry in bad taste, some was so good that only an expert could tell the difference. Innovations in jewelry production continued when Thomas H. Lowe, also from Providence, introduced the U.S. to a process for making rolled-gold "sweat" plate using heat and borax to make the gold stick to an ingot of base metal, which was then rolled into sheets of various thicknesses. The production of jewelry chains was mechanized in the mid–1800s by E. H. Perry's invention of a chain-making machine and Levi Burdon's invention for making seamless gold-filled wire (Carnevali, 307).

Mechanization continued with the invention of power presses, automatic drops, wire-bending machines and hydraulic-rocking and stamp presses. All these lowered the price of jewelry and enable unskilled workers to operate the machines. Of the 1,750 jewelry workers in Providence in 1860, 17 percent were women. The percentage of women working in jewelry production rose to 21 percent by 1880 and to 38 percent by 1899 (Carnevali, 307). Women workers were desirable because Rhode Island's labor law allowed women and children to work longer hours than the 54-hour work week legislated for men. Women could also be paid less than men for the same jobs. The 1890s saw an influx of immigrants from Russia and Italy to the United States. Many immigrant women and children found work in jewelry factories or did piecework, assembling pins and chains (Carnevali, 307). These lower costs for production brought the price of jewelry down.

The ability of women to earn and control their own money was granted to them on a state by state basis (Law Library of Congress). By mid–century some states allowed wives to own and manage property in the event of their husband's incapacity or death. But women were not allowed to manage their own earnings until later. Maine was one of the earliest states to allow women to control their wages. That state passed legislation for this in 1857. But in Rhode Island, the right for a married woman to control her paycheck was not granted until 1874, and married women in the state of Washington were finally allowed to control their earned wages in 1895. Each state enacted its own law in its own time, but as more and more women were allowed to keep their earnings, more of them bought jewelry than ever before.

* * *

Most Rhode Island jewelry manufacturers hired artists to design jewelry that other jewelers across the country bought to sell in their shops. Salesmen from Providence traveled with samples, and took orders for their wares, but as the Providence jewelry industry became big business, wholesalers came to the city twice a year to see their trade shows. By 1880 there were 142 jewelers in Rhode Island producing ¼ of all American jewelry. By 1900 the jewelry industry was the fourth largest employer in the state (Carnevali, 305). One of the largest jewelry firms in Providence was Ostby & Barton Jewelry Co., founded in 1879 by Engelhart Cornelius Ostby and Nathan B. Barton. Ostby trained to be a jeweler at the Royal School of Art in Norway and spent six years as an apprentice to a jeweler before immigrating to the United States in 1869. Ostby's business advertised that they had "the finest corps of selected designers and craftsmen in the jewelry business" ("History of Ostby & Barton"). They boasted that they were the foremost house among jewelry makers of America and that they had over 6,000 ring designs that could be made in 14 karat, 10 karat, solid gold or seamless gold plate (1917 ad appearing in *the Saturday Evening Post*). Ostby, like other American jewelers, frequently traveled to Europe to see the latest styles. Unfortunately, on his last return trip home he bought two first-class tickets on the *Titanic* for himself and his daughter, and he perished in the wreck. His daughter, Helen, survived, however, and continued to run the business with her brother Harold until the 1950s.

Charles Lewis Tiffany (1812–1902) and his partners also traveled regularly to Europe. Tiffany, Young and Ellis, a fancy-goods store located in New York City, was owned by the man who emerged as the leader of high-end American jewelry and his partners, John B. Young and J. L. Ellis. Young and Ellis retired in 1853 and the company was renamed "Charles L. Tiffany & Company." Regularly traveling to Europe to purchase large collections of jewelry, he and his designers copied or drew inspiration from these for their own assortment of work, which also included mourning jewelry. In 1862 President Abraham Lincoln bought a suite of Tiffany jewelry for his wife, consisting of a pearl and gold necklace with matching brooch, bracelet and earrings (Schon).

Tiffany items were the first American jewelry to win the gold medal at the Paris Exposition of 1867, and items from his company also won the grand prize for silverware. Tiffany jewelers, with branches in London and Paris, again won the gold medal at the Paris Exhibition of 1878. In 1887 the company purchased about one-third of the French crown jewels and sold various pieces to customers such as Mrs. Joseph Pulitzer and Caroline Astor.

Rather than send salesmen to rural jewelers to sell their jewelry, the owners of Tiffany, Young and Ellis came out with a catalog of jewelry designs first published in 1845. Known as *The Blue Book,* the company's catalog was possibly the first mail order catalog in the United States. But publishing pictures of jewelry like this was risky because other jewelers could steal the designs. Tiffany decided to discontinue its low-end jewelry business and focus on high-end, innovative pieces instead. Other jewelers had different ideas about the appropriateness of stealing or "sharing" designs. In the 1878 issue of *The Jeweler's Circular and Horological Review,* L. Sauter of Nassau St. New York, manufacturers of fine gold and hair jewelry and device work, advertised that for 50¢ they would send the customer their pattern book containing 300 designs of "the most current articles." They went on to say, "Orders for patterns from books of any other manufacturer filled at original prices upon advice of name and number of book." When department stores formed and sold goods by mail, jewelry manufacturers made deals with them to have their jewelry advertised in the store's catalogs. Fully 1/10 of the 773-page Sears 1897 catalog advertised jewelry in gold, silver, gold plate or brass. Prices ranged from 35¢ for a costume piece to $120 for a diamond ring.

As the century drew to its end, the middle class and the poor were able to afford mass produced jewelry. Everyone, even lowly shop girls, could purchase pieces of plate and paste that looked authentic. Working women had money. They could even purchase flamboyant costume jewelry that was meant to last for a short period of time. In response, high-end jewelry turned away from machine tooled items and embraced handmade jewelry of simple curves and abstract designs. C. R. Ashbee was an aesthetic jewelry designer who was a prime mover of the Arts and Crafts movement in England (Flower, 44). He designed asymmetrical work, from dull metal and polished stones. Traditional jewelers floundered. By the 1880s, wearing diamonds during the day in Britain was considered to be in poor taste. In fact, so little jewelry was worn from 1887 to 1890 that the British Jeweller's Association grew alarmed and appealed to the Princess of Wales for help (*ibid.*). She purchased some jewelry and managed to wear it on occasion, but for most of the upper class, the only tolerated jewelry was diamonds, which were taken out of their safe deposit boxes and worn on grand occasions like great balls, the opera, or events at the royal court. An article in the *Young Ladies' Journal* of 1893 said that the "taste for jewellery seems to be a thing quite of the past with our élègantes, especially that for necklaces. Brooches are extremely small, eardrops of the simplest description, and as for bracelets they have almost completely disappeared" (Flower, 44). Matching sets of jewelry were still being made, but they were thought of as being vulgar, along with anything made of silver.

7

Artists Working in Hair

After the death of Prince Albert, Queen Victoria cut off some of his hair and sent it to Garrand's, the royal jewelers, to be worked into jewelry. As soon as possible, eight pieces or more were made and given to her children. One was a gold pin fronted by an onyx cameo of the prince with a box in the back that held a lock of his hair (Lutz, 132). Queen Victoria wasn't the only one to incorporate hair from a loved one into jewelry. Grieving relatives gathered hair from the corpses of their beloved and inserted it into a piece of jewelry, or wove it into necklaces, bracelets, earrings and the like. Some were satisfied with copying patterns found in journals or instruction books, but some ordinary people used the hair as artistic material. Tapping into their creativity and their artistic sense, these people designed items, used hair as a paint medium or wove it into intricate designs and shapes they, or others, could wear.

Hair had been important to Europeans since ancient times, when they were sometimes buried with a lock of hair from their lover, spouse, child or relative so that their spirits would be reunited in the afterlife (Brett, 111). The belief was that one had to be whole before entering heaven on the final judgment day. Any spirit missing a body part, even a lock of hair, would have to search until they found it. Being buried with a lock of a loved one's hair was insurance for reunion in the afterlife.

In her instruction booklet on how to weave and make jewelry from hair, Alexanna Speight explained another ancient Greek tradition:

> It was customary to hang the hair of the dead on their doors previous to interment, and the mourners not unfrequently tore, cut off, or shaved their own hair, which they laid upon the corpse, or threw into the pile to be consumed along with the body of the relation or friend whose loss they lamented [Speight, 7].

She explained that other ancient ones believed that no one could die until a lock of their hair was severed by the invisible hand of death, and "the hair thus cut off was supposed to consecrate the dead to the infernal deities, under whose control they were believed to be placed" (*ibid.*). Speight went on to write that ancient people believed that hair could be used in magic: a witch was thought to be able to kill a man just by touching his hair, and hair was also thought to be a medicine: hair boiled in water and then thrown into a fire was thought to cure a headache. The late Angela Rosenthal, art historian at Dartmouth College, explained that hair has "often been thought of as containing the essence of individuality and personhood" (Rosenthal, 2). To Rosenthal, hair is the part of our bodies that reminds us of the entire individual when we see it, and, more importantly, when we touch it.

Hair is a part of us that stays intact for an indefinite amount of time. It is more like us than a portrait created by an artist, because it was part of our bodies. What we now know is that at the end of each strand of hair is a follicle containing the unique DNA of that person. In that respect, hair *really* is the essence of the living being. Hair is also warm and soft to the touch. Worn against our naked skin as jewelry, we can almost feel the gentle caress of the person once alive, and perhaps loved, but now passed on.

A passage from *No Name* (a book written by Wilkie Collins), which appeared in Charles Dickens' magazine *All the Year Round* in 1860, described this feeling when the heroine, Magdalen, takes a lock of hair from a white silk bag strung around her neck and says, "I can sit and look at you sometimes, till I almost think I am looking at Frank. Oh, my darling!" She then puts the lock of hair to her lips and lets it fall to her breast, "and, for one enchanted moment, Love opened the gates of Paradise to the daughter of Eve" (quoted in Lutz, 131). To the Victorian, living in a time of evangelical movements of the 1830s and 1840s and spiritualism of the 1840s and on, heaven was a real place where our loved ones dwelled. Mediums regularly communicated with the dead, and the hair of the deceased brought one closer to them. Hair was a soft reminder of those who waited for us behind death's door.

In her book on Victorian relics, Dr. Deborah Lutz quotes a letter Emily Palmer wrote to her sister-in-law, Laura, explaining why she wears a ring made from the hair of her deceased sister: "I am glad for 3 reasons. First because always wearing it—helps me always to think of her—2nd because a ring seems to be a bond of love—3rd it being round—a circle reminds one how one's love and communion with her may and will last for ever" (Lutz, 133).

Human hair is a protein filament that grows from a bulb, or follicle, in our skin. Like the nails of our fingers and toes, hair is mostly made up of keratin, and it grows faster than any other part of our body except for bone marrow. At any one time, the average person has between 100,000 and 150,000 hairs on their heads, growing at the speed of 6 inches a year. While an individual hair may seem fragile, a lock of hair is actually quite strong. Typically, 100 hairs can hold a ten-kilogram (twenty-two-pound) weight before breaking (Radford). Human hair is also elastic, can be used as a sponge, and can retain a shape. Despite rumors to the contrary, human hair does not continue to grow when we die. The appearance of growth is because our skin become dehydrated and shrinks after death. It is this retraction that makes hair and nails appear longer than they do at the moment of death.

Hair is resistant to decay and has been found on Egyptian mummies thousands of years old. Alexanna Speight wrote that when they opened the tomb of Countess D'Albini, the wife of the founder of the abbey in Wymondham, her hair was "as fine and glossy as if it had just been taken from the head of a living person" (Speight, 80–81). The countess's hair had remained a beautiful reddish or auburn color after seven hundred years! It is this imperishable quality of hair that gave the Victorians the impression that it is a part of us that escapes the ravages of death. This was a powerful reassurance to them that our souls, or our spirits, might also last for all eternity.

Some consider items made from the hair of a deceased person to be relics—part of the physical remains of a person used for the purpose of veneration. Favorite remains besides hair were teeth, bones and fingernails, valued because they also lasted a long time. Relics can also be special things that belonged to those that were holy, such as the true cross, the Virgin Mary's mantel, or Christ's crown of thorns (which is housed in

Sainte-Chapelle in Paris France). The old testament assures us that relics have special powers (2 Kings 13:21). Touching or praying to the bones of a holy person can heal you. Prayers said in front of their body parts get special consideration by God.

Christian relics generally have some connection to Jesus, the Virgin Mary, or the Catholic saints. For example, Charlemagne, king of the Franks (742–814), gave his wife a sapphire amulet containing the hair of the Virgin Mary along with fragments of the true cross (Lutz, 128). Other relics could be found by anyone who reached the end of the pilgrimage of *el Camino de Santiago* (Taylor, 233). In the crypt of the Santiago de Compostela Cathedral lie relics of Saint James and two of his disciples, Saint Theodorus and Saint Athanasius. The relics of St. James are his bones, which were taken to Jerusalem and then brought back to the coast of Spain to be buried near the Galician coast. The saint's bones were discovered in 814 AD but not authenticated by a pope until 1884, when they were put into a silver reliquary, a container, made specifically to house them. Other examples of holy relics are the blood of Saint Januarius, martyred in the 4th century AD and preserved in the cathedral at Naples, Italy; the tongue of St. Anthony of Padua, housed at Westminster Cathedral in London, England; the finger of St. Thomas, preserved in the church of Santa Croce in Rome, Italy; the head of St. John the Baptist, which can be seen in the Amiens Cathedral in France; and the head of Saint Catherine of Siena, preserved in the Basilica Cateriniana San Domenico, in Siena, Italy.

Martin Luther (1483–1546), a German priest, rejected several teachings and practices of the Roman Catholic Church and began organizing a new church in 1526. England's King Henry VIII (1491–1547) disapproved of Luther at first, but then followed suit, dissolving his country's Catholic monasteries in the 1530s with the aid of his chief minister, the Earl of Essex, Thomas Cromwell (1485–1540). At this time, large collections of relics were destroyed or disappeared. By the end of the Elizabethan age, Protestantism took hold in England, and the Catholic practice of worshiping the relics of saints was discouraged. Instead of rejecting relics completely, the populace began making secular relics for their own personal use from body parts or possessions of their heroes or loved ones, such Napoleon Bonaparte's private parts (Grovier).

Secular relics were made in many European countries. A curious assortment of secular relics can be found in the case of Galileo Galilei (1564–1642), the inventor of the telescope and teacher and defender of the theory of Copernicus (1473–1543), the Renaissance mathematician who determined that the planets revolve around the sun. As the Catholic Church believed that the center of the universe was the earth, and that Galileo's ideas were heresy, he was found guilty and ordered under house arrest by the Catholic Inquisition in 1633. Galileo was not allowed to be buried next to his family upon his death, but was placed in a small room next to the novices' chapel in the Basilica of Santa Croce in Florence, Italy. He was reburied in the main body of the basilica in March of 1737. During transfer of his body, his middle finger was severed from his hand by an admirer, Anton Francesco Gori, the founder of the city's new museum ("Galileo's Fingers"). Galileo's finger was kept privately for 100 years before the Museo di Storia della Scienza in Florence acquired it. Amazingly, in 2009 an auction house discovered two more of Galileo's fingers, one of his vertebrae, and his tooth. The tooth had been kept at the University of Padua, where Galileo taught for many years. All of these parts are now reunited, enclosed in a bell jar in the museum, and on display for everyone to see. It is amusing that the middle finger of the once-declared enemy of the church points in an upright position towards the sky (*ibid.*). Galileo's body parts are "celebrity relics," like other fragments of rulers, heroes, writers, and artists. These became popular beginning in 1500 and have remained so up until modern times (Lutz, 129). Items such as the ball that killed Lord Nelson, pieces of clothing worn during the battle of Waterloo, or the heart of King Richard I (which is in Rouen, France, while his body and entrails were buried in the cathedral in Chalus) were proof, in the time before photography, that these heroes existed and that the events really took place.

While President George Washington was alive, young girls were known to write to him asking for locks of his hair. Two of these locks are now owned by the State Museum of Pennsylvania. One of these came from Mr. John Pierie, a barber who retained a good portion of the president's hair and distributed it to his important customers. The second lock of Washington's hair was obtained from a granddaughter of Jonathan Dickinson Sergeant, a member of the Second Continental Congress. Celebrity relics are still popular today (*State Museum of Pennsylvania*). In 2011 strands of hair from George Harrison and Paul McCartney from the rock group, The Beatles, were auctioned off on Ebay. Someone paid $40,000 for strands of John Lennon's hair, and in a 2011 auction, the winning bid for locks of hair from rock and roll legend, Elvis Presley, was $150,000 (*Time Magazine*).

As in the case of George Washington's hair, not all relics come from a corpse. Items such as hair or teeth might be freely given and kept for sentimental reasons. In the case of the great English poet John Donne (1573–1631), the reason for the gift of a lock of hair caused great confusion. In his poem "The Funeral," published after his death in 1633, Donne wrote that he wore a bracelet around his arm made from his girlfriend's hair even though the woman eventually scorned him. Uncertain of the motivation behind her gift, he asked to be buried with it when he died. He wrote:

> Whoever comes to shroud me, do not harm
> Nor question much
> That subtle wreath of hair, which crowns my arm..."

Although the relationship ended in disappointment, Donne valued the hair jewelry so much that he asked that it accompany him to his grave. He ended his poem with this defiant line: "That since you would have none of me, I bury some of you."

Donne once again mentioned this "bracelet of bright hair" in his poem "The Relic," only this time he envisioned his body being dug up and his flesh decayed. The bracelet is found wrapped around his humerus—the large bone that runs from his shoulder to his elbow.

On her sixteenth birthday, Queen Victoria was given a brooch woven from her mother's hair. This wasn't mourning jewelry, because her mother was still alive (Lichten, 193). Victoria also asked Albert for a lock of his hair four days after their betrothal (Gere, 8). She put it into a diamond-set locket in the shape of a heart given to her as an engagement present by Louise, queen of the Belgians. It was common for couples to exchange hair during their engagement or around the time of their marriage. The birth of babies was also celebrated with enameled, heart-shaped lockets that contained the baby's hair. Queen Victoria put a locket containing Princess Beatrice's baby hair on a bracelet. Beatrice was born in 1857. The queen wore the bracelet when posing for a photo portrait made to celebrate her jubilee in 1897.

Queen Victoria was also fond of wearing teeth. Records of the queen's jewelry show that she owned earrings set with baby teeth, and a bracelet also made from her children's teeth (Gere, 16). She even wore an enameled, gold thistle brooch that incorporated her daughter Princess Victoria's first tooth, when visiting the French court in 1855. The tooth had fallen out in Scotland in 1847 (Bell, 18). Rather than a relic, this type of jewelry is called "remembrance," "regard" or "sentimental jewelry," and it is a symbol of affection or love. The practice dates from the 17th century, when woven hair bracelets were given as love tokens to both men and women. It then became customary to place hair under glass in rings and lockets, sometimes arranging it so that it formed initials or symbols.

But requesting hair to make sentimental pieces could sometimes be regarded as being in bad form. Lady Mary Coke (1727–1811), an English noblewoman known for her journals, wrote that a niece of Horatio Walpole, the 4th Earl of Orford, had given a lock of her hair to the Duke of Ancaster, believing that they were engaged. When he died before they could marry, her mother asked that the hair be returned. To make matters worse, she requested that "the Duchess of Ancaster order a lock of the Duke's hair to be cut off and sent to her daughter as she intended to mourn for him" (Trumback, 40). Other noble women were horrified by the audacity of such a request and saw this as a terrible imposition for the duchess, who was in the deepest sorrow for the loss of her son.

The tradition of including hair in sentimental jewelry was an ancient one and was widespread in England during the 1500s, when knights reportedly wore lockets containing wreaths or hearts made from their lovers' pubic hair (Brett, 108). Pubic hair continued to have its allure until Victorian times. Charles II of England (1630–1685) had an entire wig made from the pubic hair of his favorite mistress, which he wore to increase his virility (Rosenthal, 1). After being defeated by the Puritan Oliver Cromwell at the Battle of Worcester in 1651, Charles fled to Europe and lived under the protection of his first cousin, King Louis XIV of France. Before he left, and before he promised his cousin that he would convert to Catholicism, he sent the wig to St. Andrews, Scotland, to the Earl of Moray, who had once shown him a good time, complete with riotous drinking parties. Charles II spent the next nine years in exile but returned to London to continue his reign after Cromwell died. Charles converted only when he lay on his deathbed. In life, he was named the "Merry Monarch," and his court was a hedonistic one. The wig ended up in a men's-only sex and masturbation club called The Beggar's Benison Club, complete with masked and naked girls (Perrottet). It remained there until 1775 when the new Earl of Moray took the wig back and formed his own sex club named The Wig Club. Knowledgeable of the club's terrible loss, King George IV of England (1762–1830), an honorary member of the Benison Club, presented it with a locket containing pubic hair from his own mistress. This pubic hair, now stored in a silver snuffbox, is on display at the Museum of St. Andrew University in Scotland.

Using pubic hair in jewelry made sense in the 17th and 18th centuries, when the hair on one's head was plastered and powdered in special "powder rooms" before one could emerge into society (Rosenthal, 9). Wigs had been introduced to Britain during the reign of King Stephan (1092?–1154) in the 12th century and were so accepted by 1705 that when the Lord Keeper of the Great Seal wore his hair in a natural state, he was ordered by Queen Anne to cut it off and put on a wig (Speight, 70). Later, in the Georgian era, a wig hid the possibility that one's hair was going gray, or that a man was bald, or that a man or a woman might be suffering from syphilis. A wig also indicated a man's position in society and his occupation. The elaborate wigs women wore were testaments to their families' wealth and ability to consume luxurious fashions. Up to 2 pounds of powder were used on each powdered wig, called a peruke, and it might take a hair dresser up to

2 hours to complete a coiffeur (Rosenthal, 10). Mark Campbell, an American hairdresser who wrote the book *Self-Instruction: Art of Hairwork* in 1867, reported that military forces in the colonies of King George II were issued a pound of flour each to whiten their hair. This amounted to the purchase of 6,500 tons of flour a year. In addition to the flour, for those who could afford it, there were gold and silver hair powders to color the hair and make it shine (Campbell, 263).

The end of the 18th century saw men's wigs grow bigger—the bigger the better. Women's wigs became towers of hair sculptures. Speight describes the hairdos of the English as rising "to something like a marvelous height." The hair of women towered above those of their male companions, forcing the ladies to sleep in chairs rather than in their beds (Speight, 17). Speight, who was a hairdresser in the 19th century, recalled a gentleman saying: "The women were of such an enormous stature, that we appeared as grasshoppers before them" (Speight, 18).

The first rings to carry a lock of hair from a deceased individual appeared in the late 1600s. Queen Henrietta Maria of England owned rings containing the hair of her husband, King Charles I, who died in 1649 (Aronson, 64). This was also the time when Sir Ralph Verney's little daughter, Anna-Maria, died at only 4 years of age. Verney, the 1st Baronet of Middle Claydon, sent a mourning ring to his brother with a letter that read: "Filled with my little girl's haire; she was found of you and you loved her therefore I now send you this to keepe for her sake" (Taylor, 232). Rings like the one Verney had made were either hollow hoops into which a jeweler inserted strands of hair or ones that had a bezel onto which a jeweler placed the hair, which was then covered with a crystal or with glass. These rings were probably inscribed with the name of the deceased and the date of his or her death.

In the 1770s the Scottish artist Sir Henry Raeburn (1756–1823), who had trained as a jeweler and goldsmith in Edinburg, attached locks of hair to generic mourning brooches he painted with scenes of grieving women and funeral urns. The inclusion of hair from the deceased made the pieces more intimate. The noted British portrait artist Richard Cosway (1742–1821) used hair from the Prince of Wales, later King George IV, and his companion and possible wife, Mrs. Maria Anne Fitzherbert, to frame miniature portraits he painted of them. Cosway combined their hair and braided it, set his work into gold mountings, fastened it with gold findings, and turned it into lockets. These miniatures cost the prince 30 guineas a piece (Aronson, 23).

Jewelry containing hair, or jewelry that was primarily made of woven or braided hair, arrived in America with the European immigrants. By the late 1700s jewelers advertised their ability to make this kind of jewelry in American newspapers and magazines. Hair jewelry from this time period was fairly expensive and was only purchased by free white people of the upper and middle classes. The work was made by professionals, usually jewelers, goldsmiths or silversmiths. Placing hair in ring hoops or in brooch bezels required specialized knowledge and tools, although some hair workers, such as M. Sauvage, advertised that they worked in hair alone. Sauvage's ad, placed in 1799, read that customers could find her "at the house she resides in, on Meeting street, between George and Boundary Street" (Sheumaker, 3). Others working in hair owned their own shops. William Coleman, a goldsmith and jeweler from Baltimore, advertised that he "plats hair and forms it into cyphers, sprigs, figures, or any other devise for rings, lockets, &c. patterns of which may be seen at his shop." Once there, one could look at samples, or look in pattern books and decide on the style of weave or plait, and the object to be made (Sheumaker, 4). Some hair workers, however, were itinerant artists, which meant that they traveled from place to place. Edward G. Malbone lived in Newport, Rhode Island, but regularly traveled from Newport to Providence, Boston, New York, Philadelphia, Charleston and Savannah to find work. He would notify customers when he would arrive in their town by placing ads in local newspapers. Raphaelle Peale (1774–1825), the miniature artist mention in a previous chapter, also traveled for business. He advertised that he offered likenesses, set in gold "with plats and cyphers complete, for twenty-five dollars; the miniature alone, ten dollars." A plat was hair that Peale wove or braided before encasing it under glass on the back of his miniature. Peale liked to braid the hair of the deceased in a basketweave pattern (Sheumaker, 4).

Jewelry made from woven or braided hair became very popular in Britain and the rest of Europe from the 1830s to the 1850s. These pieces were not always memorial. Sometimes the inclusion of hair in jewelry signaled the deepening of a relationship and acted as a love token. Some hair jewelry was purely decorative and may even have been made of horsehair. Coarser and more durable than human hair, horsehair was easier to weave and was preferred for making jewelry meant for children's wear. Sometimes the horsehair was dyed red.

At the height of the fad, hair jewelry became so popular that jewelers and artists working in hair purchased human hair from hair merchants. These merchants also purchased hair for making wigs and hairpieces. In 1870, Alexanna Speight, the 19th century hairdresser, estimated that "one in every ten English woman wears a greater or less quantity of false hair mixed with her own" (Speight, 56). The most popular colors were medium to dark brown, which Speight wrote came from British or American women. Black hair

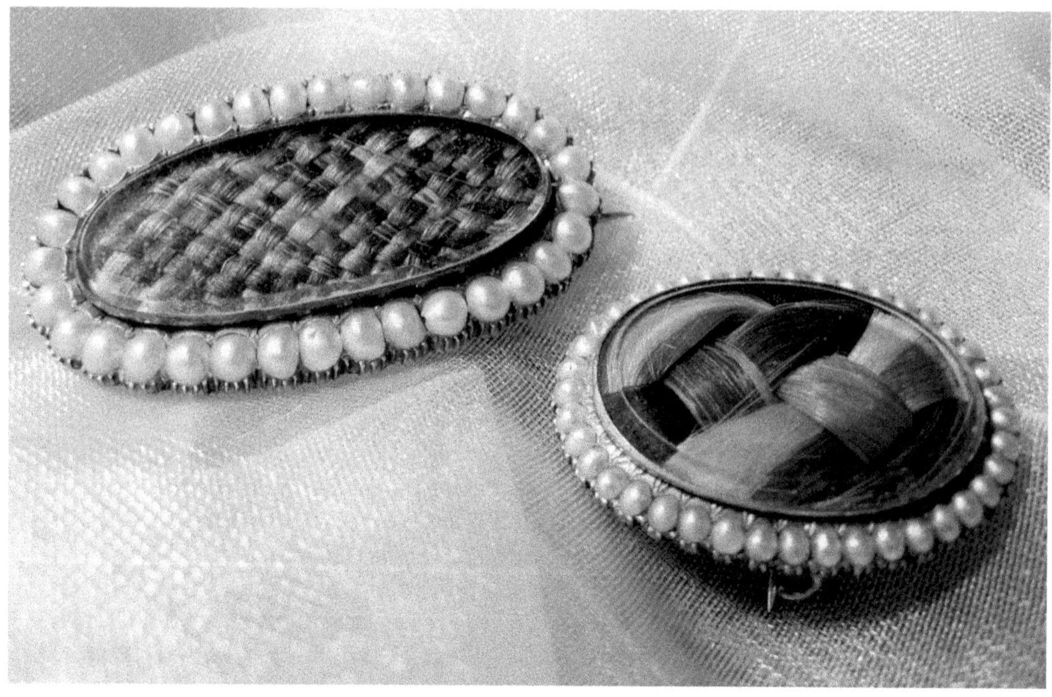

Gold brooches with hair, surrounded by seed pearls (courtesy Ann Longmore-Etheridge collection).

came from Spain or Italy, blond hair came from Germany, Holland, women from the south of France, or children as in the case of Queen Margot, the first wife of Britain's King Henry IV. Whenever she needed a new wig or hair piece, she had the heads of the king's blond pages shaved (Speight, 53). But most hair was offered up by the poor in return for money. Sadly, sometimes this was a very small amount. Francis Trollope wrote in *Summer in Brittany* that he attended a fair in the northern part of France where the hair-dealers were shearing the peasant girls like sheep and only giving them a few coins, or a brightly colored cotton handkerchief in return. He explained that normally these girls completely covered their heads with a "picturesque cap," so didn't care much for their tresses anyway (quoted in Speight, 51). Dealers in hair also got merchandise from convents and the devotees who abandoned their hair along with their other worldly goods.

An article appearing in an 1850 issue of *Godey's Ladies' Magazine* said that hairwork jewelry originated in Germany, but Mark Campbell, the American hairdresser, believed that the Norwegians were the first to make decorative jewelry entirely of hair. He went on to explain that hair jewelry was also made in Switzerland but said he believed that it was the French who perfected the art. Campbell might be right, because in the early 1800s French prisoners of the Napoleonic War settled in the Tunbridge Wells area of Kent and became famous for their skills at making hair jewelry. They created a thriving industry there, weaving hair into delicate chains (Taylor, 242). Some people also used hair for embroidery.

Writing in 1867, Campbell admitted that he made hair jewelry, but he also made accoutrements for hairdos. A hair stylist, Campbell had to buy hair, and he asserted that most if not all human hair sold originated in Europe. According to him, Paris was the greatest market for the sale of human hair in the world. In 1859 and 1860 the United States imported 150,000 to 200,000 pounds of the stuff valued at $800,000 to $1,000,000 (Campbell, 260), an amount worth more than $28 million today. At the time he wrote his book, Campbell believed that the demand for human hair was increasing. He went on to explain that a person's hair could earn them between $15 and $200 per pound depending on its hue, length and texture. Gray and white hair was valued the most, at $100 to $200 per pound. He further noted that one lucky person, whose hair measured 70 inches long, was paid $400 for 1/2 pound of the stuff.

Hair suppliers shipped both prepared and unprepared hair to the merchant. Prepared hair would be washed and scoured clean of all oil, dirt, and "unhealthy influences" (Campbell, 262). Campbell, in the middle of 19th century America, used the hair he bought to make switches, curls, plaits, fronts, wigs, and chignons, but he reserved a large amount of it for making hair jewelry. Campbell believed that all hair jewelry, either ornaments or mementos, needed to be mounted in gold finding, which one could purchase from him by mail or from one of his establishments on 737 Broadway, New York, or at 81 S. Clark Street, in Chicago. He also sold braiding tables, weights, bobbins, and forms for making hair jewelry at home.

No one invented machinery that could weave or braid hair. Hairwork was always created by hand. Those hired by an establishment to make hair jewelry were called "hairworkers." Professionals who designed and made hair jewelry began calling themselves "designers in hair" or "hair artisans." Some became real experts in the field. The most important hair designer in Britain was Antoni Forrer (1803–1889), whose shop on 136 Regent St. in London employed 50 workers. In 1848, Forrer garnered the title of "Artist in Hair Jewellery to Her Majesty" Queen Victoria (Lutz, 129). His work earned him several prizes and medals at the Great World Exhibition of 1851 in London, widely considered to be the most influential single event in the history of design (Taylor, 243). This event was organized by the queen's consort, Prince Albert, along with the inventor Sir Henry Cole. Money raise from admission to the exhibition was used to fund London's Victoria and Albert Museum. Forrer also won prizes for the set of miniature portraits of the queen and her family that he created with hair. Work by ten other hair jewelers were displayed at the Great World Exhibition. Among these was hair jewelry made by Gabriel Lemonnier, the founder of the French firm Lemonnier et Cie of Paris. Lemonnier won awards for his jewelry at the same exhibition, and also won a medal for his large portrait of Queen Victoria complete with a background filled with tombs and bouquets, made entirely from hair. In addition, he earned the title of *"Artiste dessinateur en cheveux de la Reine"* or in English, the Designated Artist in Hair for the Queen (Aronson, 68). Other expositions displayed hairwork such as the Exposition Universelle in Paris of 1855. An article in the 1858 *La Belle Assemblée* describing the fair said that a full-length, life-size portrait of Queen Victoria made entirely of human hair was on display (Flower, 22). Artwork in human hair could also be seen at the Centennial Exhibition in Philadelphia in 1876.

In 1860 H. Rushton of Clerkenwell, London, advertised that if customers mailed him their hair he could turn it into bracelets, brooches, rings, pins, studs, watchguards, Albert chains for a pocket watch, necklaces and the like. But as the century progressed, hair jewelry became less associated with sentiment and more associated with death, especially after the death of Prince Albert. Queen Victoria was very interested in her deceased husband's hair. Only 42, devastated by the loss, and with small children to raise, the queen had her royal hair jewelers make several pieces out of his hair. She even made her eight-year-old son wear a locket around his neck containing his father's hair, and one of her grown children gave her mother a bracelet combining Albert's hair with hair from the rest of the family (Lutz, 132). The queen could be seen wearing lockets containing hair from her children on a bracelet for her silver jubilee.

Taking their lead from the queen, British, European and American mourners began taking precious locks of their deceased loved ones' hair to their local jewelers where they chose a design and pattern, and left the hair to be woven and mounted into a sentimental treasure. Even famous jewelers such as Tiffany created jewelry with hair. The Rothschild collection displayed a Tiffany brooch from 1868 with braided hair from Cornelia Ray Hamilton under crystal surrounded by gold and pearls (Truong). Soon spherical earrings, rings, brooches, latticed bracelets, collars and woven chains of hair appeared on the pale arms, fingers, necks and throats of women, along with stick pins, studs, and cufflinks that adorned male mourner's clothing. Most men of this time sported woven chains of hair to support their pocket watches, and which were draped on their vests.

Designs for hair jewelry were intricate, tight and finely woven. Some jewelers found the hairwork too tedious to do themselves and hired outsiders to complete this work. Soon businesses specializing in hair jewelry production, like Linherr and Company of New York, sprang up to meet this need. An American publication named *The Jeweler's Circular and Horological Review* (horological refers to watch-making) was founded in 1869 for the purpose of giving jewelers and watchmakers in rural areas of the country information on the latest novelties. It also gave information on jewelry suppliers. O. Schwencke of Fine Hair Jewelry of 43 Maiden Lane, New York, placed a small advertisement tucked between larger ones for vulcanite jewelry and Whitby jet. The owner of

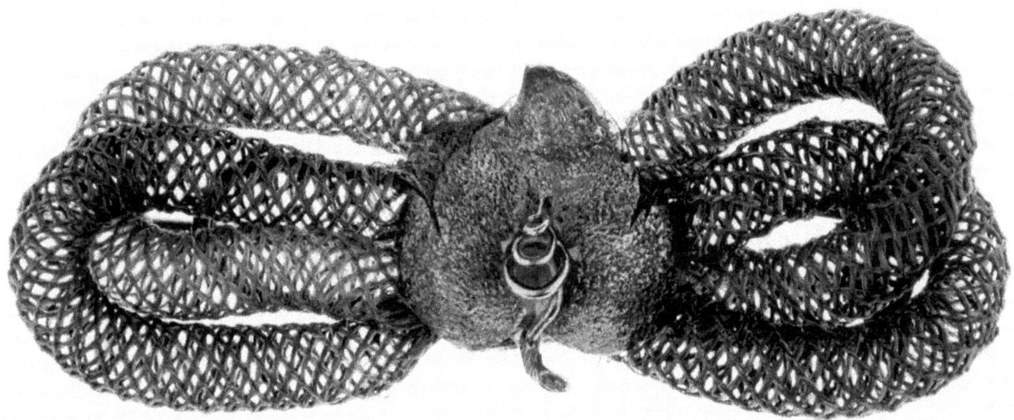

Hair work brooch, circa 1865; 2¼" × ⅞" (Minnesota Historical Society).

Schwencke's wanted to let jewelers know that solid gold findings and finishings for hair jewelry were constantly on hand and made to order at the shortest notice. Chas. T. Menge, manufacturer of Fine Hair Jewelry and Device Work located on 32 John Street in New York City also placed a small ad saying that he would send a rural jeweler a pattern book of their hair jewelry designs upon receiving satisfactory references. Mr. Menge advised, in the ad, that he could duplicate hair items from anyone else's pattern book by just giving him the number of the design and the name of the book (vol. 9, no. 9).

Unbeknownst to customers, local jewelers began shipping the precious hair gathered from corpses of loved ones to these establishments, trusting that they would complete the work. Sadly, if the hair was insufficient, or of poor texture, a hairwork manufacturer might add purchased hair to complete the piece. If the mailed hair proved so inappropriate that the job could not be completed at all, they might even substitute purchased hair entirely, returning a jewelry item made from hair belonging to a completely different individual. In some cases, the returned piece might even be a different color than the original hair! The substitution of hair, feared or real, was written about extensively in women's magazines, which noted that memorial jewelry not made from a deceased loved one's hair was valueless. This fear caused so much alarm that hairwork became a home occupation. If the work was completed at home, one was assured that no substitution was made. Besides, it was felt that the jewelry became more precious when made by loving hands.

Godey's Ladies Books wholeheartedly approved of mourners making memorial jewelry from hair of their deceased. The editors explained: "Hair is at once the most delicate and lasting of our materials and survives us, like love. It is so light, so gentle, so escaping from the idea of death, that, with a lock of hair belonging to a child or friend, we may almost look up to heaven and compare notes with angelic nature" (quoted in Rahm, 71).

Godey's December 1850 issue contained two articles with detailed instructions for making intricate hairwork at home and declared that working with hair was superior to knitting, netting and crochet because it did not have litter, dirt or unpleasant smells. In time, they offered a mail-order service and added items to purchase like clasps and pin backs. For years, the magazine continued to include instructions for different hair-weaving patterns and jewelry items made from hair. In 1853 *Family Friend,* a British magazine, published a series of articles giving readers instructions on how to make bracelets, hair nets, hair-rings, and watch guards entirely from hair. Instructions for hairwork also appeared in *Arthur's Home Magazine* and in *The Englishwoman's Domestic Magazine.* Do-it-yourself booklets were published. Mark Campbell's *Self Instructor in the Art of Hair Work* was written in 1867, and Alexanna Speight's *A Lock of Hair* appeared in 1872. Many instruction books were published by hair-jewelry-making establishments that encouraged do-it-yourselfers to buy supplies from them.

In her preface Miss Speight wrote that her main objective for writing the book was to "bring the art of working in hair within the reach of every one." She also described hairwork as an agreeable occupation for long winter evenings or long summer days. After writing about the history of hair and the horrors of the hair trade, she continued:

> We look upon the few solitary hairs which call back the dear face never more to be seen, scenes never again to be revisited, and incidents long held by the past among its own. It is not surprising, then, that these links which connect us with the past should be treasured … valued not for the goldsmith's art which it displays, but for the few hairs clustered within [Speight, 83].

She warned her readers against being the "unhappy dupe" who is deluded by a tradesman who has substituted purchased hair from some unknown poor soul, and she encouraged her readers to become their own artists by working in hair.

Speight instructed the novice artist to clean the hair with borax and soda, carefully scrape it with the edges of a knife, rinse it and cut off the jagged ends. After this preparation she suggests that they attempt to make the most complicated design one could possibly imagine, called "the Prince of Wales' feather." To complete this, one needed a curling iron, a candle or spirit-lamp, steaming hair, a palette, gum, a needle, an ivory counter, and a sugarloaf weight. Speight claimed that once this design had been mastered, the artist could easily create anything else.

The Prince of Wales' feather consists of three curls, two golden ears of barley, filigree work and three pearls, for which one needed a reel of gold wire thread, three pearls split in half, more gum, spirits of wine and a camel-hair pencil. If this didn't discourage the budding artist from trying to design jewelry or artwork from hair, she continued with more directions for making plaits and flowers but, unfortunately, seemed to have run out of steam. These directions were much less detailed, in all probability, dooming one to failure.

Speight also gave instructions on how to use hair and glue as paint, pointing out that for this, it was best to use the hair of children. With sensitivity she added, "We are, however, not insensible to a difficulty here, and we know that in the selection of hair tenderer feelings than mere suitableness will force themselves upon the amateur artist in hair" (Speight, 121). Hair used as paint needed to be finely ground and mixed with a paint medium or glue. Speight instructed the hair artist to make a willow tree by drawing directly on a tablet and then gluing down a small portion of clean hair that had previously been passed through a solution of gum. She instructed that the boughs of the tree were to be single strands of hair, and that to form foliage, one needed to cut a small portion of the cleansed hair into short lengths or sprays, which were fixed on the bough with a camel-hair pencil. To complete these pieces, the author advised that they be placed under glass and framed.

Jewelry painted with masticated hair was very popular and was worn from the early 1700s to the 1830s. Public schools were rare in the United States during this time. Literacy was not universal, so images and symbols were important. Vines growing around a tree painted with hair symbolized love or friendship. A dead tree painted with hair was the symbol of enduring love. The young lady mourning in the graveyard symbolized friendship and affection, and sheaves of wheat symbolized prosperity.

At the end of her book, Speight made the reader understand that she could provide private lessons to the beginning hair artist for a fee. She also sold the required instruments and could put the reader in touch with the best English manufacturers of jewelry, who would supply findings for lockets, brooches and bracelets.

By 1859 American ladies' magazines ran regular articles on hairwork designs. *Godey's Ladies' Book* had a monthly article on hairwork. The magazine gave instructions for making bracelets, brooches, earrings, finger rings, chains, necklaces, shawl pins, and cravat pins. They went even further, suggesting that purses, bags, bookmarks, pencil cases, guards, stud chains, scent bottles, and riding whips could all be made from human hair. They claimed that necessary supplies were readily on hand except for the frames and molds, which could be bought from a turner (a lathe worker). According to their instructions, most hair work was done around a wooden mold, which kept the hair in place until it was fixed by being boiled. After boiling, the artist could remove the hair carefully from the mold. When dried, the instructions recommended that pieces be completed by a jeweler who would provide the jewelry with clasps and such.

Mark Campbell, in the United States, stated in his preface that he wrote his booklet because interest in the art of hair work was common among all classes. His assertion was that previous to his book, information on hair art was guarded by a few, mainly dealers, who had accumulated "fortunes," and who might not have been completely trustworthy. He wrote: "Persons wishing to preserve and weave into lasting mementos, the hair of a deceased father, mother, sister, brother, or child, can also enjoy the inexpressible advantage and satisfaction of *knowing* that the material of their own handiwork is the actual hair of the 'loved and gone'" (Campbell, preface).

Once the hair was harvested, Campbell directed the hair artist to clean it. He also advised that the hair needed to be perfectly straight and tied with a string at the root. Afterwards it was to be divided into strands containing 4 to 20 hairs, which were then tied around a bobbin, fastened with a slip knot and balanced with a weight. Campbell had the eager hair artist begin by making a square chain braid around a wire or wood form so that the center of the braid remained hollow. For a small chain, he recommended size 3 wire, and suggested using 20 to 40 strands of hair. The size of the wire increased depending on how many strands of hair were used for the braid. If using 60 to 80 strands of hair to make a braid, no. 5 wire should be used. If using 100 to 120 strands of hair, he recommended using no. 7. With each strand containing 4 to 20 hairs, these patterns needed quite a lot of hair, and one can imagine the emotions one felt when cutting it off of the lifeless body of the deceased. Worse still would be approaching someone who was mortally ill to request that they allow you to cut large quantities of their hair off, or request that they cut it off themselves.

Jewelry and notions were not the only items Victorians hair artists made with human hair. They also made sculptures called "family trees," wreath wall decorations, wall pictures, and hair albums. It would be interesting to view the scalps of the corpses once the harvesting of their hair was complete. During Victorian times, men wore their hair shoulder length or shorter, but it was the fashion for women to have very long hair. Each human sheds from 60 to 200 hairs a day. Clever women saved the hair they found on their combs and brushes, untangled it, and made it into falls and hair pieces, thus saving the expensive of purchasing these. Rather than cutting all of the needed hair from the heads of the deceased, hair from these homemade hair pieces might have been used.

After the braid was completed, Campbell advised the artist to boil it in water for 10 minutes. To dry the article, one needed to place it in an oven as hot as possible without causing the hair to burn. Once dry, the ends of the hair had to be sewn together and fastened with shellac. Campbell also advised that the hair work be finished with gold fittings and recommended that the pieces be sent to him. He would complete the project using the hair that was mailed to him with a drawing of the desired finished piece (Campbell, 137). Campbell guaranteed satisfaction. He also sold potions to restore hair color and stop baldness.

The article in the December 1850 issue of *Godey's* magazine said that hairwork was a "drawing-room occupation" and described it as being elegant (Blanco, 166). For women in antebellum America, it became a popular pastime. In the mid–19th century the price one paid to purchase professional hair jewelry was quite high. Making it yourself saved this expense. Mass produced jewelry items were quickly becoming commonplace, and in contrast, hair jewelry was made by a devoted individual. It was personal; it was sentimental. It could be given to a loved one or worn against one's skin to remind us of love now lost.

In 1846 Emily Brontë explored the sentimental importance of being buried with a loved one's hair in her work *Wuthering Heights.* In Brontë's book, the main character, Heathcliff, opens a locket suspended from the lifeless body of his obsession, Catherine, and replaces the lock of hair of her husband (Edgar Linton) with a lock of his own. With this act, the reader believes he is insuring that part of him will be buried with Catherine for all eternity. Foiling his secret plot, Catherine's faithful servant, Nelly, finds the strands of Edgar's hair, wraps them around those of Heathcliff's and places them inside the locket as well, dooming the three to be forever bound. Less menacingly, in 1854 the British author Wilkie Collins declared in his popular book *Hide and Seek* that hair bracelets were one of the most common ornaments worn by women of his time; and Charles Dickens wrote in his novel *Our Mutual Friend,* written in 1864, that watch fobs made of hair were a mark of a middle-class man's respectability.

The decline in the popularity of homemade hair jewelry in England began when three lower standards for gold were added in 1854: 15 karat, 12 karat, and 9 karat. England abolished the duty on 18-karat and 22-karat gold, and then abolished the duty on silver, making conventional jewelry easier to afford. As with any fad, hair jewelry became so widespread that it became commonplace. The Romantic era of the Victorian age was ended, and with it, its extreme sentimentality. By the 1870s, the public began to be aware of the theories of John Snow and Louis Pasteur that diseases were spread by germs. Hair from a deceased body was no longer seen as being the delicate remembrance of a life now passed but was looked at as being unhealthy and something that might harbor disease.

The California gold rush of 1849 and discovery of the Comstock Lode of silver in Nevada in 1859 gave an important boost to American jewelry manufacturers. After the Civil War, the United States lowered its standard for gold, too. Because of these less expensive metals and advances in silver jewelry production, commercially produced jewelry became affordable to many in the United States, as well. In time, hair was hidden from sight in jewelry. In 1878 Brainerd & Steele of New York City advertised a patented design for lockets and sleeve buttons in 11-karat gold that contained "a concealed box for miniatures, a novelty new to the trade" (*Jeweler's Circular and Horological Review*, xxii). Although still popular, for more and more Americans, jewelry fashioned from hair was losing its appeal.

The 1870 United States census was the first to record the occupation of women. By then, almost 2 million workers were women, a total of 15 percent of the work force. Many of them worked in factories, but some were teachers, dressmakers and milliners. Women with gainful employment outside the home no longer had time to create tedious fancy-work out of hair. Jobs gave women and men financial stability, which gave the middle class the ability to purchase ready-made jewelry. While the wealthy bought 18-karat or 22-karat gold pieces of jewelry, the middle classes could buy the same styles worked in silver or lower-karat gold. The poor could buy similar styles in pinchbeck or gold-plated brass, garnished with imitation diamond paste.

As the 19th century drew to a close, catalogs such as Montgomery Ward and Sears, Roebuck and Co. advertised hair work services through mail order. Prices went down, ranging from a couple of dollars for a small item to $12 dollars apiece for a larger one. Once again the customers selected the jewelry product, mailed in their hair, and the company produced the article. Americans continued to make and wear jewelry made from hair up until the 1920s, when it eventually was seen as distasteful and "vulgar." Locks of hair might have been worn, but more and more of it was hidden from sight, placed in special or hidden compartments in lockets and charms.

Photography also replaced memorial hair jewelry. In 1849 an estimated three million Americans were being photographed each year (Bell, 17). Early images were daguerreo-types made on silver. Some of these were placed in special cases that could be turned into lockets for mourners to wear. In 1888 George Eastman (1854–1932) came out with the Kodak #1 camera, which simplified the photographic process and allowed the untrained to take amateur pictures of the ones they loved. Within a few years more than a million Americans owned their own cameras and sent their rolls of film to the Kodak Company for processing. The returned images were on paper, and the jewelry industry took note. In response, they fashioned jewelry with slots for photographs. Pictures of living loved ones quickly replaced hair relics and painted miniatures in jewelry that commemorated the dead.

To the British of the late nineteenth century, jewelry made of hair was "hideous." Machine-made goods were cheap and pretty. Working in hair was painstaking, time-consuming and just not deemed worth it anymore, although hair might still be placed in a small box attached underneath a locket or brooch. Americans grew to be less sentimental at the turn of the twentieth century. In time, death was rarely talked about, and excessive grieving was seen as a sign of psychological disease. The emotion contained in hair jewelry made for mourning was no longer tolerated. In this climate, hairwork and jewelry memorializing a deceased loved one was unacceptable. The Aesthetic style, in England, called *art nouveau* in France, valued jewelry based on natural and living things, including necklaces of beads made from semiprecious stones, and pins in the shape of insects or sports paraphernalia. René Lalique, a Parisian jeweler, paired semi-precious stones with enamel, horn and glass. The jewelry designer had great success at the Paris Salon of 1895, introducing motifs like nasturtiums, morning glories, and female nudes with long, trailing hair. Dubbed "the inventor of modern jewelry," Lalique's fame spread the Art Nouveau style worldwide, influencing jewelry design into the next century.

8

Photography and Death

Postmortem Portraits

Postmortem photographs are images taken of a corpse. Most of the surviving postmortem photographs from the 19th century are of children. Why would anyone take a photograph of their dead child? Why would anyone hire a professional photographer to come to their house and shoot an image of their dead baby? And why are postmortem photographs of the 19th century highly collectible today, with some of them costing up to $1,200 each (Miller, 9)? To answer these questions, we need to put ourselves in the place of the people of this time and study some of their history.

In the beginning of the 1700s children lived longer on average than they would a hundred years later, probably because of lower population density. A full 74 percent of babies born reached at least 10 years of age (Burns, chronology, 1640–1760). During this time the views about death and the afterlife were harsh, based on Puritan beliefs. Colonists also followed the no-nonsense approach of the Puritans when burying their loved ones. To the Puritans, everyone was born in sin. Our actions were not our fault because our lives were predetermined by an omnipotent God who controlled not only the present but the past and the future as well. Only a few "elect" humans, chosen without their knowledge, would ever ascend to heaven; the rest of us would burn eternally in the fires of hell. Concerning the corpse, the words of Samuel Willard, a colonial minister, rang true: the body was to be "commended to the cold and silent Grave where it must be entertained with Worms and Rottenness, and be turned into putrefaction" (quoted in Laderman, 52). Corpses were buried quickly and without much ceremony. This was especially true for the bodies of children. Puritanical ideas about children were that they, as all humans, were born in sin. Even babies were seen as being wayward and full of evil passions. Worse still, children did not contribute to the family and were seen as a burden rather than a blessing.

After 1760 the chances of a child reaching ten years of age dropped to 50 percent (Burns, chronology, 1640–1760). In the 19th century chances of living that long dropped even further as the death rate continue to rise. In response to the high mortality rate, parents were warned not to get too emotionally involved in their children. Dr. Stanley Burns in his work *Sleeping Beauty* wrote that parents of this time were actually "advised to be restrained in affection and aloof to their children in order not to become too attached to them" (Burns, chronology, 1677). But at the same time Calvinist ideas about the corpse softened. The idea of eternal hell and damnation did not sit well with people whose lives were short and who suffered the loss of so many precious loved ones.

148

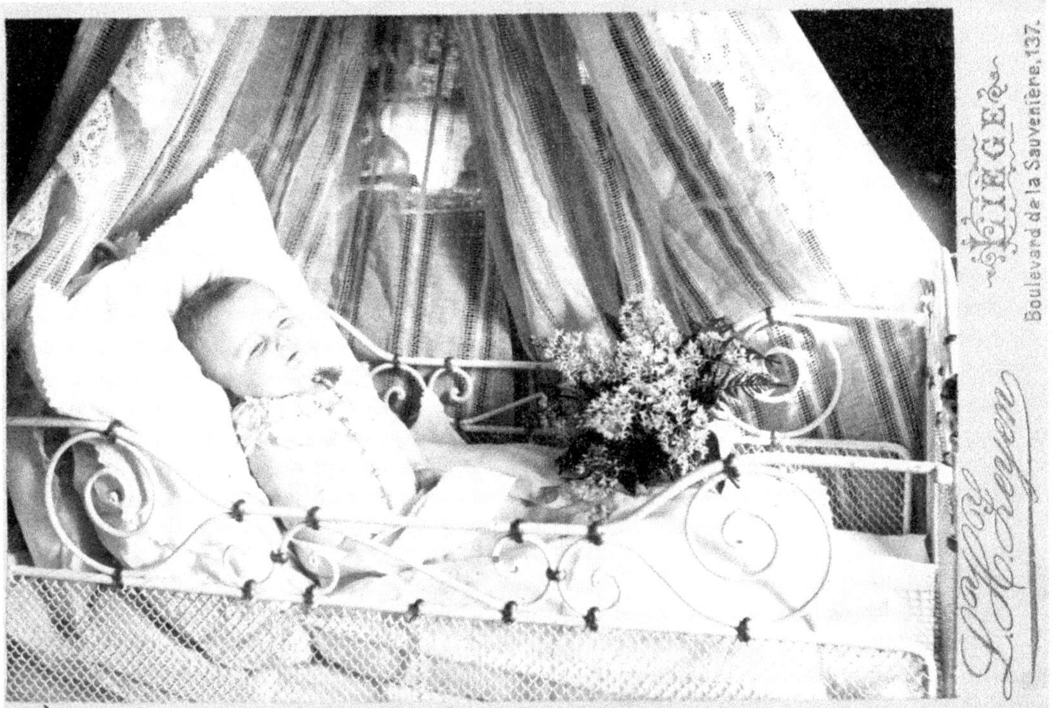

Deceased infant in cot, albumen cabinet card, circa 1890 (courtesy Ann Longmore-Etheridge collection).

In the 1730s and 1740s the Protestant faiths saw the emergence of evangelism in what is now called the "Great Awakening." Times were ripe for traveling preachers, such as George Whitefield, to usher in a new era. Whitefield preached to his emotional listeners that they could be "reborn" without sin, and in this way, gain entrance to a "Promised Land" (Whitefield, 14). Others copied his message as well as his preaching method and traveled around the colonies spreading the good word. For those who could not attend these revival meetings, Whitefield's sermons were printed and published by Benjamin Franklin in *The Pennsylvania Gazette*.

The official Protestant religion of the Puritans, based on ideas by John Calvin, was also changing. William Ellery Channing, educated at Harvard in orthodox Calvinist doctrine, became a liberal minister. He rejected the doctrine and broke away from the Calvinist church. In the 1820s Channing preached that mankind was essentially good and children were innocents, repudiating the Puritan theory of infant damnation. Channing eventually became the first minister of what was to become the Unitarian Church (Burns, chronology, 1810).

Several evangelical Protestant sects began to emerge around this time, and their religious philosophies offered people even more hope for a life after death. An important belief was in the second coming of Christ. Death was not final. At the end of days, Christ would return, and dead bodies would be reunited with their souls. God would "restore life to the dead and 'awaken' the body from its lifeless state" (Laderman, 53). Consequently, the human body gained in importance. The corpse was essential for our future eternal life, and the care of it was taken more seriously.

By the mid–nineteenth century, the Methodist Church emerged as the dominant religion in the United States (Burns, chronology, 1850). Its views on death were much more hopeful than those of the Puritans. Methodists teach that when we die, we are asleep. Their doctrine acknowledges that we do not know what happens to us after death but cites two different ideas from the Bible. The first, coming from both the Old and the New testaments, is that the dead rest "asleep" until Resurrection Day. On this Day of Judgement, we will all rise from the dead to either renewed "life, or eternal punishment" ("What Happens"). The second idea comes from the New Testament and assures us that we might ascend to heaven even sooner. In Luke 23:42, one of the thieves being crucified near Jesus calls out, "Jesus, remember me when You come into Your Kingdom!" Jesus replies "Truly I say to you, today you shall be with me in paradise." To the Methodists this indicates that when we die our souls have the chance of going straight up to the Lord. This concept is repeated in the book of Revelations 7:9 where John sees a "great multitude … from every nation and all tribes and peoples and tongues" standing before the throne of God. John could not have seen these souls in heaven if mankind needed to wait for the Judgment Day to go there ("Revelations").

Science also influenced ideas about death and the corpse. The Age of Enlightenment of the 1600s and 1700s brought with it the hopeful belief in science and the belief that science could discover the laws of God. The discovery of anesthesia in 1846 was a great turning point in American's concept of death. In Puritan philosophy, death was painful and agonizing. This was especially true because death was seen as retribution for the sins of man. But anesthetized individuals looked peaceful. People made the connection between the two states and began seeing death as peaceful as well. There was no pain, and there was no suffering. Individuals were asleep, and sleep was not frightening. It was something that we all did all the time (Burns, chronology, 1846). This was a powerful consolation to grieving parents and kin, and by the end of the nineteenth century this became the common belief, held even to modern times.

Other influences on Americans' thoughts about death from 1800 to 1860 were the sentimentality of the Romantic movement and the ideas of the closely aligned philosophy of transcendentalism, which had a huge effect on art and literature. Both philosophies emphasized the beauty of nature and encouraged intense emotionalism. In both, death, especially the death of a child, could be viewed as a peaceful sleep in which the soul embarked on a journey to an afterlife (Plante, 194). Transcendentalists believed that all souls are part of a universal spirit, the "Oversoul," or God. Upon death, the soul merely returns to the Oversoul. In his book, Dr. Burns writes that the Romantic movement came up with two views of death: the first being that it was the ultimate communion with nature, and the second was that it was an "awe-inspiring event that elevated human emotions to peak sensitivity" (Burns, chronology, 1800). Photographers, through postmortem photographs, served the purpose of recording this sentimental, Romantic and transcendent concept of death.

* * *

In the 19th century Americans developed a firm belief that there was a proper way to die called "the good death." This meant that one should die at home, and of course this home should be a good Christian one. At the time of death, one should be surrounded by family and friends who can reassure the dying person that they will all meet again in heaven (Linkman, 15). Diaries and letters from this time period show that those absent from the deathbed scene felt guilt. Attendance at the deathbed of a friend or relation and presence at their funeral was expected. Witnessing the death of a loved one taught a powerful lesson and offered reassurance for the living. Survivors would draw great comfort from the peaceful and serene expressions on the face of the dying, as this indicated the peace that we would all find in the afterlife. Postmortem photographs were important reminders of this. Postmortem photographs helped alleviate guilt for those not present at the deathbed or the funeral. It was also reassurance to those absent family members that proper treatment of the dying and the corpse had been conducted. The dead had been well taken care of, and the individual had indeed died "the good death."

Another important reason for these photographs is explained by Audrey Linkman in her book *Photography and Death.* Linkman wrote that the majority of postmortem photographs are of infants and young children. Writing about the United Kingdom, Linkman explained that poor people could not afford to bury their young children. Instead, their bodies were placed in communal pauper graves. Because there was no gravesite to visit, these postmortem photographs were important evidence that the child had been alive, and that the child had died "the good death" (Linkman, 18).

What we now call photography had its beginnings in 1839 when an image of an artist's studio, *L'atelier de l'artist,* was released to the world by the French government. This image was created by Louis Daguerre, a set designer and artist who painted panoramic work that changed with different lighting techniques. Daguerre was helped by the inventor Joseph Niepce, who unfortunately died before he realized any gain from his work. The French government acquired the rights to this process and in return gave Daguerre and the son of Joseph Niepce lifetime pensions. In 1839 the French government published instructions for the "Daguerreotypes" process as a free gift to the world.

A daguerreotype is a positive image captured on a highly polished copper plate covered with a thin layer of silver and then sensitized with fumes of iodine and bromide. Areas exposed to light form silver amalgam particles when exposed to mercury fumes. The extra chemicals not exposed by light are washed away with hyposulphite of soda to ensure they do not continue to darken and spoil the image. After this developing process, a thin film of gold chloride is deposited on the plate to give it a pleasing tone. The drawbacks of this process were that only one image could be made at a time and that there were long exposure times, making portrait work difficult. Also, the chemicals used, especially the mercury gas, could be lethal. The advantages of the process were that it was new, it was easy to learn, and the equipment needed was inexpensive. This was especially important because in 1837 America underwent a serious financial crisis that started a major recession. Wages were deflated and people needed new ways to make their fortunes. Daguerreotypy could offer some a fresh new start, and as a new technology, the field was wide open.

News of this invention arrived in America in the spring of 1839, months before directions for the process were officially published. They were brought to this country by Samuel Morse, the professor of painting and sculpture at New York University, and the inventor of the telegraph. Morse met Louis Daguerre in Paris when he was applying for a French patent for his invention. Morse, who had supported himself as a painter and portrait artist before being hired by the university, asked Daguerre to mail him details of the new imaging process as soon as the French government made them available. Daguerre did, and that summer Morse, with the help of Dr. John William Draper, the head of chemistry at NYU, mastered the daguerreotype technique. Together Morse and

Draper produced the first images of a person—a thing that Daguerre told Morse could not be done. Morse opened a daguerreotype classroom and studio in the University Building and taught the technique for two years. Although his career in photography was short, it was mighty. Morse taught the first generation of American photographers and introduced the medium to a hungry American audience when he published instructions for the process. This allowed industrious others to teach themselves ("Daguerreotype").

As more and more people learned the process, more courses of instruction in the technique became available. In 1840 Levi Hill opened a school of daguerreotypy in the Catskill Mountains area of the state of New York. The course of study varied from two to four weeks and cost $25, about $675 today. The spring of 1840 also saw the opening of the first daguerreotype portrait studio in America by Alexander Wolcott and John Johnson in New York City. Wolcott, originally a dentist, received a patent in the United States for a "mirror camera." This invention cut the posing time for a daguerreotype exposure from 30 minutes down to only 5 (Peres, 56). This greatly increased the feasibility of portrait daguerreotypes and allowed itinerant photographers to travel around, calling at houses, taking pictures wherever they could find customers. In a mere ten years, daguerreotypes reached a standard of perfection. From 1841 to 1860 an estimated 30 million daguerreotypes were taken in America (Burns, chronology, 1838) and by the 1850s several photographers were established and supporting themselves with their work.

Early daguerreotypists advertised in local newspapers to drum up business. They followed the trails set down by the itinerant portrait painters until they were able to afford to set up their own studios in cities or towns. Once a daguerreotypist set up his own studio in a large town, he might still travel as the resident photographer of smaller surrounding towns. Some of the itinerant daguerreotypists had been craftsmen; some had actually been portrait painters who switched to the less time-consuming and newer technology. Along with photographic portraits, they might also sell photographic equipment and supplies, rent local rooms and set up galleries, or teach photography to paying customers.

Photography was an equalizer. Prior to its invention, only the well-to-do could afford to have painted portraits of themselves or their loved ones. Portraits were even more desirable after an individual died. Generally, the artist portrayed the deceased as being alive but being surrounded by symbols that indicated his or her death. This genre of painting originated in Europe and traveled to the United States, rising in popularity from the 1830s to the 1860s. Portraits of deceased family members were honored relics, which were formally viewed by the family members on the birthday of the deceased, or on the anniversary of the deceased individual's death. After the invention of photography, captured likenesses were sometimes used by painters as an intermediate stage in the production of a final painted portrait. Taken before or close to death, the daguerreotype helped the artist secure the subject's likeness without him having to sketch a putrefying corpse.

We know from New York–born artist William Sidney Mount's letters and papers that he supplemented his income by painting "portraits of the dead." Alive from 1807 to 1868, Mount claimed that he disliked the work, writing that he suffered "anxiety of mind, to make my efforts satisfactory to the bereaved friends and relatives" (Laderman, 77). We know from records that Mount charged more for postmortem work and that many of his subjects were children.

But painted portraits were a luxury that the middle and lower classes could not afford. For them photography quickly became the preferred means to memorialize the corpse, giving the deceased a kind of immortality once reserved only for the rich. Even miniature portraits made by itinerant artists could only be afforded by the middle class. By the 1850s the price for a daguerreotype went down to an affordable 25¢, or $8 in current money. Daguerreotypes, portraits created in mere minutes rather than days, replaced miniature paintings. They were made of polished silver and even displayed in small, embellished cases with gold over-mats so they resembled keepsakes and charms.

Many of the early postmortem photographs have a folk-painterly quality to them, leading us to believe that folk painters and miniaturists became photographers. Some photographs show posed corpses—sitting, holding objects, or resting their heads in their hands. Photographers even touched up the images by painting open eyes on top of closed lids. But eventually, postmortem photography was influenced by the Romantic movement and the idea that death was like sleep. Photographers portrayed the deceased as sleeping or resting rather than active and alive as in postmortem paintings. These photographs of a peaceful loved one brought comfort to the bereaved. Daguerreotypes showed the corpse at home, surrounded by family members and symbols. Photographers would offer to provide "accouterments for the display of the loved ones in the home" (Laderman, 78). They might decorate the corpse by surrounding it with flowers, or add floral designs, flying angels, and other iconography to the mat or frame. Flowers, favorite toys, religious objects, a cross or a Bible were meant to keep the viewer's mind from the frightening images of decay and decomposition. These photographs were treasured and preserved in albums or displayed on the walls of parlors or bedrooms. This portrayal was meant to bring comfort to the bereaved.

Photographing the corpse was not a specialty. The most famous pioneering photographers of the times recognized how popular the genre was and sought this business. Collectors find work by Albert J. Beals, Rufus Anson, known for tinted and "finely posed images," and Southworth and Hawes, from Boston. Josiah J. Hawes was a miniature painter who became a daguerreotypist with partner Albert Southworth. Together, they are considered by the American Museum of Photography to be the first masters of the daguerreotype medium in the United States, producing the finest daguerreotypes in the world: "Their posing, lighting and presentations are unmatched" (Burns, caption 11). These photographers did not use a formula when posing a corpse. Each of their thousands of images is unique. A recent stash of 240 daguerreotypes sold in auction at Sotheby's for more than three million dollars, and the Metropolitan Museum in New York, the Boston Museum of Fine Arts, and Eastman House in Rochester, New York, all have large collections of their work.

In a speech given in 1873 to the National Photographic Association, Albert Southworth said:

> When I begun to take pictures, twenty or thirty years ago, I had to make pictures of the dead. We had to go out then more than we do now, and this is a matter that is not easy to manage; but if you work carefully over the various difficulties you will learn very soon how to take pictures of dead bodies, arranging them just as you please [Southworth, *Philadelphia Photographer*, Sept. 1873].

He then went on to describe his technique. Once the corpse was dressed and laid on a sofa, he would bend the limbs and arrange them as if they were asleep. He continued, "you may do just as you please so far as the handling and bending of corpses is concerned. You can bend them till the joints are pliable, and make them assume a natural and easy position." Southworth admitted that sometimes fluid leaked out of the mouth or nose of the corpse while moving it. In that case, the photographer would turn it over so that the liquid was ejected, wipe out the mouth and wash off the face. "Then place your camera and take your pictures just as they would look in life.... Go to the side of the head and shoot this way" rather than shooting the subject from its feet (*ibid.*).

Photographer N. G. Burges offered this advice in 1855:

> If the portrait of an infant is to be taken, it may be placed in the mother's lap, and taken in the usual manner by a side light representing sleep. If it is an older child, it can be placed upon the table, with the head toward the light, slightly raised, and diagonally with the window, with the feet brought more towards the middle of the window [Burges, 80]

* * *

"Secure the Shadow 'ere the substance fade. Let Nature imitate what Nature made," was a popular advertising slogan for postmortem daguerreotype work. The word photography means "writing with light," and that was how it was originally thought of. It was a natural medium that fit well with the new Romantic ideas of the time. "The artist stands aside and lets you paint yourself," the great American Transcendentalist Ralph Waldo Emerson noted in 1841, calling photography the "'true Republican' style of painting" (Emerson). But in the early years of the invention, few people had one made. Nor could they afford to have their likenesses painted. Postmortem daguerreotypes were the last chance for a family to capture the image of their beloved relative before they were laid into the ground. Sometimes these images are the only proof of the existence of a loved one. This was especially so for children.

Daguerreotypes of live children are very rare because of the long time needed to expose the chemicals and create the image. The photographer needed special clamps to discourage movement, and a willing model that would remain still for several minutes. Postmortem photographs of children were of better quality because their dead little bodies did not squirm or wiggle. Some photographs were "pre-mortem," taken just before death, although most photographs were taken while the corpse was on display at home. However, it was not uncommon for parents to bring their dead children to the photographer's studio to have their images captured. In this way, they could take advantage of superior lighting effects. This practice became outlawed during epidemics because of risks of contagion (Burns, caption 2).

Historians note that the end of the daguerreotype process was around 1856, the same year that M. H. Ellis published his work *The Ambrotype and Photographic Instructor, or Photography on Glass and Paper.* This book investigated new inventions in image-making. The techniques described in Ellis's work included a two-step process based on research by Englishmen William Henry Fox Talbot (1800–1877) and scientist Sir John Herschel (1792–1871) in 1839. In the first step of Talbot's "calotype"

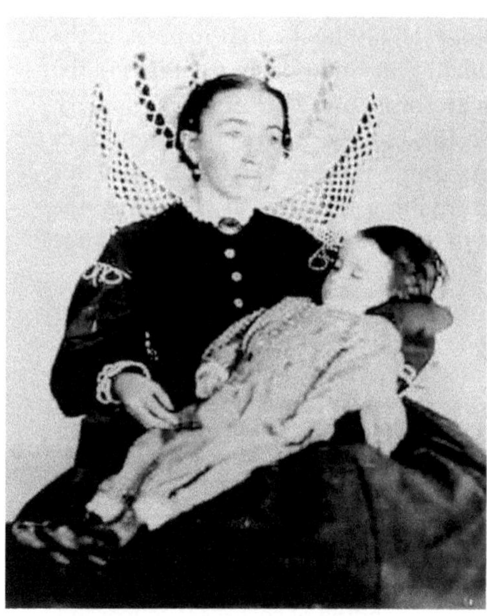

Portrait of a Mother with Her Deceased Child, **collection of the author (original from furever24k).**

process, light exposes silver salts coated on paper to create a negative of the image. This negative can then be placed on top of another sheet of sensitized paper to create a positive image. The advantage of this process is that one can create several positive images from one exposure. The disadvantage was that the paper negative blurred the final product. Inventors tinkered with Talbot's process and formulae until the negative could be made of glass, leading to the "wet collodion" glass negative process, invented by Frederick Scott Archer (1813–1857). The paper for the positive image was dipped in egg white and salt to seal it before applying the silver mixture emulsion. This technique, called the albumen print, was invented by Louis Désiré Blanquart-Evrard (1802–1872). This process had several advantages over daguerreotypy. In addition to it becoming possible to print unlimited amounts of copies from a single negative, the exposure time was reduced because of the transparency of glass. Glass and paper were much less expensive than copper and silver plates, and the photographer no longer needed metal polishers and fuming equipment. The final images, printed on paper, were as sharp as daguerreotypes, and easier

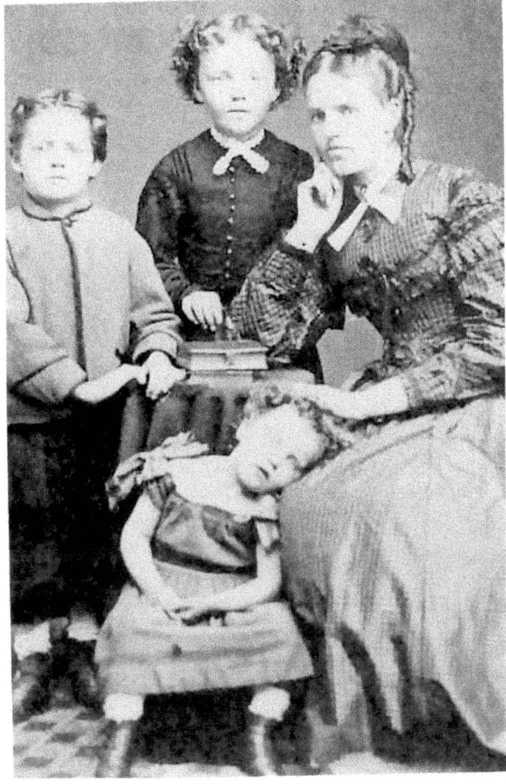

Family Portrait with Deceased Child, circa 1870, collection of the author (original from furever24k).

to see because daguerreotype images would appear negative if the viewing light did not hit the metal just right. By the end of the 1850, the wet collodion process all but replaced the daguerreotype method of photography.

Before photography, written accounts of the death of a relative were copied by hand and sent by mail to distant friends and relatives. Having multiple paper copies of postmortem photographs made this notification process easier for the bereaved. The thin memorial print would be mounted on thicker board cut to the same size as visiting cards or, from the French, *cartes de visite*. They could also be bigger—4" × 6"—and were then called cabinet cards. The bigger print gave the photographer greater freedom in poses and lighting of the corpse and allowed the photographer to retouch or hand color areas if needed. It also gave more room to add decorative floral or angel borders, and written messages including poems.

Multiple copies of the postmortem pose allowed loved ones far away to look again upon the face of their beloved. Photographers worked hard to capture a peaceful and serene expression on faces of the corpses befitting of their place in heaven. With these photos they had the important role of keeping alive the memory of the deceased. As Associate Justice of the Supreme Court, Oliver Wendell Holmes, wrote:

> It is hardly too much to say, that those whom we love no longer leave us in dying as they did of old.
> They remain with us just as they appeared in life; they look down upon us from our walls; they lie upon

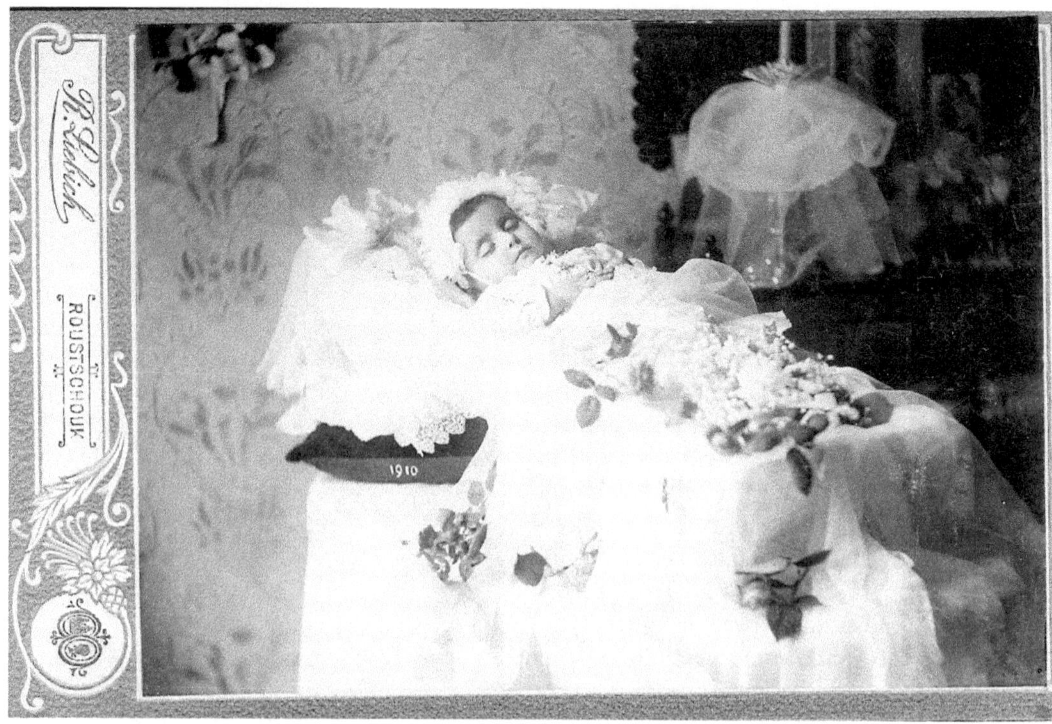

A Post Mortem Cabinet Image of a Child, 1910 (courtesy John Mathew Smith Collection).

our tables.... Parents sometimes forget the faces of their own children in a separation of a year or two. But the unfading artificial retina which has looked upon them retains their impress, and a fresh sunbeam lays this on the living nerve as if it were radiated from the breathing shape [Holmes, 14].

The 1860s and 1870s saw the soaring popularity of "stereo cards." These were photographs taken at the same time but a few inches apart to capture the image as seen from each eye. When viewed through a stereoscope viewer, the images are superimposed upon one another to appear 3-dimensional. This technology was invented in the 1830, but gained in popularity with the advent of the paper photographic print. Postmortem stereo cards exist of individual corpses, but the majority seem to have been mass produced. Postmortem photographs of famous people became a small part of the retail portraiture market. There is a difference between postmortem work and photos of the deceased "lying in state." Christians believe that the memory of worthy people "could exert a positive and beneficial influence on others. The sale of these images was probably justified on moral grounds" (Linkman, 18). It is believed that even Queen Victoria of England commissioned a postmortem of Prince Albert in 1861, which stood on a table in her daughter, Princess Alice's, bedroom. There are 6½" × 8½" albumen prints of Abraham Lincoln as he was laid out in his casket in New York City, but there are also memorial prints and stereoview cards of a live Abraham Lincoln surrounded by symbols such as fallen leaves and arrangements of flowers, which signified his death. The New York photographer Jeremiah Gurney, Jr., took several photographs of Lincoln in his casket. When Secretary of War Edwin M. Stanton heard about this, he had the plates and prints confiscated and destroyed; however, he kept one of them for himself.

In the image, Admiral Charles H. Davis (navy) and General Edward D. Townsend (army) stand at the head and feet of the slain president. This image was taken by Gurney on April 24, 1865, in City Hall, New York City, which still stands. All of Gurney's images were sequestered by Secretary of War Edwin Stanton, who saved only this one print, from a stereoview, and told no one. His son, Lewis, found it in his deceased father's files in 1869 and sent it in 1887 to John G. Nicolay for the authorized biography of Lincoln, where it never appeared. The image was finally found in Nicolay's papers in the Lincoln Presidential Museum in 1952 by a 14-year-old summer intern, Ron Rietveld. Rietveld went on to teach history at California State University, Fullerton, for many years.

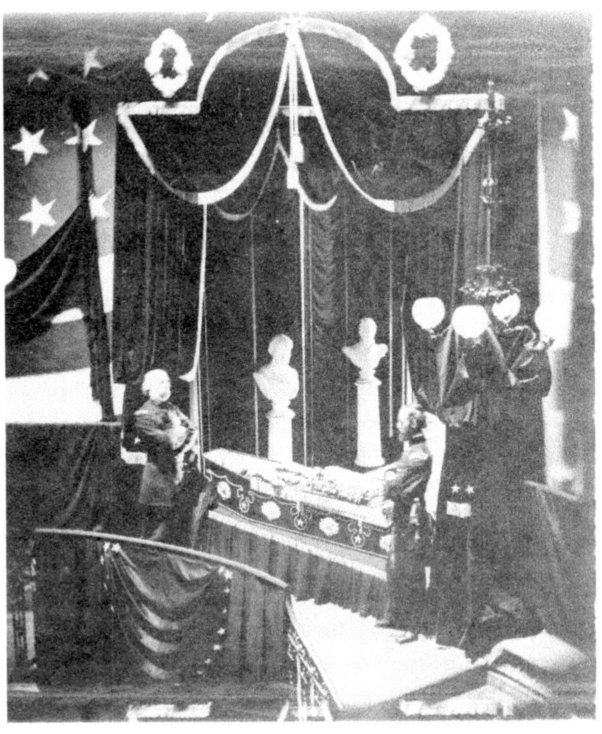

Abraham Lincoln Lying in State, **from stereogram (courtesy Abraham Lincoln Presidential Library and Museum, Springfield, IL).**

Even before the assassination of Lincoln, stereographs and photographs of famous corpses were mass-produced and sold to a hungry population. This form of photography was made popular by the London photographer William England and was found in the United States in the late 1850s. Even the death images of famous thieves and criminals could be found for sale. This was the case for the infamous Reuben (Rube) Burrows, train robber and outlaw, killed in 1890. It was also true for Jesse James. A stereoview of him lying in his coffin made by A. A. Hughes went on sale to the public in 1882.

Mathew Brady and the Civil War

Dying the "good death," at home, surrounded by loved ones was impossible for soldiers during the Civil War. Relatives mourned not only their cherished family members but also the ability to comfort them and ease their transition into the afterlife. The bodies of soldiers killed on the battlefield had to be disposed of quickly, before their bodies decayed and caused a health risk to the living. This may account for the popularity of photographs of war dead during this time. Another contributing factor was that the lead American photographer of the era, Mathew B. Brady (1822–1896), turned his attention away from portraiture and towards documentation of the Civil War. He was the first to mobilize field photography, and he shot some photographs, sent crews out to shoot more, and exhibited and then sold these photographs in his gallery. Without him we might never have had photographs of the Civil War.

Brady and his crew of technicians took his cameras and portable darkrooms out onto the battlefields of the first major battle of the Civil War, called the First Battle of Manassas by the Confederate soldiers and also known as the First Battle of Bull Run by the Union army. This major encounter shocked the North and the South with its 5,000 casualties and made the country realize that the war would not be decided by a single victory, as many had believed.

Today art historians seem to either love or hate Mathew Brady. They love him because he set the style of American photography, but they hate him because he slapped his name on the work of others and gave no credit to the professionals who worked under him. However, there is no denying that by July 1861 and the onset of the War Between the States, he was one of the most successful photographers of his times and had photographed all of the famous Americans of the age. He owned a self-operating studio on Broadway in New York City as well as one later opened on Pennsylvania Avenue in Washington, D.C. The name "Brady" was a "brand" name. While he did not create all of his own photographs, and hired others to do the work, all photographs produced in his establishments bore his name. Instead of working in the darkroom, Brady spent most of his time luring famous people to his establishment and getting them to sit for him. As his business grew, he was careful to hire the best operators and chemists. He also hired women to paint finishing touches on the photographs.

Lacking formal education, scholars believe that Mathew Brady learned the daguerreotype process from Samuel F. Morse after—in his twenties—learning the trade of jewel case manufacturing. Brady sold the cases he made to daguerreotypists who used them as mounts for their images (Cobb, 29). But Brady was an entrepreneur, and he recognized the opportunities the new technology held. Despite his very bad eyesight, he set up a daguerreotype studio of his own in New York City and sought every opportunity to photograph celebrated Americans. Brady also drew the public to his work by opening the Daguerrean Miniature Gallery in 1844, only five years after the technique was given to the world. Seeing the reaction by the public in viewing images of subjects such as President Zachary Taylor and artist John James Audubon, Brady realized that people also wanted to purchase images of these illustrious individuals, so he had lithographic prints of famous people rendered from the daguerreotypes by Francis D'Avignon and sold them in a publication called *Gallery of Illustrious Americans*. Brady also entered his work in fairs and won prestigious prizes (Trachtenberg, 45). In 1851 Brady attended the World's Fair at the Crystal Palace in London, exhibiting 48 daguerreotypes of his Illustrious Americans series. For this exhibition, he was awarded the metal for first place (Trachtenberg, 38).

While in England, Brady met Alexander Gardner (1821–1882) and learned wet-plate technology from him. Gardner, a well-educated chemist and photographer from Scotland, moved to the United States in 1856 to work for Brady. Gardener's brother James soon joined him and was hired as his assistant. The studios began using the Woodward Solar Camera, which enabled the technicians to enlarge photographs to 17" × 21" and make life-sized portraits. These Brady called "Imperial Prints" and sold for $50 to $750 each. The Gardner brothers also experimented with artificial electric light, which made the photographic process easier. Although Thomas Alva Edison invented the first commercially successful incandescent light bulb in 1879, the electric arc lamp was invented by the Cornish scientist, Sir Humphry Davy, in 1802. Several followed, creating various electric lights. From glass plate negatives, Brady's studios could make unlimited amounts of pictures, some of which he exhibited in his own galleries that he named Brady's of Broadway and Brady's National Photographic Art Gallery. Brady cleverly filled these galleries with portraits of illustrious Americans to draw people to his establishments. Once there, he hoped to convince them to have their own pictures taken for $5 to $150 a shot.

In order to get politicians and famous visitors to sit for him, Brady kept himself in the public eye and sought the company of influential people such as P. T. Barnum. He also took images for free or offered reduced rates to favored customers. For example, to get Franklin Pierce, the president of the United States from 1853 to 1857, to sit for a portrait, Brady charged him only $15 instead of the going rate of $50 (Cobb, 62). Brady knew that the president's portrait would draw people to his establishments and some individuals would become his new customers. Brady also got his staff to make copies of the photograph in the more popular *carte de visite* size and put these on sale.

Brady's portrait gallery idea and promotional efforts proved to be a success. On June 21, 1858, the *National Intelligencer* newspaper wrote this about Brady's new studio in Washington, D.C.:

> Those who have not yet seen this charming gallery would do well to while away an hour in scanning this array of beauty, diplomacy, living senatorial and clerical celebrity, besides the speaking, almost startling likenesses of the great ones who have passed from the earth.

Some of the celebrated people on display were President James Buchanan and his cabinet members in a composite photograph; presidents Millard Fillmore and Zachary Taylor; writers Washington Irving and James Fenimore Cooper; politicians including senators Daniel Webster and John C. Calhoun; and House Speaker Henry Clay. Brady's studio is even credited with making the inaugural portrait of Abraham Lincoln. By 1860 Brady was barely 40 years old and was estimated to have negative images of 10,000 famous people (Trachtenburg, 43). *Harper's* magazine wrote of Brady: "Nowhere else can so extensive and in one sense so valuable a collection of art treasures be witnessed. For the past twenty years there has hardly been a celebrity in this country who has not been photographed here" (quoted in Trachtenburg, 42).

But portraiture was looked down upon by artists of the Romantic and Transcendentalist time. They believed that art should serve a higher purpose and that artwork should have an important moral function. In the hierarchy of painting the genre of historically themed work was ranked the highest, with biblical themes coming in a close second (Trachtenberg, 84). Samuel Morse discontinued his photography studio after only two years and returned to painting as his main medium, ever bitter that he had to support himself with portrait work instead of devoting himself entirely to work on history themes (Trachtenberg, 36). Other artists, such as William Page, a friend of Brady's and a painter, used photography as a sketching tool. Because it was too like the person and showed defects, Page did not believe that photography would ever amount to a real art form. Perhaps because of these sentiments and Brady's desire to prove them wrong, Brady jumped at the chance to add historical images to his repertoire. He became fascinated with documenting the Civil War. This was history in the making, and many major battles of the war were within a few hours' ride of his Washington, D.C., studio. Alexander Gardner, who was managing this studio, also took an interest in "photojournalism," and while still keeping his job with Brady became the official photographer for General George B. McClellan, general-in-chief of the Union army from 1861 to 1862. Gardner was given the honorary rank of captain (Cobb, 50). Because of their artistic differences photographing the Civil War, Gardner and Brady broke off their relationship, and Gardner opened his own studio in Washington, D.C., in 1863.

Brady copyrighted the first war views in and around Washington, taken in July 1861. These consisted of images of soldiers of the Twelfth New York Regiment at Camp Anderson. But when the first major battle, called the First Battle of Bull Run, broke out on July 18, 1861, Brady rushed to document it, having received special permission from President Lincoln and his secretary of war, Edwin M. Stanton, to photograph on the war's battlefields.

Brady was not the first, however, to photograph images of war. In 1854 the Englishman Roger Fenton (1819–1869) traveled to Russia to photograph scenes of the Crimean War. Fenton's landscape scene inspired Alfred, Lord Tennyson's poem "Charge of the Light Brigade." But because of the long exposure times needed for the sensitized glass plates, Fenton was only able to capture images of stationary or posed objects and landscape (Daniel). This would be the case for Brady, too.

Brady set out for the battlefield with chemicals and two wagons full of equipment. On his way, he photographed encampments and troops. The Confederate forces were greatly outnumbered. Everyone thought that the battle would be easily decided in favor of the Union and that the war would soon end. Brady spent time shooting peripheral shots, mimicking themes of historical painting. His images show portraits, scenery, and groups of soldiers. He shot images of the Roman Catholic chaplain assigned to the 69th New York State Militia encamped at Fort Corcoran. He also photographed Professor Thaddeus S. C. Lowe and his gas tanks; Lowe attempted to make observations of the Confederate troops from a balloon (Cobb, 51). What was missing was pictorial war correspondence, that is, images of the actual fight; because when the battle broke out, it was much fiercer than Brady or anyone else imagined it would be. Brady's photographic plates needed to be prepared in the portable darkroom and kept wet throughout the entire process. His exposure times were anywhere from 5 to 10 seconds. His large cameras needed to rest on tripods, and his lenses were not designed to capture action. There are reports that during the battle Brady and his wagons got lost in the woods and had to be rescued. Other reports say that Brady sustained another eye injury, further weakening his already poor vision.

Brady returned to the city. He was shaken by his experience but eventually created an album that he named *Incidents of the War*. This album also included a view of the White House with a herd of cattle used to feed the troops pasturing on the lawn. His album was praised by the *New York Times*, which wrote:

> Mr. Brady, the Photographer, has just returned from Washington with the magnificent series of views of scenes, groups, and incidents of the war which he has been making for the last two months.... The public is indebted to Brady of Broadway for numerous excellent views of 'grim-visage' war.... [His photos,] made with arduous and perilous toil will do more than the most elaborate descriptions to perpetuate the scenes of that brief encounter [*New York Times*, August 17, 1861, quoted in Trachtenberg, 71].

Brady wanted more than just portraits and landscapes of this great historical time, but he was no longer eager to observe the fighting himself. He spent the early months of 1862 organizing field units and training his crews. He even had specially designed, horse-drawn darkrooms built. When the Battle of Antietam occurred in September 1862, he sent his best men to document what they found.

Alexander Gardner and his assistant James Gibson arrived at Antietam two days after the fighting. This battle, the first to take place on Union soil, was a bloody one, with almost 20,000 wounded and 3,500 dead, including several generals on both sides. Lee's army withdrew across the Potomac and back into Virginia while the Union burial details were hard at work on their grim task. Brady's crew found dead horses and soldiers still lying where they had fallen when they arrived. Other corpses, now bloated and rotting, had been moved and were set in neat rows awaiting burial (Trachtenberg, 74). Gardener was inspired. This was to be the first time anyone had attempted to capture images such as these—the aftermath of war—and he set to work shooting 95 images of the scene. Along with views of shattered trees and weary soldiers were images of the deceased. In fact, 75 percent of the images shot were of corpses (Frassanito, 27). One shot was of a dead white horse belonging to a Confederate officer. The horse impressed viewers with his peaceful appearance in death—his head gracefully turned to one side, his legs folded neatly beneath him. Brady's team took five photographs from different angles of the dozen or so dead soldiers lying on Hagerstown Pike. They took photographs of the contorted bodies filling what would later be called Bloody Lane and continued to shoot images of the fallen at Miller and Sherrick farms and Dunker Church.

Brady exhibited these photographs in his New York gallery, calling the exhibition "The Dead of Antietam." These images were described as gruesome and shocking, recording the final agonizing moments of the soldiers' lives. They exposed the terrible effects of shells and bullets on human flesh. But the public, at the same time as being horrified, were intrigued. His exhibition was a huge success, attended by what the *New York Times* reviewer called "crowds of people." Customers were also able to buy copies of these photographs to put into their home albums. Photo albums were new in the 1860s, just in time for the Civil War. Everyday people would purchase photos of the war and display them in their albums on coffee tables with the photographs arranged as they wished. Photographs of the dead always sold the best (Trachtenberg, 84). The reviewer continued:

> Of all objects of horror one would think the battlefield should stand preeminent, that it should bear away the palm of repulsiveness. But, on the contrary, there is a terrible fascination about it that draws one near these pictures, and makes him loth to leave them. You will see hushed, reverend groups standing around these weird copies of carnage, bending down to look in the pale faces of the dead, chained by the strange spell that dwells in dead men's eyes [*New York Times,* Oct. 20, 1862].

An article appearing in *Harper's Weekly* said that viewers even brought magnifying glasses with them to the exhibition so they could examine details of the photographs, perhaps searching for their sons, fathers or husbands among the dead.

Artists had previously depicted the death of soldiers in battle. For example, the American painter Benjamin West portrayed "The Death of General Wolfe" a century before, but no one had ever portrayed the grim realities of casualties like this, and the viewing public responded eagerly. Brady's team not only had made individual photographs of dead soldiers they could sell, but also had used stereo cameras used to make stereograms for home viewing in 3D. If they wanted, and could afford them, customers could purchase hand colored photographs that looked even more realistic. Brady's success with the "Dead of Antietam" photographs started a craze, and he realized the entrepreneurial opportunities of continuing this type of work. Half of the major battles of the Civil War were in Virginia and within traveling distance of his Washington, D.C., studio.

For more distant battles, Brady bought photographs and negatives from other photographers without distinguishing them from his own studio's work.

Alexander Gardner saw the same opportunities the photos of the war offered, but he was not happy with the quality of some the images Brady bought. He also grew bitter that he was not being credited for his work. Gardner's photographs were lumped together with all the rest, exhibited and sold with the words "Photographed by Brady" stamped on them even when Gardner used his own equipment. He had the right to feel slighted. After all, it was he who had done the hard work of creating the popular images of Antietam, and he had not received any acknowledgment. To this day Gardner has not received as much credit as he deserved. Gardner left the employment of Mathew Brady. He continued working for the military and photographed the Battle of Fredericksburg. By the spring of 1863, he and his brother were able to open their own studio in Washington, D.C., stealing away some of Brady's most accomplished crew.

Shortly after the establishment of Gardner's studio, on July 1, 1863, the Battle of Gettysburg began. It ended on July 3 with an estimated 50,000 casualties and at least 8,000 dead. The number of soldiers slain on the battlefield in these two days equaled the number of troops lost during the American Revolution, excepting those who died later from their wounds (HistoryNet). Gardner knew that photographs of dead soldiers sold well, but he also became engrossed with the idea that photography could change people's views about war. With Timothy O'Sullivan and James Gibson as his crew, he rushed the 77 miles from Washington, D.C., to the Pennsylvania town. Taking all of his equipment with them, the group probably arrived on the morning of July 5. The crew were not only the first photographers to reach the Gettysburg battlefield but also the only photographers to arrive before the dead had been buried. William Frassanito, a historian who analyzes the photographs of the Civil War, believes that the dead were all buried by July 6. Frassanito also believes that Gardner's main interest at Gettysburg was to photograph the dead, noting that he did not shoot scenery or important parts of the town such as General Lee's headquarters. Of the 60 negatives taken at the site, 75 percent of these were of "bloated corpses, open graves, dead horses, and related details of wholesale carnage" (Frassanito, 27).

The battle had taken place over a 25-square-mile tract of land surrounding the town. The corpses had been lying there for four days, and to add to the deteriorating conditions, it had rained the day before they arrived. During the battle, horses were deliberately shot to cripple the mobility of the enemy. More than fifteen hundred animal carcasses were strewn everywhere. In the hot summer weather, gases generated by the decomposition process bloated the bodies of men and beasts, which were surrounded by or covered in blood. Flies encircled the heads of the dead and crawled on their faces and sightless eyes. The Army of the Potomac buried the soldiers. The task of burying the horses rested with the militia. Anyone caught stealing from the battlefield was given the choice of being arrested or helping with this ghastly task (Frassanito, 150).

The bloating expanded the dead soldiers' middles, popping the buttons of their trousers and shirts. Burial team members tied ropes around the limbs of the dead and dragged them into position at the burial site, often, but not always, close to where they fell. The dragging and the bloating caused many a dead soldier's pants to burst open and then fall down below his hips. Their pockets had been picked clean and turned inside out, and their shoes and their guns were removed to be used by those continuing the fight.

Gardner and his men followed the burial teams as they dug a grave, put a body in and then dug another grave next to it, using the dirt from the second to cover the first.

The Union troops were ordered to bury their own fallen first, so by the time Gardner and his crew reached the site, the remaining bodies were most likely those of Confederate dead. But the colors of uniforms varied greatly depending on where the soldiers came from and what material was available. The resulting black and white prints made it seem that both Union and Confederate soldiers lay side by side together on the bloody battlefields. These men, all Americans but separated by different beliefs, were united in death. The sentimentality captured in these images was very appealing to viewers of the time.

Gardner and O'Sullivan took most of the shots while Gibson was busy in the travelling darkroom developing the fragile glass plates. The men shot 8" × 10" photographs and also stereograms. Sometimes they shot both of the same scene if they found it to be of particularly interest. Close-up shots focused on the dead soldiers, while stereo images were able to capture a little more of the landscape behind. Frassinito summed up the importance of these images: "They were the only men to photograph the battlefield while its dead still lay exposed, revealing, as only a photograph can, the true horrors of Gettysburg. And finally, Gardner's views are the earliest in existence that show the field as it basically looked to the soldiers who fought there during the first three days of July 1863" (Frassinito, 34).

At first Gardner was wary of the putrefied and decomposing corpses, and mostly shot images of the burial team hard at work at their grim task. But as time passed, he, O'Sullivan and Gilbert lost their fear of the dead enough to experiment with staging their shots to create maximum visual impact. To make a better composition, the men placed an artillery shell on the ground next to a body. In another image they laid a rifle across a soldier's leg, close to his dismembered hand. While some critics are horrified that Gardner moved bodies and props around, they must remember that the field of photojournalism

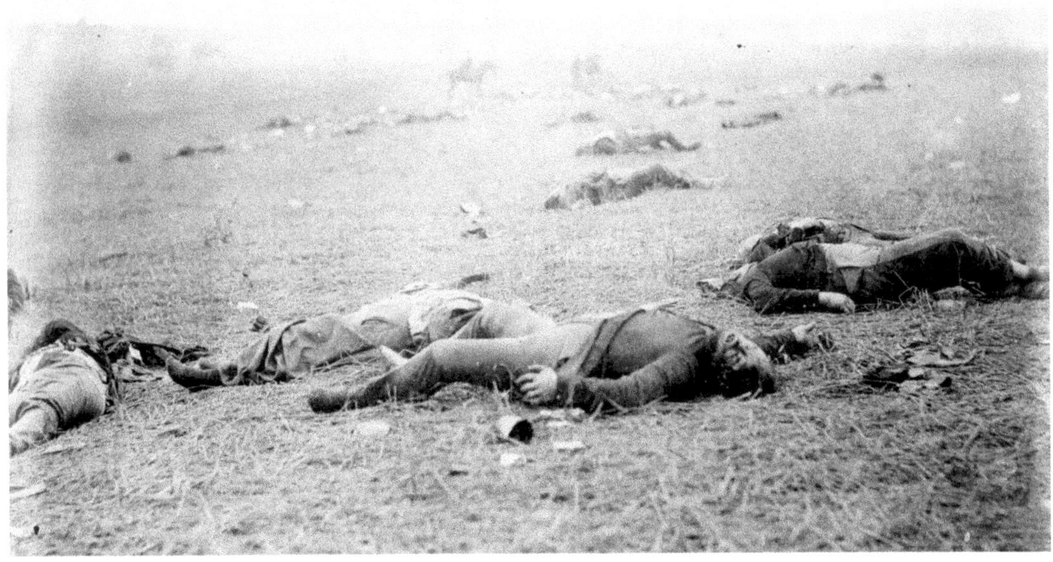

Timothy H. O'Sullivan, *Incidents of the War: A Harvest of Death*[:] *Dead Federal Soldiers on Battlefield at Gettysburg, PA*, in Gardner's *Photographic Sketch Book of the War*, vol. 1, page 36 (Library of Congress, Prints and Photographs Division).

had not yet been invented—these men were inventing it. In addition, the corpses were continuously being shifted around as the soldiers prepared to bury them. Gardner didn't see anything wrong with moving some to get a more powerful shot. Gardner wrote that his team spent nearly an hour to "achieve a sentimental composition" of the first soldier found lying in the field in what would be called Devil's Den. This image, which Gardner entitled "The Home of the Rebel Sharpshooter, Gettysburg," is considered by the Gettysburg National Military Park to be one of the most iconic images made of the war. Frassanito describes the process the team went through to get the shot: "In what must have been a flash of creative excitement, the cameramen chose to improvise. Returning to the position they had just photographed, Gardner's men placed the slain youth's body onto a blanket … and in all likelihood carried him themselves some forty yards up the slope" (Frassanito, 191).

For this same photograph, the cameramen propped a rifle next to the corpse. The fact that it was of a kind that a Sharpshooter would never use didn't matter to these civilians. They also put a knapsack under the soldier's head so the camera could get a better view of the face. Frassanito believes that this corpse was one of the last to be buried, because the crew shot six images of the same soldier.

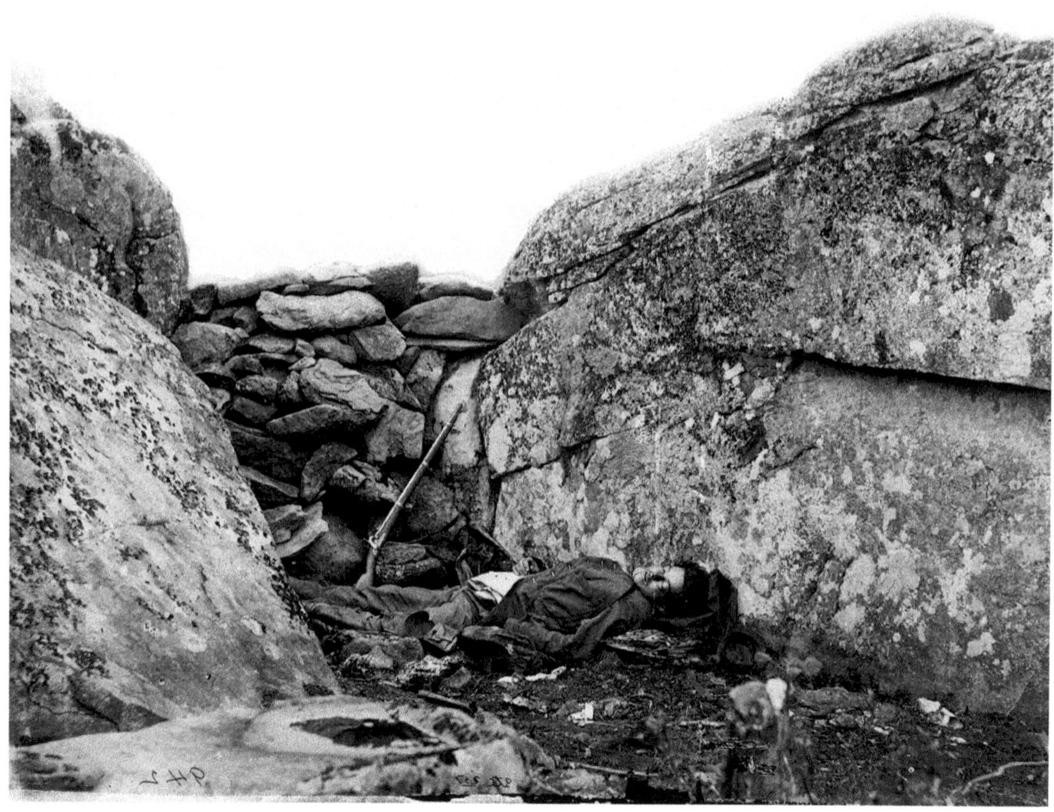

Timothy H. O'Sullivan, *Gettysburg, PA. Dead Confederate Soldier in Devil's Den*, photograph July 1863 (named *Home of the Rebel Sharpshooter, Gettysburg*, by Gardner). Wet collodion negative (Library of Congress, Photographs Division).

Gardner titled another iconic image from this shoot "Incidents of the War: A Harvest of Death, Gettysburg, July 1863." This image was shot by O'Sullivan and printed by Gardner (Gardner's plate number 36—see fig. 23). Scholars have determined that these soldiers died during the second day of battle on the Rose Farm land. The Confederate soldiers had lain the bodies of their comrades out for burial but had to abandon their work when new Union reinforcements came. Gardner maintained that the image illustrated a useful moral by showing the "blank horror of war, in opposition to its pageantry." He continued saying that photographs, in great detail, should be an "aid in preventing such another calamity falling upon the nation" (Trachtenberg, 99).

Gardner and his men were the only ones to photograph the dead of Gettysburg. But Alfred Rudolph Waud (1828–1891), the best sketch artist of his time, drew pictures of the actual battle and remained to draw pictures of the aftermath, coming into contact with Gardner. Waud, born in England, trained at the Government School of Design, now called the Royal College of Art. He immigrated to the United States in 1850 with the intention of continuing his work painting theatrical scenery. In 1860 he was hired as a staff illustrator for the *Demorest's New York Illustrated News*, which sent him to cover the movements of the Army of the Potomac, the Union's army, in the East. Waud did not shy away from depicting the dead or dying in his work. He also drew his scenes as accurately as possible. During the Battle of Gettysburg, he was employed by *Harper's Weekly* magazine. Most of his sketches were turned into woodcuts, reproduced and published in it (Frassanito, 173).

Gettysburg had its own resident photographers, Charles and Isaac Tyson. They had owned and operated the town's Excelsior Gallery and Tyson Brothers' Photography Studio since 1859. Unfortunately, they lacked the portable equipment to take photographs out-of-doors. They did stay open during the first hours of the battle as hordes of Union soldiers rushed to have their photographs taken before they went into the fray. When it appeared that the Rebels would take over the town, the brothers closed up shop and did not return until days after the battle was over. A month after the battle, they began making a series of 18 different views of the area on 8" × 10" plates to cater to the tourist crowd and relic seekers. A year later they produced 100 stereo views of the scenery, but they were not there for the battle or its aftermath (Frassanito, 41).

Neither was Mathew Brady's team. It reached the battlefield on July 6 after the burial detail had completed its work. Brady himself did not arrive in Gettysburg until July 15. Brady and his men took 30 photographs of the scenery where the battles took place. They also shot famous landmarks, including the headquarters of General Robert E. Lee. By then Brady had the advantage of knowing what sites were considered most important, knowledge that Gardner and his team had lacked. Brady's team often posed one of his lone assistants gazing off toward a distant field or looking as if he were contemplating the recent events. The team's panoramic images of scenery and buildings serve as an important record of the area's appearance directly after the battle, but they did not sell well.

The money was with photographs of the dead. That was what the public wanted, and that was what they bought. This caused another photographer, Peter S. Weaver, to attempt to counterfeit scenes of the dead. Weaver attended the dedication ceremony of the Soldier's National Cemetery at Gettysburg in November 1864, where he cajoled some of the soldiers participating in the event to pretend to be corpses in Devil's Den. Weaver made six photographs of the men pretending to have fallen in battle. Regrettably, they lay in theatrical poses, looking too healthy to be real. The fact that there were no leaves on the trees also added to the improbability of the photographs being authentic depictions of the July fight (Frassanito, 185).

In those days, the size of the negative was generally the size of the print. In Gardner's case he used a single-shot 8" × 10" camera and a stereo camera. The stereo slides were the most popular and made the most money for the firm. Each stereo negative was a double image and smaller than the albumen prints. These could be used as *cartes de visite*, the most popular and best-selling item, because they could be put into home albums. Stereo cards, viewed in a stereoscope or a stereo viewer, were pretty much a standard size. A very popular stereoscope was invented by Oliver Wendell Holmes (1809–1894), who purposely did not patent it so that it could be easily afforded by all. His son, Oliver Wendell Holmes, Jr., became a famous member of the Supreme Court of the United States. In the late 1860s there were approximately 6,000 photography studios in the United States. Photographers not only made original pictures but also bought images from other photo artists that they assembled into albums or stereo sets and sold in their shops. Stereo viewers were popular entertainment in the era before electricity and the phonograph. Every home had at least one, and every family needed stereograms to view. Images of the dead were always included in sets of the Civil War for both albums and stereo viewers.

Gardner sold his photos in mail order catalogs. Prices for his prints ranged from 50¢ to $1.50 each. In 1865 Gardner produced his own album, called *Gardner's Photographic Sketch Book of the War*. The same year, George P. Barnard, a photographer from Connecticut, produced *Photographic Views of Sherman's Campaign*. Lacking an inexpensive way to duplicate photographs, each of Gardner's albums contained 50 original photographs and sold for $150, which translates to $2,000 today. Gardner continued his photography career, shooting portraits of President Lincoln and then, sadly, of the president's funeral. Gardner was also the only photographer allowed to be present at the hanging of Lincoln's convicted assassins. You can still purchase a poster of this photograph for $14.99. At the time, these photographs were sold to the public and were also made into engravings to be published in national magazines. For a while, Gardner continued with photography. He was hired to make portraits of Native Americans who came to Washington to sign treaties, and he made stereograms of proposed railroad routes. In 1871 he gave up photography and helped found an insurance company. Gardner died in Washington, D.C., in 1882.

In 1865 Mathew Brady began selling published sets of prints entitled *Brady's Photographic Views of the War*. He followed this with *Brady's Album Catalogue* and *Incidents of the War*. His photographs were also used to make artists' lithographs, engravings or woodcuts and published in periodicals. In 1869 Brady published his catalog of war photographs entitled *National Photographic Collection of War Views and Portraits of Representative Men*. This included 700 scenes of battle and 2,500 portraits. But Gardner's departure seriously hurt Brady's business. Gardner took some of Brady's best photographers with him, including Timothy O'Sullivan. Brady could not find a good replacement to manage his Washington studio, and his business fell off. Brady reduced the price of his war albums from $75 to $50 but they still did not sell well. The Washington gallery could not pay its bills. He was sued by creditors and had to declare bankruptcy.

He was able to buy back his gallery, but for $7,000 he could only afford half the space. When Boss Tweed of Tammany Hall was arrested in 1872, Brady had no one in

New York to protect him from his creditors (Cobb, 62). Brady went into bankruptcy and he and his wife moved his equipment to his Washington, D.C., gallery before the New York marshals could seize it. Believing that his photographs of the Civil War were important, Brady petitioned Congress to buy them, haunting the halls of the Capitol Building. To stave off further creditors, he assured them that when Congress purchased his Civil War photos all would be paid.

President Grant's secretary of war, William W. Belknap, purchased some negatives from Brady for a mere $2,500. But by then, the public had lost interest in the war and the death it had brought. The Library of the War Department assessed the value of Brady's photographs, and in March of 1875 Congress appropriated a lump sum of $25,000. This was in exchange for the clear title to all of Brady's war scenes. This meant that 5,712 wet plate collodion negatives of various sizes were given to the government and now reside in the National Archives. Unfortunately, this price was far less than the estimated $100,000 or more Brady spent to produce and acquire the work, and he was in dire financial straits (Cobb, 64). By 1880 Brady's Washington studio was run down. He and his wife lived in the gallery until one of his employees sued him for non-payment, and that was the final straw. In 1881 Brady's National Photographic Art Gallery closed forever, although Brady continued working in various photography shops for the next fifteen years.

In the late 1880s Stephen Crane (1871–1900), author of the classic novel *The Red Badge of Courage,* used Brady's images of the war for his opus *Battles and Leaders of the Civil War.* This book was based on Cranes' popular series of articles for *Century Magazine,* which appeared from 1884 to 1887. But the photographs were no longer popular with the public, and Crane was criticized for using them because they were too realistic (Trachtenberg, 77). Brady died in a charity hospital in New York City in 1896, believing still in the importance of his Civil War work.

Spirit Photography

New York City was also the site for the 1869 trial of another photographer, William H. Mumler (1832–1884). Mumler appeared before a judge in that city charged with fraud for capturing images of what he said were spirits of the deceased in photographic portraits. To some, these photographs were powerful proof of the existence of immortal souls. The public believed that photographs depicted reality and that photography was an infallible process. It didn't lie, so it followed that if someone was able to take a photograph, or several photographs, of the spirits of the dead, this was scientific proof that these spirits existed. But to others, such as Elbridge T. Gerry, the lead prosecutor in the case, these spirit photographs only affirmed ideas of the spiritualist movement, which he believed was a revival of pantheism and blasphemy. These photographs threatened Christianity and its beliefs in original sin, resurrection and final judgment. To Counselor Gerry, believing that resurrection occurred at the moment of death even denied the divinity of Jesus Christ.

The counselor for the defense, John D. Townsend, likened Mumler's spirit photography technique to the invention of the telegraph, developed only 25 years earlier. Townsend answered the question of why ghosts didn't appear in every photograph, only in Mumler's, by saying that electronic communication between people hundreds of miles apart was only possible for some people—those who understood Morse Code. So it followed that Mumler

HARPER'S WEEKLY.
A JOURNAL OF CIVILIZATION.

Vol. XIII.—No. 645.]   NEW YORK, SATURDAY, MAY 8, 1869.   [SINGLE COPIES, TEN CENTS.
[$4.00 FOR YEAR IN ADVANCE.

SPIRITUAL PHOTOGRAPHY.

The case of the people against William H. Mumler, of 630 Broadway, is one so remarkable and without precedent in the annals of criminal jurisprudence that we devote this page to illustrations bearing upon it. The charge against Mr. Mumler is that, by means of what he terms spiritual photographs, he has swindled many credulous persons, leading them to believe it possible to photograph the immaterial forms of their departed friends.

The case has excited the profoundest interest, and, strange as it may seem, there are thousands of people who believe that its development will justify the claims made by the spiritual photographer. We shall not attempt to give an expression to our own opinions, but simply to follow the developments of the case through the testimony offered during the first few days of the trial.

It is through the instrumentality of Marshal Joseph H. Tooker that the case has been brought before the courts. He deposes that he was ordered by Mayor Hall to investigate the case, which he did by assuming a false name, and by getting his photograph taken by Mr. Mumler. After the taking of the picture the negative was shown him, with a dim, indistinct outline of a ghostly face staring out of one corner; and he was told that the picture represented the spirit of his father-in-law. He, however, failed to recognize the worthy old gentleman, and emphatically declared that the picture neither represented his father-in-law, nor any of his relations, nor yet any person whom he had ever seen or known. With this evidence the prosecution rested.

The counsel for the defense have brought forward a number of witnesses who testify to the genuineness of spiritual photographs taken for them by Mr. Mumler. William P. Sneed, a photographer, of Poughkeepsie, testifies that Mumler succeeded in producing spiritual photographs at his gallery in Poughkeepsie, and he was unable to discover how it was done. Judge Edmonds, one of the most distinguished advocates of Spiritualism, deposed that he had two photographs taken by Mumler; the spirit form in one of them he thought he could recognize, but not the one in the other. He said: "I believe that the camera can take a photograph of a spirit, and I believe also that spirits have materiality —not that gross materiality that mortals possess, but still they are material enough to be visible to the human eye, for I have seen them; only a few days since I was in a court in Brooklyn when a suit against a life assurance company for the amount claimed to be due on a certain policy was being heard. Looking toward that part of the court-room occupied by the jury, I saw the spirit of the man whose death was the basis of the suit. The spirit told me the circumstances connected with the death; said that the suit was groundless, that the claimant was not entitled to recover from the company, and said that he (the man whose spirit was speaking) had committed suicide under certain circumstances; I drew a diagram of the place at which his death occurred, and on showing it to the counsel, was told that it was exact in every particular."

A large number of witnesses deposed that they recognized the forms of departed friends (in some cases of those long dead) in the photographs taken for them by Mumler. The most striking case was that of a gentleman of Wall Street, whose deceased wife's features both he and his friends distinctly recognized in a photograph taken for him in this way.

If there is a trick in Mr. Mumler's process it has certainly not been detected as yet. To all appearances spiritual photography rests just where the rappings and table-turnings have rested for some years. Those who believe in it at all will respect no opposing arguments, and disbelievers will reject every favorable hypothesis or explanation. Mr. Mumler has certainly been very fortunate. He has been believed in, in the first place, by a large number of people. He has obtained, again, a good price for his photographs; for who could expect spirits to be called "from the vasty deep" for less than ten dollars per head? And, finally, he has been prosecuted, and thus extensively advertised. Beyond this, the trial, like all legal prosecutions of this nature, will amount to nothing.

In addition to our illustrations of specimens of Mr. Mumler's spirit photographs, we give also representations of similar photographs taken by Mr. Rockwood of this city. The latter were taken by natural means, but not so as to escape detection as to the trick resorted to to secure the result. Mr. Mumler has certainly the advantage of a longer experience in the business.

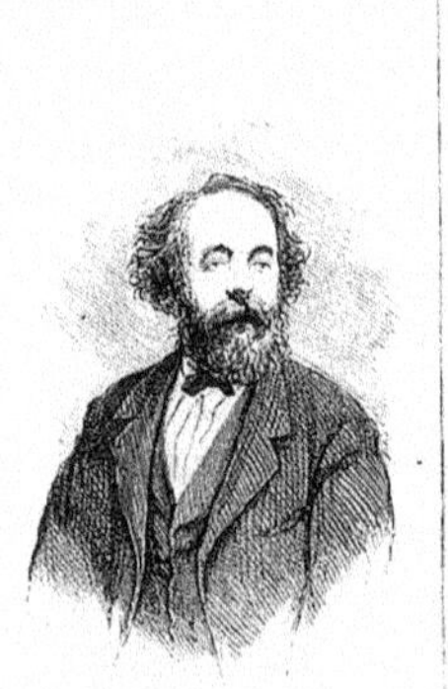

W. H. MUMLER.

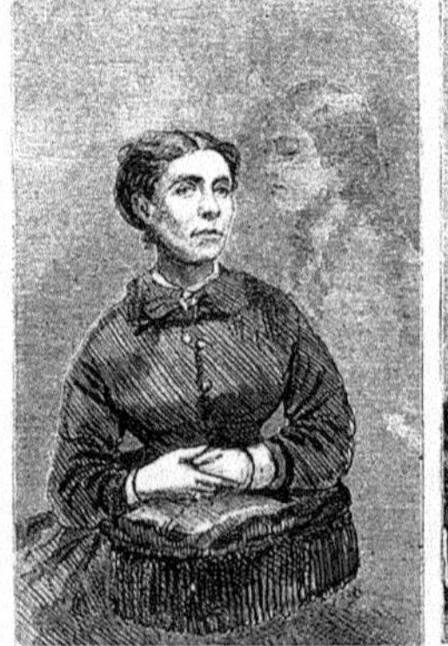

MRS. W. H. MUMLER.—BY MUMLER.

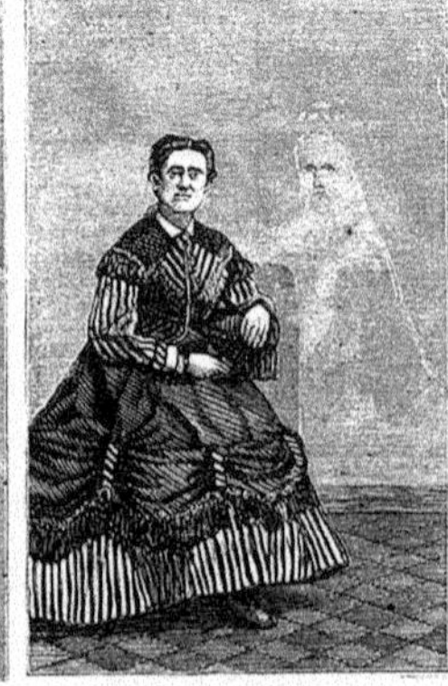

SPIRIT PHOTOGRAPH BY MUMLER.

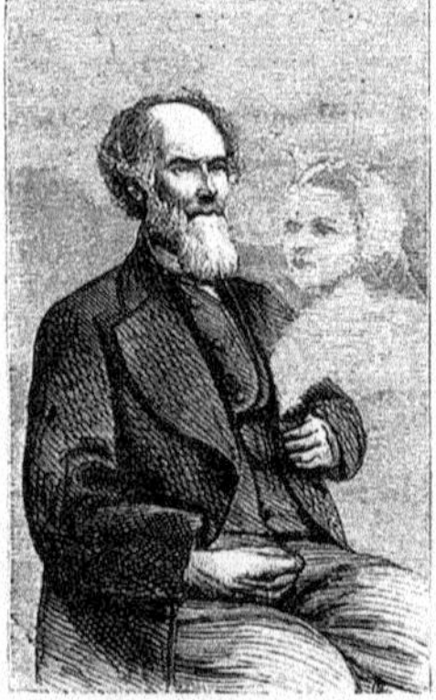

SPIRIT PHOTOGRAPH BY MUMLER.

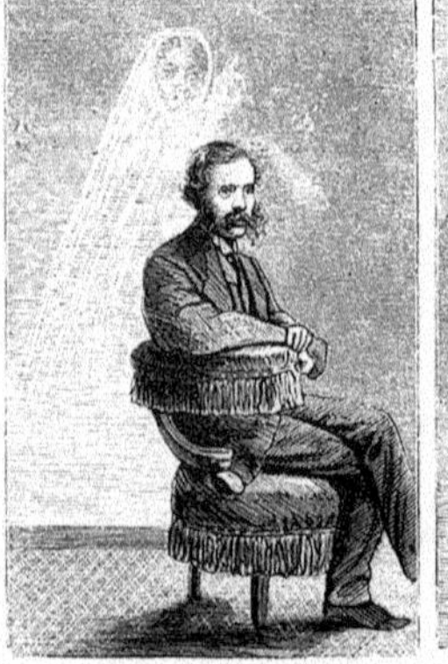

SPIRIT PHOTOGRAPH BY MUMLER.

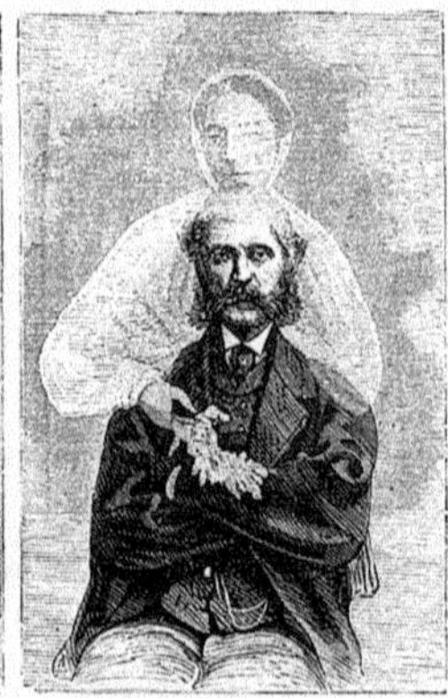

SPIRIT PHOTOGRAPH BY MUMLER.

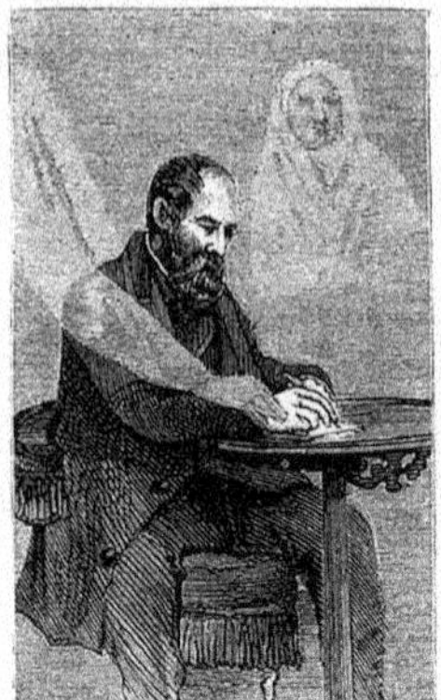

SPIRIT PHOTOGRAPH BY MUMLER.

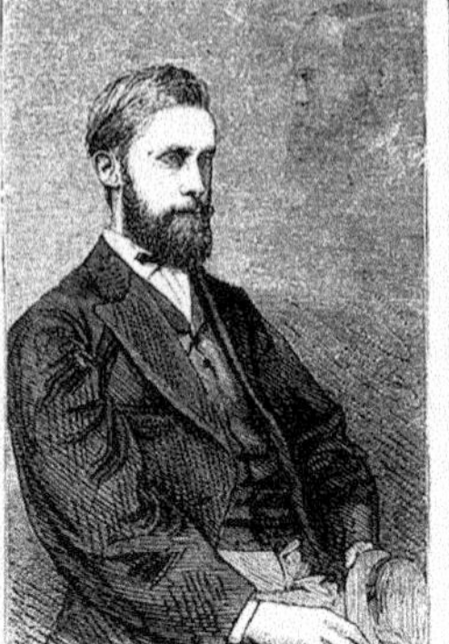

P. V. HICKEY.—BY ROCKWOOD.

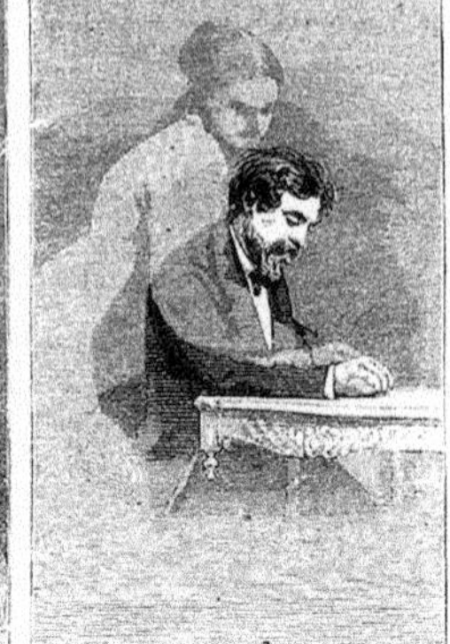

C. B. BOYLE.—BY ROCKWOOD.

SPIRITUAL PHOTOGRAPHY.—[Specimens Furnished by Mumler and Rockwood.]

William H. Mumler, cover for *Harper's Weekly*, May 6, 1865 (author's collection).

had a special relationship to spirits that other photographers lacked. The *New York Times* had mixed opinions on the subject. Reporting on the trial, one headline read, "A Stupendous Fraud—Pretended Spiritualistic Portraits of Deceased." Another article said that these spirit photographs demonstrated "untold powers of the yet-to-be-known" (Kaplan, 19). For many people, spirit photographs were a "miraculous message from the afterlife" (Becker). They offered hope and proof that the spirit of a loved one survived after death. And hope was desperately needed at this time.

Communication technology was advancing so rapidly in the middle of the nineteenth century that the idea that spirits could communicate with the living through photographs seemed plausible. The telegraph was an amazing but little-understood invention that changed the course of history, allowing Union forces to win the Civil War in part because of its invention and President Lincoln's ability to embrace this new technology. In ancient times the leader of a nation was the leader of the nation's army. If these kings and queens didn't fight, they at least had to be present at important battles. Examples of this are England's King Henry V, who led his forces in Agincourt in 1415, and Queen Elizabeth I, who gave a rousing speech to her troops at Tilbury in 1588. This was also seen in the early 19th century with Napoleon Bonaparte. Not only did Napoleon serve as emperor of much of Europe; he also led his troops in battles from 1804 to 1815. If a leader did not go to battle, he or she waited hours or days for couriers riding horseback to deliver news of the course of events. If a reply were needed, there would be the lag time necessary for the couriers to repeat their journey with a response. Tom Wheeler, the author of *Mr. Lincoln's T-Mails: The Untold Story of How Abraham Lincoln Used the Telegraph to Win the Civil War*, explains that President Lincoln was able to keep a close watch over his armies using communication by telegraph. Lincoln not only could gather information but could also disseminate information to his generals in the field over the wire. He could encourage his troops when necessary, and if there were decisions to be made, he could draw on the expertise of advisors close at hand and send word back to the field immediately. This made him able to participate in military operations more than any other American president had previously been able to do. The instant communication the telegraph afforded President Lincoln allowed him to truly be the commander-in-chief of the armed forces of his country. But the telegraph would not have been possible without the discovery of electricity.

The ancient Egyptians and Greeks wrote that they observed static electricity. They knew that rubbing amber, the gemstone made from fossilized tree resin, with fur or wool created sparks and became magnetic. But it wasn't until the 1640s that the English scientist Sir Thomas Browne (1605–1682) named the phenomena *"Electricus,"* from the Greek and Latin words for amber. In 1745 Dutchman Pieter van Musschenbroek of Leiden (1692–1761) invented a primitive battery called the Leyden jar. Soon after, the American statesman and inventor Benjamin Franklin (1705–1790) experimented with it, running wires from a Leyden jar across the Schuylkill River to simultaneously ignite alcohol flares on either bank. Benjamin Franklin named the Leyden jar a "battery" because the electrostatic charge it produced reminded him of a "battery" of cannons. Franklin also conducted experiments proving that lightening was electricity.

In 1800 Alessandro Volta (1746–1827), from Italy, discovered how to create a continuous source of electrical charge. Named the "voltaic pile," this device producing a direct current of electricity demonstrated to the world the possibilities of this energy. Sixteen years later, Englishman Francis Ronalds (1788–1873) came up with the idea of using electricity as a communication device, building the first working electrostatic telegraph in his backyard. Unfortunately, the wires carrying the electric current were insulated with glass, and his creation was rejected by the British Admiralty as too impractical to use. Ronalds didn't publish his *Descriptions of an Electrical Telegraph* until 1823. Soon afterwards, several other scientists began tweaking his invention. Their efforts made telegraphy more and more practical, and by the end of the 1830s telegraph poles and wires accompanied European railroad lines. The city of Munich was even wired up in 1835. In the United States, the scientist David Alter (1807–1881) invented the first American telegraph, but he did not advertise his idea, so very few people knew of it. It was left to Samuel Morse, mentioned previously for his contribution to photography, to develop and patent an electric telegraph system in 1837. Morse also invented the Morse Code, a binary method to communicate letters. This was a breakthrough in communication. The code allowed the transmission of at least fifteen words a minute, making the system practical to use for almost instantaneous communication.

At the onset of the Civil War, the Confederate army destroyed railroad tracks and cut telegraph wires, but Andrew Carnegie (1835–1919), a young railroad supervisor, was drafted into the Union army to make repairs on both. As a teenager, Carnegie worked as a telegraph messenger boy and was one of the rare individuals who could decipher Morse Code just by listening to it. This knowledge of telegraphy helped him become the personal assistant to Thomas Scott, the superintendent of the Pennsylvania Railroad. Scott was a very influential acquaintance of the young man. He helped get Carnegie this promotion and helped him gain financial success.

Electricity made the telegram possible, and while to many in the early to mid–1800s, electricity was a magical thing used by clever entertainers to produce amusing parlor tricks, they had heard of Volta's experiments proving that electrical energy made certain wires glow. Although it wasn't until the 1870s that electric light bulbs were patented, and it wasn't until the 1880s that Thomas A. Edison (1847–1931) developed the first system to generate electricity for home use, people were still conscious that something invisible could travel through wires, making auditory and visual effects. It is not difficult to understand how many people, especially those in grief over the loss of a loved one, drew the conclusion that the "animal energy" that Luigi Galvani and Franz Mesmer proved we possessed was separate from our human flesh, and that this energy existed after the death of an individual in the form of a spirit or a soul. It seemed only logical that this force could be captured in a photograph.

Through the spiritualist movement, and mediums such as Kate and Maggie Fox, spirits of the dead were very real to many people of the time, and communication with them seemed possible. Spiritualism was at its height of popularity from the 1840s to the 1920s, when so much death surrounded people that the belief in the immortality of the soul and communication with spirits was a great comfort, especially for grieving parents of innocent children. According to spiritualist ideas, death gives everyone a second chance to live. The belief was also a comfort to relatives of the hundreds of thousands of soldiers who did not die the "good death" during the Civil War, and whose bones lay hundreds or thousands of miles away in the cold, hard earth. Belief that spirits of the dead could communicate with the living allowed people to de-emphasize the mortal remains of their loved ones in favor of thoughts of their eternal spiritual energy.

Spiritualism was not a fringe cult. At the peak of the religion's popularity, Spiritualism claimed eleven million followers, and eight million of these were American, totaling ⅕ of the country's population. The religion also spread to several different countries. Even today there are Spiritualist churches and adherents to the belief in spirit communication. What's more, Spiritualists' ideas became incorporated into current religious creeds and are embraced by many without their knowing it. These ideas are the belief that everyone has spirit energy that continues after we die, and the belief that when our spirit leaves our body it travels to a spiritual existence that is superior to our earthly one. To spiritualists, our fate in the afterlife does not depend on our behavior on earth. Most souls will go to a "better place," a place they called the "Summerland"—the heaven we think of today, where we will be reunited with loved ones and continue to learn and grow.

As early as 1848, four years after the invention of Morse Code, Katie and Maggie Fox summoned spirits in front of audiences that heard them respond to questions with clicking or rapping noises very similar to the clicks of a telegraph, except that these messages came from the "great beyond." Soon, other people discovered that they also had the ability to act as mediums and communicate with the spirits of the dead. The spirits not only answered questions with rapping noises; they also were able to summon enough energy to perform feats such as moving furniture around, blowing out candles, and making occasional brief appearances.

Spirits departed earth for the Summerland or heaven, but might not some of them have the energy to return and watch over those they left behind? In order to record a photograph, one needs energy. The energy from light acts invisibly on chemicals and glass to create the image. Following this line of thought, could not this bioelectric or animal energy, turned into spirit at our death, act as light and record its image in a photograph? This is exactly what occurred when William H. Mumler (1832–1884) took a photograph of himself in 1861.

Mumler did not start his career as a photographer but worked as the principal engraver for Bigelow Brothers and Kennard Jewelers, the leading jewelers in Boston, where he was well respected by the jewelers who entrusted him with their precious creations. When Mumler was approximately 30 years old, he went to Helen F. Stuart's photography saloon at 258 Washington St. in Boston to learn the process of photography from a friend. Jewelers had been creating cases for daguerreotypes for over decade, so his interest in the new process was not unusual. Mumler knew Ms. Stuart because she also worked in the jewelry industry, making mourning jewelry from the hair of the deceased. In the studio, Mumler took a picture of himself. He focused the camera on a chair and then ran over to sit and pose. When he and his friend developed his portrait, he noticed that it contained a blurred image beside him that resembled the form of a person. Mumler thought that he had not cleaned the glass plate well enough and took another shot, being more careful. But this time the blurred image appeared even clearer. To his surprise, it resembled his cousin who had passed away twelve years before (Pearsall, 120). Mumler had known about spiritualism but did not believe in it at the time. However, he showed his photo to a Dr. H. F. Gardner, a physician from Harvard, who believed and told him it was the real deal. Gardner wrote an article about Mumler and his spirit image that appeared in the *Herald of Progress*, a journal published by Andrew Jackson Davis, the well-known Spiritualist. The article was republished in Boston's *Banner of Light*. Davis jumped to accept the legitimacy of spirit photography because it was visual proof of spiritualist ideas. Davis saw photography as a new science that would verify the existence of the soul after death. He wrote in his work *Death and the After-Life*: "A gentleman who is an expert in science says that he can demonstrate that the photographic instrument can photograph invisible substances. … Art has made the nearest approach to painting unsubstantial shadows, so that the human eye can, with admiring satisfaction, look upon them" (quoted in Kaplan, 8). The article, widely read in Boston, contained Mumler's address, and people flocked to his residence to see the photo. Soon, several individuals urged him to take their portraits, too. More often than not, the phenomenon repeated itself, and the spirit of an assumed deceased person appeared. Mumler took a photograph of Dr. Gardner in 1862 that showed him surrounded by his deceased children. This picture particularly impressed the public because Gardner was a physician and an educated man.

Mumler continued his engraving work, taking off only two hours a day to make photographic portraits that often contained spirit images. Mumler became a Spiritualist and married a woman who claimed to be a medium. As he continued to work, he believed more and more that he had the special talent of being able to photograph spirits. He also thought that his wife as a medium had the ability to call spirits for him to photograph with her magnetic abilities. Several patrons swore that they had overseen Mumler's camera and darkroom techniques and had made certain that he had not done anything deceitful with his camera or in the processing phase. Still the ghost images appeared on his prints. Mumler's photographs revealed not only the spirits of dead relatives, but also spirits of famous people. Mumler likened his spirit photographs to passing a current of electricity through a vacuum tube, an experiment made by the English engineer Prof. C. F. Varley of London: "The light was so feeble that it could not be seen, and the operators doubted if the current were passing. But at the same time photography was at work, and in thirty minutes a very good picture was produced of what had taken place" (quoted in Kaplan, 136).

Mumler used this example to explain that phenomena invisible to the human eye can be seen and recorded by the photographic lens. He also cited ultra-violet rays and electricity. He asked:

> What is electricity? [It is a] force that is silent and invisible as it travels over the wire and performs its work. The medium in electricity is the vacuum tube. When connected to a battery we can see electricity as light…. Mediums stand in the same relation to spirits as vacuum tubes do to electricity: they supply the necessary elements by which spirits are enabled to be seen; whether those elements be aura, magnetism, or anything else [quoted in Kaplan, 136].

Even the editor of the *British Journal of Photography* weighed in by likening spirit photographs to florescence: "Hence the photographing of an invisible image, whether that image be of a spirit or a lump of matter, is not scientifically impossible. If it reflect only the florescent or ultra-violet rays of the spectrum, it will be easily photographed, although it will be quite invisible even to the sharpest eyes" ("Editor of the 'British Journal,'" 421).

But not everyone appreciated Mumler's spirit photographs or the ideas of spiritualism, and Mumler was denounced in the Boston newspapers. Even Dr. Gardner denounced him, writing in 1863 that while he believed that Mumler was able to produce real spirit photographs, in two instances there was "evidence of deception" (Kaplan, 58). Mumler's engraving business was ruined, and he and his family were forced to leave town. He moved to New York City and took up spirit photography as his only career. He advertised spirit photos for sale in publications such as *The Religio-Philosophical Journal*. But his most successful strategy for getting customers was to print up pamphlets and place them on chairs of Spiritualists meetings before the public was admitted.

A reporter from the *New York Sun* published an article on Mumler that drew so many new customers that Mumler was able to purchase his own studio. He attracted famous and influential clients and even created a portrait of Mary Todd Lincoln with the spirit of her husband, the deceased President Lincoln, behind her.

Even P. T. Barnum sat for a spirit picture. In his book *Humbugs of the World*, he described what he found in Mumler's studio:

> Mothers came to the room of the artist, and gratefully retired with ghostly representations of departed little ones. Widows came to purchase the shades of their departed husbands. Husbands visited the photographer and procured spectral pictures of their dead wives. Parents wanted phantom-portraits of their deceased children … [All those who] sought to look on those pictures were satisfied with what had been shown them, and, by conversation on the subject, increased the number of visitors. [Barnum, 79–80].

Barnum believed that Mumler practiced some kind of "humbug," but he could not prove it. He did recall that the wife of a statesman had a photograph taken at Mumler's establishment showing the ghost of her newly departed brother. According to Barnum's account, the woman was delighted with the photo but even more delighted when it turned out that her brother was still alive. Barnum noted that even this mishap didn't shake her faith in spirit photography. Rather than not believe, she chose to accept that a demon assumed her brother's spirit form to fool her (Barnum, 84). Barnum was charged the exorbitant fee of $5.00 per

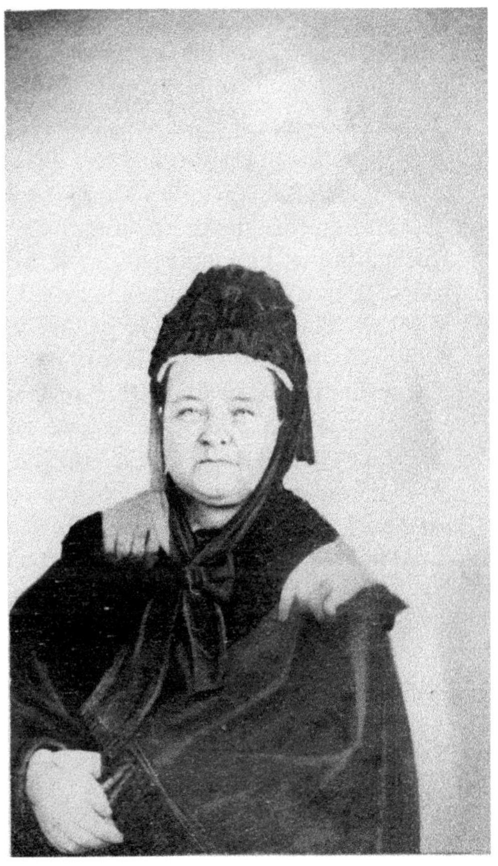

William H. Mumler, photograph of Mary Lincoln with the spirit of Abraham Lincoln (from the Lincoln Financial Collection, courtesy Allen Public Library and Indiana State Museum).

photograph but wrote that in time Mumler's fame spread so among the spiritualist crowd that he had to raise his fee to $10 a shot so he would not be overwhelmed with business.

The spiritualists were delighted with spirit photographs. Mumler's pictures not only proved the immortality of the human soul but also showed what life after death was like, refuting the harsh beliefs of conventional Christianity. Mumler's photographs showed that spirits of the dead kindly watched over the living. In a spirit photograph an unfelt arm might be seen draped across one's shoulders, proving that the dead were with us and could still feel love. The photographer had no control over which spirit would appear, meaning that the dead had autonomy and retained their own free will. They retained the same physical appearance they had in life, too. The ghosts were dressed in the latest fashions and were all well coifed. Some wore jewelry, and some carried wreaths of flowers. Journalist W. T. Stead's spirit even stood near a potted plant. To Jen Cadwallader, writing in *Modern Language Studies*, this conveyed that

> [The spirit world is a] perfected, beautified version of the world we live in. Except for the absence of sin, death, and defect, the next world is recognizably our own, with landscapes, towns, homes,

> people. It is the world as one would wish it to be. The spirit photograph seems to uphold this vision of perfection…. Love and compassion appear to be the only motivation behind the spirits' visits, suggesting that all "rougher" emotions have been transcended [Cadwallader, 18].

Mumler's images of spirit repudiated the idea of suffering of the soul and affirmed that the afterlife is one of immortality and blissfulness, with the soul free of temptation and sin.

In 1869, six years after Mumler established his photographic business in New York, P. F. Hickey, the science editor of the *World* newspaper, complained to the mayor of New York City that he suspected deceit. Hickey was a member of the American Institute's Photographic Society, and he believed that Mumler was making such a mockery of photography that no one would believe its veracity and reliability. An undercover officer, Joseph Tooker, was sent to investigate. Tooker sat for his portrait, saying that he wanted the spirit of his deceased father-in-law in it as well. Mumler produced the portrait and on it was an indistinct blur. Tooker said that Mumler told him that if he looked at the blur long enough it would resemble the face of a relative. Mumler then charged the officer $10 for 12 photographs. The officer arrested Mumler on two felony charges and one misdemeanor. Mumler could not make bail. He was sent to jail to await a preliminary examination before a judge who would determine if the case should go to a grand jury.

Prior to his arrest, Mumler's spirit photographs were first written about in Spiritualist magazines, then in photographic journals. But news of his trial was reported in New York City newspapers and picked up by the national press such as *Harper's Weekly* magazine and *Frank Leslies's Illustrated Journal*. Spirit photography became a topic for the tabloid press. The trial came to represent a showdown of scientific logic versus Spiritualist beliefs, and several of the most distinguished Spiritualists, including Andrew Jackson Davis, were present in the audience during the hearing.

The trial lasted seven days. The prosecution called in several former customers of Mumler as witnesses, but none of them were dissatisfied with their pictures. He also called in experts who explained how a photographer could create deceitful spirit photos. Members of the American Institute made double exposures to demonstrate how these spirit photographs could be made, but no one was able to swear that these were methods Mumler used. Witnesses also pointed out that the same "spirit" appeared in a photograph Mumler made in Boston and a photograph made in New York, and that the ghost actually looked a lot like a person who was very much alive.

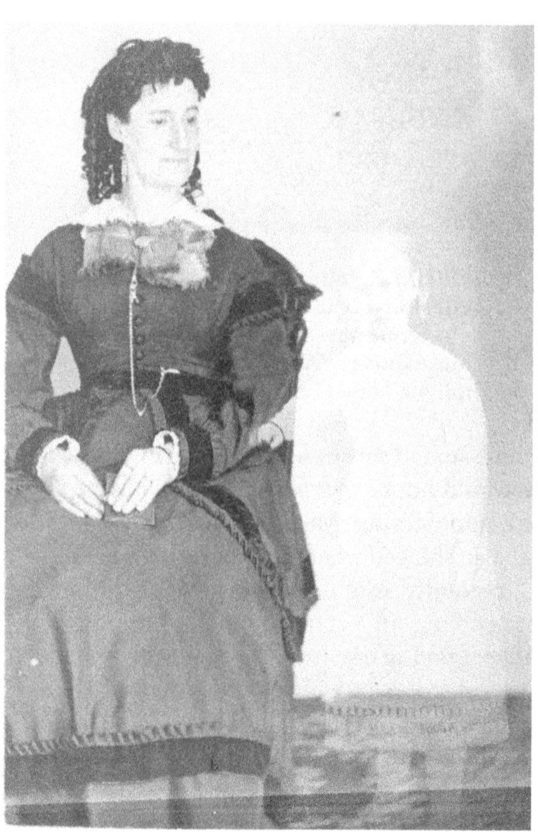

Mrs. Tinkham, 1862–1875, albumen silver print (digital image courtesy Getty's Open Content Program).

Mumler spoke in his own defense, stating that he was a spiritual medium who produced spirit likenesses. He argued that he was not an artist and in fact was a poor photographer. So poor, in fact, that he did not know how to do the photographic tricks mentioned by the prosecution. He pointed out that magnetism was a force that could not be seen, but existed. He claimed that his wife, a medium, had "magnetic" abilities that made spirits appear, introducing the idea that the camera might be able to record energy the human eye could not see. He also stated his belief that he was an instrument in the hands of those who dwelled in the "invisible world" (Kaplan, 241). One of his witnesses, William P. Slee, a photographer from Poughkeepsie, had worked with Mumler for several days developing photographs. Slee testified that he could not discover Mumler using any trickery to produce his work.

The judge, Joseph Dowling, acquitted Mumler, saying that the prosecution failed to make its complaint by not being able to figure out and definitively show how Mumler produced his work. But the judge added, "However I may be morally convinced that there may have been trick and deception practiced by the prisoner" (Kaplan, 27).

The judgment was a victory for Spiritualism, but it was a bitter victory for Mumler himself. The defense cost him $3,000, more than $50,000 in today's currency and a huge sum at the time (Becker). While in jail, his gallery and his studio in New York City had been rented out from under him, and he had nowhere to work. He tried to sell his work in gallery shows but was not able to make enough money to remain in New York City. He moved back to Boston where he still owned a house, where he lived quietly until he died in 1884. Shortly before his death Mumler destroyed his negatives; however, his photographs are on still on display in museum around the country. Modern photographers have studied these and can still not figure out how some of them were made.

Mumler was not the only photographer claiming to be an instrument of otherworldly forces. In England, Frederick Hudson (1812–1889) shot photographs of Mr. Samuel Guppy in 1872 while his wife, Agnes Nichol Guppy, a famous medium, sat in a nearby walk-in cabinet, summoning the spirit that

Mumler Studio logo, from the backside of the Mary Todd Lincoln Mumler photograph (from the Lincoln Financial Collection, courtesy Allen Public Library and Indiana State Museum).

appeared in the print. When news of this photograph got out into the public, Hudson was inundated with other spiritualists wanting spirit photographs of their own (Pearsall, 120). Admitting to wanting to make his customers happy, Hudson was caught several times retouching his photographs. He even dressed up as a ghost to pose in them himself. But when investigated by the respected photographer James Beattie, no trickery of any kind was to be found. Mr. Thomas Slater, an established optician and amateur photographer, brought his own equipment to Mr. Hudson's studio. This equipment included items such as a new camera and new glass for the plates to guarantee that no trickery was performed. The photograph Slater and Hudson produced contained a spirit on it. Slater continued to make spirit photographs of deceased individuals in his own house. One was of a mysterious spirit of a woman dressed in black and white flowing robes. Slater did not recognize her, but others in his family saw that it was the image of his own mother. Alfred R. Wallace writes in his work *Miracles and Modern Spiritualism*: "The fact that any figures, so clear and unmistakably human in appearance as this, should appear on plates taken in his own private studio by an experienced optician and amateur photographer, who makes all his apparatus himself, and with no one present but the members of his own family, is the real marvel" (Wallace, 199).

Edouard I. Buguet (1840–1901) was not as lucky as Hudson. A French photographer, Buguet had a considerable reputation in France for producing spirit photographs of famous individuals and their departed loved ones. In June 1874 Buguet even opened a studio in London on Baker Street, but soon afterwards he was arrested for fraud by the French government. To the dismay of those in the spiritualist movement, Buguet pled guilty. Buguet confessed that his spirit photographs were created with double exposures. He was also found to use cardboard cutout figures and other paraphernalia to depict the deceased (Becker). His supporters found his confession difficult to believe. They declared Buguet innocent and feared that he had been bribed or terrorized by the Catholic Church to confess his guilt. Was this because the images looked so much like the deceased that they could not have been faked?

Some individuals claimed they could see auras or spectral illusions. Could a spirit photographer record images that no one else could see? Or did the spirit photographers have eager customers who were prepared to see what they wanted to see in order to ease their grief?

Spirit photography had high-profile supporters well into the 20th century. These included the physicist Sir William Crookes, a pioneer of the vacuum tube; author Sir Arthur Conan Doyle, the creator of the Sherlock Holmes stories; and J. Traill Taylor, the editor of the *British Journal of Photography*. In 1891 Alfred Russell Wallace, a noted British scientist and the co-creator of the theory of evolution, made a thorough study of psychic experiences and came to the conclusion that at least some spirit photographs were genuine and needed to be scientifically investigated. His ideas only gained him ridicule and loss of prestige among his peers, making it doubtful that the scientific establishment would ever initiate a study of these photographs or take a study of the psychic powers needed to create this work seriously (Pearsall, 118).

Today, images are usually digital, and anyone can use software to add whatever "ghosts" he or she likes. Yet spirit photographs made without computer enhancement continue to appear, and these intrigue us enough to be themes for pseudo-scientific television shows. Images of spirit photographs fill up pages and pages of the Internet. Some of the most famous modern images are of the Brown Lady of Raynham Hall, the famous ghost first seen in 1835 whose image was shot in 1936, and the recent photograph of the Pink Lady of Greencastle shot in Indiana by Guy Winters.

When looking at spirit photographs made prior to the invention of computer imaging we can see that some of them are obvious staged phonies. The ghosts were created by nefarious means such as double exposures taken of posed models during or after the initial portrait was shot. Other "ghosts" can easily be explained away as being light leaks or mistakes in processing such as careless handling of chemicals, paper or the plates. Grief-stricken viewers interpreted these blobs and blurs as resembling their lost dearly departed because they so desperately needed to believe that their existence did not end with their deaths, especially if their deaths were untimely or violent. Their souls survived—our souls will survive! These spirit photographs gave hope to viewers and believers that they would be reunited with loved one eternally and live in an idealized place beyond our earthly woes.

Among the thousands of spirit photographs there are some that defy explanation. Even trained photographers cannot figure out how they were created, and one cannot exclude the possibility that some of these are real.

9

Art and the Corpse

Graveyard Design and Tradition

Graveyards of the 19th century were filled with mournful statues, monumental grave markers and sumptuous carvings. They were laid out in intricately designed parks, filled with exotic plants and trees. Landscape architects, sculptors, stone carvers and masonry architects sprang up, and those who were proficient at this work were hired to build extravagant gardens dedicated to death. To fully appreciate the effect death had on artists who created this work placed in cemeteries of the 19th century, we need to understand what became of the corpses of loved ones. To put the sepulchral monuments, statues and carvings of the 19th century in perspective, we must delve into historical graveyard designs and the traditions that cultivated them.

Act V of Shakespeare's play *Hamlet* opens in a graveyard with two churchwardens digging a fresh grave. As they work, they uncover one and then another skull, which they toss to the side. When Prince Hamlet and his friend Horatio enter the scene, another skull is uncovered. This time the gravedigger identifies it as belonging to Yorick, the court jester, to which Hamlet exclaims: "Alas, poor Yorick! I knew him, Horatio: a fellow of infinite jest, of most excellent fancy: he hath borne me on his back a thousand times; and now, how abhorred in my imagination it is!"

Shakespeare wrote his play in 1601, a mere six years before the Virginia Company of England founded Jamestown, the first permanent British settlement to survive on the North American continent. The playwright labeled the gravediggers "clowns," had them speak disrespectfully about the dead, crack jokes, sing bawdy songs and drink "a stoup of liquor" while performing their grim task. In the scene, the prince ponders the fate of once noble men, speaks of worms and bones, and complains about the stench of the graveyard. Although this play takes place in the Danish town of Elsinore in the fourteenth or fifteenth century, the Bard may just as well have been talking about graveyards of his own time, when the majority of Christian men and women were buried in consecrated land adjacent to a church. This practice satisfied the religious belief of the time that all dead first went to purgatory and benefited from being in earshot of regular prayers.

Seventeenth century English aristocrats and the very elite could be buried inside the church, and the bodies of lesser nobility might be placed in a vault in the churchyard, but the rest of the deceased didn't dream of having their own individual grave in a permanent spot. Their main concern was that the Church accept their bodies in sacred ground. What happened after that was not much of a concern.

In the United Kingdom, families were asked to help the ailing British wool industry by purchasing and then wrapping the corpse in a shroud made of good British wool. The necessity of a British shroud became law with the passing of The Consumption Statutes of 1660 and 1678. This shroud completely enveloped the body and was tied at the head and at the foot (Mytum, 21). If the deceased's family had some money, they might place the corpse of their loved one in a locally made coffin for burial. If money was tight, they rented a public coffin to carry the shrouded corpse to a common, unmarked grave (Mytum, 21). Churchyards were places for the disposal of their corpse.

In Shakespearian times, burials were shallower than they would later become. Accounts of St. Saviour's Southwark Parish in London from 1613 state that coffins for adults were placed in holes dug 5½ feet deep. For those without a coffin, a 4½-foot-deep hole sufficed (Mytum, 21). Because churchyards were small, bodies were buried one on top of another in a practice called overburying. They remained in the ground only for as long as it took for them to decompose—about six or seven years. To find empty spaces in the churchyard, gravediggers pushed iron borers into the ground, which sometimes led to the rupture of buried coffins and the escape of decomposition gasses. Disturbing earlier burials also brought bones to the surface, some of these with flesh still attached. Body juices are rapidly absorbed in dry and warm soil. The muscular part of the body also decays or dries up quickly. The face of a dead body buried in free soil takes three to four months to be destroyed. In the fourth month the thorax and the abdomen, where the worse gases come from, putrefy (Loudon, 4). But some parts of the corpse, such as the upper part of the thigh, resist decomposition for four or five years, and bones do not decay for decades or even centuries if buried in a dry climate (Loudon, 3). In Shakespeare's times churchyard bones were intentionally dug up and removed to an ossuary. There, they were mixed indiscriminately and dried, after which they were placed in a charnel house located under or adjacent to the church. When these houses were filled, the human bones were sent north from London and crushed in mills to be used as organic fertilizer (Linden-Ward, 25).

Jews of Shakespeare's day were considered "aliens" and were forbidden to own land for any purpose, but they were permitted to lease land from Christians to bury their dead. The oldest Jewish burial grounds in London are in the East End and date from 1657, 1696 or 1697. The oldest Anglo-Jewish burial ground outside of London is in Dublin, Ireland, and dates from 1718 (Kadish, 59). Unlike the practices of the Christians, the ancient Jewish religious principle in regard to burial was that the burial place be located outside the city walls (Kadish, 61). Jews also had a separate grave for every coffin and did not reopen a grave to add another corpse to the hole. Christians, whether Protestant Church of England or Catholic, were buried in their parish churchyard adjacent to their parish church. Puritans, Calvinists, Quakers, Independents, Presbyterians, and others were called "Nonconformists" or Dissenters. These people petitioned the Corporation of the City of London for their own burial ground and received approval to create a small graveyard at Bunhill Fields in 1665. Graves were sold in "perpetuity" in this unconsecrated ground until the land ran out in 1832 (Linden-Ward, 23). Even though the ground was not considered holy, families still had to pay burial fees to the Church of England until the Reform Act of 1832 (Sayer, 117). Once called "Bone Hill" because of the cartloads of bones buried there from the charnel house of St. Paul's Cathedral in 1547, Bunhill Fields had once been an ancient Saxon burial ground. Many of Cromwell's associates were buried there, as was the writer of the famous religious work *The Pilgrim's Progress,* John

Bunyan, buried in 1688, along with the founder of the Quakers, George Fox, who was buried in 1691 (Linden-Ward, 23). The last burial in Bunhill Fields took place in 1852. The bodies buried there totaled 124,000. But for most, burial outside sacred consecrated ground was extreme punishment. It meant that those souls could never enter the pearly gates. Burial on unconsecrated ground was reserved for suicides, lunatics, the excommunicated, executed criminals, and sometimes their families. The bodies of these individuals might be buried in shallow graves, but more often than not they were hung or left completely exposed to the elements for wild animals to consume.

Christians in medieval and even Renaissance times did not like nature or wilderness. Wilderness was the place outside the Garden of Eden. It was the place Adam and Eve were banished to as punishment for their original sin. The wilderness was also where wolves roamed, and English wolves were said to be large and ferocious. Packs of them desecrated churchyard burials, digging up corpses and eating human flesh. This easily available diet led to an increase in the number of wolves, which made them even more threatening to the living and especially to small children. Hungry and unafraid, wolves entered British towns and villages in winter to dig up and feast on the dead. Although rarely seen in England by the late 1600s, they were still so plentiful in France that the government passed an edict in 1695 decreeing that all French cemeteries be enclosed within a solid wall and locked gates to deter the ravaging beasts (Linden-Ward, 16). (The last wolf in Scotland was said to have been shot in the late 1880s, although there are current efforts to reintroduce them to maintain the deer population of Scotland).

Wolves still roamed the forests of 17th century New England when the Pilgrims landed in Massachusetts, and to protect their graves and livestock, the settlers built their houses in a cluster around a central common area that contained their grazing and burial grounds. Later, large stones called "ledger stones" were placed over the graves to prevent the wolves from digging them up and dining on the corpses. These slabs of rock, sometimes called "wolf stones," had a flat surface and were rectangular, covering the entire grave (Mytum, 29).

The Puritans began arriving in North America in 1630. Puritans were followers of John Calvin (1509–1564), the French theological reformer who broke from the Catholic Church and wanted further purification of the Christian religion. As protestors, or Protestants, their beliefs differed from those held by the Catholic Church and the Church of England, which had been reinstated by the Act of Supremacy 1558 during the reign of Henry VIII's daughter, Queen Elizabeth I. Puritans placed more emphasis on Old Testament scriptures and believed that in the wilderness of the New World they could more exactly follow the word of God. To them, salvation after death was predetermined by God and not completely dependent on one's behavior. Still, there was salvation for some, so they needed to keep their bodies intact and in their original burial places in order for God to find and save them. The Puritans conducted their religious services in meeting houses separate from the burial grounds, which were in their town center. They kept the wolves away from the graves with wooden fences (Linden-Ward, 17) and put bounties on wolf heads and pelts, eliminating most of these animals by the mid–eighteenth century.

Colonists in America allowed their animals to graze on their burial grounds where grass grew freely on the graves, but in the seventeenth century churchyards of England, Scotland and Ireland, the dirt was so over-saturated with gas and fluid from decomposing bodies that barely anything grew except the ancient yew trees that had been planted

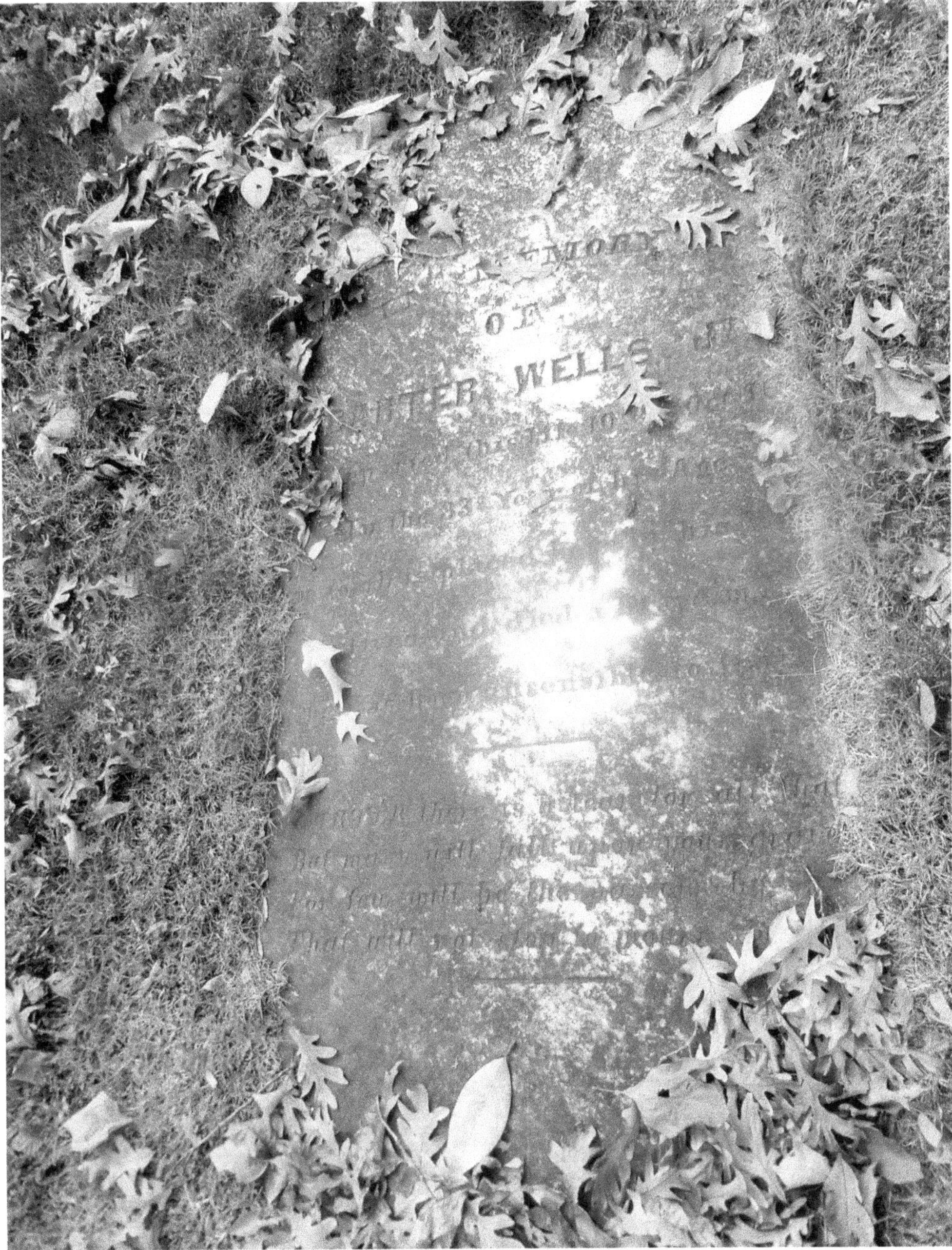

Ledger Stone, or "Wolf Stone," in Hollywood Cemetery, Richmond, Va. (author's photograph).

centuries before. Yew trees can live for more than 1,000 years. They were planted in almost every churchyard in the kingdom because they are such practical trees (Linden-Ward, 17). The wood from the yew is pliable; good for making longbows and also good for needed church repairs. Priests also used yew branches instead of palms for Palm Sunday services, but these trees were few. British clergy worried that trees in a churchyard would lure people back to paganism which, in Shakespeare's time, had never completely disappeared because Germanic, Romanic, Celtic and Slavic people living in the area had mixed their ancient pantheistic paganism with Christianity.

Pre-Christian Europeans had "natural" religions, and plants were often part of their rituals for their dead. Some envisioned the afterlife as the Greek Elysium, a beautiful garden where it is always spring. Gallo-Romans, Barbarians, and Merovingians buried their dead in open fields (Linden-Ward, 15), and an ancient folk custom was to plant trees and flowers on the graves (46). The Celts buried their dead near wells, rivers, and sacred trees. The British antiquarian John Weever (1576–1632), writing about ancient British funeral monuments, retold a story from the Roman historian Tacitus, who reported that Saxons did not bury their dead at all. Instead they laid corpses on the ground and covered them with "turfs, clods or sods of earth" (Weever, vi). According to Weever, the more important the deceased was, the higher the stack of turfs. These mounds were called "beries, baroes, or burrows," a term that was incorporated into the names of many British towns such as Jedburgh, Glastonbury, and Canterbury. Weever also wrote that Stonehenge was the "sepulcre," or burial place, of Britains slain by the Saxons when they raided the land after the withdrawal of Roman troops. Stonehenge has been found to be much older than this, so anything Weever wrote needs to be investigated further.

Cypress trees were planted in graveyards in southern Europe and Muslim countries. Ancient Greeks believed that the god Apollo turned a beloved child, Cyparissus or Kyparissos, into a cypress tree. Ovid related that the youth accidentally killed his pet stag and begged the god to let his tears flow forever. The sap of the cypress tree resembles tears, and the tree became the symbol of mourning, death and immortality. Cypress trees were planted on the edge of graves of the French elite. Walnut trees were planted in Poitou, France, and elms in Northern Europe. In southern Europe, rosemary was commonly planted near graves and allowed to grow into a hedge. This plant was valued because of its strong odor and the belief that it retarded the putrefaction of the corpse (Linden-Ward, 17).

Several trees, like the rowan and oak, were important or even sacred to the Anglo-Celtic Druid priests of Britannia, who, Julius Caesar reported, sacrificed humans to their gods by burning them alive in bonfires of wood. Trees were also important to the Teutonic Saxons, who held that certain trees captured the spirits of the dead. In 723 CE the British Saint Boniface of Wessex supposedly traveled to Germania and cut down the sacred oak that contained the spirit of Donar, or Thor. Thor was the Teutonic god of storms, strength and protection of mankind, whom the Saxons believed whispered messages through the branches of the sacred tree (Linden-Ward, 16). Catholics rejected the idea of these pagans. Counter-Reformation leaders banned all plants from graveyards after the Council of Trent in 1563. Fearing a resurgence of paganism, in 1577 the Italian cardinal Charles Borromeo declared a formal ban on planting trees, shrubs, vines, flowers and grasses in graveyards. He was later declared a saint. But the yew tree had been a favorite of the British since pagan times. When Christianity was brought to the islands in the 4th or 5th century, the lowly but long-lived yew was planted in all the Christian churchyards due to a belief that the tree roots would find the mouths of the dead and quiet them (Linden-Ward, 17). By Shakespeare's time, the yew tree was tolerated as a symbol of immortality. It was allowed to continue to grow in Christian churchyards because British clergy deemed it too unattractive to inspire anyone's worship (Linden-Ward, 17).

Burial practices of the 17th century differed a great deal from those of ancient times. The Ptolemies of ancient Egypt buried their dead outside their cities in "necropolises," or "cities of the dead." One of these near the Nile Valley village of Tuna al-Gabal was recently discovered by Cairo university students using radar. More than 30 mummified humans were discovered next to a necropolis in which thousands of mummified animals lay. The remains of the humans are believed to be more than 1,500 years old (E. Rosenberg). The Old Testament tells us that the Jewish patriarch Abraham and matriarch Sarah were buried in the Cave of Machpelah, or Ma'arat HaMachpelah, which Abraham purchased from Ephron the Hittite 3,700 years ago. Years later, his son Isaac and his wife Rebecca, and Jacob and his first wife, Leah, were buried there as well. Jacob's second wife, Rachel, died giving birth to her second son, Benjamin, so she was buried in a grave on the road to Ephrath. On top of the grave, Jacob set a pillar that was still in existence at the time of the writing of the Bible. Rachel's tomb is called "Kever Rakhel" in Hebrew and "Qubr Raheel" in Arabic. Sacred also to Muslims, and known as the Sanctuary of Abraham, the cave of Abraham Sarah, Jacob and Leah was discovered around 1119 CE by a monk named Arnoul beneath a building where he prayed.

Athenians buried those slain in battle outside their city in a place called a *ceramnicus.* The Etruscans, who preceded the Romans, buried their dead on the outer banks of their fortifications or in underground rooms. The ancient Roman poet Virgil (70 BCE–19 BCE) wrote that the Romans cremated their deceased, gathered their bones and then placed them in an urn, which was stored in a monument. According to other Roman historians, they also buried their dead. The Roman Jewish community tunneled underground to store their dead around 100 CE. These Jews believed that when God sent the Messiah to resurrect them and lead them to a new Jerusalem, they needed all their body parts to rise from the dead. A hundred years later, Roman Christians joined them in carving tunnels to place the bodies of their dead while waiting for Christ's return. These catacombs had carved recesses in the tunnel walls where shrouded bodies were placed. These cavities were arranged in rows and stacked one on top of another. A slab of marble or tile with the name of the deceased secures the tomb. All Christian catacombs in Rome are property of the Catholic Church.

The second law of the Roman legal code, named the Twelve Tables and later the Theodosian Code, prohibited Romans from burying their dead inside their city walls. Following customs of the Etruscans and Greeks, Romans built tombs for several miles on their main roads such as the Via Appia (Appian Way). Street graves can also be seen in other cities including Pompeii. These sites were for the wealthy, the famous, or members of powerful families, and were given to them by a public vote (Coltman, 11). Markers for these grave sites were erected in a variety of forms. Some could be simple mounds of earth or a heap of stones. Others were shaped like pyramids, towers, temples, columns and even palaces. More commonly, a memorial stone in the shaped of a small column was placed on the side of a road. The top of the column was carved to resemble a head, which was probably painted; the names of the persons and an inscription recorded the family. Weever (xiii) tells us that it was a Roman custom to decorate these monuments with sweet-smelling flowers at least once a year.

Weever also wrote that the British continued to bury their dead outside their cities and town walls in "sleeping places" until Gregory the Great (Pope Gregory) became leader of the Catholic Church from 590 to 604 CE. This pope allowed "monks, fryars and priests" to offer sacrifices for the departed souls, and "for their more easy and greater profit," it was allowed "that the places of sepulture should be adjoining unto their churches" (viii). Later, the clergy got permission to bury people inside the church as well.

The first archbishop of Canterbury, Augustine, who converted King Æthelbert to Christianity around 598 CE, was buried in the porch at the entrance to the church of St. Peter and Paul, more commonly known as St. Austin's near Canterbury. Weever tells us that it was Cuthbert, the eleventh archbishop of Canterbury (d. 760), who obtained a dispensation from the pope to make churchyards into burial grounds, located within town and city limits. Both Augustine and Cuthbert were later made into saints.

By Weever's times, not every grave had a marker. As he explained:

> Sepulchers should be made according to the quality and degree of the person deceased, that by the tombe every one might be discerned of what rank he was, living … therefore it was the use of reverend antiquity, to interr persons of the rustic or plebeian sort, in Christian burial, without any further remembrance of them, either by tomb, grave-stone, or epitaph [quoted in Mackie, 41].

Whether buried inside or outside the church, those who warranted a marker for their graves had to abide by strict rules of etiquette. According to Weever, the marker for persons of lesser gentry was a flat gravestone. "Gentlemen of eminence" had a lifelike sculpture of themselves, from the waist up, and without any arms, carved on something called a "term" placed on a pedestal raised from the ground. Nobles, princes and kings were placed in tombs also raised from the floor (Weever, xi). These memorials, like the one in Westminster Abby memorializing King Henry VII, were topped with life-size, realistic statues of the deceased, carved from alabaster and marble, and embellished with polished metals like copper and brass.

When Henry VIII became Supreme Head of the Church of England in 1534, he was able to marry the infamous Anne Boleyn, and he shut down corrupt churches and monasteries, confiscating their silver and gold. But he made little change to traditional church practice despite the desire of the Puritan reformers to rid religion of Roman "superstitions." His son and heir, King Edward VI, was crowned in 1547 when he was only nine years old. Raised as a Protestant, Edward and his regents made some important changes to the new religion, but he died at the age of 15, and the throne went to his older sister, who was raised a Catholic. Nicknamed "Bloody" Mary, the queen reversed Edward's reforms and had many English Protestants burned at the stake. Mary also only lived a few years, after which her younger half-sister Elizabeth was crowned the queen.

Elizabeth I had been raised a Protestant. The Act of Supremacy of 1558 re-established the Church of England's independence from Rome and designated her as the "Supreme Governor" of the Church. The new title was given to her because many were concerned that a woman could not be the head of a church. The Act of Uniformity of 1558 forced all citizens to go to church once a week or pay a penalty; it also set the liturgy of the English Book of Common Prayer. Despite these reforms, Elizabeth continued to support the hierarchy within the church consisting of deacons, priests, bishops, the Archbishop of Canterbury, and her at the top, even though she gave little guidance as to its direction. The most important thing to her was that her subjects were loyal despite a papal bull, issued in 1570, encouraging the British Catholics to remove her from the throne. When Queen Elizabeth died in 1603, her distant cousin James Stuart was crowned, uniting the kingdoms on the British Isles. James was born in 1566 and was crowned king of Scotland when he was only 1 year old. Although he had been the head of the Presbyterian Church of Scotland (which had been granted many of the reforms the Puritans wanted for their English church), he opted for the status quo when he came to the English throne. His son, King Charles I, married a Catholic and was eventually beheaded in 1649.

In Shakespeare's time, churches supported their members from baptism to death and even after that. One paid burial fees to the church, which kept it functioning. One also paid for prayers said for the dead, which supposedly helped shorten the amount of time souls stayed in Purgatory. Members of the Church of England had conflicting ideas about the existence of Purgatory, but they still believed that praying for the dead was helpful. Being interred in a church where constant prayers were said was best, but a churchyard burial still allowed some benefits. The east side of the church, nearest the altar, was the choicest location for an external grave because the prayers there were the loudest. If this was not possible, the south or west sides were where passers-by might see your grave and be reminded to pray for your soul. Because of this, it was important to have a memorial to mark your grave.

In the early 1900s, Herbert Batsford (1861–1917) published his photographs of typical mural monuments and tombstones found in English parish churches and churchyards to inspire artists and architects to preserve these traditional British forms. Batsford explained that memorial stones located within and without the walls of British churches were made "to hold the memory of the dead, to defeat oblivion … and to reflect the dignity of those who stood, in varying degree, pre-eminent among their fellows in their lifetime" (Batsford, 1). He believed that the inside of a church should have wall panels and realistic busts of those deceased set in niches in the wall as in Renaissance times, and that wall panels memorializing the dead should have lengthy inscriptions at their centers that determined the artistic basis of the design. These inscriptions should be surrounded by ornaments of death and the deceased's shield or coat of arms (Batsford, 4). From the 15th century on, the funerals of all English aristocratic arms-bearing families were supervised by the Court of Heralds, also known as the College of Arms. Founded by King Richard III, this group, or corporation, was created to ensure that no social-climbing family displayed a coat of arms or had grand funerals to which they were not entitled.

Along with wall panels, Batsford's photographs show highly carved ledger stones and table tombs carved with great skill by those called "monument masons" or "monument designers." None of these artists signed their work, and unfortunately, little is known about them. The English did not use the word "sculptor" to describe an artist working in three dimensions until after Shakespeare's time in the mid–17th century. Full sized, lifelike statues of important deceased nobles, called effigies, placed on tombs were said to have been sculpted by Italian artists brought to England in the time of King Henry VIII (Batsford, 12). But it is evident that some locals learned the trade of carving and were able to do excellent work. In the time of Shakespeare, English sculpture was at its infancy. Nicholas Stone (1586–1647), son of a quarryman, was known specifically for his funerary monuments. Apart from being an artist, he was a mason and an architect. Trained in Holland, he was appointed master mason to King James I in 1619 and was also master mason to King Charles I until his death. Another sculptor who achieved a reputation at this time was Edward Pearce or Pierce (d. 1698). The son of a painter by the same name, Pearce created funerary busts but also worked as a mason and a carver for the architect Sir Christopher Wren. Despite his reputation as a sculptor working in wood and stone, few of Pearce's works survive.

Ledger stones covered the entire graves of anyone lucky enough to be buried inside the church. These were cut from marble or some other hard stone and laid in the floor or in the pavement. Aside from an inscription, ledger stones were adorned with a carved medallion containing the deceased's shield of arms, with crest and mantling. Batsford's photographs show that table tombs also stood in the interior of English churches, or in the churchyard if there were limited space inside. Some table tombs were ledger stones raised up on columns to prevent grass or weeds from growing over it. Some were placed on a closed rectangle resembling a chest made of stone. Horizontal sculptures of the deceased, made by the Italian artists, rested on the top of the older chest tombs and are usually found inside the church. Batsford's photographs show that the sides of chest tombs have much more surface area for artists to design. Some were left blank, but others were filled with inscriptions, varied heraldic adornments and other ornamentation.

A popular decorative element on all memorials was a "putto" (from the Latin *putus*, boy), a cherub head with wings and drapery. These are illustrated by Batsford's photograph of a tablet in St. Dunstan-in-the West, London. This memorial, dated 1685, shows a carved angel head with wings on a cloud carved onto the bottom of a panel. The sides surrounding the inscription are decorated with vegetation, ending in spirals near the angel's head. A photograph of another monument located in St. Vedast on Foster Lane in London, dated 1672, shows a monument containing a carved cherub head with wings at the bottom. In the center of the monument is an urn with a putto on each side. In the corner of each side of the arch is a skull. These winged, chubby boy babies were popular icons in the Renaissance. Representing cupids, or angels, it was believed that these babies served God and represented innocence.

Early colonists of high status in Virginia, as in Britain, could also be buried inside the church with a ledger stone placed on the floor covering their grave. These settlers were not Puritans. Instead they were members of the Church of England, or even Catholics, and they continued the same burial practices that were carried out in their homeland, even burying their dead in an east–west orientation, placing the head of the corpse on west side of the grave and its feet pointing towards the east. This alignment was so that when they were resurrected on Judgment Day, they would face the rising sun and the direction of Jerusalem (Gilson, 86). But this practice was not consistent in colonial American graveyards. Burial grounds were first placed in consecrated ground in the

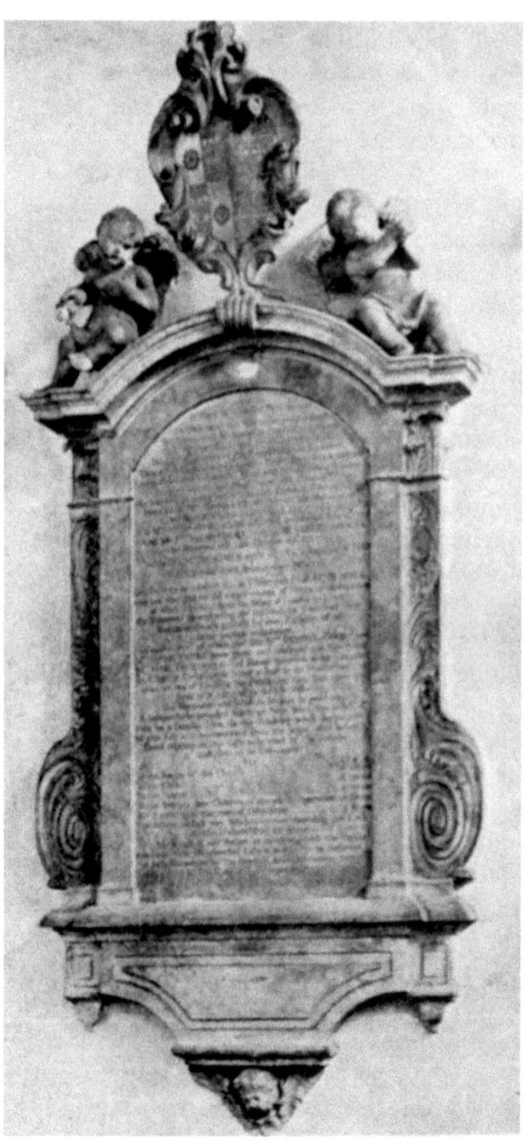

Wall memorial, St. Vedast, Foster Lane, London, 1672 (Herbert Batsford, 1916).

middle of town, and then, following the English tradition, in churchyards or inside the churches when these were built (Mytum, 20). Records of Bruton Parish Episcopal Church of Williamsburg, Virginia, relate that burial in the chancel of the church (the part near the altar) cost the deceased, or her or his family, 1,000 pounds of tobacco, or €5 paid to the minister (Mackie, 45). The family also had to give the grave digger or sexton 10 extra pounds of tobacco for his labor. Virginia had small churches, and as in England, burial in the church was restricted to those of rank. Few North American churches have been excavated, but in Jamestown, Virginia, two internal church burials were found marked with monuments. One was for a knight and had brasses set into the memorial. The other was for a cleric (Mytum, 18). Seventeenth century Virginia grave markers were imported, pre-carved, from Britain. The local stone was not very good, and the early colonists were not trained in stone carving. Most British people at the time were agrarian and rural. The British colonists in America continued this rural tradition of planting crops and caring for animals. In the words of Governor William Bradford, "They were not acquainted with trades nor traffic ... but had only ben used to a plain country life and the innocent trade of husbandry" (Deetz, 59).

American colonists with imported markers for their graves were the wealthy few. England passed a Navigation Act in 1651 restricting imports to the new land. More restrictions were enacted in the 1660s and 1670s. These acts limited goods headed for America to items bought only from English or Scottish merchants and transported on English ships. Even if a grave memorial was originally made in Italy, it had to be bought from an English or Scottish middleman, which increased the cost.

The gravestones used in 17th century England were the headstone, coped stone, coffin stone, ledger stones, body stone, chest-tomb, bale-tomb, pedestal-tomb and table-tomb. Some of these were so elaborately carved that they must have originated on the continent. Grave markers imported to Virginia were the headstone, chest-tomb, ledger stone and a few table-tombs (Deetz, 55), although in the Chesapeake Tidewater area of America, the majority of the graves did not have upright headstones.

* * *

When the first European explorers came to North America, they brought diseases that killed millions of native people in a very short span of time. Large populations of the original people died even before Europeans and Africans settled into an area, making it seem that the continent was sparsely populated. There must have been burial monuments and grave sites for the deceased, yet we know little about them, and the Native American Graves Protection and Repatriation Act (NAGPRA), enacted in 1990, limits and restricts further excavation of their remains and burial sites. While this important legislation keeps their graves and memorials undisturbed, it also keeps them unexplored. What little we know comes from the writings of missionaries and early colonists. Père Pierre Biard (1567–1622), a Jesuit missionary from Grenoble, France, wrote that the Algonquian family of tribes tied the bodies of their deceased into fetal position and placed them seated in a deep hole that they covered with sticks. Pilgrim leaders reported that they discovered this same type of burial covered with a mound of earth. Other colonists reported finding pits containing deceased Native Americans covered with stones. What we believe is that burial customs among the indigenous people varied from tribe to tribe, and that their practices may have influence the burial of the colonists ("New England Native American").

In alignment with the interpretation of the Bible by John Calvin (1509–1564), the French theologian and leader of the Protestant Reformation, the Puritans wanted to purify the Church of England of what they believed were Catholic superstitions. Doubtful that the British king would allow this, shipload after shipload of Puritans arrived in Boston harbor, with immigration tapering off during the English Civil War of 1642–1651. By 1642 more than 20,000 Puritans had settled in New England. Still loyal to the British Crown, they were hopeful that the ocean between them would allow them the freedom to build a new society. The Puritans of Plymouth Colony joined with those from the Massachusetts Bay Colony, the New Haven Colony and the Connecticut Colony to form the New England Confederation in 1643. Unlike the British colonists in Virginia, who hoped to return to England as wealthy men, the Puritans were skilled tradesmen, farmers and merchants, who came with their families to stay. As their first governor, John Winthrop (1588–1649), reminded them, their communities were to be "cities on a hill," bright lights for the rest of the world to follow. The Puritans built their towns around a central meetinghouse that also served as a church and central gathering place. They established graveyards on unconsecrated ground set at a distance from where they prayed. John Calvin (1509–1564), a leader of the Protestant Reformation, wrote that on the day of burial, "The dead body ... be decently attended from the house to the place appointed for Publique Buriall, and there immediately interred without Ceremony" (Linden-Ward, 22). Calvin wrote that praying, reading and singing "are no way beneficial to the dead, and have proved many ways hurtfull to the living, therefore let all such things be laid aside." Puritans did not build memorials to honor their dead. Even the tomb of John Winthrop on Copp's Hill was barely marked (Linden-Ward, 95).

Puritans and Calvinists had ambivalent feelings about death. They believed that they were born wicked. They hoped that if they lived a good life, they would be saved. Death "was to be welcomed by the saved, and feared by those 'not chosen'" (Rainville, "Mortuary Variability," 556). However, no one, not even the most devout, could guarantee that they were chosen for eternal life. Puritans believed in Christ, but their God was all powerful. Their lives were predetermined, and no human had any assurance that they would receive God's mercy, nor could any human exert influence over what was to be. Puritans called death "the great change" (Hijiya, 347). Death inspired their awe and fear and was the gateway to heaven, but it was also punishment for their sins.

By 1660 great numbers of Americans had never even seen England, and their lifestyle and burials reflected their new way of life. While some buried their dead in churches or churchyards, like those in Virginia's Burton Parish Church, most colonists had moved away from their towns and lived on their own farmland. They preferred burials in their own backyards or in the less desirable plots of their own farmland. Carved stones marking a grave were rare. Most of those discovered are ordinary field stones either left unmarked or with text scratched onto them. Early graves may also have been marked with one wooden post or with two wooden posts set in the ground parallel to the body of the deceased with a post at the head and foot and a board in between. This type of marker, resembling the headboard of a bedstead, is a regional style from southern England where they are called "grave rails" (Deetz, 121). Wooden memorials like these were actually found intact in South Carolina. Gravestone researchers Elizabeth A. Crowell and Norman V. Mackie III believed that thousands of graves were either unmarked or marked with wooden markers, although they found no evidence of wooden markers in the middle Atlantic region of colonial America (Crowell, 9). These markers would be difficult to impossible to find. Wood from hundreds of years ago would decompose. If the land were tilled for farming or dug up for development, the post holes would be destroyed. However, mention of wooden markers was found in documents from New England, Georgia and Maryland (Mytum, 26). Later posts were made from stone with one post marking the head of the corpse and another one marking the feet; a wooden rail joined the two together. Text was either written or carved on the rail, occasionally embellished with a design.

New Netherlands didn't mind wooden grave markers. Even the wealthiest had cedar posts or simple upright markers for their graves (Stone, 143). With its capital called New Amsterdam at the southern tip of Manhattan Island, New Netherlands was founded in 1624 by the Seven United Netherlands. It stretched along the east coast of North America and up the Hudson River. The area remained under Dutch control until 1664, after which it was alternately occupied by Dutch and English forces until the Treaty of Westminster ceded the area to the English in 1674. This province had a very diverse population including Flemish, Belgian Walloons, French Huguenots, Scandinavians, Irish Scots, Germans and those from the Lowland provinces. There were also small numbers of Turks, Jews, Poles, Italians, enslaved Africans, free Africans and Native Americans.

What we know about slave burials comes from either the 18th or 19th century or from recent excavations, like the 6.6-acre site discovered in 1991 in New York City outside the settlement of New Amsterdam, containing from 15,000 to 20,000 free and enslaved African Americans. Scholars from Howard University researched and excavated the site. The secretary of the interior designated the burial ground as a National Historic Landmark in 1993, and George W. Bush made it a national monument in 2006 through a presidential proclamation administered by the National Park Services.

In Southern plantations people were buried on private land. These burials were in clusters, suggesting that slaves or indentured servants were buried at a distance from those of the owners of the land. It is probably that African Americans in both Northern and Southern colonies had their own separate burial grounds in the 17th century. Plantation documents mention them, and while they give hints that they were located near mills or near the slave quarters, they give no specifics about actual locations of the graves (Mytum, 21).

Once unkempt and neglected, with fallen, or tilted stones collecting lichen and moss, these old graveyards and gravestones are a link to the country's past. Ignored by most for many years, some intrepid admirers covered the stones with paper and made crayon rubbings of their surfaces, which they framed and hung on their walls. Others vandalized these resting places and stole a gravestone or two to decorate their yards and patios. Now we recognize that these places and objects are important links to America's history. From them we can gain genealogical, historical, medical and anthropological knowledge. As examples of America's first sculptures, they are also important in the field of art.

Early Stonecutters and Grave Markers

Exploring the gravestones made in the 17th and 18th centuries is important because the stone carvers who made them were the first sculptors in America. The stones have been studied extensively by historians and archaeologist, but they have not been looked at enough as artwork made by artists that influenced the development of the American aesthetic.

The imagery on American gravestones is abstract and perhaps symbolic rather than realistic. This was enormously different from work artists were creating in Europe. We must remember that the artist known as Donatello created his bronze statue of David in the mid–1400s. Michelangelo, another famous Renaissance sculptor, lived from 1475 to 1564. He created his world-famous statue the *Pieta* in 1498 and his own statue of David in 1504. All of these sculptures were expressive and lifelike work. When the Puritans were colonizing the American northeast in 1622–1625, the sculptor Gian Lorenzo Bernini was creating his *Apollo and Daphne,* a delicate and very realistic work commissioned by Cardinal Scipione Borghese. This sculpture consists of two figures carved in marble portraying the ill-fated love of the god for the hapless nymph whose heart was pierced by Eros with a lead arrow, ensuring that she would spurn all advances. Bernini delicately carved her flowing hair and the thin leaves sprouting from Daphne's fingers symbolizing her metamorphosis into a laurel tree. In creating this statue, Bernini made his work highly ornamental and highly emotional, in keeping with the Baroque style. While British sculptors lagged behind the masters of Italy in artistry, sculptors such as Nicholas, John Bushnell and Edward Pearce could at least carve the human form and probably a good likeness of their patrons. Across the Atlantic, the stonecutters of America carved childish figures of skulls, flowers and fruit. Lack of skill might have accounted for this, or the religious adherence to the second of God's commandments given in Exodus 20:4: "Thou shalt not make unto thee any graven image, or any likeness of any thing that is in heaven above, or that is in the earth beneath, or that is in the water under the earth" (King James Bible). The evolution of their work explains, to a certain extent, America's romance with popular images and its ambivalent feelings about the visual arts that exist even to this day.

The first serious publication on the topic of gravestone art was written by Harriette Merrifield Forbes (1856–1951) and published in 1927. It contains photographs of gravestones located predominantly in Massachusetts; however, she also photographed stones in other New England states as well as in Long Island, New York. Ernest Caulfield (1890–1972) took photographs of gravestones of Connecticut in the 1950s while researching epidemics of diphtheria and scarlet fever. Allen Ludwig published his study *Graven Images: New England Stonecarving and Its Symbols, 1650–1815* in 1966. Businessman Daniel Farber and his wife Professor Jessie Lie Farber, who worked at Mount Holyoke College, spent 20 years collecting rubbings and photographing gravestones. Prof. Farber became interested in gravestone art when she saw an exhibition of rubbings at New York's Whitney Museum of American Art in 1974. Approximately 15,000 pictures of more than 9,000 gravestones were digitized by the American Antiquarian Society and are available online at the Farber Gravestone Collection at http://www.davidrumsey.com/farber/about.html.

While these resources are impressive, important research was done by Edwin Dethlefsen and James Deetz (1930–2000) in the mid–1960s. These academics looked at grave markers as important archeological artifacts in their article "Death's Heads, Cherubs, and Willow Trees: Experimental Archaeology in Colonial Cemeteries," published in *American Antiquity* magazine. The authors categorized the designs on gravestones and connected them to changes in religious philosophy of the times. Since they confined their research to Massachusetts, several other researchers investigated stones and memorials from other areas of the United States. Some corroborated the hypotheses of Dethlefsen and Deetz while others discovered that gravestone ornamentation varied by location and the ability of the local artists and carvers. Even Deetz, in later work, admitted that before the late 18th century, "Carvers working only twenty miles apart were evolving very different motifs" (Deetz, 122). There was a lot of regional variation in New England gravestone carving, and many designs have no counterpart in England. These local styles were not only "radically different from contemporary English designs, but also from each other" (Deetz, 122). James Deetz formed the opinion that the early British American colonies consisted of "peasant societies." Aside from those working in professions such as governance, religion and education, most of the population could not travel and had little knowledge of the wider world.

Back in Britain, Oliver Cromwell died in 1658. His son, Richard, became lord protector of the Commonwealth but was not liked by the army or the Parliament and was made to resign. Fearing that the kingdom would fall into anarchy, the governor of Scotland, George Monk, First Duke of Albemarle, marched into London with an army, resulting in a general election, an attempt at another civil war. This resulted in the return to power of the heir to the throne, Charles II, in 1660. According to Deetz, the British American settlers of this time lived in hundreds of tiny communities, isolated by poor modes of transportation. Escaping war and upheaval in their homeland, they developed conservative values "characterized by close ties to kin, suspicion of outsiders, change, or innovation" (Deetz, 60). Meanwhile, the Renaissance had been transforming Britain through the 16th and 17th centuries, and with it came cultural transformations that were not known about in America. Only the wealthy elite sailed back and forth between continents, and in their travels they saw the latest styles. Although these cosmopolitan travelers were few, they brought new ideas to the American colonies.

By the end of the 17th century and the beginning of the 18th century, more and more Americans wanted their graves, or the graves of their loved ones, marked with tablets carved of stone. With the increase in demand, professional workers set up shop on American soil. Known as stonecutters, they established a new enterprise and trained their children and grandchildren to take over the family business, establishing gravestone-carving dynasties that influenced the look of American gravestones for a hundred years. Some stonecutters came with sketchbooks of designs based on what they had seen in their homelands, but some created designs from their own imaginations to fit their customers' aesthetics. These artists developed skills in carving local stone and became the pioneers in the visual art of sculpture in America. One of these artists, called "The Stone Cutter of Boston," trained servants or apprentices, like the mysterious artist who signed his work with the initials, J.N. These men ventured out to other towns and established businesses of their own.

Harriette Merrifield Forbes (1856–1951) photographed the early gravestones of New England in the late 1800s, when photography was a difficult, technical medium. This was before the invention of the Brownie camera and flexible film. She then pored over probate records and other documents to research the men who carved the stones. Her work, a rambling narrative discussing the stone carvers and her photographs, was published decades later in 1927 and became the basis for later academic research.

Forbes discovered that the earliest New England gravestones were made from stone found in or adjacent to the site. Called field stones, these are rough markers with carved inscriptions. Some of the stones were "wolf stones" covering the entire grave. Some of these were so large that they covered the surface of several unnamed graves at once (Forbes, 50). Field stones had no ornamentation and only an inscription containing the name of the deceased, birth and death dates, and perhaps an epitaph. A large majority of the lettering was crude, but many were executed surprisingly well. Stones deliberately cut to be used as grave markers showed more skill. In the vicinity of Boston, Massachusetts, this stone was usually slate.

While historians believed that slate was imported from Britain, Forbes disagreed. She accepted that the earliest slate might have come from England or Wales, but when she examined hundreds of ship bills, she did not find any slate gravestones listed on them (Forbes, 6). She also referenced the Reverend Francis Higginson, who wrote in 1633 that there was "plenty [of slate] at the Isle of Slate in Massachusetts Bay" (Forbes, 8). Her research uncovered acts passed in 1633 and 1650 under the General Court Rule of the Massachusetts Colony that decreed that any man could use this slate for free. Slate was used not only for gravestones but also used for hearths, sinks, doorsteps, and shingles. Early quarries opened in Attleborough, Wrentham, Bellingham and towns around the Narragansett Basin. Later, quarries were established in Harvard and Lancaster, as well as in Vermont, Rhode Island and Connecticut. Once the quarries opened, stone carvers arrived and opened new shops.

In all likelihood, the earliest stone carvers were itinerant and travelled from quarry to quarry to carve the stones. The chronicler of the Hayden Genealogy wrote that the Hayden Stone Pit in Connecticut was worked by William Hayden as early as 1654 and probably earlier, since a gravestone for the Reverend Ephraim Huit dated 1644 came from there. The author explained that when suitable slabs for a gravestone were quarried, the men leaned them up against the front of their shops. This way, when a death occurred, the customer had a number of stones to choose from. According to Forbes, the genealogist explained that the customer paid for the grave marker and told the owner of the quarry what should be written on it. When there were enough orders, an itinerant carver was hired to live on the premises and carved all the slabs at one time (Forbes, 11).

While early Boston gravestones were carved from slate, Connecticut markers were carved from local red sandstone. Both of these stones held up surprisingly well to the elements, keeping the carvings and inscriptions crisp for centuries. A low-grade marble was found in Newbury, Massachusetts, in 1697, but as in the Virginia colony, the noble class of New England still imported their marble grave markers from England. An early marble ledger stone with pillars for the father of Sir William Pepperell, a baronet, was imported as late as 1737 and stands in the graveyard in Kittery, Maine. The cost of this was 34 pounds, 11 shillings and 4 pence, about $7,000 today.

Forbes grew so acquainted with the gravestones she photographed that she began to notice "little peculiarities" that became like "the handwriting of a friend" (Forbes, 16). She began to identify the different carvers by their style and eventually linked their names to probate and estate records (Forbes, 16). Although many were trained on American soil, new stone carvers continued to immigrate from England. Others came from Scotland and Ireland, where gravestone ornamentation was not frowned upon.

The English Protestant kings and queen tried to create a Church of Ireland, but this was not embraced by the Gaelic-speaking population, which remained Catholic and faithful to the pope. The patron saint of Ireland, St. Patrick, had trained in France before converting the Irish to Christianity in the 5th century CE, and the Irish had a close relationship to that country which had remained Catholic in Reformation times. Irish men seeking freedom of religion traveled to France, where colleges were established specifically to train them to become Catholic priests. These men returned to their homeland having absorbed French aesthetics and traditions. Despite the fact that the new church was con-

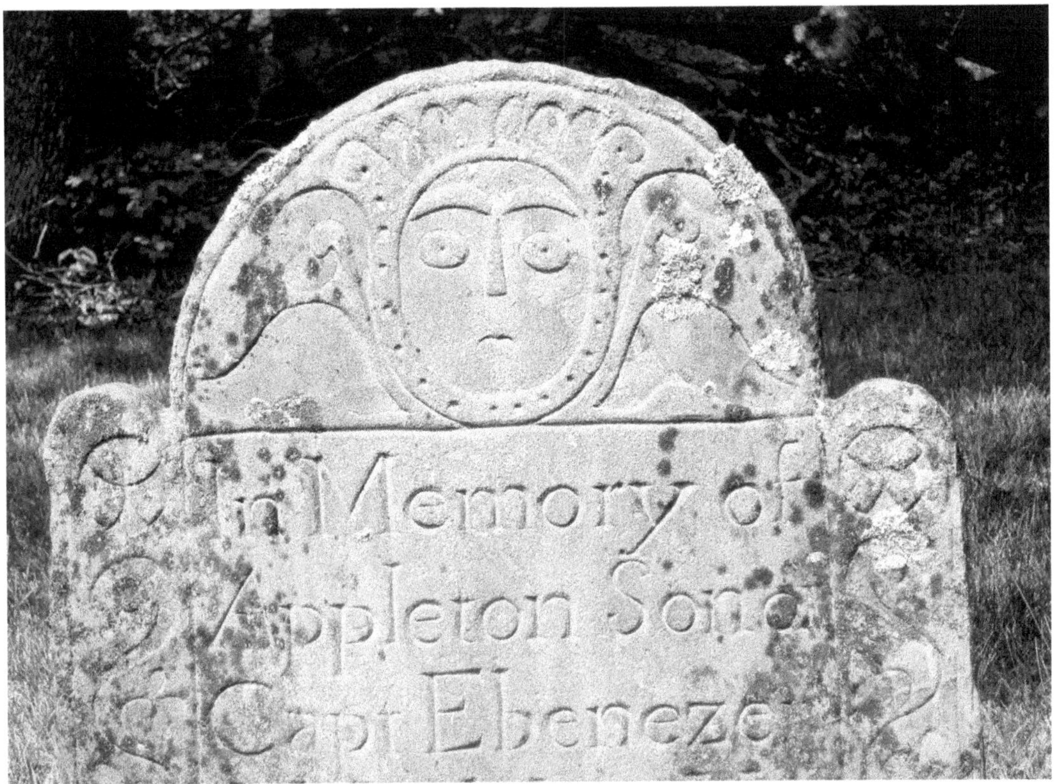

Antique headstone, Abington Burial Ground, Connecticut, 2009 (Don S. Rogers).

sidered the state religion, most Irish people remained Catholic despite severe discrimination. Irish Catholics fought for their land and their rights in what is known as the Irish Rebellion of 1641 but were defeated by Oliver Cromwell's army, plague and famine, resulting in the death of about 1/3 of their population.

Religion was also a deadly conundrum for the Scots, who had undergone the Protestant Reformation in the mid–1500s and established a Calvinist church. However, an estimated 1/3 of the population remained Catholic, which led to the religious civil wars known as the Jacobite rebellions. The Catholic Jacobites were tragically defeated by the British at the Battle of Culloden in 1745. Despite these conflicts, gravestones with mortality symbols on them started to appear in Ireland in the 16th century and by the 17th century were being produced in the lowlands of Scotland. A favorite European image that appeared in Ireland was the image of a skull with a long bone in its teeth. This symbol, carved around 1557 on the nave of Lismore Cathedral, in County Waterford, memorializes the MacCragh family. We also see carved effigies of men of status on sepulchral monuments soon after they appeared on the European continent. The Irish continued to carve effigies of the deceased longer than most of the rest of Europe ("Gravestone Symbolism").

The Scots desired to identify their buried deceased not only with the person's name and relevant dates but also with the crest of their clan, or their heraldry. Carved objects on tombstones might also identify the person's occupation, and carved mortality symbols reminded onlookers that everyone must die. In 1627 Scottish masons carved a full complement of mortality symbols on the north wall of the cathedral in Enniskillen for the British Cole family. These included a skull, crossed bones, bell, hourglass and coffin.

While few of the early stonecutters left records, probate registries from the mid–17th century recorded the purchase of gravestones in the Massachusetts colony, and wills recorded the prices stonecutters were paid from the estates of the deceased. Looking at colonial records, Forbes discovered that stone carvers had other occupations, and she hypothesized that in the early days of the colonies there were not enough deaths to allow one to concentrate solely on carving gravestones. Other occupations for stonecutters included masonry, bricklaying, surveying, farming, and working in slate. A surprising number of grave carvers were cordwainers, men who made or repaired leather goods; braziers, those who made things of copper and brass; or joiners, those who made and carved furniture. These men had their own shops and would have been familiar with creating decorative borders. Craftsmen would have carving or engraving tools on hand and could easily transfer techniques from one medium to another. Forbes believed that they worked on gravestones when they had the inspiration or when they were not occupied with other work. Stonecutters didn't wait until someone died to carve a stone. Some were pre-carved with decorations and an epitaph of the artisan's choosing. Some of these were in Latin, which few could read but added dignity to the grave. The pre-decorated stones were put on display in the artisans' shops. When someone died, the customer could choose one of these pre-cut stones and know exactly what he or she was going to get. Of course, the stonecutter left a blank area where he could add the name of the deceased and the dates. Using this method of production, the stone might even be ready in time for the funeral (Forbes, 12). Inventories show unfinished carved gravestones in the estates of deceased carvers. These were passed on to their kin and might not have been immediately sold. Because of this, stones from a known stone carver appear in graveyards dating long past the death of the artist.

The oldest gravestone that Forbes found in the Boston area with artwork on it was made by the artist she named "the Stone Cutter of Boston." This was made for the grave of Ann Erinton, who was laid to rest in Cambridge in 1653. Forbes described the design on the stone as half a rosette engraved on the tympanum. Also known as a lunette, a tympanum is the large arc found at the top and center of a gravestone. A rosette is a round, stylized flower, but the design on this particular stone also resembles either a setting sun with protruding rays, which would have been the symbol for death, or a rising sun, which would have been the symbol of resurrection. Under the tympanum and between the shoulders of the stone is a flat area called the tablet. This is where stonecutters engraved the name of the corpse, the date of his or her death, and an epitaph. The typical colonial gravestone had two smaller and lower arcs are on either side of the tympanum. These would top off what is known as the shoulders of the stone. This three-arced configuration made the headstone resemble a colonial bed headboard, an apt metaphor for the state of the deceased. The word *tympanum* is also used in architecture to describe a decorative arc placed above a building's main doorway. Comparing a gravestone to a door was also appropriate because the Puritans considered death to be the portal to the afterlife.

A document describing the erection of a tomb for Mr. Zachariah Symmes around 1670 also refers to *the* stonecutter at Boston, again indicating that there was only one person in the city who carved gravestones (Forbes, 21). The price for this tombstone, which included masonry work, cost 12 pounds including the burial cloth. Sixteen additional shillings were paid to cart the stone to the graveyard (Forbes, 20). This sum would be approximately $3,000 today. Identified by Forbes for his unique style of lettering, the same artist began carving a winged skull, called the "death's head" symbol, on his stones. This symbol had been commonly used in printed advertisements of deaths in England since Elizabethan times (Ludwig, 236). Proceeding tentatively, the artist then began decorating the bands underneath the shoulders of the stone with spirals and curves. He also made footstones for some graves that were smaller versions of the same shape. The Stone Cutter of Boston also embellished the stones' inscriptions with Latin epitaphs such as *Tempus edax rerum* (time is the devourer of things) and *Memento te esse mortalem* (remember you are mortal).

Whoever the Stone Cutter of Boston was, his work continued to become more elaborate. Although he rarely deviated from putting the death's head design in the center, he began to carve in high relief, adding more depth and shadows to his work. He created flowers in the borders and carved little heads with scalloped hair in the shoulder arcs. These faces vaguely resembled the putti that were being carved at the same time in Europe, but they were much simpler and much less detailed. Forbes believed that the Stone Cutter of Boston had enough skill to carve, in high relief, the elaborate stone for the grave of John Foster buried in Dorchester in 1681. Instead of the usual death's head symbol, the tympanum design contains a scene with a skeleton, an angel, a smiling sun and a globe. Frieze work on the tombstone he created for Joseph Tapping, buried in the first Anglican church in Boston, King's Chapel, in 1678, also shows an angel embracing a skeleton. The intricate shape of the stone resembles others being made in Britain at the

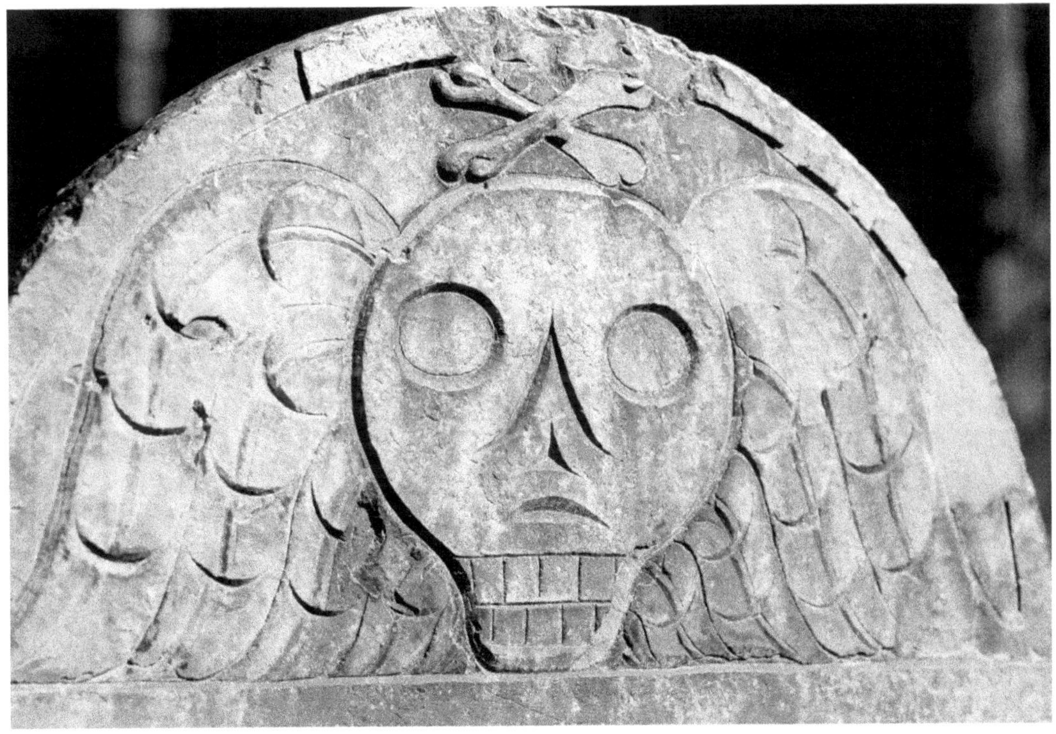

Death's-head symbol (Jana Schwartz).

same time. If these truly were his work, one wonders why the Stone Cutter of Boston repeated the same death's head imagery over and over again for his Boston area clients. This leaves us to believe that either there was more than one stonecutter in the Boston area at this time, or the one man was capable of doing more intricate work than his customers wanted or could afford.

Forbes wrote that we can see the artistry of the Puritans in their carved tombstones (Forbes, 2). Despite the fact that few colonists were able to read, and hardly any could read Latin, she believed that the beautiful lettering alone gives us insight into the Puritan aesthetic sensibility and deepest feelings about death. But Linden-Ward in her book *Silent City on a Hill* reminds us that the influential Puritan minister, Increase Mather (1639–1723), sermonized that "to praise the dead is to praise corruptible flesh … to praise memory is to worship the dead" (Linden-Ward, 26). In her opinion, Puritan graveyards were meant to mortify pride and the ambition to amass gain in this world. To Linden-Ward the graveyards around Boston, tightly clustered, with every inch of available space occupied, do just this. Yet despite his words, Mather did not want his own son's grave to go unmarked or undecorated. Forbes discovered that in 1688 Mather hired a stonecutter named William Mumford (1641–1718) to carve a headstone for his son, Nathanael Mather, which marked the young man's Salem grave.

William Mumford had been a servant to Henry Shrimpton, a brazier, who engraved copper and brass. Mumford must have picked up carving and design skills from this artisan, because his carvings were decorative rather than creative and changed little over time. All of his gravestones contain a death's head set into the center of the tympanum of the stone. Plain disks, or sometimes rosettes, decorate the arc of each shoulder, topping off a descending border of figs, flowers and leaves. The wings of the death's head were always carved in the same manner, looking like the overlapping petals of a marigold blossom. This lack of creativity was not as surprising as the fact that Mumford, being a Quaker, carved images on grave markers at all.

Quakerism arose in the mid–17th century with the belief that every individual had his or her own access and connection to God. Quakers believed in equality and rejected the Calvinist idea that only a select few would be saved. Although many of the followers of the religion became wealthy, they advocated simplicity in dress and speech. Each Quaker community was allowed to make its own decision about allowing gravestones in their burial places, but Quakers frowned upon undue ornamentation and expressions of social distinction. They would have objected to the decorated gravestones Mumford carved. Several in his community were even against simple grave markers made of wood, feeling that these venerated the dead. They preferred being buried in unmarked graves (Bromberg, 79).

When his master died in 1666, Mumford inherited five pounds from his estate. Soon after, he had enough resources to marry a woman named Ruth Copp and purchase a house from her father on Copp's Hill. Ruth's dowry came with ten pounds and ten acres of land in Braintree, Massachusetts, a place noted for its excellent slate. Although Mumford was a Quaker, he was connected to the Mather church through his wife, who was a member. All of his children were baptized there (Forbes, 28). While the Stone Cutter of Boston lived, Mumford was referred to in documents and bills as a mason and a slater. When the Stone Cutter of Boston either retired or died, Mumford's reputation as a carver of gravestones grew. By 1700, Mumford was referred to in documents as being "the" stonecutter of Boston, indicating how successful he was at this work.

In 1695 Mumford charged one pound even for stone markers for Moses Draper, buried in Copp's Hill, and for Captain Samuel Ruggles, buried in the Eustis Street Burying Ground (Forbes, 30). Although the stone for the captain is larger and more elaborate, both of these tombstones have winged death's heads in the center of the tympanum with similar flower petal designs for feathers on the wings. Blank disks fill the rounded arcs of the shoulders, topping off the side-border flower designs. The stone Mumford created for Increase Mathers' son in 1688 has the same death's head in the center, and the same border designs on each side as the others. It deviates in that there is a carved flower in the arc of each shoulder instead of a blank disk, and the border pattern continues under the inscription tablet, emphasizing the square area where the deceased's name and epitaph are carved.

Aside from his carving business, Mumford was involved in several successful business ventures and had enough clout and money to purchase land and pay for the building of the brick Quaker Meeting House on Boston's Brattle Street. When the congregation outgrew this place, he bought another lot and had a larger meeting house built. Around this new meeting house was the Quaker graveyard where the dead were buried in unmarked graves or lay under very plain, unadorned stones.

Mumford also made stones for the deceased of Newport, Rhode Island, where his married daughter, Elizabeth, lived. The earliest gravestone in the Newport cemetery dates from 1696. Made of plain red sandstone, the marker is for Mr. R. Smith. This graveyard also contains stones cut by the Stone Cutter of Boston. One of these was made for Mumford's relative, Ann Mumford, who died in 1697/8. Mumford himself chose to be buried in the common graveyard on Copp's Hill rather than in the Quaker burial grounds. Mumford's widow, Ruth, and his three surviving daughters marked his grave with a large double stone made from Connecticut sandstone. The carving on this stone is so similar to Mumford's known work that Forbes believed he must have carved it himself before he passed in 1718 (Forbes, 34).

Another carver who was a contemporary of Mumford signed his initials, J. N., in several places on the stone he carved for John Cleverly, buried in Quincy in 1703. This stone has the typical bedstead shape and a death's head at the top of the tympanum, but underneath is an hourglass flanked by two opposing peacocks. Forbes was not able to find any records of payment to a carver with those initials, but she did find other stones signed in the same manner. An example of this is the one carved in 1705 for the Reverend Edward Tompson, buried in Marshfield, Massachusetts. Instead of the death's head image, this stone has a vase with flowers surrounded by curling leaves on the tympanum. Flowers are carved into the arcs of the shoulders; the borders are made of stems filled with more flowers and leaves that serpentine along the sides. J. N. was also able to copy the style of Mumford in the stone he carved and signed for the Reverend Ichabod Wiswall, laid to rest in Duxbury, Massachusetts, in 1700.

Although the stone for Deborah Thomas, in Marshfield, dated 1696, was not signed, Forbes believed that it was also carved by this mysterious man. This stone has a winged putto head at the center top of the tympanum instead of the death's head. It also has lily flowers carved in deep relief. Forbes believed that the stone carved for Ruth Carter, who died in 1698, was also carved by this artist. Each scroll on the shoulders contains a realistic skeleton standing on a chest tomb. One looks out and faces forward, while the other has turned its back to the inscription as if it is walking away. An urn with a single flower occupies the center of the tympanum space. Its leaves arabesque to the edges and fill the entire area. Flowers carved in low relief also fill the tympanum of the stone carved for Thaddeus MacCarty in 1705. Another stone, carved for Sarah Nisbett in 1698 and located in Milford, Connecticut, has winged putti on the tympanum on either side of a squat urn filled with what appears to be fruit. Forbes hints that the J. N. initials might stand for John Nichols, a joiner who had relatives and lived in the areas where these stones are found. Or it might have stood for John Noyes, a Boston silversmith born in 1674 (Ludwig, xxxiii).

The Lamson family lived in the waterfront area of Boston called Charlestown. Forbes believed that the patriarch, Joseph Lamson, was an apprentice to the Stone Cutter of Boston because his early work bears a strong resemblance to that of the older man. Forbes identified Lamson's work by his rare use of lower-case letters along with the capitals in his inscriptions. He also carved the word "the" instead of the more commonly used "ye." His carvings demonstrate good symmetrical design skills, but his figures are crude and almost comical, showing that he never acquired drawing ability. What Forbes calls "little men" busily at work depicted on his tombstones seem like childish caricatures of the human form. These can be seen below the death's head and on either side of the hourglass he carved for John Hammond in 1709. The heads carved on the top of the shoulder arcs might also have been attempts at the putti icon. The faces Lamson carved on the shoulder arcs were even more simplified in the finely carved tombstone for Per Tufts, made in 1700. The price for a gravestone had gone down. The stone Lamson created for Richard Kaets in 1717 cost his family two pounds and twelve shillings on condition that it be carted to the burying ground (Forbes, 43).

An exception to his poor execution of carved faces is the winged cherub head carved in 1711 for John Fowle, who lies in Charlestown's graveyard. In his book *Graven Images*, Allan Ludwig called the stone Lamson carved for John Russell "surely one of the finest stones in New England" and a masterful blending of the glyptic and modeling modes of stone carving. If these truly were his, one wonders if Lamson was abstracting his other figures intentionally. It is possible that his Puritan customers objected to realistic portrayal of the human form in order to avoid idolatry. Lamson's children, Nathaniel and Caleb, continued in this line of work but did little to explore form or material. Instead, they produced the same boring death's head image on stones, with fewer and fewer decorative elements as time went by.

While he lived and was able to work, Mumford's stones were the preferred ones for Boston area burials. Being involved in so many other ventures, he undoubtedly trained apprentices, and Nathaniel Emmes probably was one. The first record of a payment for a gravestone to Emmes was in 1717, the year before Mumford's death. Soon after this, he became the most important stonecutter in the Boston area. Forbes did not record the cost of this stone, but in 1718 Emmes was paid one pound, ten shillings for a stone he created for Nathanael Newell (Forbes, 58) The work of Emmes resembled the work of Mumford, although cruder and even less imaginative. Instead of the blue slate that Mumford used, Emmes at first preferred a red colored slate that unfortunately did not hold up as well. Still, from 1717 to 1753 Forbes found that 87 estates made payments to him, which were probably all for gravestones (Forbes, 58). In time, Emmes returned to using the higher quality blue slate stone, and his work grew neater and more organized. This might have been because his sons Joshua and Henry began helping him. After his death, Emmes sons continued carving stones; however, it was William Codner, Emmes' pupil or apprentice, and not his children, who was paid 40 pounds to carve the coat-of-arms on the stone for William Clark in 1743. For some reason Codner was not able to copy the design from the inlay piece set on the floor of the Clark mansion, and the estate had to pay Thomas Johnson, described as an "artist," fifty-seven pounds to make a drawing of the heraldry for Codner to use. The carved coat-of-arms on the gravestone is bordered with garlands of fruit, which might have also been drawn by Johnson or copied from the mantel in the Clark mansion.

Working from pictures had become a specialty of Codner, who carved several portraits of deceased individuals on gravestones for upper-class families of Charleston, South Carolina, which was called "Charles Town" at the time. A select number of portrait effigies had been made in New England, such as the one made for the Rev. Jonathan Pierpont in 1709 (Ludwig, 236), but the first monument of this kind in Charleston marked the grave of the Reverend Nathan Bassett, who died in 1738. Codner was so proud of the work he did on this stone that he carved his name on the base of the monument. Carving stone portraits of individuals was important to Greek and Roman civilizations, and by the early 1700s it had become popular with the English, who were entering the neoclassical movement in the arts. Charleston was a cosmopolitan port city where travelers brought their new ideas. In Charleston the stonecutters' abilities were not stifled by New England Puritan dogma and worries about idolatry. Codner's work demonstrated that he could sculpt well enough to capture the likeness of an individual, and he was hired, in 1744, to carve the portrait of the Reverend Grindall Rawson on his gravestone in Mendon, Massachusetts.

Edwin Dethlefsen and James Deetz studied some of the graveyards Forbes photographed around the Boston area in the 1960s. Noting the lack of artistry in most of them, they described the gravestones as "folk products" (Dethlefsen, 502). Even Forbes admitted that by the middle of the 18th century "the cutting of an ordinary gravestone had got to be a rather monotonous and dull art in Boston" (Forbes, 62). The research of Dethlefsen and Deetz tied the different images found on stones to changing religious attitudes toward death in Colonial and Federal period America. They also announced to the academic world that the study of gravestones gave valuable information about personal and societal values and social organization of this time (Dethlefsen, 503). These researchers found that despite unique designs reflecting the work of local artisans, three basic motifs for the tympani of gravestones were common among all the burial grounds. These were the death's head, which was the most common motif of the oldest stones, the winged cherub head, also called the winged soul head (which I believe is closely linked to European putti), appearing after the middle of the 18th century, and the urn and willow pattern that appeared at the close of the 18th century and the beginning of the 19th. They noted that in time, the work on the death's heads and the cherub stones grew less complex (Dethlefsen, 503). They also noted that the form of the arced, shouldered bedstead gravestone gave way to a square shoulder shape when decorated with the urn and willow design.

The death's head is an abbreviated symbol of the winged skeleton that appears in Northern European Renaissance art. This symbol represents either the spirit liberated from the body, or the angel of death—the divine messenger of God. The skull is representative of the entire skeleton. It is easily identified and easier to carve than all the rest of the bones. Plus, a skull takes up less vertical room on the tympanums of the gravestone, while the wings, a nice decorative element, add symmetry to the skull and fill up the entire arch of the stone. Dethlefsen and Deetz noted that the gnashing teeth of the early New England death's heads moved down and eventually resembled a collar, while a smiling mouth was added under the nose, reflecting a more hopeful view of the afterlife. They believed that the death's heads represented the remains of the body, while the cherub heads represented the immortal components of the deceased (Dethlefson, 507). They wrote that the urn and willow motif does not represent either the body or soul of the deceased individual and is a depersonalized image instead (Dethlefson, 507). Others have pointed out that the urn and willow tree are symbols for the graveyard, placing the emphasis on the bereft rather than on the deceased.

When Dethlefson and Deetz looked at English gravestones they saw a similar change of motifs occurring more than half a century earlier. Cherub heads were popular in England at the beginning of the 18th century, but it wasn't until the 1720s that they appeared in a small number around the Boston area in Cambridge and Charlestown, appearing on the grave markers of the elite such as Harvard College presidents and their wives, high church officials, the governor's daughter and a visitor from London. They noted that the purchase of cherub head stones resembled a battleship-shaped curve in time. At the beginning of the use of this design, only a few elite individuals ordered a carved cherub head on their headstone, while the rest of the population continued to ask gravestone carvers to produce the standard death's head skulls (Dethlefson, 508). By the middle of the century cherub heads were in highest demand, only to be eclipsed in popularity at the end of the century by the urn and willow design.

In his individual research Deetz found that early on, the death's head symbol was replaced by the cherub head symbol on gravestones in Newport, Rhode Island. Newport was an important port city and a leader in commerce and intellectualism. The primary religion in Newport was Baptist and the city was noted for religious tolerance (Deetz, 117).

Death's and cherub head gravestones from Boston are found in other graveyards from colonial times. In an article written for *Historical Archaeology* magazine, Gaynell Stone explains that Long Island had no quarriable stone. This meant that all early gravestones, except for field stone markers, had to be imported. Twelve percent came from Massachusetts, 20 percent from Connecticut, 27 percent from New York City, and 8 percent from Rhode Island. The pattern of substitution of motifs compared favorably to those found by Dethlefson and Deetz with the willow and urn eventually overtaking death's head and cherub designs (Stone, 147). In Long Island, the Dutch were twice as likely to use field stone memorials as the English, except for the Quakers. Long Island Quakers tended to choose natural stones with a pointed top. Researchers also found that wooden markers were used in Long Island Quaker cemeteries and that some of these were carved with designs. The Dutch language was used on stones until 1817. Their inscriptions faced east so that one didn't have to walk on the grave to read them, unlike the English stones, which faced west. This changed in time, however, and all decorations faced west (Stone, 153). We know that Native American were servants and slaves to the Dutch settlers of Long Island, but there is only one wood post marking a Native American grave in Long Island from this time. The others were buried beneath cobbled mounds (Stone, 149).

The Hill family of Connecticut carved winged cherub heads on gravestones and sent them to customers in Long Island. In 1783 the family moved to Sag Harbor, where they eventually discontinued making the cherub heads and explored other motifs such as plain lettering, ornate floral designs, and urn and willow decorations. Artists had to be flexible because the location of the graveyard and the ethnicity of the customer affected the choice of the gravestone design (Stone, 152). By the early 1800s transportation

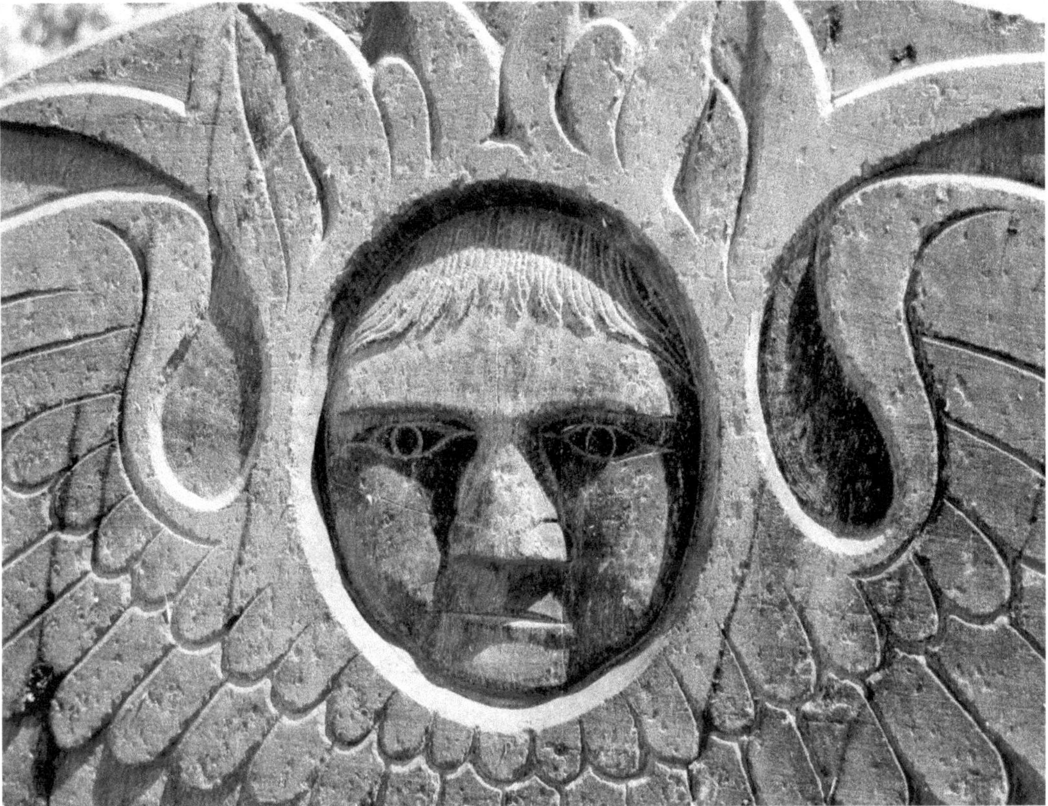

Winged cherub head, Eliot Burying Grounds, Roxbury, Massachusetts (Paul Neumann).

improved, and gravestones from New York City's cutting center dominated the Long Island trade. Shipping fees were included in the price. The oldest of these stones were plain lettering, but some contain ornate calligraphy for the "in memory of" portion at the head of the stone. Also from New York came cherub heads with or without wings. Stones decorated in the urn and willow design followed (Stone, 152).

Elizabeth Crowell studied gravestones in the Middle Atlantic region of America including graveyards in Philadelphia; Cape May County, New Jersey; tidewater Virginia; and southern Maryland. She discovered that by the 1740s people from St. Mary's County in Maryland were able to import their gravestones from Philadelphia, as did those living in Cape May, New Jersey. Limestone was quarried in Montgomery and Chester, near Philadelphia, making gravestones affordable to a wide segment of the population. However, Philadelphia was a Quaker stronghold, and gravestones imported from there throughout the 18th century were very plain and without ornamentation of any kind.

In the southeastern cities, including Charleston, South Carolina and Savannah, Georgia, urban burials took place in churchyards and rural burials took place in the village burial plot. When people moved to their own plantations, they found themselves at great distances from population centers. Even though English settlers of Georgia preferred being buried in the consecrated ground of a churchyard, people took to burying their dead in family cemeteries on their plantations or their farms. It wasn't until the 1780s that roads improved enough to make churchyard burials possible again (Crowell, 13).

There was a dearth of local stone in the southeast, which meant that gravestones had to be imported. The cost of shipping was added to the cost of the stones, which made them very expensive and an indicator of socio-economic status. Information taken from wills, estate inventories and family papers tell us that the majority of gravestones found in tidewater Virginia prior to the American Revolution were imported from England, but after experiencing dramatic economic growth around 1750, colonists from the South other than the rich were able to import gravestones from England as well (Gorman, 91). A coat of arms carved onto a grave marker indicated that the individual was a member of the gentry. If not, a carved skull and crossed bones design was popular on these imported stones. For Protestants this symbol signified the brevity of life. For Catholics this symbol encouraged the family to pray for the deceased, decreasing the time they would spend in purgatory. Some of these stones were even signed with the carver's name.

About half of all gravestones found in South Carolina and Georgia were imported slate tablets from New England, carved by our country's first sculptors, the stone carvers. On them is the same imagery of death's heads, cherubs and willow and urn patterns. Dethlefsen and Deetz believe that the popularity of the cherub heads coincided with the "Great Awakening" of Puritanism in 1740 that stressed the existence of an afterlife. They also believe that the urn and willow design came into popularity with the founding of Unitarianism and Methodism in the last decade of the 18th century (Gorman, 89). But Frederick Gorman and Michael DiBlasi note that the popularity of these gravestone designs lagged these events in the deep South. The cherub head, introduced in New England in the 1720s, didn't reach its peak of popularity in the South until 1790; and with the passing of the "Non-Importation Agreement of 1767" by South Carolina and Georgia, there was a decrease in gravestone importation from Britain. Indigenous stonecutters in these two states bought blank slate stones from Northern stone quarries and created their own innovative local designs. Motifs such as bird heads, angels, anchors, skeletons, and the wreath and torch appear on South Carolina gravestones. The hourglass, the cross, Father Time, the shroud and masonic emblems appear on stones in the cemeteries of Georgia. Common to both states (besides the death's head, the cherub head, plain inscription, and urn and willow designs) are portraits, sunflowers, rosettes, and the skull and crossbones (Goerman, 79).

The earliest slate headstone from New England, found in Charleston, South Carolina, is dated 1710 (Nelson, 103). It is believed that Southern clients communicated directly with the New England stonecutters, such as Josiah Manning and the Lamson family, who began signing their work in an effort to attract new Southern customers. New England stonecutters such as John Bull, a carver from Newport, Rhode Island, traveled to Southern cities and advertised in 1773 that he would take orders for stones (Nelson, 97). George Allen, also from New England, traveled with a stock of blank stones and lived in Charleston in 1787. Allen advertised that he had "Slate Tomb Stones and Gravestones, of an excellent quality, which he will furnish with inscriptions only or ornaments with coats of arms, crests, or other sculpture" (Nelson, 97). Any unused stones were bought by local artisans such as David Merry, John Saxon and Richard Baylis, who advertised in local directories that they were stonecutters ((Nelson, 97). South Carolinians preferred portrait stones and Northern carvers eagerly complied. Historians are not sure if the artists worked from paintings of the deceased or drew their own sketches from the corpses. By the 1750s Anglicans from South Carolina had the cherub head design replaced by portraits of the deceased on their stones. These predated the popularity of these images in New England by 30 years. These portraits might not be totally realistic, but in the days before *Godey's Ladies' Book*, they are remarkable pictorial references of the hair, wig, clothing, and jewelry styles of the times.

William Codner was the first to do a portrait stone for a Charleston customer. He was paid to created so many of this type of stone that Forbes believed he must have been able to get a good likeness of the deceased. After him portrait stones were sculpted by Daniel Hasting, the Parks of Groton, and John Stevens of Rhode Island. William Park immigrated from Scotland in 1756 when he was fifty-one. Working in the Boston area, Parks came to America with a large variety of designs and the skill to carve exquisite flowers on the side borders of his stones. But Forbes believed he learned to do portrait work from a New England drawing primer, because his faces all looked the same (Forbes, 71).

John Stevens, listed as a mason, bought land in 1705 in Newport, Rhodes Island, where he made simple, shallowly carved gravestones. When he died in 1736 at 90 years of age, his sons John and William continued the business. John is believed to have carved many of the coats of arms in the Farewell Street Burying Ground, Newport's cemetery (Forbes, 93). This man also repaired shoes, built houses and made chimneys. His son, also named John, continued the family business and even began signing his work with "Cut by John Stevens Junr" on the bottoms or on the backs of his stones (Forbes, 96). It was probably this John Stevens who was hired to make the portrait stone for Phillis Lyndon, the African American servant or slave to Governor Josias Lyndon who was a member of the church of Pastor Ezra Stiles. Phillis was the wife of Zingo Steven, the slave of John Stevens who was able to buy his freedom and continue working in the shop as a stone carver. Phillis's grave is in a separate section of the Newport cemetery reserved for people of color. The portrait on her gravestone shows her wearing a kerchief covering her hair and makes an attempt at portraying realistic features. Either John Stevens or Zingo created stones for other African Americans as well as Caucasians. In 1781 Stevens advertised that his stones are "superior to any commonly found in America" (Forbes, 96). The Steven's family continued carving gravestones until they sold the shop in 1927, when it was bought by John Howard Bensen. The shop was still in operation on the same site in 2017.

Ancestors of the Stevens family came from Oxfordshire, England. Ancestors of another stone-carving family named the Bighams came from Ulster Province of Ireland and settled on the Appalachian frontier around 1730. The Scots-Irish Bighams had little contact with New England stonecutters, and although they were able to carve similar designs, their choice of decoration was a coat of arms showing the clan identification of the deceased. Western Pennsylvania was far away from the College of Arms, the official authority on British heraldry, and the Bigham stone carvers took advantage of this by adding or subtracting heraldic elements and placing them in unique configurations instead of duplicating the full coat of arms containing the crest, the mantling and the shield.

In the 1760s Samuel Bigham, Sr., moved to Steele Creek, North Carolina, where a number of Scots-Irish Presbyterians had established a church. It was there that they set up a stone carving shop with at least six different stonecutters. According to Edward Clark's article "The Bigham Carvers of the Carolina Piedmont," Samuel Bigham, Jr., was the most skilled carver (Clark, 37). He also identified himself as a stonecutter, even signing his name with the initials "s. c." on legal documents. Samuel junior's two brothers,

William and Hugh, were also stonecutters along with two apprentices, James Sloan and William McKinley. Stones from the Bigham shop have a variety of traditional British designs on them such as the Scottish thistle, the tree of life and the dove of promise. The dove symbol, sometimes portrayed with an olive branch in its beak, was most often carved on the tympanum of a stone marking the grave of a child or an adolescent.

While in operation from 1740 to 1820, this family of carvers created more than 800 stones. Their early work shows an allegiance to their Scots-Irish heritage. As time went by, heraldic shields showing clan identity gave way to symbols that represented the patriotism they and their customers felt for their new country. On one stone carved for a relative, Andrew Bigham, who died in 1788, a carver sculpted the seal of the Commonwealth of Pennsylvania instead of a coat of arms. On another stone carved for Robert Bigham in 1777, the sculptor carved thirteen stars on a heraldic shield. Each star represented one state of the United States. It is interesting to note that this was completed before the Revolutionary War was won (Clark, 57). The Bigham family of carvers did not follow the formula of carving death's heads, cherubs, or willows and urns. In their gravestone carvings they were able to tell the story of their family and their customers' journey from immigrant to American citizen.

* * *

Looking at these American gravestones, especially those from rural areas of Colonial and early Federal period times, one might believe that they show a purely American style of art. These simplified images even seem to act as harbingers of the Abstract Art movement of the late 19th and early 20th centuries. But Allen Ludwig casts doubts on this theory, noting the similarity to imagery found on Romano-British stones. He also explained that some symbols such as the rosette, the setting or rising sun, leaf designs, and the skull are common to cultures all around the world. In his book is the image of a British woodcut advertising the death of Mrs. Rebekah Sewall. On it are printed images of skeletons, hourglasses with and without wings, skull heads, crossed bones, and heavily decorated borders with icons found on the gravestones of America. This demonstrates the influence English symbols and design had on American stonecutters. Another way American design was influenced by British iconography was through "emblem books." These European books containing prints of drawings, poetry and prose were very popular up to the 18th century and served as inspiration for border design and symbolic imagery. By the end of the 18th century, printing techniques had improved to such an extent that European and British books and illustrated journals arrived on American shores. These introduced Americans to neoclassical design and were a great homogenizer of fashion and taste. Gravestones inspired by archaeological discoveries in Italy and Greece may have seemed out of place in the wilds of America, but their discovery renewed interest in what Ludwig called "Imperial Rome" and "Olympian Greece." These influences first appeared in America in the 1780s, and Ludwig confirms that by 1800 almost every burial ground in New England except for those in isolated, rural areas had gravestones in this new style. The urn in the urn and willow pattern probably represented the urns used by ancient Greeks and Romans to hold ashes of their deceased. The weeping willow tree originated in China. Able to propagate from virile twigs, the tree followed merchants along the silk route and was brought to England in the mid–1700s and to North America by colonists. As an image for the bereaved, the willow is mentioned in Psalm 137 as being the tree in which the Hebrews hung their harps and wept.

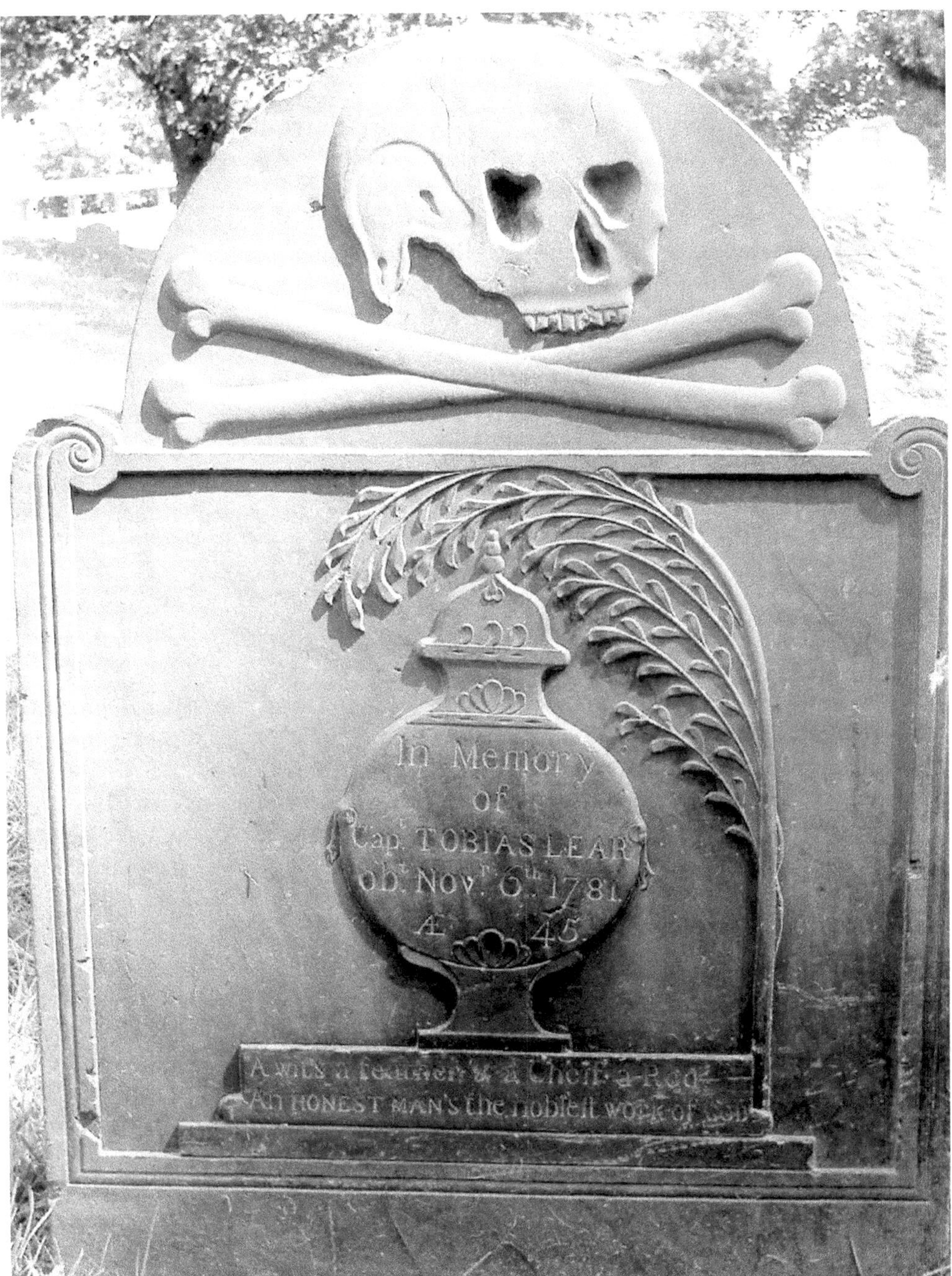

Skull and Crossbones, Urn and Laurel **(courtesy Heather Salek).**

The urn and willow became a widespread design for tombstones, and while there are some variations with aesthetic interest, many carvers came up with a design and then did not deviate from it. Stonecutters such as the grandsons of William Park became less artists and more businessmen. They expanded their shops and reproduced urn and willow gravestones with "deadly mechanical commercial flatness" (Ludwig, 337). Some carvers, such as the Scots-Irish William Young, didn't have contact with other stone carvers. His work was sought after and better liked than the urn and willow stones younger men carved. Young continued carving gravestones decorated with thistles, bunch-berries, tulips and other flowers until he was 80 years old in 1791 (Forbes, 80). But others, like Benjamin Day, kept ready-made head- and foot-stones in stock, complete with an urn and a willow tree drooping over an oval that contained the words "Here lies" or "In Memory of." A blank space was left for the name of the individual and his or her dates. On the bottom of the stones, in small letters, was a bland epitaph appropriate for either saint or a sinner, such as "An honest man's the noblest work of God" or "Death levels all both the Wicked and the Just" (Day, 8). At the base, Day put his name and the address of his shop as an advertisement.

The quarrying of slate became mechanized. It took two men ten hours using picks to cut slate 6 inches wide, 5 inches deep and 24 feet long. By 1839 the Pin Hill quarry owned by Benjamin Day in Harvard had a converted mill. Stone saws moved back and forth, powered by a water wheel and a crank. Saws were kept wet and a slurry of sand in the slit of the stone, called the kerf, did the cutting (Day, 10). Once he found his style, Day's work became mechanical. Like other gravestone producers, he rarely varied it.

Death and the Landscape Artist: The English Garden

Over time, European churchyards became dangerously overcrowded. Concerned individuals and the rich searched for new ways to dispose of their corpses, employing architects, landscape artists, and designers to help with this task. Churchyard burials were outlawed in Paris in 1773 in response to concern about "exhalations" from the receptacles of the dead (Smith, 18). The consecrated cemetery of Saints-Innocents was the first to cause alarm. Founded in the 10th century, it was the oldest Parisian graveyard. By the mid–18th century it served 22 parishes, in addition to receiving the dead from the Hôtel-Dieu hospital, which included epidemic victims. Over eight centuries an estimated 2 million Parisians were buried there, mostly in twenty-foot trenches that were dug thirty feet deep. The trenches were nothing more than open pits filled with shrouded dead bodies, covered by planks of wood, and left open for months on end until they were filled to capacity. When filled, they were covered with a thin layer of dirt. Over the centuries, the added soil had raised the churchyard so much that it was 8 feet above the level of the street. Bodies didn't stay in the pit for long. The standard burial was only two years; then the bones were sifted from the earth and the process began all over again. Two years is not enough time for the human body to decompose on its own, so powdered lye and quicklime were added to hasten the process (Linden-Ward, 19).

The elite could pay for the privilege of being buried inside a church, or in a small family tomb, but this cost dearly because the Catholic church had a monopoly. The remains of the lesser nobility and the bourgeoisie were thrown with the rest of the masses into a putrid and horrible—but consecrated—hole. This was the norm in all Catholic countries during this time. As can be imagined, the pits stank. At the end of the eighteenth century foul odors were understood to be unhealthy, and Parisians wanted change.

As early as 1713 residents near the royal botanical garden in Paris complained of polluted air. The lieutenant-general of the Paris police, Marc-René D'Argenson, discovered that this was caused by two burial pits built to hold 10,000 dead but that held more than 10,000 more. D'Argenson demanded that quicklime be added to the trenches and that they be mounded over with 400 additional cartloads of dirt (Linden-Ward, 21). He issued new regulations limiting the size of burial pits to ten feet deep, nine feet wide and 48 feet long. No more than seven layers of bodies would be allowed, which meant that the pits could hold no more than 500 dead. But the regulation was impossible to enforce. The problems were the same throughout the country, and in 1776 King Louis XVI authorized towns to purchase land outside city limits to create new graveyards. Unfortunately, civil decrees and secular efforts failed to change the Church-run burial system, which relied heavily on burial fees.

In 1779 gases from a communal trench in the Cimitière des Saints-Innocents began to seep into several houses bordering it, and people started getting sick. A year later a cellar wall collapsed, uncovering thousands of decaying cadavers (Mytum, 289). The inspector general, Cadet de Vaux, made a report on this hazardous condition to the Royal Academy of Science in 1783 and recommended that Saints-Innocents be closed. But it wasn't until 1786 that the archbishop of Paris, Monseigneur Leclerc de Juigné, finally agreed. The land was deconsecrated (Linden-Ward, 22). The French Royal Society of Medicine supervised the sifting of bones from the soil and their relocation, a process that took two years. An ossuary, named "the Catacombs," (after the burial tunnels of Rome) was consecrated. Architect Héricart de Thury was hired to supervise the placement of these bones in neat and orderly "artistic arrangements." The public could enter and view these catacombs for a fee (*ibid.*).

Conditions in London were no better than they were in France. Even though there were over a hundred parish churchyards in that city, some of them had been used for centuries and dated back to Roman and Saxon times. For example, in 1845, the churchyard of St. Martin-in-the-Fields in the northeast corner of Trafalgar Square contained an estimated seventy thousand burials (Linden-Ward, 25). Because churchyards were small, there was the need to use and reuse every inch of soil, and the accumulation of dirt from successive burials added height to the churchyards so that they towered over the entrances to the churches.

John C. Loudon (1783–1843) was a Scottish botanist and garden designer who criticized the burying practices of his day, saying that they were "disgusting" and caused disease and even death to the living (Loudon, 4). A major concern of his was the noxious gases that corpses emitted and the living inhaled. Although they might not be noticeable for 3 or 4 days, gasses escape the decomposing corpse through the nostrils and mouth. A corpulent cadaver might swell so much before it was removed from the house that it was ready to burst. Dead bodies also contain fluids. If the burial was too delayed, the fluid might drop from the coffin before it could be taken from the house. Once buried in free soil, this fluid mixes with rain and is carried to a natural outlet, or to a well, where it may contaminate drinking water. If buried in a wooden coffin in free soil, to a depth of 5 or 6 feet, the gas and fluids would be mostly absorbed and not be contaminants. But if a corpse was placed in a catacomb, a vault or brick grave under a church, or even was set into a lead-lined coffin buried in the churchyard, the fetid matter had nowhere to go. It remained in the enclosed space, or coffin, until it decayed. Louden doubted that even "hermetically sealed" catacombs were truly airtight, and he thought that there were usually crevices in the leaded coffins. In his time there had been spontaneous explosions in catacombs, requiring undertakers to make repairs. He recommended that to avoid this problem coffins needed to be tapped and the gas burnt as it escaped (Loudon, 4).

Loudon also decried the practice of interring a number of bodies in the same grave without enough earth over each corpse to absorb escaping material from decomposition. He described how in 1813, coffins were inserted into cells in the boundary wall of Poland's Warsaw, which were hermetically sealed with stucco. The name of the deceased was then traced with an iron instrument onto the wet plaster. However, as in France, the poor were buried in trenches in open ground without coffins, and naked, dead soldiers from the battle of Bautzen were put into large square pits. In the countryside, families who couldn't afford the fee to be buried in a churchyard were dropped from the parish coffin into holes dug by the roadside.

Loudon noted that grave-diggers complained of "intolerable suffering" when they reopened family graves. The crowded burial ground was so full of gas, and the earth stank so badly as the grave diggers got within 2 to 3 feet of the last coffin, that they needed to drink a lot of rum to anesthetize themselves enough to finish their job. He added,

> It is only requisite to stand for a minute or two beside a grave which has been opened down to the last-deposited coffin, to experience the suffocating effects of the effluvia of decomposition, which escapes even from a coffin which has perhaps been only deposited a week or two, and the wood of which is of course perfectly sound [Loudon, iii–iv].

Loudon warned that the public should understand the danger they were in from living near churchyards that were full but were still over-burying. These neighbors should not drink water from wells dug in the vicinity of burial grounds. No one should attend services in a church or chapel with a graveyard or vaults attached (Loudon, 4). Loudon was hired to plan a new cemetery in Cambridge, England, and wrote down his suggestions in his work *On the Laying Out, Planting and Managing of Cemeteries and on the Improvement of Churchyards,* which he self-published in 1843 and which became a standard reference for what came to be known as the "garden" or "rural" cemetery movement. While he believed that the main object of a burial ground was the disposal of the remains of the dead so that their decomposition didn't injure the living, the second object was to act as a sort of cultural institution that would improve morality and the taste of all classes, especially that of the masses.

Burial grounds of his day were feared. Solitary and deserted, they were nightmares, gloomy horrors, and were shunned. Loudon would have the dead buried in a "cemetery," a word not used until the 19th century, taken from the Greek word meaning "a place to sleep." Instead of being surrounded by black, fetid dirt in which nothing could grow, the graves would be marked by beautiful monuments and "properly planted" with cedar, spruce, cypress, yews and honeysuckle. A cemetery such as this would be a place of meditation, a place for moral instruction, a school of instruction for "architecture, sculpture, landscaping-gardening, arboriculture, botany and neatness, order and high keeping" (Loudon, 12). A cemetery like this would be a place where deceased loved ones were surrounded by love. In a place such as this, the dead would inspire the living to be virtuous. Death and the grave are solemn realities, but nature can soothe. A cemetery, properly planned and well tended, can be "the sworn foe to preternatural fear and superstition" (Loudon, 11).

Gardens had become very popular in England and in Europe in the 18th century. While the wealthy and famous had to bury their dead in a consecrated churchyard and were unable to lay them to rest in a beautiful place, they could create a beautiful garden to memorialized them. From 1738 to 1773 Charles Hamilton developed a garden he named Painshill in Surrey, England, that is still open today. Castle Howard's park in Yorkshire had an obelisk built, dedicated to Lord Howard and erected by his son. Still in operation and open to the public for a fee, this park contains the Greek-inspired Temple of the Four Winds and a mausoleum in which the lords of the castle now rest. Originally buried in the parish church yard, the family members were re-interred in the mausoleum in the mid–1700s. This became the first Anglican burial site not connected to the Church, built in England, since ancient times (Linden-Ward, 41). The design and construction of this building were by Nicholas Hawksmoor (1661–1736), who was a leading architect of the English Baroque style.

Another architect, Rombert Adam (1728–1792), designed a Gothic mausoleum for Claremont Gardens in Surry. The ninety-foot-tall, colonnaded Rockingham Mausoleum, built in Wentworth Park in Yorkshire in 1791, was designed by architect John Carr (1723–1807). This building had busts of the Marquis of Rockingham's friends on the first floor and an empty sarcophagus on the second, topped with a Roman cupola on the third (Linden-Ward, 48).

These melancholy structures placed in English gardens were criticized because they were based on "heathen" mythology, but some, like the Irish statesman and philosopher, Edmund Burke (1727–1797), supported them, believing that they encouraged sublime, solitary contemplation of mortality. Sentiments such as these, while they elicited melancholy, could also lead to refined taste. They gave sublime pleasure and so were beneficial to society.

The end of the 18th century saw a new attitude towards death, with more emphasis on the melancholy sentiments of the mourner. It was believed that landscaped gardens could inspire sublime thoughts. In 1790 the Reverend Archibald Alison (1757–1839) from Scotland wrote *Essays on the Nature and Principles of Taste,* declaring that observations of things of beauty triggers a "series of mental suggestions of divine power and love" (quoted in Linden-Ward, 50). Sentiments like this signaled that English gardens were elevators of taste and gave them even more legitimacy. Attention was paid not only to garden horticulture but also to objects placed in the gardens, such as urns, busts of ancestors, ruins, temples, triumphal arches, broken columns and mausoleums, which could be empty or filled. Foliage imbued the viewer with the gentle and awesome power nature has to make humans reflect on higher ideals; the funerary art and architecture initiated serious reflection on the meaning of life and death.

English garden design was embraced by the French after the 1763 Treaty of Paris ended the French and Indian War and the Seven Years' War between Britain and France. Having heard about this new type of garden, tourists from the continent traveled to England to take a look. Many of the elite, such as René-Louis, marquis de Girardin (1735–1808), returned to the continent inspired to create gardens of their own. At the time, gardens in France had been orderly and linear in the Baroque style. The English garden was planted to inspire melancholy and to look natural and disordered. This arrangement reflected the coming philosophical move from neoclassicism to Romantic thought. Philosopher Jean-Jacques Rousseau (1712–1778) spent the last six weeks of his life at Girardin's garden at Ermenonville. The marquis hired workers from Scotland and England to build his garden, and place 50 urns, broken columns and ruins on it. Girardin became the leading authority of English garden design in France. When Rousseau unexpectedly died, Girardin decided to bury him in his garden even though it was forbidden by the Catholic Church. On July 4, 1778, at midnight, a group of dissenters accompanied the embalmed body of Rousseau to a tomb built on an island in his garden that Girardin called the Île de Peupliers. However, Rousseau's bones were not allowed to rest in peace. In 1794 they were moved to the Panthéon in Paris and placed near the remains of another famous writer and philosopher, François-Marie Arouet, otherwise known as Voltaire.

In addition to Rousseau's tomb, Girardin also had built the "Altar of Dreams" in his garden. This was a semicircular temple of philosophy dedicated to Michel Eyquem de Montaigne (1533–1592), one of the most significant French philosophers. Girardin buried other individuals in his garden and also built empty tombs called cenotaphs, which he dedicated to individuals he admired. A guidebook was written for Ermenonville in 1788, and visitors who could afford the price of admission could tour the gardens with the likes of Thomas Jefferson and Benjamin Franklin. Also touring the gardens were kings, queens and leaders of Europe, including King Louis XVI, Queen Marie Antoinette, and later Napoleon and Robespierre. The garden inspired the queen so much that she had *le jardin anglais* created at Versailles. The French king put mock funerary monuments in the gardens of his hunting chateau, Rambouillet; however, the queen replaced the sad ruins with an Austrian hamlet and a *Temple d'Amour* (Temple of Love) (Linden-Ward, 59).

The English dissenter clergyman Joseph Priestley was encouraged by Benjamin Franklin to continue his research on plants. Believing that fire and corrosion was caused by an element named phlogiston, he discovered that plants emitted what he called "dephlogisticated air" (Linden-Ward, 65). Priestly delivered a paper about this to the Royal Society in London in 1772. Shortly after this, Jan Ingenhousz or Ingen-Housz (1730–1799), a Dutch biologist, discovered the process of plant photosynthesis, and the corrosive and flame-inducing element was understood to be oxygen. These discoveries began to convince people like Rousseau's friend Jacques-Henri Benardin de Saint-Pierre (1737–1814), a writer and a botanist, to extend the English garden idea to include cemeteries where plants could nullify the noxious gases created by the decomposition process. St. Pierre went on to advocate that burial places be located outside of cities, in rural, garden settings, or even on an island in the middle of the Seine. He described a suburban cemetery where monuments to the dead were distributed tastefully on land that was planted in a natural pattern with indigenous and imported trees, shrubs and grasses (Linden-Ward, 66). St. Pierre published a philosophical treatise that mentioned gardens in his work *St. Pierre's Studies of Nature*, written in 1784. This work was translated into English and widely read in England and in the United States. In the section entitled "The Pleasure of Ruins," he pointed out that humans have a universal "taste" for ruins (St. Pierre, 308). He hypothesized that this was because they derived pleasure in contemplating danger from a position of personal security. Ruins included in gardens are picturesque. That they look like they have been weathered by time, give "pleasure by launching us into infinity; they carry us several ages back, and interest us in proportion to their antiquity" (St. Pierre, 309). He continued to write that the ruins of Greece interest us more than those of Italy, and the ruins of Egypt interest us more than those of Greece. He wrote: "The ruins in which Nature combats with human art inspire a gentle melancholy. In these she discovers to us the vanity of our labours, and the perpetuity of her own.... The interest of ruin, however, is greatly heightened when some moral sentiment is blended with it" (*ibid.*).

Although St. Pierre believed that no ruin could inspire sentiments as sublime as nature could, he continued in the next section, "The Pleasure of Tombs," to describe the feeling of patriotism one gets when viewing the tombs of founding fathers, and the inspiration one gets from tombs of men of virtue such as Socrates. St. Pierre's garden cemetery would combine nature and places of solitude, with obelisks, ruined columns, pyramids and urns decorated with bas-relief and medallions. The French Revolution also made people wonder why tombs were only for the privileged, and the call was for funeral honors to be the same for all. Before this, however, the French had revived their practice of throwing cadavers into burial pits for the unfortunate thousands who lost their heads to the guillotine.

The first important rural garden cemetery was created in Paris in 1804. It was named *Cimetière du Père-Lachaise* (Père Lachaise Cemetery) after the confessor of King Louis XIV, Father Francois de la Chaise, who at one time lived on the land. The cemetery sprawled over one hundred and ten acres in what was then countryside. Winding paths and flights of steps were built on the acreage to help mourners navigate the varied terrain. The new cemetery was thought to be too far away from the city, and it was not blessed by the Catholic Church, so burials in the new cemetery were few until the administrators began transferring the remains of famous French people such as the playwright Molière and the poet Jean de La Fontaine. Soon afterwards, people became eager to have their relatives buried next to such illustrious citizens, and the neoclassical monuments and mausoleums they built to mark their graves were so crowded that they almost touched one another. By 1830 the cemetery contained more than 33,000 graves, and its directors found that they had to expand it several times. Although Belfast had opened a non-sectarian cemetery outside its city limits in 1774, and reform was taking place in other parts of Europe, it was *Père Lachaise* that had a huge effect on cemetery design.

In England, the Rosary Cemetery was established in 1821 by the nonconformist minister Thomas Drummond, but reforms to Church of England burial grounds were slow to come. Church leaders such as the archdeacon of York wanted to maintain control of burials and the income they provided. It took a statute from Parliament in 1836 to form the private York Cemetery Company, which broke the archbishop's control. A new garden cemetery was built and the first burials occurred the following year in what locals described as the "Père de la Chaise of York" (Mytum, 291). Sadly, city graveyards continued to function, spreading their noxious fumes, until the Burial Acts were passed by the British Parliament in the 1850s, which officially closed them down. By this time, attitudes about death had changed even more. The interment of a loved one needed to be a dignified service. Relatives wanted to erect memorials and visit the graves. Over-burying was no longer tolerated by a public convinced that errant bones caused by digging up the deceased did not look good on decorative flower beds.

In 1836, Parliament passed a statute creating seven new rural cemeteries for London. These were Kensal Green, opened in 1833; West Norwood Cemetery, opened in 1836; Highgate Cemetery, opened in 1839; Abney Park, Brompton, and Nunhead, opened in 1840; and Tower Hamlets, opened in 1841. The British Parliament passed another statute creating the London Cemetery Company. Stephen Geary was hired as the architect, James Bunstone Bunning was the surveyor, and David Ramsey, a garden designer of renown, became the landscape architect. Built on seventeen acres of steep hillside overlooking London, Ramsey filled Highgate Cemetery with exotic plantings that complimented architecture built in the Tudor, Gothic, and classical styles. Highgate quickly became the preferred burial site for Londoners. The cemetery was eventually consecrated by the Church of England, setting two acres aside for dissenters.

The Reverend Alison's essays on nature and taste was reprinted in Edinburgh in 1811 and then in Boston the following year. English poet laureate William Wordsworth (1770–

1850) also describe the value of a rural garden cemetery. In "Essay upon Epitaphs," published in 1810, Wordsworth wrote: "A grave is a tranquillising object: resignation in course of time springs up from it as naturally as the wild flowers, besprinkling the turf with which it may be covered, or gather round the monument by which it is defended" (Owen, 59–60). He reminded those writers of epitaphs that the grave monument "is intended to be permanent" (*ibid.*). This was a far cry from the common pits found in churchyards of his time.

* * *

American elites besides Jefferson and Franklin also paid admission to tour English gardens such as Studley Royal, near Ripon in North Yorkshire, created on the estate of John Aislabie (1670–1742). Aislabie was the disgraced chancellor of the Exchequer, the British national treasury. Aislabie spent 20 years creating his masterpiece, now a World Heritage Site, located in the valley of the River Skell. Aislabie created a formal garden with a "moon pond" (a spot designed to be viewed at night), decorated with classical statues of the Roman gods, Bacchus and Neptune, and the Greek physician and philosopher Galen. He also had workers construct a Greek temple dedicated to Hercules. When his son, William, inherited the property, the temple was redesigned and named the "Temple of Filial Piety." William bought more land adjacent to the garden and expanded it. This land contained the 12th century Fountains Abbey, a Catholic monastery partially destroyed in the time of Henry VIII. Around 1770 William built the Temple of Fame. Not open to the public, this temple supposedly contains a statue of Anne Boleyn. The temples and the ruins of the abbey are meant to serve as reminder of the transitory quality of life.

Another famous English neoclassical garden is Stourhead, in Wiltshire, built by Henry Hoare the Younger (1705–1785), a member of the financial elite. Stourhead gardens are now part of Britain's National Trust. Hoare's life was marked by tragedy when his mother, wife, and two children died within a period of a few years. Never remarrying, he created the landscaped garden and spent the next 40 years developing it. Although he had 50 gardeners to help him, and Architect Henry Flitcroft (1687–1768) to lay out the garden design, Hoare became known as "Henry the Magnificent" because of his gardening abilities. Hoare had workers dam the River Stour to form a lake and built edifices such as the "Chinese Umbrella," the "Turkish Tend" and the "Hermitage" on the path to the "Temple of Apollo." Stourhead was inherited by Sir Richard Colt Hoare, Henry's grandson, who was inspired by the landscape painters of his times. Sir Richard made many changes to the garden. He planted several more trees and added laurel and rhododendron as under-plantings. In addition, he had a building inspired by the Roman Pantheon built near the lake in 1754.

But the most famous English landscape garden of this time was Stowe, in Buckinghamshire, owned by the Temple family. This garden also evolved from a formal, Baroque design to become a pioneering English landscape garden. Buildings in the Stowe garden bear names like "the Temple of Ancient Virtues" and "the Temple of Bacchus." Among several other edifices is the "Queen's Temple," built in 1742 but remodeled in 1772 to resemble ancient Greek architecture, and "The Chinese House," dating from 1738. This was the first known building in England built in a Chinese style. These were placed in areas of vegetation with names like "The Elysian Fields" and the "Grecian Valley," where the "Temple of Concord and Victory" stand. The Temple of Ancient Virtue, built in 1737, has four niches containing four life-sized statues. They are of Epaminondas, an ancient

Greek general; Lycurgus, the ancient Greek law maker; Homer, the poet; and Socrates, the philosopher. All of these were made by Peter Scheemakers (1691–1781), a Flemish sculptor who lived in London. Scheemakers probably learned the art from his father, who was a sculptor. He also studied in Denmark and in Rome. Statues of seven Saxon deities placed in the garden were created by Jan or John Michiel Rysbrack (1694–1770), another Flemish sculptor and son of a painter. Inspired by the deities who gave their names to our days of the week, these sculptures were set around an altar in the area between Roger's Walk, lined with chestnut trees, and Nelson's Seat. Both Scheemakers and Rysbrack established studios in London and were considered the top sculptors of their day. The Temple of British Worthies was built in 1734 and contains busts of 15 notable British men such as John Milton, the poet, and the playwright William Shakespeare. Also included are Sir Walter Raleigh, Sir Francis Drake, and John Locke, made by Rysbrack and Scheemakers (Linden-Ward, 37). Rysbrack also sculpted the bust of Queen Elizabeth I, also included in this curved, roofless structure. Buildings and statues were not the only edifices on the property. Looking like it's set into a little hill is what is known as "Dido's Cave." This rustic-looking alcove, built in the 1720s, was turned into a memorial for the Marchioness of Buckingham in 1781 at her death by her son, the First Duke of Buckingham (Linden-Ward, 39).

While actual bodies might not have been buried in the mausoleums or memorials located in these landscape gardens, the purpose of them was to mingle with the seasonal flow of nature and elicit strong emotions and reflective moods in those who meandered there. The craze for gardening continued into the 19th century. For those who did not have the room or could not afford to build neoclassical architecture, objects placed in gardens that helped one attain a meditative mood also gained in popularity. These included obelisks, columns and urns, which became popular home garden decorations in England and abroad. Artisans even made less expensive copies of these items out of wood painted to look like stone. Neoclassical objects and busts of the deceased were reminders of things that had passed. They came to represent feelings of loss and mourning even when one was not touring a garden. The symbol of a column, or the symbol of an urn or obelisk on a print, embroidered in needlework or carved into a headstone, served as reminders of these feelings of meditation and loss.

* * *

English colonists in America continued the practice of crowded churchyard burials even though there was plenty of room in the new land. In Boston the dead were crowded into three original burial places: King's Chapel, in use from 1630; Copp's Hill, in use from 1660; and Old Granary, also in use from 1660. After a time, these burial grounds had so little space left that the dead were over-buried four deep or placed in common trenches. In 1756 a fourth graveyard was opened in Boston that was used for African Americans (mostly slaves), Catholics, and strangers who died while visiting (Linden-Ward, 25). In New Haven, Connecticut, Senator James Hillhouse, a Federalist, wanted to bury his family members on his own property, but he feared that their graves would be destroyed if, in the future, his property were sold. In 1796 he convinced 30 other people to go in with him in purchasing six acres that would be used for a permanent resting place for members of their families. The purchase was made, and family plots were established. There were also free plots for the president and fellows of Yale University, one plot to each ecclesiastic society, one for people of color, one for the burial of strangers. Three were left over for paupers. Because purchasing burial plots in graveyards not affiliated with a church was such a novel idea, the remaining plots did not sell well. Built before Père Lachaise cemetery in Paris, no one had ever heard of such the idea. This was an entirely new way to dispose of the remains of the dead. This tract of six acres was flat, devoid of noteworthy vegetation or topography except for a few poplar trees, and the owners made little landscaping improvements. Despite this, the cemetery became a major attraction for visitors. Basil Hall, a Scotsman, wrote that it was "one of the prettiest burying places I ever saw" (French, 43). It was a vast improvement over the British and Anglican churchyard, where mourners "sank ankle deep in rank and offensive mold, mixed with broken bones and fragments of coffins" (*ibid.*). What was first called the New Burying Ground, now named the Grove Street Cemetery, gained in fame, but it was the Mount Auburn Cemetery in Massachusetts that set the standard for a new movement in burials called the rural or garden cemetery.

Rural or Garden Cemeteries in America

Sir Walter Scott (1771–1832), the widely read Scottish writer, was an avid gardener who surrounded his home in Abbotsford with exotic plants and trees from around the world. Scott bought up surrounding farms until his estate, located in Scotland near the banks of the River Tweed, grew from the original 110 acres to 1,400 acres. He and his workman, Tom Purdie, planted hardwood trees among the evergreens and created over 100 walking and horse trails. Outside the house, which he called "Conundrum," Scott designed three outdoor garden "rooms" laid out in the old Regency style.

In 1827 and 1828 Scott wrote two brilliant essays about gardening for a journal called the *Quarterly Review* in which he explained the imagination and tenacity needed to design and create a garden (Linden-Ward, 50). To paraphrase Scott, gardens took such a long time to grow that they would not come to fruition in the designer's lifetime. Because of this, it took a true artist to imagine the results. Scott believed that gardening was a fine art. Those who designed and developed gardens were artists, a separate breed from the lowly men who raked, weeded and planted seeds. Scott's essays explained his belief that the "artist gardener" was a sculptor whose media were plants and the earth, creating art for an audience that has not yet been born. Although he didn't have the vocabulary of today, Scott laid the groundwork for what we now understand are "earthworks" and "conceptual art." Sir Walter's ideas were important to the United States because he was an honorary member of the Massachusetts Horticultural Society, whose president was Judge Joseph Story (1779–1845) and whose members included Harvard professor and physician Dr. Jacob Bigelow (1787–1879) and Henry A. S. Dearborn (Linden-Ward, 50).

The urban population in the United States more than doubled, from 6 percent to more than 15 percent of the total population, in the decade from 1800 to 1810. The rapid growth caused housing congestion and also congestion in the old church graveyards. Disease spread rapidly in urban areas. In 1822 an outbreak of yellow fever in New York City killed 16,000 inhabitants. When it was noticed that the disease was especially virulent in the vicinity of the Trinity Church burying grounds, a special investigative committee was appointed by New York City's Board of Health. This board recommended a prohibition on inner-city burials. Unfortunately, the recommendation wasn't followed for another 15 years (French, 42). Boston church graveyards also ran out of space. In the

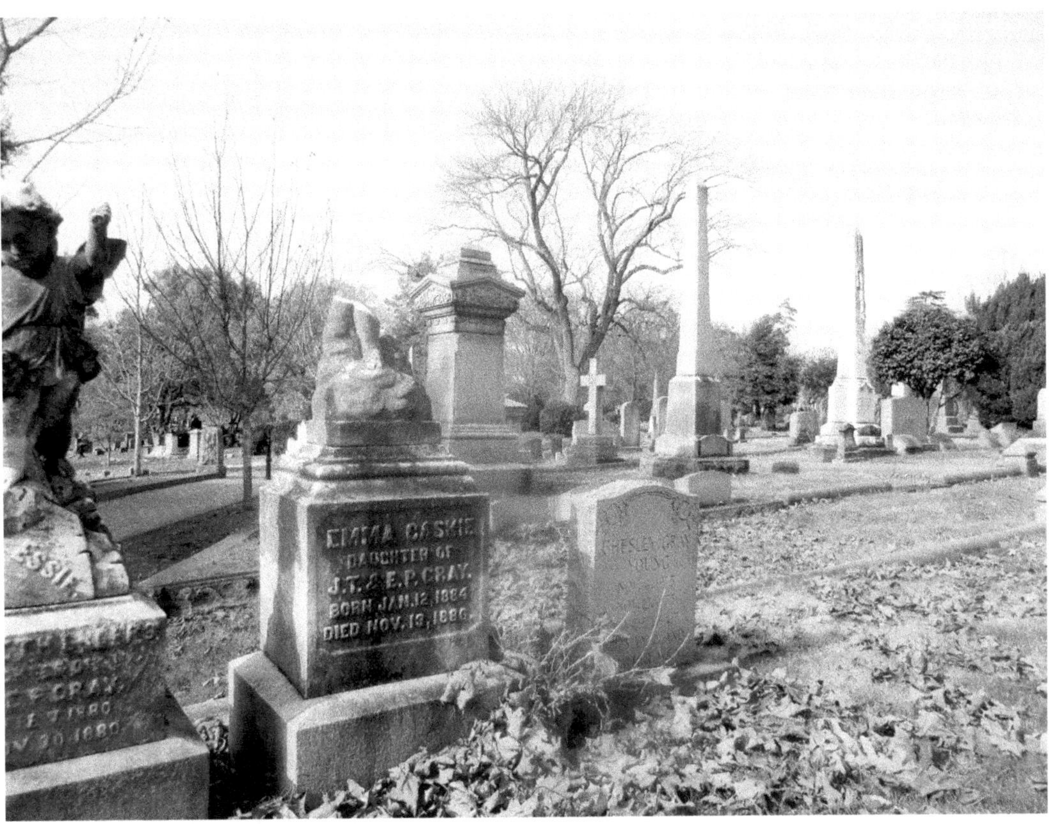

Garden Cemetery, Hollywood Cemetery, Richmond, Va. (photograph by author).

same year, 1822, Boston clergy petitioned their city council to allow burials in the cellar vaults of their churches. Boston officials created their own special committee to investigate. In the report they wrote of their findings, the committee not only rejected vault burials but recommended that all burials within the city be stopped. Unfortunately, Boston political leaders also didn't act on the recommendation of the committee, so Dr. Bigelow, the author of the report, decided to act on his own.

Dr. Bigelow began the movement to establish a new cemetery outside the city of Boston, and he enlisted members of the Horticultural Society to help with this plan. These men were aware of the Père Lachaise Cemetery in Paris because it had become famous for its inspirational monuments, winding paths, elegant trees and luxuriant vegetation, all of which helped visitors think about heaven. These men were also familiar with "the New Burial Ground" in New Haven and thought they could improve upon that idea. They would base their cemetery on Père Lachaise Cemetery but combine it with a garden based on English landscape garden ideas. This would be nonsectarian, a place of meditation, a place of instruction and a place, open to the public, where noble ideas and patriotism would thrive.

The Massachusetts Horticultural Society would purchase the land and establish a corporation to create and maintain the rural cemetery. Half of the acreage would be this burial ground, which was expected to repay the society for their half of the purchasing price. The other half of the acreage would be used as the society's experimental garden.

The society envisioned that the entire acreage would be a park, open to foot traffic from sunrise to sunset every day except Sunday. Those with horses and carriages could pick up free tickets from the society that would allow them entrance during open hours. This cemetery and garden would be fenced and would be supervised by paid staff so relatives need not worry that loved ones would be dug up and sold to medical schools for dissection or experiments. There would be a gatekeeper, a supervisor, a secretary and gardeners. Gravesites would be available to any and all that could pay for a plot, regardless of race or creed. It would be democratic. Farmers, mechanics, and small businessmen could even buy plots or pay with their labor or services instead of their cash.

This cemetery would be "beautiful, attractive and consoling, not gloomy and repulsive" (Bigelow, 128). It would be a place of repose, a place where nature combined with art and architecture to guide the morality and the character of the living. The cemetery would be a cultural institution as well as a place of repose. It would be a place where people erected inscribed columns, obelisks and monuments to their dead so that others could read of their history and accomplishments. These monuments would serve as models of elegance; they would elevate the public taste in architecture. The statues erected in memory of the deceased would heighten the sensibilities of the viewer and bring high art to all that visited there. The dead would instruct the living. The cemetery would instruct morality and character and elevate artistic taste.

The concept behind this new cemetery was innovative. The Boston Common, the 50-acre area in the middle of the city, had been used as a place for public hangings until 1817. It was also used as a grazing field for cattle until 1830, when the bovines were finally outlawed and it attained its designation as a park. Central Park in New York, the first designed urban park in America, wasn't built until 1857. The new country also had few public art museums and fewer public statues or monuments. Work on the Washington Monument began in 1848 and was not completed until 1885. The Statue of Liberty did not reach American soil until 1885 and was not dedicated until 1886. The oldest museum, containing a hodge-podge of items, was founded in Charleston, South Carolina, in 1773, but not opened to the public until 1824. Another museum was founded in Philadelphia in the 1770s by the artist Charles Wilson Peale. This contained many of his own paintings and seems to have been more of a gallery. Peale would go on to help found the Pennsylvania Academy of Fine Art, which organized annual art exhibitions but did not have its own museum building until 1876. The Metropolitan Museum of Art in New York City didn't open until 1870, and Boston's Museum of Fine Arts also didn't open until 1876.

An act of the legislature enlarged the powers of the Massachusetts's Horticultural Society, enabling it to purchase land to be used for a consecrated cemetery and an experimental garden, both of which would be under constant inspection by the society's gardener so they would be neat and well kept. The corporation promised that the graves would remain there in perpetuity; the buried would have undisturbed rest, and "that what the earth has once covered it shall not again reveal to light." The founders also promised that unlike Père Lachaise Cemetery, the monuments would not overwhelm the plants and trees, and "the resources of art shall not be wasted in vain efforts to delay or modify the inevitable courses of nature" (Bigelow, 128).

To the founders of this new rural cemetery, burial in it surrounded the deceased with "everything that can fill the heart with tender and respectful emotion; beneath the shade of a venerable tree, on the slope of the verdant lawn, and within the seclusion of the forest; removed from all the discordant scenes of life" (Bigelow, 139).

Judge Story had recently lost a daughter to scarlet fever. At the consecration of the new cemetery, he confessed in his sermon that what was needed was affectionate and pious care of the dead. This was not only for their corpses, but for those left behind who were filled with natural tenderness felt for the deceased (Bigelow, 149).

Another intention of the cemetery would be to honor the nation's great men and women. The trustees lamented that the early settlers of our country were heaped one upon each other, deposited in loathsome vaults, or laid beneath the gloomy crypts of churches. Story declared that this practice was not worthy of Christianity. Burial in a rural garden would honor the dead and honor the country's heroes. Monuments and statues marking their graves would influence the living, who would be inspired to follow their examples. The trustees likened the cemetery to a school in religion and philosophy. It would be a place where the dead would guide the living in terms of morality. It would build character.

A favorite picnic spot for Harvard College students was chosen as the site for this cemetery and experimental garden. The land was purchased in 1831. Located four miles outside of Boston, the property followed the Charles River near the college and contained woods, hills, valleys and streams. The highest point rose over 100 feet above the river. From the top of the hill one can see Dorchester Heights, most of Boston, Cambridge and the college. The students called the area Sweet Auburn, from Oliver Goldsmith's idyllic poem "The Deserted Village" (1770). The founding members of the cemetery named it Mount Auburn, preferring this to the property's original name, Stone's Woods (French, 44). Plots soon went on sale and were quickly bought.

Rural cemeteries in garden settings were common on Southern plantations. For example, Thomas Jefferson made plans for a private garden burial place when he designed Monticello in 1771. George Washington's resting place at Mount Vernon also shows a typical private garden burial site, but the founders of Mount Auburn cemetery warned that gravesites on private land could be sold and passed on to someone else who would not show the gravesite respect. An advertisement for Mount Auburn warned: "The mother of Washington lies buried in a field, the property of a person not related to her family, and in a spot which cannot now be identified" (Bigelow, 138). It also mentioned that the expense of a lot or burial in the Mount Auburn cemetery was considerably less than that of a common tomb or burial beneath a church.

The corporation needed 100 subscribers to purchase burial plots to repay the Horticultural Society for their half of the purchasing price of the land. However, after only a few years the cemetery became so successful that the trustees decided to turn the entire property into a cemetery and not bother with building an experimental garden after all. Fearing that the cemetery plot owners would have too much to say about Horticultural Society business, members of the corporation renegotiated the original contract in 1835, and the cemetery and the Horticultural Society split apart. Since the Horticultural Society had originally purchased the land, the agreement stipulated that the cemetery, now a separate corporation, would pay the society 1/4 of all the money they earned from the sale of burial plots. This turned out to be very lucrative for the Horticultural Society. The cemetery ran at a profit, which in some years amounted to $40,000 (Bigelow, 27). The society used this money to erect two buildings in Boston for their use. The Mount Auburn Cemetery Corporation continued to run at a profit of hundreds of thousands of dollars from the sale of plots, and the trustees used this money to preserve, improve and embellish the cemetery (Bigelow, 34).

The cemetery was designed like a European landscape garden. It contained carriage avenues and graveled footpaths that blended in with the topography. Avenues were named after trees; footpaths were named after flowers. After the first year of operation the trustees purchased another twenty-four acres of land on the west side. Sixteen additional acres from the original farm were added in 1854. The minimum family plot measured 15 by 20 feet and initially sold for $60.00. These could be fenced with metal or stone fencing, not wood. Single interments were put in the St. James lot on Cypress Avenue, enclosed with a slight fence; the charge for this was $10 a gravesite. This fee was later increased to $12 with an additional charge of 50¢ for a stone bearing the number of the occupant and corresponding to the record book.

The first burial in Mount Auburn was conducted for a child of Mr. James Boyd on July 6, 1832. The second person buried there was Mrs. Mary Hastings on July 12th of the same year (Bigelow, 23). Grave markers had to be made of stone that was not slate. There were no restrictions on the style of gravestones, but they needed to be approved by the trustees (French, 48). Bigelow designed the gate of the cemetery in Egyptian Revival style. He also designed the Washington Tower, a circular tower that predated the Washington Monument by more than 30 years. The Bigelow Chapel was constructed in neo-Gothic style. This building was made of granite and became the place where religious services for the dead could be performed. Marble busts and statues were placed in this building so that they were not exposed to the elements. In 1872 the trustees commissioned a statue of the sphinx to be made by artist Martin Milmore (1844–1883), an Irish-American sculptor. This was to commemorate those fallen in the Civil War. The sculpture was carved from a 40-ton block of Maine granite and lugged to the artist's Boston studio by horse and carriage.

Mount Auburn quickly became the model for rural cemeteries in the country and around the world. Besides being a burial ground, it was also the first designed landscape open to the public in North America, and it doubled as a place where people could escape the congestion of city life. When Mount Auburn first opened, it rivaled Mount Vernon and Niagara Falls as a tourist destination. People crowded into the cemetery to enjoy nature, art and architecture rather than to mourn the dead. Entry was allowed by foot, and also on horseback or in carriages, but this had to be halted when some began driving recklessly through the grounds, disturbing the paths and annoying other visitors. In 1832 the trustees voted that no horses or carriages except those for a funeral would be allowed on the grounds. However, this was soon amended so that owners of cemetery plots (called "proprietors") were issued tickets that allowed them to enter with their vehicles. Speed limits were enforced, and owners had to ensure that their horses were properly controlled.

The popularity of the cemetery stimulated the creation of city parks and influenced Frederic Law Olmsted (1822–1903), who grew up to become America's premier landscape architect and the designer of outdoor spaces including New York's Central Park, San Francisco's Gold Gate Park and the Niagara Reservation in Niagara Falls, New York. Other cities followed Boston's lead and opened garden cemeteries of their own. Philadelphia opened Laurel Hill Cemetery in 1836. New York City opened Green-Wood Cemetery in what is now Brooklyn, in 1838. In the same year, Mount Hope Cemetery opened in Rochester, New York, followed by Green Mount Cemetery in Baltimore and Worcester Rural Cemetery in Worcester, Massachusetts. Allegheny Cemetery opened in Pittsburg in 1844. Spring Grove Cemetery opened in Cincinnati in 1845; Cave Hill Cemetery in Louisville, Kentucky, opened in 1848; Hollywood Cemetery opened in Richmond, Virginia, in 1849; and Magnolia Cemetery opened in Charleston, South Carolina, in 1850.

Monuments to Death

Rural cemeteries became prestigious places for burial. Monuments and sculpture glorifying the deceased and his or her accomplishments were no longer frowned upon but were welcomed and encouraged. From the beginning, art was an important part of these cemeteries. Monuments were to be instructive and inspirational. Inscriptions were to give the living an awareness of history. The American society was a mobile one, constantly flooded with immigrants. In 1838 Levi Lincoln, the governor of Massachusetts, declared that the generation who had created the country were all but forgotten. In the dedication ceremony of the Worcester Massachusetts Rural Cemetery, he said he hoped that the new cemetery would give people a sense of historical continuity and renewed patriotism. His hope was that these cemeteries would give our American society roots and remind the citizens of the debt they owed to the founders of our nation (French, 48). The *Boston Evening Transcript,* a daily afternoon newspaper, urged owners of Mount Auburn plots to hire the best American sculptors to make Mount Auburn a treasury of art as well as a treasury of scenery (French, 49). Sculpture was no longer reserved for the wealthy but could be viewed in the cemetery by anyone with a ticket, and tickets were given out for free in the office of the corporation. In 1848 an estimated 30,000 visitors acquired tickets to tour Laurel Hill Cemetery (Lichten, 217). Making these memorials and sculpture to honor the dead encouraged American artists to become sculptors and work in three-dimensional media.

In the early 19th century, the state and federal governments were great patrons of early American sculptors because they wanted to have statues of famous founders of our country grace the buildings that were being built all across the land. These commissions were given to sculptors, usually Americans, who had achieved some sort of reputation; however, most of these had moved to Italy where they were able to hire assistants to help them with their work. Customers wishing to memorialize their loved ones with sculpture in their garden cemetery plot hired sculptors of lesser reputations. But it is in the garden cemeteries of the early Victorian era that we see the creativity of the time. Millions of people in America and abroad came to believe that spirits of the dead communicated with the living, and that after death, souls went to a garden place called the "Summerland." Individual gravesites in garden cemeteries were guaranteed to stand in perpetuity, and these monuments honored the dead. To these people, the deceased might possibly be present, even though unseen, and this had to have completely changed their attitudes towards burial. Instead of thinking that the graveyard was merely a place in which corpses decayed, graveyards became park-like cemeteries, where relatives could be mourned but also honored and praised.

Victorians believed in an afterlife, but they were materialistic and believed that we lived on in this world through our accomplishments. Those who could afford it erected great monuments to their dead that explained who they were and what they had done. One's secular achievements became as vital as one's piety, and an important use of a cemetery was to teach and remind the living of the value of the deceased. Realistic statues portrayed the deceased as they were when they were healthy and often included some

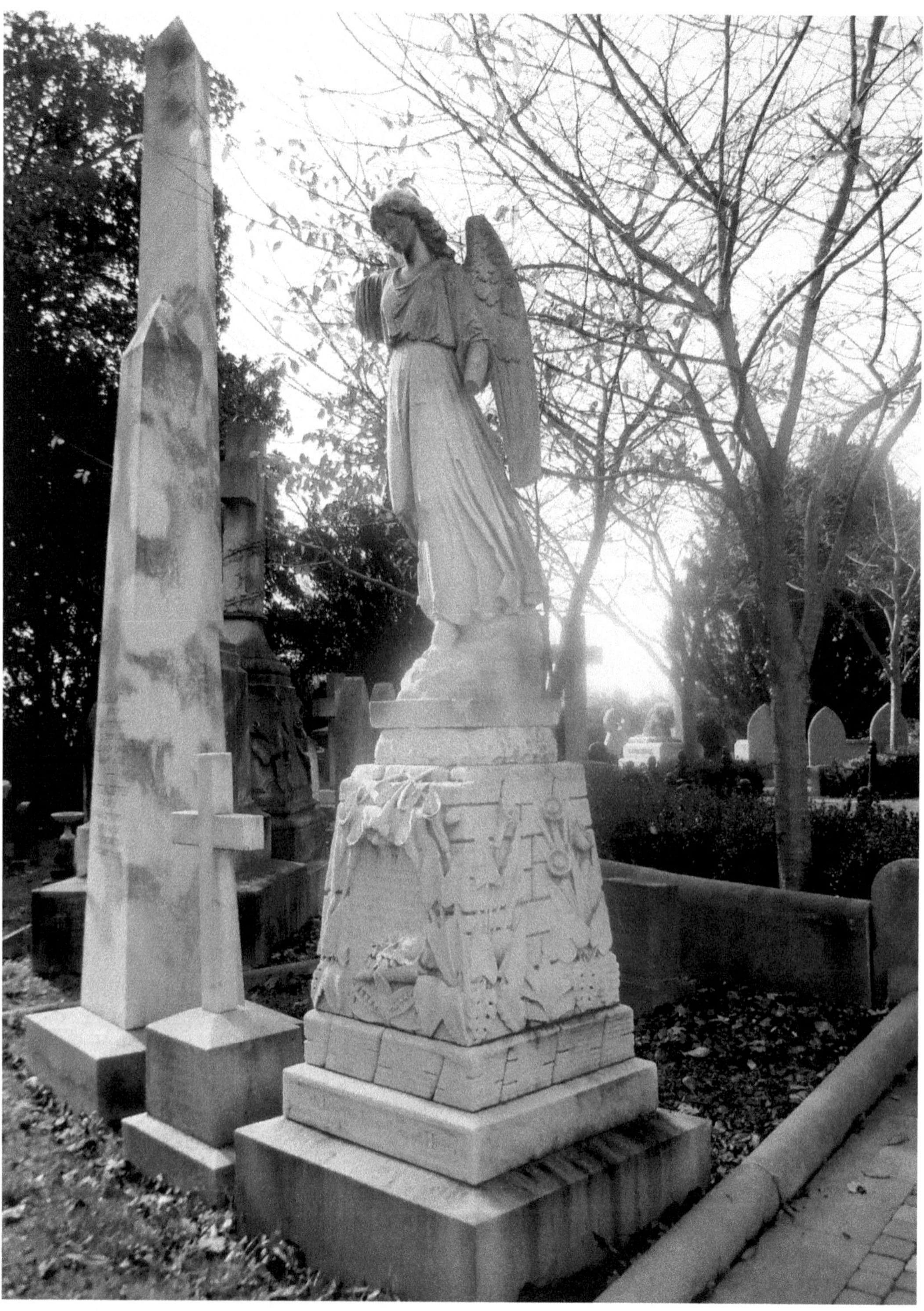

Angel statue, anonymous sculptor, Hollywood Cemetery, Richmond, Va. (photographed by the author, 2017).

objects associated with their occupation. Statues for women were not realistic portraits of the deceased but instead were meant to evoke ideas of grief, religion or resurrection. Sprinkled in between these were statues of angels portrayed in various stages of grief. The ideas and emotions these statues evoked were not only for the family but were also for the visitor, who would learn moral concepts while sharing in the sentiments the loss aroused. Whether symbols of power or symbols of grief, elaborate gravesites reminded visitors of the wealth and the power of those left behind. The burial became a way to achieve immortality for the family as well as for their dead. An important concept of the early garden cemeteries was to create a shared history for Americans. These statues of the dead, combined with monuments to our heroes, gave those who could afford it the ability to narrate the ideas of who we were supposed to be.

Unfortunately, sculptors of cemetery statues are difficult to identify. Victorian garden cemeteries were not required to keep records of burials, let alone the names of artists who made individual cemetery statues. Those that did have records had no guidelines or instructions on how to maintain them. Some garden cemeteries went out of business and were neglected for a time, losing the records they had. Some are now maintained by non-profit institutions with little staff. Researchers are scarce and need to spend time discovering who is buried in the plots rather than discovering sculptors' names. Rules for photographing statues and releasing information on the deceased vary from cemetery to cemetery. There is no governing body for these cemeteries, so each burial place developed rules of its own.

Graveyard sculptures were not cataloged. Some were created by the top artists of their time, while some of them were not unique, rather being one of several copies of a popular funerary art. Many sculptures standing in graveyards, left open to the elements for over a hundred years, are now in disrepair. But some cemeteries, such as Green-Wood in Brooklyn, New York, have embarked on expensive restoration and preservation projects, raising funds to clean and repair the sculptures they have. This money might be raised by family members, like the great-grandson of Gordon W. Burnham, who raised money to preserve the granite angel carved by John Moffitt that stands over the grave of his great-grandfather Gordon W. Burnham (1803–1885). Burnham was the owner of the Benedict & Burnham Manufacturing Co., the largest manufacturer of brass and copper fixtures in the United States at the time of his death. Little is found about John Moffitt other than that he was trained in England and might have been British. Moffitt carved several sculptures for the deceased residents of Green-Wood Cemetery. Three of them are located inside the Durant Mausoleum, where very few people are allowed to go. Moffitt also carved detailed reliefs on the main gates, made repairs to the Steinway family mausoleum for a mere $350, and carved the "Ages of Man" friezes on the exterior of the Fort Hamilton visitors' lounge.

With the exception of carved figureheads for boats, there were very few statues in America prior to the revolution. Puritans and Quakers rejected ostentation and did not build monuments to anyone. The British erected only a few statues, and those that they did, such as the statue of King George III that stood on the Bowling Green in Manhattan, had been torn down by protesters and slaves during the rebellion. Colonial forefathers just disappeared, leaving hardly a trace, without even a gravesite remaining as evidence of their existence. As new immigrants rushed to the country after the Revolutionary War, the importance of remembering the country's virtuous early leaders and war heroes grew, as did the belief that their memory would stabilize American society and perpetuate high ideals. One of our country's founding fathers, Dr. John Warren, a surgeon during the American Revolution, believed that Athens and Rome fell because they had forgotten their fundamental principles. He urged Americans to seek out the sacred repositories of the dead, "the relicks of your martyred fellow citizens, and from their dust receive a lesson of the value of your freedom!" (Linden-Ward, 97). Besides being a physician, Dr. Warren was also a member of the Masons and the founder of the Harvard Medical School. His brother, Joseph, the president of the Provisional Congress, died fighting the British in the Battle of Bunker Hill. America's first native-born architect, Charles Bulfinch (1763–1844), was hired by King Solomon's Lodge of Masons to design a memorial to the fallen hero. Built of wood, the column was erected on Bunker Hill in 1789. It stood on a pedestal and was topped by a globe but was torn down in 1811, when real estate speculators decided to lower the hill in order to build expensive houses on the site (Linden-Ward, 98).

In 1785 Benjamin Franklin invited the French sculptor Jean-Antoine Houdon to accompany him to the United States to make a bust of George Washington. A very wise man, Franklin may have realized how important it would be to the new country to have a three-dimensional portrait of the first president, or he may have just liked the sculptor's work. Franklin had had Houdon carve a bust of himself a short time before and seemed pleased with the results. Carved busts, portrait sculptures of just the head, neck and upper chest of an individual, were popular at this time before the invention of photography. Houdon accepted the invitation and after landing in the United States, spent fifteen days with Washington, making wet clay models and a plaster cast of the president's head (Taft, 15). The artist returned to France six months later and spent the next two years working on the bust. In neoclassical tradition, he carved some fabric on one side to represent a toga and left the other side bare. When the bust was completed, it was shipped to the United States and arrived in Richmond, Virginia, where it was installed in the state capitol Rotunda in 1788. The sculpture and the plaster cast have been used as models for many other statues of our first president, including the profile of Washington found on old postage stamps.

In the early days of the republic, artists came to and went from the shores of America, and there were no native sculptors working in stone. Even George Washington had to import marble reliefs from Italy to put into his Mount Vernon home (Taft, 5). No one in the new country could have carved a marble bust such as this except perhaps Patience Lovell Wright (1725–1786). She was a realistic modeler, but she worked in wax and eventually moved to London before the Revolutionary War. Wright was originally from Philadelphia. After her husband died, she earned money to support herself and her children by creating realistic wax figures. Modeling in wax was considered a low art and not taken as seriously as carving marble pieces. The wax needed to be kept warm, and to do this, Wright put blocks of the stuff in entertaining crevices on her body as she did her work. Marble is more durable than wax, and the translucent material was said to resemble human skin. Marble was also a favorite material for sculpture from ancient Greece and Rome and was popular in the neoclassical style. Still, for a short time in the American colonies, Wright supported herself and her family by charging customers admission to view her life-sized wax sculptures of famous people. To make them look even more realistic, she filled the eye sockets with glass eyes. Wright toured her wax figures through Philadelphia and Charleston, South Carolina, until opening a wax museum in New York City in 1770. Unfortunately, the building burned down the next year and much of her work was lost. Hoping for better luck, she moved to London, England, where she sculpted

Benjamin Franklin in wax. With his help and the help of his wife, she met and sculpted King George III and members of the royal family. She opened another wax museum in London, predating Madame Tussauds by about 50 years (Taft, 15).

After the American Revolution, Giuseppe Ceracchi (1751–1801), a sculptor born in Rome, also sculpted a realistic bust of George Washington. Originally from Italy, the artist came to America in 1791 with the dream of having Congress pay him $30,000 to sculpt a colossal monument he called *The Goddess of Liberty*. Sculpture like this wasn't a priority for the new legislators, and Congress declined. Two years later the artist returned to the States and tried to raise money for his work from private sources, but failed. Once more he returned to France and was eventually executed by the guillotine for conspiring against Napoleon I. Luckily, before his demise, he had George Washington sit for him, which enabled him to make the bust. Thomas Jefferson, statesman George Clinton, Alexander Hamilton, founding father John Jay and naval commander John Paul Jones also sat for him and had their sculptural portraits done (Taft, 17). Memorial busts of founding fathers and military heroes, in the neoclassical style, complete with carved drapery on one shoulder, were immediately popular in the early days of the republic, and every state house and federal building wanted several. Plaster casts were made of these and exhibited in art academies in the North and in the South.

William Rush (1756–1833) is considered by some to be America's first major sculptor who had a great deal of skill. Unfortunately, he modeled works in clay and wax and completed his large works in wood, even though these pieces, like the *Nymph of the Schuylkill,* were intended to be placed outdoors. The *Nymph* originally stood in Centre Square, Philadelphia, and then was moved to Fairmount Park until it started to decay. Rush learned the art of wood carving from his father, who was a ship's carpenter. Rush also was an apprentice to Edward Cutbush, who carved figureheads for ships. Rush's original works, made of cedar or pine, have disintegrated or disappeared, but studies for them in plaster or clay remain to show us what they were like. Rush went on to teach art, becoming an administrator of the Pennsylvania Academy of Arts, which he founded with Charles Wilson Peale.

John Frazee (1790–1852), was the first American-born artist to carve a marble portrait bust. The tenth child born to his mother in Perth Amboy, New Jersey, he was raised in poverty. At age eleven he was hired out to an abusive farmer; two years later he was apprenticed to a bricklayer, who also opened up a tavern. For the next five years, the teenager took care of the bricklayer's farm, laid bricks by day and waited tables at night. On his one day off, Sunday, he practiced his penmanship (considered a very important talent) and practiced drawing and carving skills. In the summer of 1808 the bricklayer had Frazee chisel his name, Lawrence, onto a stone tablet on a bridge to identify that his company had built it. Frazee's ability to chisel the name was considered so remarkable that he was hired as a stonecutter by Peter De Windt Smith of Haverstraw, New York. When he had learned all he could from Smith, Frazee opened his own stonecutting business in 1814. He later moved to New York City to open a marble yard with his brother, where he carved mantel pieces, marble church memorials, and gravestones, concentrating on perfecting his lettering style (Tuckerman, 572). Although many of Frazee's marble tombstones have been harmed by exposure to the elements, they were considered to be very creative, with intricate borders, natural designs and unique letter spacing and style. The first attempt at carving a figure came when his oldest child died in 1815. On this gravestone, he attempted to carve the personification of grief.

Frazee was able to see plaster casts of European sculpture at the New York Academy of Fine Arts in New York. Although discouraged by the director of the academy, painter John Trumbull, who believed that it would take another 100 years before anyone in America could become a sculptor, Frazee became a student of the academy, carved a bust of his mother, and exhibited it there. This work, completed in 1815, was the first marble bust chiseled in America carved by a native-born American (Taft, 32). Members of the old St. Paul's Church in New York saw the piece and commissioned the artist to create a wall monument dedicated to the recently deceased John Wells, a prominent lawyer. The memorial, completed in 1825, contained a bust of the man, for which Frazee was paid $1,000 (which would be about $25,000 today). The artist carved the work using drawings that had been made from Wells' corpse. In the neoclassical tradition, the bust rests on a ledge carved with typical neoclassical bric-a-brac including books, draped fabric and a lamp (Taft, 33). There is also a tablet containing a long inscription carved in Frazee's unique lettering style. His next important commission came in 1831, when the artist was hired by Gulian C. Verplanck, a congressman from New York, to make a bust of the recently deceased John Jay, the first chief justice of the United States. Another bust that he made, of Nathaniel Prime, led to Frazee obtaining important commissions from the Boston Athenaeum, including the carving of a bust of the living politician, Daniel Webster. Webster was a very difficult subject to get to sit still. He reportedly delivered a speech on the floor of the Congress while Frazee was modeling him (Taft, 27). Frazee never abandoned his marble business and stuck to carving busts rather than attempt to carve an entire figure.

Frazee did not go to Italy to study or to complete his work, and neither did Hezekiah Augur (1791–1858), the son of a carpenter, and a shoemaker's apprentice. A self-taught American sculptor, Augur first invented a lace weaving machine, which resembled a lathe used to make piano legs. He also invented the bracket-saw. Discovering that he had amassed wealth from his inventions, Augur turned his attention to art, which he considered a pleasant "pastime." Professor Samuel Morse saw promise in Augur's wood carvings and convinced him to work in marble (French, 49). Working without a model, the first bust he carved in this material was of the Roman god Apollo. He then produced the head of President George Washington and another of the ancient Greek poet Sappho. These made him famous but earned him few orders. Eventually he just gave up, having completed very little work.

The first American sculptors were isolated from each other. William Rush from Philadelphia knew he was an artist, but Hezekiah Augur, who lived in New Haven, Connecticut, could not earn money from his work and did not take it seriously as an occupation. John Frazee, in New Jersey and New York, carved busts and memorials but continued working in his marble yard and gravestone carving business. The next generation of American sculptors moved to Italy and did little to create a distinct American sculptural tradition. These were Horatio Greenough, originally from Boston; Thomas Crawford, originally from New York; and Hiram Powers, from Cincinnati. In Italy they could learn sculpture techniques and hire workmen to help them make their art. Italy had the best marble in the world, and sculpture was appreciated in Europe. Travel guides made stops to artists' studios a regular part of the "Grand Tour." Rich tourists were shown numerous clay models. They could choose one of these, have the work carved from marble, and, when complete, have it shipped to their homes. Tourists also sat for their portrait busts, modelled first in clay, and completed later in marble and shipped. When sculptors needed more work, Greenough and Crawford returned to the United States to drum up business, especially lucrative government commissions. However, Powers, made internationally famous by his creation *The Greek Slave* (first exhibited in 1843), never needed to return; he remained in Italy until his death in 1873. In pre–Civil War America more than one hundred thousand people paid to see Powers' *The Greek Slave*, a statue of a nude, teenage girl in chains, as it toured the United States. Many Americans being oblivious to the suffering of actual American slaves, the statue was considered to be the greatest work of sculpture known to history and the most beautiful representation of the female form executed in its time. Poets wrote poems about it, and the statue was chosen to be the centerpiece of the American exhibit at the Crystal Palace Exhibition in London in 1851. A copy of *The Greek Slave* was made for the Corcoran Gallery in Washington, D.C. (Wecker).

A problem for American sculptors in the early days of the United States was the lack of interest in art. To paraphrase the famous words John Adams, our second president, wrote to his wife, his generation needed to study politics and war so that their sons could study mathematics and philosophy, "in order to give their children a right to study painting, poetry, music, architecture, statuary, tapestry and porcelain" (Adams, letter posted May 12, 1780). During the Revolution and the early years of the republic, there were more important things to do than create works of art. When civic-minded groups, the government, and garden cemeteries created the demand for sculptures, there was a perceived lack of materials and a lack of professionals possessing the knowledge to accomplish the work and teach the techniques.

The marble first found in the land was of an inferior quality. There also were no bronze-casting facilities. Bronze, although very heavy and difficult to heat and mold, was long lasting when used for outdoor sculptures. Even though it would discolor, bronze was less likely to be destroyed by the elements. Foundries were established in America to make tools and cutlery, but the technology to cast large pieces of art didn't exist until the middle of the 19th century. When garden cemeteries first awoke an interest in erecting sculpture as memorials, American sculptors had to rely on European foundries in places such as Munich, Paris or Rome. An early attempt to cast artwork in bronze in the United States was made by Henry Kirke Brown (1814–1866), who established a small foundry in his own studio. He was not able to create very large work and so established a relationship with the Ames Manufacturing Company of Chicopee, Massachusetts, before the Civil War. His student, John Quincy Adams Ward, also became a sculptor of note. Ward was hired by the Ames company to make models for bronze statues in 1861, which eventually allowed customers to bypass the artist and choose from a number of mass-produced sculptures for their graves.

Brown was born in Leyden, Massachusetts, and died in Newburgh, New York. He studied painting in America under the portrait painter Chester Harding, but from 1842 to 1846 he traveled to Italy to learn how to sculpt. Unlike many of his contemporaries who worked and lived in Italy and became influenced by Italian style, Brown took his cues from the Hudson River School painters and wanted to sculpt work that was distinctly American. He returned to the United States and opened his own studio in New York City, where he was employed carving marble portrait busts. Some of his clients actually were Hudson River painters such as Asher B. Durand and Thomas Cole.

Brown was interested in working in bronze, and he moved to Brooklyn, where he was able to set up his own foundry with the aid of French workmen. Here he successfully cast small sculptures and medallions that were sold to middle-class subscribers by an organization called the American Art-Union. When the family of George Hogg were looking for a sculptor to make a statue to place over his grave, they chose Brown. The statue, named *Angel of the Resurrection,* was erected in 1850 in the Allegheny Cemetery in Pittsburgh, Pennsylvania. Brown made another bronze statue for the William Satterlee Packer memorial. Packer died in 1850 and was buried in Green-Wood Cemetery, in Brooklyn, New York. In 1853 Brown made the heroic statue for Dewitt Clinton's grave memorial and decorative low-relief panels for its pedestal, also erected in Green-Wood Cemetery in 1853. This statue is the second-oldest large bronze cast to exist in America. Clinton was a New York politician who led the construction of the Erie Canal. He had died in 1828, but was dug up and reburied in Green-Wood in the successful attempt to make the cemetery appeal to an elite clientele.

In 1853 Brown also received the commission to make a bronze memorial statue of George Washington that was paid for by donations from New York City merchants. An equestrian statue, it was completed and installed, with much fanfare, in Union Square in New York City on July 4, 1856. The statue measured 14 feet by 16 feet and was 20 feet in height (Tuckerman, 575). Another very famous American sculptor, Horatio Greenough, who lived and worked in Italy, was supposed to help with its creation, but he backed out of the deal once the money was secure. Brown helped to create the National Statuary Hall in the United States Capitol building. He gained several major commissions and was instrumental in popularizing the use of bronze as an art material (Metropolitan Museum of Art).

The first step in the process of creating a neoclassical bronze sculpture like those of Brown was to draw sketches to work out ideas and decide on the design. This might include three-dimensional studies to work out the detail or difficult parts of the work. Once the idea for the sculpture is finalized, the sculptor made a small model of the work measuring only 4 to 6 inches in height. For this he or she used clay, modeling wax, or plastiline (also called modeling clay—a combination of clay and oil that does not harden). If all went well, a larger model would be made, perhaps a foot in height. If areas needed further refinement, additional three-dimensional sketches were made, until a model one foot tall was formed. When the artist was certain of the design wanted, he or she would model the life-sized statue out of clay, which was constantly sprinkled with water to keep it moist and covered with damp cloths at night so it wouldn't dry out. Unfortunately, unsupported clay would collapse under its own weight, so the sculptor first needed to build an armature—a skeleton—made out of wood or metal pipes. The metal would be bent into shape for things like arms, fingers and legs. The armature was placed on a revolving stand and the artist then covered it with clay. Details were modeled with bone and wood tools, and fingers were used to carve fine detail (Stone, 22).

Once the modelled figure was completed to the smallest detail, an inside and an outside mold was made from it. Molten metal was poured into the space between the two molds. When cooled, the metal was dipped into acid to take off the impurities and give it the gold color of bronze. If the cast was good, a workman called a "chaser" smoothed off the seams. If it was done in pieces, another workman called a "mounter" joined the pieces together. When the statue was mounted on its base the chaser worked with the sculptor to make any last-minute changes.

The first model for a statue to be cast in bronze in the United States was made by the English artist Ball Hughes. This was for an effigy of Nathaniel Bowditch, an early

American mathematician and astronomer. The statue, which stands in Mount Auburn Cemetery, was paid for by subscriptions after Bowditch's death. Markings on the statue say that it was executed in Paris in 1847 and recast in 1886 (Taft, 116). The director of the cemetery, John Bigelow, explained in his memoirs that Hughes, who had been contracted to make and deliver a completed work, had only been able to make the model, and after several years the cemetery voided his contract. What Bigelow called "a benevolent friend" (Bigelow, 52) came to the artist's aid, and the bronze cast was finally made. Unfortunately, it was so imperfect that in 1853 holes in the statue had to be repaired and the entire thing had to be painted a bronze color (Taft, 97). Dr. Bowditch was so revered that the trustees had the mold recast in bronze at the later date.

Because foundries were used to make cannons and cannon balls needed for the Civil War, the Ames Manufacturing Company of Chicopee (mentioned previously) turned its attention away from sculpture and towards making munitions. The first large bronze statue actually cast in an industrial foundry in the United States was the seven-foot tall statue *Citizen Soldier*, a memorial made in remembrance of the fallen soldiers of the Civil War, dedicated during America's first observance of Memorial Day. The sculpture was modelled by Irish-born artist Martin Milmore (1844–1883) (Reynolds, 9). Milmore had immigrated to the United States with his family when he was seven years old and was able to study with the painter Thomas Ball of Charlestown, Massachusetts, before he moved to Italy. The statue was placed in Forest Hills Cemetery in Roxbury, Massachusetts, only two years after the war ended in 1867.

Milmore's bronze *Citizen Soldier* depicts a Union soldier resting on his rifle, looking down contemplatively at the gravestones below. This statue launched Milmore's career and was duplicated several times for northern towns such as Waterville, Maine, which in 1876 raised close to $1,600 to purchase an exact duplicate to place in the middle of their Monument Park. Their statue was cast at the Robert Wood & Co. foundry in Philadelphia, Pennsylvania, which we can assume cast Milmore's original. The bronze statue was placed on a base or a "pedestal," and the base had to have a foundation to stabilize the monument. In both Waterville and Roxbury, the base is made of granite. The price of the base and foundation, plus a $16 fee for shipping, cost the citizens of Waterville almost $1,000 more. Even though Milmore went on to create the *American Sphinx*, a bronze statue for the Mount Auburn Cemetery, in 1872, the duplication of his *Citizen Soldier* began a statue industry where people could bypass the artist and purchase ready-made art from the foundry.

Marble, the hardened form of white limestone, a popular material for English funerary markers, was found in Newbury, Massachusetts, in the late 1600s, but it was inferior to its European counterpart and not very durable. Those wanting marble gravestones or monuments had to have them shipped from England because of British laws, and the stone probably originated from Carrara, Italy, where the finest marble was found. At the end of the 18th century, a better-quality American marble was found in western Massachusetts, and when Vermont was settled, an even better white marble was found. Dorset, Vermont, became the major center for marble production in the country, and the first gravestone from Dorset marble was produced in 1790 (Bauer, 89). Stone carvers including Ebenezer Soule and Zerubbabel Collins moved to Vermont and began carving white marble gravestones in the 1770s. Zerubbabel, the son of the Connecticut stonecutter and cabinet-maker Benjamin Collins, is considered one of the most talented marble stone carvers of his time by the Connecticut Gravestone Network. Although he carved cherub heads with the same bulbous noses as those of his father, the younger Collins surrounded the tablets of his stones with elaborate flower filigrees. Beginning in the early 19th century, customers began to prefer the light-colored marble stone for grave markers, and other Vermont marble quarries opened up in West Rutland, Sutherland Falls, Pittsford and Columbia.

Forty years later, marble was also discovered in northwest Georgia, and although it was coarser and inferior to Vermont marble, it still sold well in Southern states. This marble came in shades of white, black, gray, pink and even purple and green. Called the Murphy Marble Belt, these layers of marble extend from Alabama to North Carolina. Pickens County, Georgia, was the heart of the Southern marble industry. Plans to quarry the stone began in 1832 when Irish stonecutter Henry Fitzsimmons (1802–1845) leased the land on Marble Hill. Three years later he was operating a water-powered marble finishing mill on the east branch of the Long Swamp Creek (Davis, 368). When he had enough orders he would ship the tombstones and monuments by a six-mule-team wagon to principal markets as far as North Carolina. After Fitzsimmons' death, George L. Summey from South Carolina and William Hurlick, a former partner of Fitzsimmons, resumed the business and named it Perseverance Quarry. In 1860 the quarrying company employed 20 workers and an untold number of slaves. In 1860 a new owner installed a steam powered marble mill and employed 40 to 50 workers at a time. In 1884, what was then known as the Georgia Marble Company paid the new railroad to build an extension to its quarries. Once cut from the cliffs and removed to the railroad, the marble was hauled to the finishing plant where about 200 "specialized craftsmen, including Irish, Italian, and Scottish stonecutters, carved the stone into finished monuments and building materials" (R. S. Davis, 375). Some of the craftsmen settled there and were buried beneath the ornate marble monuments the company made.

When these inexpensive sources of marble were introduced to the American population, there was a rapid shift to its use for grave markers and grave monuments. Marble quickly replaced gravestones made from local sandstone or slate in popularity. Although designs and lettering on marble did not hold up as well as they did on local stones, study results published in *Scientific America* magazine found that Vermont marble was more durable and stood up better to American weather conditions than marble from Italy. Writing in 1879, the researchers stated: "The depth of most Vermont quarries now is such that better marble is obtainable than was produced by them three years ago" (Henderson, 272).

The Hudson River opened for use as a waterway in 1822. New York's Erie Canal was completed in 1825, and the Champlain Canal connecting the Atlantic Ocean to the Hudson River was completed in 1827. All of these waterways made shipping marble westward easier. At the same time, Carrara, Italy, constructed a pier that made the loading of marble onto ships more efficient. No longer subject to British laws, Italian marble could be shipped directly to the east coast of America and then sent westward via the Erie Canal. As far west as Ohio, the use of local sandstone and Euclid bluestone diminished in the 1830s, replaced by marble. As in the East, local stone was used only for the bases of monuments. By the 1880s, however, granite became the medium of choice for these.

Stonecutters and monument makers liked to work in marble because it was easy to cut and carve either by hand or by waterpower with mid–19th century tools. American customers of the 19th century, like their British and Europeans counterparts, also liked to use the material for grave markers because it reminded them of those from ancient

Egypt, Rome and Greece. But marble was also a building material, used outside for columns of buildings and inside for floors, baseboards, stairs, railings, door frames, wall panels, mantels, and cornices. The exterior of the House and Senate extensions of the Capitol Building in Washington, D.C., is made from marble from western Massachusetts; marble from Georgia was put in the connecting corridors in the East Front, while Italian marble was used for the grand staircases and the Senate chamber ("Marble"). Built near the end of the century, the Georgia state capitol building used Indiana limestone for its exterior but Georgia marble for the interior floors, steps, and wall.

Marble gravestones became just a small part of a larger industry. As the industry became more commercialized, carvings on gravestones became less creative and more mechanized. Customers chose the willow tree, urn or column patterns from design books. These patterns were copied onto the stone by workers, rather than by artists, standardizing gravestone design. Towering monuments were the grave markers of choice. These symbolized the new defiant and arrogant feelings towards death influenced by Darwin's evolutionary theory, technological innovations, and economic growth.

* * *

Garden cemeteries were laid out like cities, with neighborhoods for the wealthy and neighborhoods for the poor. Wealthy families had architects create elaborate marble monuments for their dead, inspired by classical Greek and Roman or Gothic design. Their plots were encircled by fences made from marble. Less expensive cast-iron fences enclosed the plots for the rest. Nineteenth century Americans were used to fences in their burial grounds. They had originally been erected to keep cattle from grazing on the graves. Cemeteries such Mount Auburn banned the use of wood for fences in favor of wrought-iron railings or marble or granite posts with chains.

In the 1830s over 40 new fences were erected in Mount Auburn each year. From 1842 to 1857 this number rose to 71 per year (Linden-Ward, 260). The popularity of fences created a boom in ornamental ironwork, creating private areas in some cemeteries that caused people to complain. Spring Grove Cemetery in Cincinnati, founded in 1845, was the leader in the abolition of internal cemetery fencing. Instead of iron railings separating family plots, curbstones identified where each family plot was. The founders of Spring Grove conceived it to be a "lawn cemetery," an idea that became popular after the Civil War. Cemetery fences were also removed because of the Social Gospel Movement, a religious movement that arose in the second half of the 19th century. This movement discouraged hoarding and encouraged what they believed was Christ's practice of sharing with the less fortunate.

The sides of sarcophagi had richly carved marble friezes or were faced with bronze reliefs. Inscriptions were written on tablets listing important achievements accomplished by the deceased. Marble monuments inspired by Egyptian design, called obelisks, sometimes called "shafts," were extremely popular and sprang up like weeds in the garden cemeteries of America.

In ancient times obelisks were built in pairs, with one on each side of the entrance to an Egyptian temple. Carved from a single piece of stone, they taper from a square or rectangular base to a pyramid at the top. Egyptian obelisks were carved with hieroglyphs, which were often a dedication to a pharaoh or to a god. Many obelisks were transported to Rome in Cleopatra's time. In our modern era, originals were given as gifts, such as the one in New York City's Central Park, which was originally dedicated to Thutmosis III.

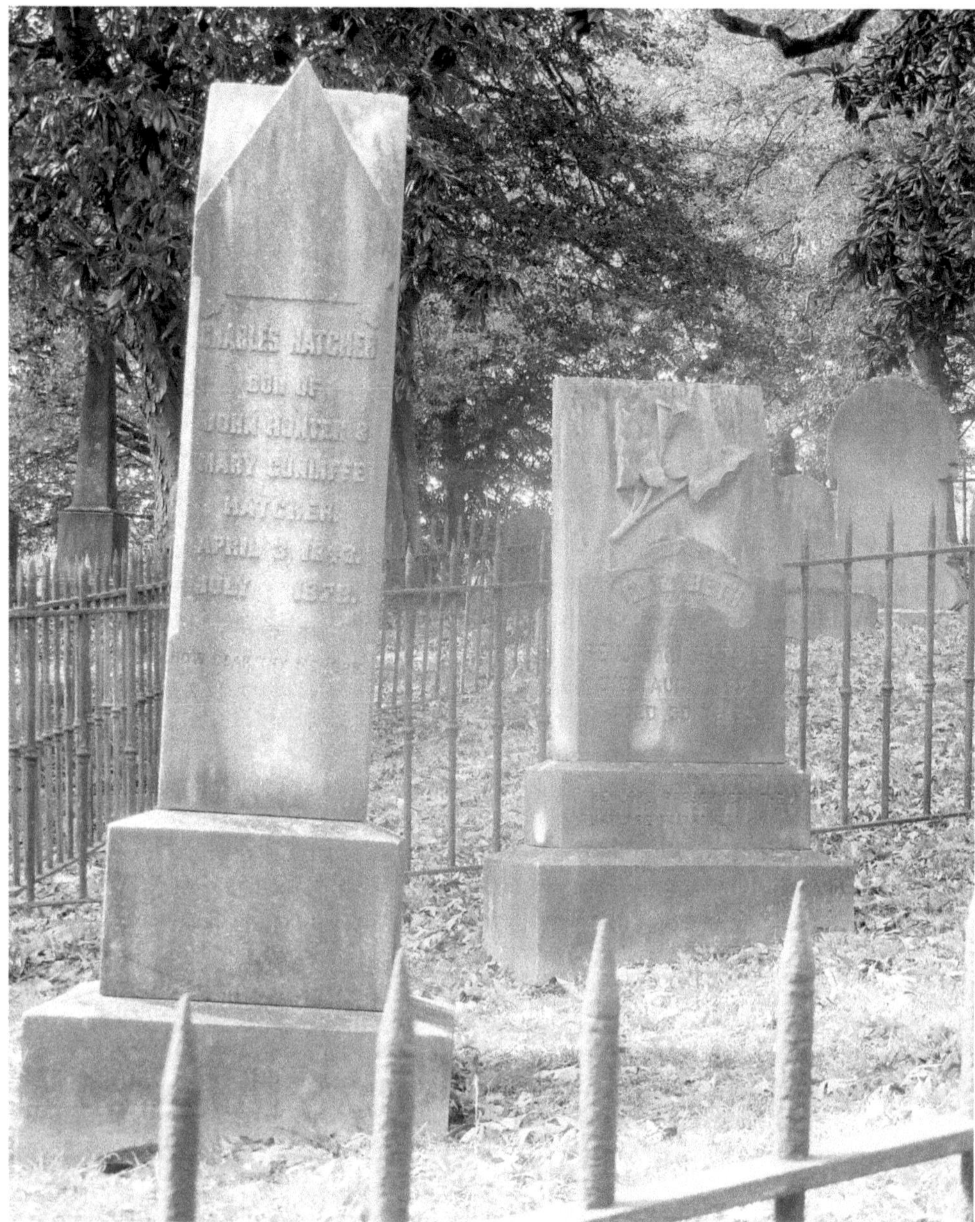

Iron fencing around family plot, Hollywood Cemetery, Richmond, Va. (photographed by the author, 2017).

This obelisk, made of red granite, was created to stand in Heliopolis, Egypt, but was later moved to Alexandria. In 1879 the 244-ton piece was offered to the United States by the Khedive of Egypt, who was also the viceroy of the sultan of Turkey, in an attempt to stimulate trade. It arrived in New York City in 1880, but a special reinforced bridge had to be built to allow it to reach its final destination (Cooke, 149). The largest obelisk, and also the tallest stone structure in the world, is the one erected to honor the first president of the United States, President George Washington. Called the Washington Monument,

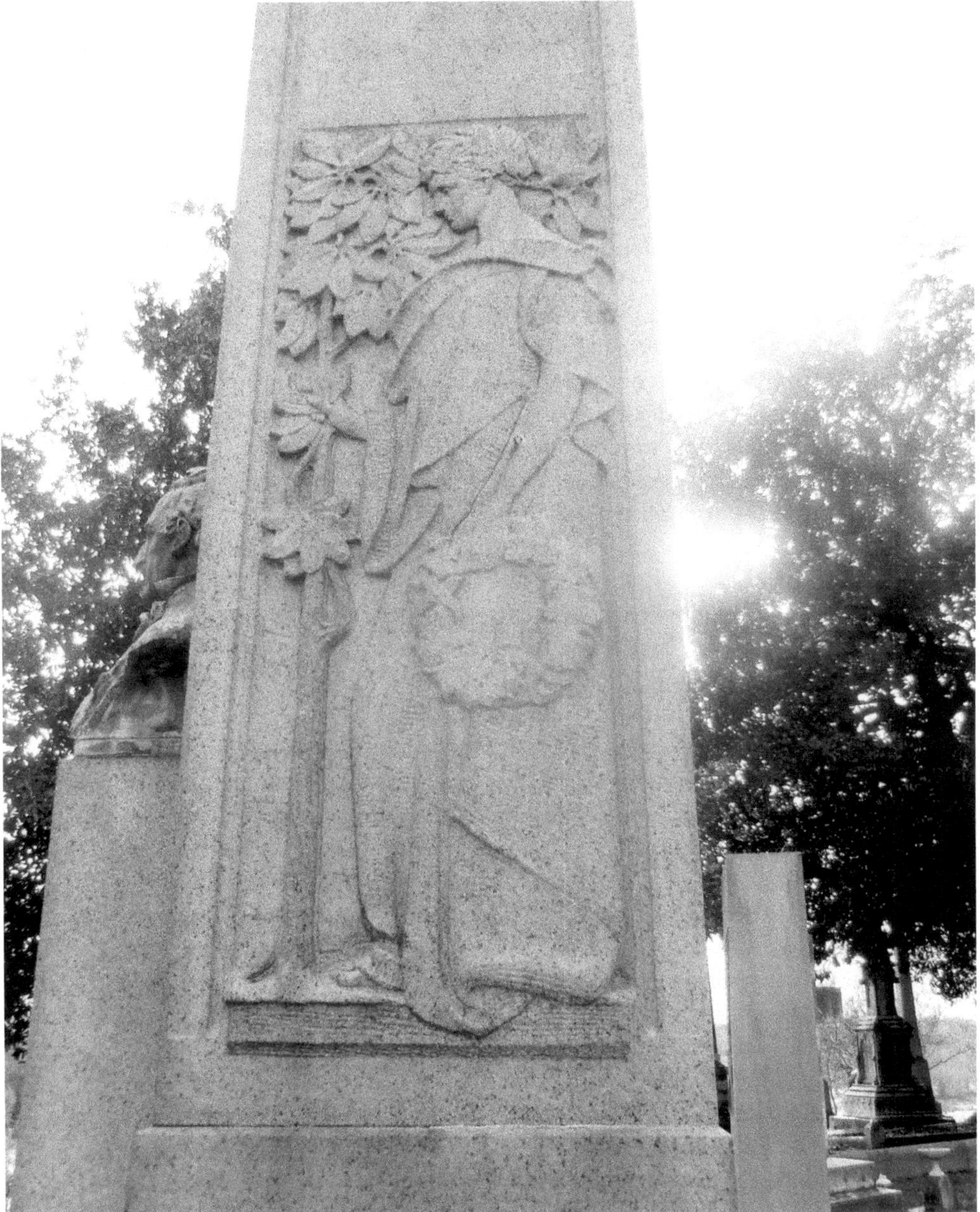

Carved relief frieze on President John Taft's memorial obelisk, Hollywood Cemetery, Richmond, Va.

it was erected in Washington, D.C. In addition to marble blocks quarried in Maryland, New England granite and bluestone gneiss (a material that resembles granite) were used for the exterior. The monument is 555 feet tall and contains an observatory and 898 interior stairs. The cornerstone for this structure was laid in 1848 by the Washington National Monument Society, but construction was halted until 1877 because of the Civil War and lack of funds. The building cost $1.2 million in private funds and was not completed and opened to the public until 1888. The Washington Monument was to have statues at its base, but the society ran out of money to complete the original design. Another obelisk was erected at the site of Bunker Hill in 1843. This commemorative piece made of granite stands 221 feet tall, and there are 294 steps leading to the top. The sculptor, Larking Goldsmith Mead, designed a shaft for the National Lincoln Monument in Oak Ridge Cemetery in Springfield, Illinois. Made from granite from Biddeford, Maine, this obelisk is 117 feet tall and stands on top of the final resting place of the former president, his wife and three of his sons. The obelisk rests on a base in the middle of a 12–1/2-acre plot. It is surrounded by sculptures, the most popular being the bronze face of Lincoln created from a marble relief carved by Gutzon Borglum (1867–1941), who went on to carve the faces on Mount Rushmore. Borglum's original was modeled after a plaster cast of the president's face made when he was alive. Borglum's son, Solon, created *Azrael*, the Angel of Death, a statue for the Charles Schieren Memorial at Green-Wood Cemetery.

Construction of the Jefferson Davis Monument in Kentucky was begun in 1917 and was completed in 1924. The monument to Davis, who was born in Kentucky, is 351 feet tall. Poured in place, is believed to be the tallest concrete cast obelisk in the world. Visitors ride an elevator to the top rather than climbing the steps.

People assumed that a shaft would also be put up to honor President Ulysses S. Grant after his death, but by the 1880s so many obelisks had been built that the form became a joke and was mocked in magazines such as *Puck* and *American Architect and Building News*. Henry Van Brunt, writing in the *North American Review*, said that these shafts showed a narrow range of conventional memorial types conceived by "untaught stonecutters" (Kahn, 215). In 1888, the Grant Monument Association was formed, which solicited memorial and grave designs from artists, architects and sculptors who competed for cash awards. The only material that could be used was granite, or granite combined with metal, and the memorial was to cost no more than $500,000. Sixty-five designs were submitted. Five were the top winners, and three of these were for shafts (Kuhn, 218). By then, the judges believed that the shaft was typical American design, but there was a public outcry. There were so many obelisks in Green-Wood Cemetery and all over the continent that the form had lost its meaning. A subcommittee was formed to refine the parameters. The memorial was to house the sarcophagi of Grant and his wife and contain a meeting hall, an area to display Civil War relics, and an observatory. The American architect John H. Duncan from New Orleans, who had been raised in Binghamton, New York, was declared the winner with a design inspired by a monument called the *Tropaeum Alpium*. This monument was built by the Romans for Emperor Augustus, celebrating their victory over the ancient Alpine tribes. The original design envisioned Grant's tomb to be surrounded by statues, which the committee was not able to afford.

The Importance of Memorial Sculpture for Emerging Artists

Memorial sculpture was very important for emerging American artists. The federal and state governments of the new country raised funds to erect statues to honor American heroes. These statues graced the new government buildings that were springing up all across the land. Politicians felt it was important for American artists to create these works rather than hire Europeans, and a whole generation of sculptors were able to land important commissions that kept them busy for most of their careers. Regular citizens also wanted to memorialize their dead in sculpture, and this was encouraged by cemetery corporations. In the original envisioning of American garden cemeteries, sculpture was to play an important part. Statues depicting moving representations of grief, statues reminding mourners of resurrection, or stirring tributes to the dead in stone were to dot the landscape and blend in with the stately monuments, flowers and the trees. To get the ball rolling, cemetery trustees set aside money to purchase and erect sculpture in public areas. An example is Laurel Hill Cemetery's celebrated sculptural group, *Old Mortality and Sir Walter Scott* by James Thom (1802–1850), prominently exhibited at its entrance gate. Laurel Hill Cemetery in Philadelphia had once been a country estate with beautiful views of the Schuykill River. Now a designated National Historic Landmark, it has over 33,000 monuments and over 11,000 family plots (Lichten, 217). The cemetery was designed by Scottish-American architect John Notman (1810–1865) and was completed in 1839. The famous sculptural group *Old Mortality, His Pony, and Sir Walter Scott* was inspired by Sir Walter Scott's novel *Old Mortality*. Carved from red sandstone, the group was brought to America from Britain and first exhibited in New York's Crystal Palace for the Exhibition of the Industry of All Nations, where it made quite a sensation in 1853. The group was given to the cemetery by the artist, Thom, who eventually became a United States citizen and died in New York (Lichten, 217). The fact that Thom came from Britain is not a surprise. The figure of Scott measured 6 feet tall. Sculpture of this size was a rare commodity in America. American sculptors who wanted to work that large had to move to Italy.

In the 19th century the first step in carving a large stone statue began with creating a life-sized clay model. From this, a mold was made which was used to create a plaster copy of the original. This plaster copy was then duplicated onto a marble block using calipers and a grid. American sculptors working in Italy had Italian "assistants" helping and instructing them in this task. Something called a "pointing machine," or a *macchinetta di punta* in Italian, was also used. This ingenious contraption, invented in the 1700s by either the French sculptor Nicolas-Marie Gatteaux or British sculptor John Bacon, had several metal arms ending in needles. One arm was placed on the plaster model and a corresponding one made certain that the marble was drilled to the correct depth. This process was repeated as many times as needed until the marble was covered with holes. Then a *scarpellino* ("chiselman") cut the marble down to the bottom of all the holes, creating a rough draft. For the next step a more skilled *scarpellino* smoothed out the marble and made certain that the measurements were correct. When it was practically finished, the sculptor would add any finishing touches needed (Stone, 22). Studying this process in Italy and having a studio filled with Italian "assistants" seemed to become a prerequisite to becoming an American sculptor in the 19th century.

One important émigré was Horatio Greenough (1805–1852), who was commissioned by Congress to create the massive memorial sculpture of George Washington in celebration of the hundredth year of his birth. Greenough came from a wealthy Bostonian family, and his family wealth and social position made him very different from the first generation of American sculptors. His family owned a marble sculpture of the Athenian statesman Phocion, which, like those in Washington's Mount Vernon, probably was imported from Italy. This statue stood in the family's garden and inspired him every day of his youth, as did the journals and illustrated portfolios the family possessed. Seeing his interest in art, the child was introduced to William Smith Shaw, the director of the Boston Athenaeum, the oldest independent library in the United States. Shaw gave the preteen free access to the fine arts room of the library and let him draw and copy anything he wished. At the same time, Greenough learned clay modeling techniques from Mr. Solomon Willard of Boston, marble carving techniques from Mr. Alpheus Cary, Boston's stone carver, and he was invited to work alongside visiting artist M. Jean-Baptiste Binon, from France (Taft, 37).

Greenough was the first American of a high social standing to choose art as his profession, giving it new respect among the elite. As a boy, he knew he wanted to be an artist, but his father insisted that he attend and graduate from Harvard University, where he studied anatomy. In his spare time, he continued to model in clay and copy original drawings belonging to the school's library. Even before his graduation ceremony, in 1825, Greenough sailed to Europe and went to Rome where he spent his days drawing and modeling. In the evenings he drew from the nude at the *Accademia di Belle Arti di Roma*, or Rome's Academy of Fine Art. On this trip, he fell ill from malaria and returned to the United States, where he modelled the bust of President John Quincy Adams. As soon as he was able to, he returned to Italy, but this time to Florence to study with Lorenzo Bartolini (1777–1850), a famous artist and teacher, who was a bridge from neoclassicism to Romantic portraiture. Other American sculptors following Greenough to Florence were Larkin Goldsmith Mead, Thomas Ball and Hiram Powers.

Greenough didn't seem to make funerary statues, but through the patronage of writer James Fenimore Cooper, Greenough earned a commission from the United States Congress in 1832 to make the memorial statue of George Washington that was to be placed in the Capitol Building's rotunda to commemorate the 100th year of the former president's birth. The artist worked on this piece steadily and completed it in Italy in 1843. It took 22 oxen to haul it from his studio in Florence to Genoa, where it was placed on a ship for America. Envisioning the nation's first president as the Greek god, Zeus, Greenough carved the figure bare-chested, with one arm raised to the heavens. He carved a draped toga over the other shoulder, which also covered the president's lap. Hailed by some, like Massachusetts politician Edward Everett, as being the greatest work of sculpture of its day, the finished work was so huge that it didn't fit through the Capitol Building's doors. Weighing 12 tons, it was also too heavy for the building's floor and had to be erected outside instead on the eastern front of the Capitol. Here it was hated by the public and ridiculed by journalists who thought the statue looked like Washington had just emerged from his bath and was reaching for his clothing located down the street in the Patent Office. It is now on display in the National Museum of American History ("Landmark Object").

Horatio Greenough died in 1852. His younger brother, Richard Saltonstall Greenough (1819–1904), also became a sculptor, and in 1854 was hired by Dr. James Bigelow, the director of Mount Auburn Cemetery, to create a sculpture for the cemetery that would be sheltered in the newly constructed chapel to commemorate the state's illustrious dead. So many people had bought plots in the cemetery that it had a huge monetary surplus, and Bigelow reminded the trustees that the vision of Mount Auburn was the union of art and nature. The trustees allocated $15,000 to purchase three marble statues which were to represent distinguished persons of American history and be made by "proper artists" (Bigelow, 65). The cemetery had already received the marble statue of their important cemetery founder, Judge Story, which had cost $5,000, funded by private subscriptions immediately following the judge's death in 1845. The statue had arrived from Italy in 1855 and was placed in the vestibule of the Boston Athenaeum. The contract for this statue was with William W. Story, the judge's son. The artist was originally given five years to complete the job but needed an extension. In Bigelow's own words, the four sculptures and busts were to be as "elaborate works of art" as those not uncommonly seen in Europe but "occasionally seen in this country" (Bigelow, 62). The other statues would be of John Winthrop, the first governor of Massachusetts, sculpted by Richard Greenough in Florence; John Adams, the second president of the United States from Massachusetts, sculpted by Randolph Rogers; and James Otis, an early Massachusetts leader of the resistance against Britain, modelled and nearly completed by Thomas Crawford in Rome but probably finished by artisans in his studio after Crawford's death. Despite the fact that the trustees almost rescinded the artists' contracts in 1856, the sculptures were completed, and Bigelow believed that they would be important factors in separating Mount Auburn Cemetery from its imitators:

> Mount Auburn, in most respects, takes precedence of other cemeteries which have been founded in imitation of it…. It exceeds all similar establishments in this country in the size and durability of its larger constructions, and is about to lead, instead of following them, in the interest of its historic and monumental sculptures [Bigelow, 72].

Thomas Crawford had settled in Rome, joining other expatriate sculptors such as Edward Sheffield Bartholomew, Randolph Rogers, William Henry Rinehart and women sculptors led by Harriet Goodhue Hosmer. When Crawford died, William Wetmore Story, son of Judge Story, a principal founder of Mount Auburn Cemetery, became the leading American sculptor in Rome.

Richard S. Greenough (1819–1904) was the younger brother of Horatio Greenough. Born in Boston like his brother, he was educated at the Boston Latin School. Unlike his brother, his father did not force him to graduate from Harvard. At 17 he began studying sculpting. He went to Rome in 1837 and became part of the second generation of American expatriate artists living there. The younger Greenough divided his time between Europe and America. He married and was elected a fellow of the American Academy of Arts and Sciences in 1855. His best-known work is a memorial statue of Benjamin Franklin (1856) that stood in front of Boston's Old City Hall.

Randolph Rogers (1825–1892) 1856 completed the memorial statue of John Adams for the cemetery of Mount Auburn in 1856 near the start of his career. He was born in Waterloo, New York, but grew up in Ann Arbor, Michigan. After developing an interest in woodcuts and wood engraving, he moved to New York City in 1847. The young man took a job as a clerk in a dry goods store and was fortunate to have his employer send him to Italy to study sculpting. In 1848, he was a student of Lorenzo Bartolini in Florence. In 1851 he opened his own studio in Rome and supported himself by modeling works in clay and supervising Italian artisans as they carved busts of tourists. Rogers' first large-scale work, the statue named *Ruth Gleaning*, made in 1853, was very popular. Twenty replicas were produced and sold by his studio. His next large work was *Nydia, the Blind Flower Girl of Pompeii*, 1853–54. This was inspired by the best-selling novel *The Last Days of Pompeii* by Edward Bulwer-Lytton. Seventy-seven replicas were made and sold of this in marble. In 1855 Rogers received the commission from the United States government to make the great bronze doors for the east front of the U.S. Capitol. Rogers chose to depict scenes from the life of Christopher Columbus. These doors were modeled in Rome, cast in Munich and installed in the Capitol in 1871. In 1873 the artist became the first American elected to Italy's *Accademia di San Luca*. He was knighted by King

Umberto I in 1884. Rogers left his papers and plaster casts to University of Michigan, even though he had settled permanently in Italy and became a prominent member of the Roman art community.

Besides the sculpture made for Mount Auburn Cemetery, Thomas Crawford (1814–1857) got an important commission to make bronze statues for a Richmond memorial monument honoring historic Virginians including Patrick Henry and Thomas Jefferson, with an equestrian statue of George Washington on top. Crawford and his team of artisans modeled the work in Rome and cast it in Munich. The artist was born in New York City, and at age 19 was an apprentice to stonecutter John Fanzee and his partner Robert Eberhard Launitz, a Russian immigrant who had learned marble carving in Rome. Crawford left for Europe in 1834 and the next summer was a pupil of Launitz's former teacher, the internationally known sculptor Bertel Thorvaldsen. Crawford's first work was the six-foot tall *Orpheus and Cerberus*, created in 1839. Bought by the Boston Athenaeum in 1843, this work is now displayed in Museum of Fine Arts in Boston. Crawford followed this piece with a succession of groups, single figures, and bas-reliefs. In his brief life, the artist completed a lot of work for the United States Capitol building in Washington, D.C., including the marble pediment entitled *Progress of Civilization*. A statue completed by Crawford's studio is perched on the top of the Capitol dome, entitled *Freedom Triumphant in War and Peace*. This work is now known as the *Statue of Freedom*. His career ended in 1854 with failing eyesight caused by cancer of the brain. He died in 1857 and is buried in Greenwood Cemetery in Brooklyn, New York.

We are certain that William Henry Rinehart (1825–1874) made several sculptures specifically placed over graves in garden cemeteries. As a child, he worked on his father's farm in Union Bridge, Maryland, until the age of 18 when he became assistant to the neighborhood stonecutter. In 1844 he started an apprenticeship in the Baughman and Bevan stone yard and studied sculpture in what is now known as the Maryland Institute College of Art. He went to Italy in 1855 but returned two years later to open a studio in Baltimore where he made busts and fountain figures for the United States Post Office in Washington, D.C. He also was commissioned to make sculpture that is on the House of Representatives' side of the United States Capitol Building. In 1858 he returned to Rome. Except for trips made in 1866 and 1872, he remained in Rome for the rest of his life. His most important patron was William T. Walters, who founded Baltimore's Walters Art Gallery, now the Walters Art Museum. On Walters' recommendation, American patrons traveled to Rome to meet Rinehart and commission work from him. His classic piece, *Sleeping Children*, is a funereal group for the Sisson family lot in Green Mount Cemetery in Baltimore. Another one of his bronze sculptures is *Love Reconciled with Death*, also found in Green Mount Cemetery. This was commissioned by Walters after the death of his wife, who had contracted pneumonia in London while touring the unheated Crystal Palace Exhibition. The bronze work was cast in Munich in 1866 and installed in Baltimore the following year. Rinehart returned to the United States and traveled as far as California before returning to Rome. Suffering from tuberculosis, he spent the last years of his life completing the many commissions he had accepted for funeral groups, ideal figures and realistic portrait busts. The last work he completed was entitled *Victory Over Death*. His own body was returned to Baltimore and buried in Green Mount Cemetery. A cast was made in Munich from his marble statue *Endymion*, and a sculpture made from this was placed over his own grave. Endymion was a beautiful shepherd boy who was loved by the moon and granted eternal youth but also eternal sleep, by all powerful Zeus. As the executor of Reinhart's estate, Walters gave funds to the Maryland Institute School of Art and Design, which established the Rinehart School of Sculpture in 1896. Rinehart is considered to be the last American sculptor to work in the neoclassical style. Aside from his funerary statues, his work, mostly of the human figure, are in the collections of museums such as New York's Metropolitan Museum, the National Gallery of Art in Washington, D.C., and Boston Museum of Fine Arts.

Robert Eberhard Launitz (1806–1870), the Russian immigrant, a mentor for Thomas Crawford, also made funerary statues. His uncle was a sculptor, and he advised his nephew to train with him in Rome. Launitz continued his training under a leading European neoclassical sculpture, Bertel Thorvaldsen, and moved to New York City in 1828, where he was hired by John Frazee and eventually became his partner for a short while. Launitz sculpted several funerary statues for the Frankford Cemetery in Frankfort, Kentucky. His monument to General George H. Thomas stands in Troy, New York. But he is best known for the grave statues he carved for cemeteries in Brooklyn, New York, including the Fireman's Memorial, the bas-relief of a grieving Native American for the Do-Hum-Me Indian Princess memorial, and the Charlotte Canda Memorial that he made with Frazee that stands in Green-Wood Cemetery.

The story of Charlotte Canda tugged at the heartstrings of Victorian America. The memorial was originally designed by sixteen-year-old Charlotte to stand over the grave of her beloved aunt, who had recently died. When Charlotte was riding with her father on the trip home from her seventeenth birthday party, a storm broke out that spooked the horses. Charlotte was thrown from the carriage, hit her head and was killed. The devastated father used the plans Charlotte had drawn for the aunt's memorial and added symbols of his own: a star to symbolize immortality and a butterfly to symbolizes her spirit, now freed. Charlotte's fiancé, Charles Albert Jarrett de la Marie, a French nobleman, was so brokenhearted over the death of his beloved that he took his own life a year later. Charlotte was initially buried in the churchyard of Old St. Patrick's Cathedral in Manhattan but was dug up and reinterred in Green-Wood Cemetery on April 29, 1848. Word of the sad story and beautiful gothic monument spread, causing visitors to flock to the cemetery, making it a major tourist attraction of its time.

Green-Wood Cemetery in Brooklyn was founded in 1838 and is now a National Historic Landmark. It is spread out over 478 acres and contains over 600,000 graves. Wealthy Victorians made significant art purchases to place over their final resting places. The directors and the trustees, as in Mount Auburn Cemetery, commissioned artists to enhance the property with sculpture. One of the first orders was for John M. Moffitt (1837–1887) to make figures for the eastern entrance to Green-Wood Cemetery representing the four ages of man. Moffitt was born in London and was apprenticed to a London sculptor. When his apprenticeship was complete, he came to America, arriving right before the Civil War. He specialized in sculptures for cemeteries, churches and military memorials. Moffitt learned how to carve granite, and besides the work done for Green-Wood, he made the sarcophagus for General Griffin A. Stedman that is in Cedar Hill Cemetery in Hartford, Connecticut. Stedman died in 1864 but was probably not buried until 1875. The general's accoutrements, his coat, a flag, his belt and sword, are carved on top of the bier. Lettering of the names of battles in which he fought are on the folds of the flag and on his coat. Besides the bas-reliefs for the Visitor's Cottage at Green-Wood, Moffitt also made a granite statue for the Burnham family, the *Artic* statue for the Brown family memorial, and many others in Green-Wood Cemetery.

Granite and Concrete Grave Markers

According to the *Marble Workers' Manual*, in 1850 there were more than 14,000 stone and marble cutters in the United States. Marble was cut with steel plates, aided by sand, water, pumice and cloth. By the end of the Victorian era, monuments and tombstones were being sold in the Sears, Roebuck and Company catalog, which advertised that they offered a complete line of new and modern designs in monuments and tombstones and added only a small percentage of profit. If a customer paid in full, they could avoid the 25¢ to 50¢ charge on delivery (COD). The catalog complained that most retail marble cutters used inferior grades of marble and charged high prices because customers, in their grief, didn't question the cost. Sears and Roebuck got their marble from the ACME Blue Marble Quarries of Vermont. They had the latest types of polishing machines and employed the most expert artisans, "men whose life has been devoted to this class of work" (Sears, 2). Any tombstone or monument took four to six weeks to complete. Markers cost from $4.88 to $7.87 depending on the size and type. Elegant markers cost $4.90 to $8.00. And for 50¢ more, one could purchase a foot stone. It would cost $18.40 for a monument meant for adjoining markers for a father and mother or a husband and wife. One could also purchase a rustic cross with clinging vine design at $35.33. Lettering was 6 cents per letter. For the grave of a child, one could buy a sleeping lamb carved on top of the tombstone for $11.65 to $112.88. Sears' gravestones also came with stock inscriptions like "Sleep on sweet babe, / And take they rest; / God called thee home, / He thought it best" (Sears, 40). Another epitaph was "She came to raise our hearts to Heaven / She goes to call us there." Verses cost 2.5¢ a letter. The family name on the upper base, or letters raised from the panel, cost 15¢ each and were 2 inches high.

Marble is porous. It doesn't weather well, especially in northern climates. Within decades many marble memorials were illegible. With improvements in railway transportation a new material, granite, started to be shipped and explored for use for grave markers and memorial sculpture. Early granite came from New England quarries including the Barre granite industry in Washington County, Vermont. By the 1870s stone carving companies such as Scotch and Quincy were advertised granite funerary monuments (Bauer, 91).

A catalog from the New England Granite Works from Hartford, Connecticut, stated that they owned a quarry in Westerly, Rhode Island, that had white statuary granite. They bragged that they had devoted half a century to the embellishment of American cemeteries and had an extensive collection of original designs. The company complained about the "cheap marble figures" found in cemeteries all around the country, saying that they were made by Italian apprentices and have no "merit of art or of individuality." Their company had a statuary works division headed by Mr. Carl Conrads, "whose work will compare favorably with that of any sculptor in this country, and his statue of Alexander Hamilton in Central Park has received the highest praise, and is the only statue of granite ever admitted to the park" (*Cleveland Leader*). Carl H. Conrads (1839–1920) was trained in Germany and emigrated to the United States when the Prussians overtook his family's town. Conrads was an artilleryman in the Civil War, then moved to Hartford, Connecticut, in 1866 where he worked for James G. Betterson at the New England Granite Works until 1903. He worked on the 81-foot-tall *National Monument to the Forefathers* with other artists. The sculpture, dedicated in 1889 in Plymouth, Massachusetts, contains five figures and was the largest granite monument in the world.

But granite was difficult to carve and expensive to cut. The stone didn't replace marble until technological improvements in carving, grinding and polishing techniques were made, such as the use of carborundum as an abrasive and the 1890 development of pneumatic drilling technology. Sandblasting techniques also made carving monuments and statues from granite easier. When these tools were invented, immigrants from Ireland, Scotland, Finland and Italy came to America, bringing their skills with them to the granite industries of Quincy, Massachusetts; Barre, Vermont; and Westerly, Rhode Island. Many of these became master carvers; some even signed their names to their work. The deterioration of marble was so pronounced that by the end of the century, some cemeteries were no longer accepting marble stones or monuments at all. Granite became the replacement stone. The list of the New England Granite Works' customers went from coast to coast and included every major cemetery in the country. The Sears, Roebuck and Co. catalog began selling granite makers along with the marble ones. In San Diego County, granite became the favorite over marble in the 1890s, probably because a local granite source was found.

New Jersey cemeteries of the late nineteenth and early twentieth centuries had grave markers made of concrete. Concrete markers were less expensive than marble or granite. Concrete could be poured and markers could be mass-produced at lower costs. The "poor man's marble," concrete became the material of choice for those with limited budgets (Mallios, 447).

Funeral Arts

As more members of a family died, family plots grew. Usually there was one central monument and many smaller grave markers, surrounded by a fence. This is the case of the Warner family monument located in Laurel Hill Cemetery, carved by Alexander Milne Calder (1843–1923), a Scottish-American sculptor and grandfather of the 20th-century artist who invented kinetic mobiles. The sculpture in Laurel Hill is the larger-than-life figure of a woman lifting the lid of the coffin of William Warner, releasing a face embedded in a cloud of smoke, which presumably is his soul. Along with sculptures, Egyptian mausoleums and towering obelisks were popular from 1850 to 1880. By the end of the century, marble statues started to be mass produced, causing Laurel Hill Cemetery in Philidelphia to issue rules. Critics wrote that the factory-produced monuments and angels were hideous stone shapes that marred the landscape.

As the century continued to its end, cemeteries were no longer seen as our nation's public parks. Filled with towering monuments and sad depictions of grief and death, they were no longer places of solace and meditation. Sorrowful, mass-produced angels portraying misery were criticized as "artistic horrors ... stereotyped pieces of stone" (Sample, 546). One no longer needed tickets to enter Laurel Hill Cemetery. Other garden cemeteries had been built. None had fulfilled their purpose of improving American society. None had made the vain correct their vanities, made the greedy less greedy, or strengthened morality. Besides, there were more things to do in each city. As in Philadelphia at the end of the century, cities had museums and organized sports.

World War I, followed by the world-wide influenza epidemic of 1918, had a great effect on the way people in Britain and America mourned. Around 41 million people, civilians as well as military personnel, were killed in the war. Four hundred and twenty

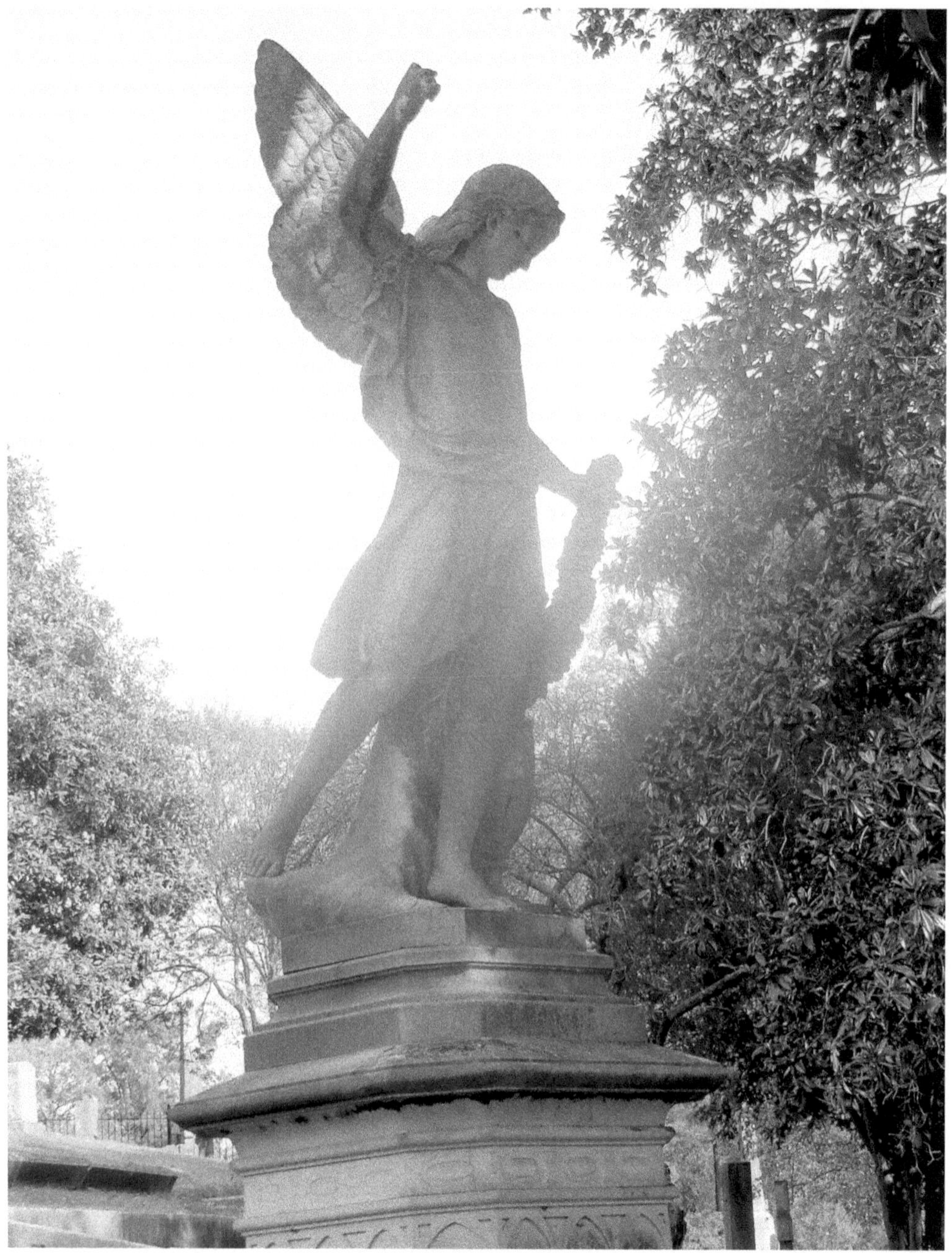

Angel statue, anonymous sculptor, Hollywood Cemetery, Richmond, Va.

thousand of these were Americans. Influenza claimed another 50 to 100 million worldwide (Barry, 2004). More than half of those killed by the pandemic were young adults in their 20s and 30s with good immune systems, lowering the American life expectancy figure by 10 years. To reduce the chances of getting the flu, gauze masks were required by law in San Francisco and then in San Diego. Funerals were limited to 15 minutes by law in many cities. Prescott, Arizona, even forbade people from shaking hands (Mallios,

441). The disease traveled in waves, spread by travelers landing in seaports, military camps and railroad stations. Suicide rates skyrocketed. Arrogance that had dominated the late nineteenth and early twentieth centuries was crushed, replaced with fear, cynicism and humility.

On the other hand, spiritualist mediums continued to channel spirits. And although some spirits wished to do harm and investigators found that many mediums were charlatans, the importance of the body waned as the importance of the spirit or soul grew. Western optimism in an afterlife to which the spirit would return flourished, as did the belief that when we die, we go "to a better place." The decrease of the importance of the body was reflected in the burials of the dead. Smaller, two-dimensional grave markers appeared on graves. After World War I, cemetery architects advocated getting rid of grave markers altogether (Sample, 546). Technological improvements in lawn-mowing equipment called for the removal of plot fences and rough terrain. There was a movement to have "lawn cemeteries," consisting of flat graveyards with markers set level with the ground. There even was a rise in cremation of the remains. Communal grieving was at a minimum, and individual mourning became private. This was not unique to the United States. In England the number of grave monuments reached its height in the 1880s. After that time there was a steep decline (Sayer, 116). Interestingly, before the 1880s there was no funeral industry. Bodies were taken care of by the family or religious groups. After the 1880s the dead were seen as a new market to explore.

Arterial embalming was first practiced by Dr. Frederick Ruysche between 1665 and 1717 in Amsterdam, Holland. Dr. William Hunter of Scotland used a solution of turpentine and resinous oils. French chemist Jean Nicholas Jannel combined aluminum acetate and aluminum sulfate and injected it into the carotid artery (Miller, 22). But the father of modern embalming technique was Dr. Thomas H. Holmes (1817–1899), who discovered and promoted a safe embalming fluid in 1863. He and his colleagues embalmed and shipped home thousands of soldiers from Civil War battlefields and started the mortuary industry.

Holmes charged $100 to embalm an officer and $25 to embalm an enlisted man, and he boasted that he had personally embalmed over 4,000 men in a process that kept the body sanitary and without decay (Burns, 1863). This process was not generally accepted but was made more palatable to the public when used on the assassinated president Abraham Lincoln, whose body toured American before being buried in Illinois. By 1878 the "trocar" was patented. This is a surgical instrument that enables the withdrawal of fluid from a cadaver, making chemical embalming easier. Using a special needle and an injection pump, a body could be embalmed without opening it up and removing its vital organs. In 1882 Dr. C. M. Lukins established the Cincinnati School of Embalming. In 1883 the first national association of undertakers, the Funeral Directors National Association of the United States, was formed.

By 1891 the American Association of Cemetery Superintendents began the promotion of "perpetural care" grave keeping. This lessened even more the family's interaction with the deceased (Burns, 1891). In 1892 the *Embalmers Monthly* journal was created for nonmedical embalmers. Trade magazines were established for the funeral industry (*ibid.*, 1892). As time passed, professionals were trained, and corpses were handled in a more organized way. Death was announced in the hospital, where doctors made certain that the person was really dead. The death was recorded. The body was then sent to specialists, where it was embalmed and made ready to be buried or cremated. Although many survivors wanted to view the corpse, the dead could be "moved from hospital room to burial plot or urn without making any public appearance" (Laderman, 2). There was little to no need to have contact with it any longer. Burial in a tended graveyard, or placement in a communal crypt with a plaque on the sealed door that designated the person's name, meant that there no longer was a need to even tend a grave, freeing the mourner from the horrors of death and encouraging thoughts of the soul's journey to heaven. The body had served its purpose; there no longer was any use of it. The spirit of the person lived on in memory and probably in heaven, watching from above.

Burial sites were forgotten and many without endowments for their upkeep fell into disrepair. But colonial and 19th century monuments and statues are making a comeback. Interest in them has revived. Cemeteries that were once neglected are now on the historical registry. Monuments and statues that were devastated by pollution and the elements are being restored. These cemeteries are being recognized as part of our shared history. They are being saved and repurposed with a schedule of planned activities including Halloween festivities, concerts, ghost walks, historical talks, scheduled nature-sketching classes, organized bird watching, and several other uses. As our urban areas become more congested, garden cemeteries contain precious "green spaces" that make them valuable once more, and academics have become interested in them as places to research art and architecture, symbolism, language and poetry.

It is not uncommon to see school buses bring children to garden cemeteries to read inscriptions about the people that went before them. Descendants of original lot owners form "Friends of" societies and raise money for the upkeep of grounds and preservation of monuments, sculptures and buildings. These people are joined by genealogists, historians, joggers, bicyclists, and cemetery neighbors who want to ensure that these places remain intact and still green for generations to use. While more and more people meander through the hills and valleys of obelisks and memorials, hosts of angels look down from their perches above a grave on a new generation who are recognizing that they are an important part of our heritage.

Epilogue

In the nineteenth century many artists responded to death by using it as inspiration for their work. Others immersed themselves in the occult and turned away from realism in favor of depicting the spiritual that exists in all things. This eventually led them to explore new ways of visualizing the world. They used new colors and new forms that led them down the path of abstraction and nonrepresentational work—the art that dominated the greater part of the twentieth-century art scene. Death was the driving force behind the American sculpture tradition. Memorial monuments and gravesite statues encouraged Americans to carve marble and work in bronze, studying these sculpture techniques in Italy. American Victorians erected giant monuments to their dead and then hired sculptors to model postmortem sculptures of our heroes, and angels who forever mourn over the graves. Victorians admitted photographers into their homes to photograph their loved ones laid out in their parlors, or they brought the corpses of their children to the photography studio and allowed the photographer to twist their arms and legs to get a good pose. Americans of the Victorian Era brought magnifying glasses to galleries so they could search for loved ones among the photographs of the dead lying in battlefields. They bought photo albums and stereo cards of their wars and their dead lying in the bloody fields.

Death made artists out of ordinary people, too. They became fashion designers, sewing clothing for themselves and their families. They became costume designers, draping their bodies with yards of black fabric, desiring to make their grief visible to all. They became jewelry designers and fashioned jewelry from the body parts of the deceased. The Victorians of the 19th century became performers. Some became mediums who communicated with the dead, but all of them designed ritualized procedures for coping with death, loosely based on the practices of European royalty from a century before. As if they were dancers in a choreographed ballet, Victorian men and women learned the steps that they expected of themselves, and followed them, using their communities and the world as their stage.

In response to death, Americans created new religions including Spiritualism and the new philosophy of Theosophy. In doing this they were seeking comfort in the belief that we were not all born in sin and that we would not all forever burn in hell. Several great artists, writers, scientists and thinkers of this time became followers of Spiritualism and Theosophy, and this is reflected in their work. Although many Americans did not accept this new theology, they borrowed the Spiritualist idea that heaven was a wonderful place and incorporated it into their traditional religions. In doing so, they made sense of dying by changing their religions to include hope—the hope of the survival of the spirit, the hope of reincarnation, or the hope of continued existence in a better place.

But in the 19th century death also became commercialized. Entrepreneurs realized that money could be made from grieving loved ones and figured out ingenious ways to capitalize on this. Designers encouraged people to buy new mourning clothes for each individual death. Charles Frederick Worth always made samples of his dresses in black, probably with the need to supply widow's weeds with rapidity in mind. The immediate need for mourning garb contributed to the off-the-rack sale of clothing. This encouraged uniformity in dress and further removed women from being able to design how they looked. As the era progressed, headstones and statues of angels were mass-produced, eliminating the artist and any influence the mourner might have had in the creation of a marker identifying a loved individual's grave. Prices came down, but mass-produced products depersonalized final resting places so much that even epitaphs became standardized. And mourning warehouses, desiring to expand their business, produced books that encouraged elaborate mourning rituals, then sent salespeople to the homes of the newly deceased to drum up business and encourage mourners to purchase items that they didn't need and couldn't afford. Finally, care of the corpse became an industry. This removed the mourner even further from the death of a loved one. The results of this is that today mourning is private and can actually be seen as an excessive response to a loss.

Is death really an end? In response to spiritualism, mediums conducted performances that gave assurances to people that the dead still existed and were interested in their lives. In our own time, television shows star mediums who claim they can communicate with spirits of the dead, and as one medium is disgraced or debunked, others rise to take their place. As part of my research for this book, I drove my old car with a broken air conditioner down Miami highways to see a medium who claimed that she communicated with the dead. The 19th century belief that spirits of the dead continue to exist and watch over those alive was a driving force behind the creation of Victorian mourning rituals, and I needed to see the reality of this myself. The temperature that day was more than 90 degrees, and the humidity was almost 90 percent. I had no idea where I was going and had to follow the GPS on my phone, which meant that my windows had to be closed in order to hear the directions. Plodding my way through manic drivers that dangerously darted back and forth between the lanes, I was filled with conflict. I hoped that I would make it to the venue alive and on time. Usually a skeptic, I hoped that the experience would give me a better understanding of this interest in communicating with the dead. On the other hand, I was also frightened that someone from my crazy family would try to contact me in front of an audience. Fortunately, they didn't, and I was not disappointed with what the medium had to say.

The medium at first spoke to the crowd. She explained that spirits of the dead have higher vibrations than the living do, and that to communicate we must raise our vibrations as they must lower theirs. When she started her readings, she came up with a correct and very unusual name for someone's departed loved one. She knew that another audience member had recently tattooed the face of her departed fiancé on her back; that a young man's wife had died, leaving him to raise his baby boy; that someone's uncle was very assertive when he was drunk; that someone else had brought a necklace that her dead mother had worn to the show; and several other things that amazed us all. With each reveal of a correct answer, the audience let out a collective gasp, astounded that the medium knew these intimate details of audience members' lives and the lives of their departed ones. I came to the venue a nervous skeptic and left thinking that what the medium said was at least 80 to 85 percent correct. But once home, I began to reflect on the messages the spirits gave. The dead souls did not give the medium any profound information. They didn't reveal the meaning of life; they didn't give the audience any clues about who God is; they didn't give us information about what waits for us beyond death's door. The dead who communicated seemed to have the same personalities they had when alive. Some were bossy, some joked around, and some were laid back. Most gave the medium descriptions of how they passed. They died from their "head"—a head injury or stroke, or they died from their "chest"—a heart attack or pleurisy, and so on. If the medium actually was in communication with spirits of the dead, their personalities were still recognizable, and they didn't have much to say except to reassure us that they still were there, wherever *there* was.

Death is one thing all humans have in common. Death is permanent, and death can seem senseless and very sad. Performance mediums, artists, alleviate this sadness with the quasi-religious belief that when we die, we are reborn or we go to heaven, a "better" place, the "Summerland." Of course artists, just as most people of the 19th century, thought about death. Artists responded by creating art. What is interesting is that today we are so horrified by death that very few of us are aware of this, want to think of artists in this way, or want to look at their work in this light.

Bibliography

Adams, Charles Francis. *Letters of John Adams: Addressed to His Wife*, vol. 1. Charles C. Little & James Brown, 1841.

Alison, Archibald. *Essays on the Nature and Principles of Taste*. Boston: Cummings & Hilliard, 1812.

"All New: Locks of George Washington's Hair." State Museum of Pennsylvania, Aug. 5, 2014. http://statemuseumpa.org/locks-george-washington-hair/.

American Printing History Association. https://printinghistory.org. Accessed Oct. 16, 2017.

"America's War." U.S. Department of Veterans Affairs. Accessed June 21, 2015. http://www.va.gov/opa/publications/factsheets/fs_americas_wars.pdf.

"The Ancient and Mystical Order Rosae Crucis." Rosicrucian Order, https://www.rosicrucian.org/history. Accessed Oct. 26, 2018.

Arditi, Jorge. "The Feminization of Etiquette Literature: [Michel] Foucault, Mechanisms of Social Change and the Paradoxes of Empowerment." *Sociological Perspectives*, vol. 39, no. 3 (Autumn 1996). 417–434.

Arnold, Wilfred Niels. "The Illness of Vincent van Gogh." *Journal of the History of the Neurosciences*, vol. 13, no. 1 (2004), 22–42.

Aronson, Julie, and Margorie E. Wieseman. *Perfect Likeness: European and American Portrait Miniatures from the Cincinnati Art Museum*. Yale University Press, 2006.

Bach, Jennifer L. "Acts of Remembrance: Mary Todd Lincoln and Her Husband's Memory." *Journal of the Abraham Lincoln Association*, vol. 25 (Summer 2005). 25–49.

Bachner-Melman, Rachel. "Freud's Relevance to Hypnosis: A Reevaluation." *American Journal of Clinical Hypnosis*, vol. 44, no. 1 (July 2001). 37–50.

Baker, Peggy M. "The Godmother of Thanksgiving: The Story of Sarah Josepha Hale." Pilgrim Society & Pilgrim Hall Museum, 2007. http://www.pilgrimhallmuseum.org/pdf/Godmother_of_Thanksgiving.pdf.

Bambach, Carmen C. "A New Drawing by the Young Raphael and Its Source in Donatello." *The Burlington Magazine*, vol. 149, no. 1256 (Nov. 2007). 772–778.

Barillari, Alyssa. "Tibula." Salem Witch Trials: Documentary Archive and Transcription Project. Accessed Jan. 15, 2016. https://dh.virginia.edu/project/salem-witch-trials-documentary-archive-and-transcription-project.

Barnum, Phineas T. *Humbugs of the World: An Account of Humbugs, Delusions, Impositions, Quackerie*. New York: Carleton, 1866.

Batsford, Herbert. *English Mural Monuments & Tombstones*. London: B. T. Batsford, 1916.

Bauer, Andrew, J. T. Hannibal, et al. "Distribution in Time, Provenance, and Weathering of Gravestones in Three Northeastern Ohio Cemeteries." *The Ohio Journal of Science*, vol. 102, no. 4 (Sept. 2002), 82–96.

Becker, William B. "Do You Believe? A Final Thought on Spirit Photography." The American Museum of Photography. Accessed July 15, 2015. https://www.photographymuseum.com/finalth.html.

Behrendt, Stephen C. *Royal Mourning and Regency Culture: Elegies and Memorials of Princess Charlotte*. New York: St. Martin's, 1997.

Bell, Jeanenne C. *Answers to Questions About Old Jewelry 1840–1950*. 5th ed. Iola, WI: Krause, 1999.

Bennett, Bridget. "Spirited Away: The Death of Little Eva and the Farewell Performances of 'Katie King.'" *Journal of American Studies*, vol. 40, no. 1 (2006), 1–16.

Berg, Maxine, and Helen Clifford. *Consumers and Luxury: Consumer Culture in Europe 1650–1850*. Manchester University Press, 1999.

Besant, Annie, and C. W. Leadbeater. *Thought Forms*. New York: Theosophical Publishing Society, 1901.

Bigelow, Jacob. *A History of the Cemetery of Mount Auburn*. Boston: James Munroe, 1860.

Blachowicz, James. *From Slate to Marble: Gravestone Carving Traditions in Eastern Massachusetts*. Vol. 1, 1770–1870. Evanston, IL: Graver, 2006.

Blanco, José, and Patricia Kay Hunt-Hurst. *Clothing and Fashion: American Fashion from Head to Toe*. Santa Barbara, CA: ABC-CLIO, 2015.

Blavatsky, H. P. "Is Theosophy a Religion?" *Lucifer*, vol. 3 (Nov. 1888).

_____. *Isis Unveiled: A Master-Key to the Mysteries of Ancient and Modern Science and Theology*. Theosophy Trust, online, 2006.

_____. *The Secret Doctrine: The Synthesis of Science, Religion and Philosophy*. Theosophical University Press, original date of publication, 1888. Online edition, http://www.theosociety.org/pasadena/sd/sd-hp.htm.

Blotkamp, Carel. "Annunciation of the New Mysticism: Dutch Symbolism and Early Abstraction." In *The Spiritual in Art: Abstract Painting 1890–1985*. Maurice Tuchman, Judi Freeman, Los Angeles Museum of Art, eds. 89–90. New York: Abbeville, 1987.

_____. *Mondrian: The Art of Destruction*. London: Reaktion, 1994.

Boime, Albert. *Revelation of Modernism: Responses to Cultural Crises in Fin-de-siècle Painting*. Columbia: University of Missouri Press, 2008.

Braid, James (author), and Donald Robertson (ed). *The Discovery of Hypnosis: The Complete Writings of James Braid, the Father of Hypnotherapy*. National Council for Hypnotherapy, London, 2009.

Braude, Ann. *Radical Spirits: Spiritualism and Women's Rights in Nineteenth-Century America*. 2nd ed. Bloomington: Indiana University Press, 1989.

Brett, Mary. *Fashionable Mourning Jewelry, Clothing and Customs*. Atglen, PA: Schiffer, 2006.

Bromberg, Fracine W., and Steven J. Shepard. "The Quaker Burying Ground in Alexandria, Virginia: A Study of Burial Practices of the Religious Society of Friends." *Historical Archeology*, vol. 40, no. 1 (2006). 57–88.

Brown, Nell Porter. "Land of the Living." *Harvard Magazine*, May–June 2017. https://harvardmagazine.com/2017/05/land-of-the-living.

Buck, Louisa. "Without Parallel: Georgiana Houghton's Spirit Drawings." *The Telegraph* (London), Sept. 2, 2016. Accessed Oct. 26, 2016. http://www.telegraph.co.uk/luxury/art/georgiana-houghton-spirit-drawings-at-the-courtauld-gallery-revi/.

Buell, Denise Kimber. "The Afterlife Is Not Dead: Spiritualism, Postcolonial Theory, and Early Christian Studies." *Church History*, vol. 78, no. 4 (Dec. 2009). 862–872.

Burges, N.G. "Taking Portraits After Death." *The Photographic and Fine-Art Journal*, vol. 8, no. 3 (Mar. 1855).

Burnap, George Washington. *The Sphere and Duties of Women: A Course of Lectures*. 3rd ed. Baltimore: John Murphy, 1848.

Burns, Stanley B., MD. *Sleeping Beauty: Memorial Photography in America*. Santa Fe: Twelvetrees, 1990.

Buser, Thomas. "Gauguin's Religion." *Art Journal* (College Art Association), vol. 27, no. 4 (Summer 1968). 375–380.

Cadwallader, Jen. "Spirit Photography and the Victorian Culture of Mourning," *Modern Language Studies*, vol. 37, No. 2 (Winter, 2008): 13.

Calahan, April. *Fashion Plates: 150 Years of Style*. New Haven, CT: Yale University Press, 2016.

Campbell, Mark. *Self-Instruction: Art of Hairwork, Dressing Hair, Making Curls, Switches, Braids, and Hair Jewelry of Every Description*. New York: M. Campbell, 1867.

Carrier, David. "Gavin Hamilton's 'Oath of Brutus' and David's 'Oath of the Horatii': The Revisionist Interpretation of Neo-Classical Art." *The Monist*, vol. 71, no. 2 (Apr. 1988). 197–213.

Cashman, Sean Dennis. *America in the Gilded Age*, 3rd ed. New York University Press, 1993.

Cellania, Miss. "The Bell Witch of Tennessee." *Mental Floss*, Oct. 18, 2012. http://mentalfloss.com/article/12828/bell-witch-tennessee.

Champlin, Carroll D. "The Cultural Contribution of International Expositions." *The Phi Delta Kappan*, vol. 20, no. 4 (Dec. 1937). 115–117, 142.

Chapin, Davie. *Exploring Other Worlds: Margaret Fox, Elisha Kent Kane, and the Antebellum Culture of Curiosity*. Amherst: University of Massachusetts Press, 2004.

Chief Seattle, 1854 speech. Reprinted in *Seattle Sunday Star*, Oct. 29, 1887.

Childe-Pemberton, William S. *The Romance of Princess Amelia: Daughter of George III (1783–1810)*. London: G. Bell, 1910.

Clark, Edward W. "The Bigham Carvers of the Carolina Piedmont: Stone Images of an Emerging Sense of American Identity." In *Cemeteries and Gravemarkers: Voices of American Culture*, Richard E. Meyer, ed. Logan, UT: University Press of Colorado, 1989.

Coates, James. *Photographing the Invisible: Practical Studies in Spirit Photography, Spirit Portraiture, and Other Rare but Allied Phenomena*. London: L. N. Fowler, 1911.

Cobb, Josephine. "Matthew B. Brady's Photographic Gallery in Washington." *The Bulletin of the Columbia Historical Society*, Washington, D.C., vol. 53/56 (1953/1956). 28–69.

Coltman, O. A. "The Evolution of Memorial Art—V." *Stone*, vol. 4, 11–13.

Conan Doyle, Arthur. *The History of Spiritualism*. Vol. 1. London: Cassell, 1926.

Connolly, Thomas J., et al. "The Archaeology of a Pioneer Family Cemetery in Western Oregon, 1854–1879." *Historical Archaeology*, vol. 44, no. 4 (2010). 28–45.

Cooke, Jim. "The Obelisks of Greater Dublin." *Dublin Historical Record*, vol. 56, no. 2 (Autumn 2003), 146–160.

Coote, J. *A Biographical Memoir of the Much Lamented Princess Charlotte Augusta of Wales and Saxe Coburg: Illustrated with Recollections, Personal Anecdotes and Traits of Character, Not Generally Known, from the Most Authentic Sources*. 4th ed. London: J. Barfield (Printer to H.R.H. the Prince Regent), 1818.

Cornelius, Charles O. "Early American Jewelry." *The Metropolitan Museum of Art Bulletin*, vol. 21, no. 4, part 1 (Apr. 1926). 99–101.

Courteaux, Oliver. "Charles Frederick Worth, the Empress Eugénie and the Invention of Haute-Couture." Napoleon.org: The History Website of the Fondation Napoleon. Accessed Dec. 3, 2016. https://www.napoleon.org/en/history-of-the-two-empires/articles/charles-frederick-worth-the-empress-eugenie-and-the-invention-of-haute-couture/.

Cox, Richard J., and Debra Day. "Stories of a Pleasant Green Space: Cemetery Records and Archives." *Archival Issues* (Midwest Archives Conference), vol. 33, no. 2 (1011). 88–99.

Crowell, Elizabeth A., and N. V. Mackie. "'Depart from Hence and Keep This Thought in Mind': The Importance of Comparative Analysis in Gravestone Research." *Northeast Historical Archaeology*, vol. 13, article 3 (1984).

Cunningham, Patricia A. *Reforming Women's Fashion, 1850–1920: Politics, Health and Art.* Ohio: Kent State University Press, 2003.

Curl, James Stevens. *The Victorian Celebration of Death.* Stroud, UK: Sutton, 2000.

Current, Ira. "The Brady Bit." *Photographic Society of American*, vol. 70, no. 6 (2004). 33–35.

"Daguerreotype." Library of Congress. Accessed June 25, 2015. https://www.loc.gov/collections/samuel-morse-papers/articles-and-essays/collection-highlights/daguerreotype/.

Daniel, Malcolm. "Roger Fenton (1819–1869)." The Met: Heilbrunn Timeline of Art History. Accessed Oct. 26, 2015. https://www.metmuseum.org/toah/hd/rfen/hd_rfen.htm.

Davey, Richard. *A History of Mourning.* McCorquodale, London, 1890.

Davis, Robert S. "The Story of the Georgia Marble Dynasty." *Georgia Historical Quarterly*, vol. 89, no. 3 (Fall 2005). 368–388.

Day, Marilyn. *Benjamin Day Stone Carver, Lowell, Mass. (1783–1855).* Pelham Historical Society, Pelham, NH, Hayes-Genoter History and Genealogy Library, 2005.

De Chenneviéres, Henri. "The Court-Balls of Marie Antoinette." *The Connoisseur*, vol. 1, no. 2 (Winter 1886–1887), 1–7.

"The Death of George Washington." George Washington's Mount Vernon. Accessed Oct. 14, 2016. http://www.mountvernon.org/digital-encyclopedia/article/the-death-of-george-washington/.

Deetz, James. *Flowerdew Hundred: The Archaeology of a Virginia Plantation, 1619–1864.* Charlottesville: University of Virginia Press, 1993.

_____. *In Small Things Forgotten: An Archaeology of Early American Life.* New York: Anchor, 1996.

Deetz, James, and Edwin S. Dethlefsen. "The Plymouth Colony Archive Project: Death's Head, Cherub, Urn and Willow." *Natural History*, vol. 76, no. 3 (1967). 29–37.

De Valcourt, Robert. *The Illustrated Book of Manners: A Manuel of Good Behavior and Polite Accomplishments.* Cincinnati: R. W. Carroll, 1866.

Dethlefsen, Edwin, and James Deetz. "Death's Heads, Cherubs, and Willow Trees: Experimental Archaeology in Colonial Cemeteries." *American Antiquity*, vol. 31, no. 4 (Apr. 1966). 502–510.

DeVoll, Matthew. "Emerson and the Realms of Mesmerism: 'Where Angels Fear to Tread.'" In *The Occult in Nineteenth-Century America*, ed. Cathy Gutierrez, 83–117. Aurora, CO: Davies Group, 2005.

Dewey, D. M. *The Mysterious Noises Which Are Supposed by Many to Be Communications from the Spirit World.*, Rochester, NY: D. M. Dewey, 1850.

Dolan, Therese. "The Empress's New Clothes: Fashion and Politics in Second Empire France." *Woman's Art Journal*, vol. 15, no. 1 (Spring–Summer 1994). 22–28.

Donne, John. "The Funeral." Poetry Foundation. Accessed Mar. 28, 2017. https://www.poetryfoundation.org/poems/44102/the-funeral-56d2230f8b508.

"The Editor of the 'British Journal of Photography,' on the Possibility of Spirit Photography." *The Spiritual Magazine* (London, England), Sept. 1, 1869.

Eldredge, Charles C. "Nature Symbolized: American Painting from Ryder to Hartley." In *The Spiritual in Art: Abstract Painting 1890–1985*, ed. Maurice Tuchman, Judi Freeman, and Los Angeles Museum of Art, 113–129. New York: Abbeville, 1987.

Ellis, M. H. *The Ambrotype and Photographic Instructor or Photography on Glass and Paper.* Philadelphia: Myron Shew, 1856.

Ellison, Betty Boles. *The True Mary Todd Lincoln: A Biography.* Jefferson, NC: McFarland 2014.

Eltzroth, E. Lee. "Georgia Photographers: The First Generation, 1840–1860." *Georgia Historical Quarterly*, vol. 92, no. 1 (Spring 2008). 37–64.

Emerson, Ralph Waldo, journal entry quoted in *American Journal of Photography*, June 1858.

Erbsen, Wayne. *Manners and Morals of Victorian America.* Asheville, NC: Native Ground Books and Music, 2009.

Evans, Henry Ridgely. "Madame Blavatsky." *The Monist*, vol. 14, no. 3 (Apr. 1904). 387–408.

Evans, Joan. *A History of Jewellery, 1100–1870.* New York: Dover, 1953.

Fant, Åke. "The Case of the Artist Hilma af Klint." In *The Spiritual in Art: Abstract Painting 1890–1985.* Maurice Tuchman, and Judi Freeman, Los Angeles Museum of Art, eds. New York: Abbeville, 1987. 155–163.

Farber, Jessie Lie. "Early American Gravestones: Introduction to the Farber Gravestone Collection." *American Antiquarian Society*, 2003. http://www.lunacommons.org/luna/servlet/FBC~100~1.

Farrar, Mrs. John. *The Young Lady's Friend.* Boston: American Stationers, 1838.

"Fashion Plate Collection." Fresno State Digitized Collection: Henry Madden Library. Accessed Dec. 13, 2016. http://cdmweb.lib.csufresno.edu/cdm/landingpage/collection/fashion.

Faust, Drew Gilpin. "Death and Dying." National Park Service. https://www.nps.gov/nr/travel/national_cemeteries/death.html

Flanders, Judith. *Inside the Victorian Home.* New York: W. W. Norton, 2003.

Flower, Margaret. *Victorian Jewellery.* London: Cassell, 1951.

Forbes, Harriette Merrifield. *Gravestones of Early New England and the Men Who Made Them 1653–1800.* Boston: Houghton Mifflin, 1989.

Fornell, Earl Wesley. *The Unhappy Medium.* Austin: University of Texas Press, 1964.

Francaviglia, Richard V. "The Cemetery as an Evolving Cultural Landscape." *Annals of the Association of American Geographers*, vol. 61, no. 3 (Sep. 1971). 501–509.

Frassanito, William A. *Gettysburg: A Journey in Time.* Gettysburg, PA: Thomas, 1975.

French, Harry Willard. *Art and Artists in Connecticut.* Boston: Lee & Shepard, 1879.

French, Stanley. "The Cemetery as Cultural Institution: The Establishment of Mount Auburn and the 'Rural Cemetery' Movement." *American Quarterly*, John Hopkins University Press, vol. 26, no. 1 (Mar. 1974). 37–59.

Fried, Michael. "The Structure of Beholding in Courbet's 'Burial at Ornans.'" *Critical Inquiry*, vol. 9, no. 4 (June 1983). 635–683.

"From Fashion Plate to Social Reform: The Story Behind Godey's Lady's Book." Past Is Present: American Antiquarian Society Blog, March 10, 2011. http://pastispresent.org/2011/good-sources/from-fashion-plates-to-social-reform-the-story-behind-godey%E2%80%99s-lady%E2%80%99s-book/.

"Galileo's Fingers to Be Displayed in Florence Science Museum." *The Guardian*, June 8, 2010. https://www.theguardian.com/culture/2010/jun/08/galileo-fingers-museum-florence.

Garman, James C. "Viewing the Color Line Through the Material Culture of Death." *Historical Archaeology*, vol. 28, no. 3 (1994). 74–93.

Garoian, Charles Richard. *Performance Art Teaching as a New Pedagogy*. Stanford University, Ph.D. dissertation. Ann Arbor, MI: University Microfilms International,1984. Accessed Sept. 2, 2015.

Gauguin, Paul. *Paul Gauguin's Intimate Journals*. Brooks Van Wyck, trans. New York: Crown, 1936.

Gere, Charlotte. *Love and Art: Queen Victoria's Personal Jewellery*. Essays from a study day held at the National Gallery, London, 5 and 6 June 2010. Royal Collection Trust © HM Queen Elizabeth II, London, 2012.

Gere, Charlotte, and Judy Rudoe. *Jewellery in the Age of Queen Victoria: A Mirror to the World*. London: British Museum Press, 2010.

Gilmartin, Sophie. "The Sati, the Bride and the Widow: Sacrificial Woman in the Nineteenth Century." *Victorian Literature and Culture*, vol. 25, no. 1 (1997). 141–158.

Gilson, William. "Stone Faces." *New England Review (1990–)*, vol. 30, no. 4 (2009–10). 79–101.

Gnann, Achim. "A New Attribution to Raphael." *Master Drawings*, vol. 36, no. 2 (Summer 1998), 198–204.

"Godey's Lady's Book." The Online Books Page. http://onlinebooks.library.upenn.edu/webbin/serial?id=godeylady.

Goetheanum. https://www.goetheanum.org/en/.

"Going Once, Going Twice … Most Expensive Lock of Hair." *Time*. Accessed Mar. 29, 2017. http://content.time.com/time/specials/packages/article/0,28804,1917097_1917096_1917086,00.html.

Gollin, Rita K. "The Matthew Brady Photographs of Nathaniel Hawthorne." *Studies in the American Renaissance*, 1981, ii. 379–391.

Gombrich, E. H. *The Story of Art*. Phaidon, Oxford University Press, New York, 1951.

Gorman, Frederick J. E., and Michael DiBlasi. "Gravestone Iconography and Mortuary Ideology." *Ethnohistory*, vol. 102, no. 4 (Sept. 2002). 82–96.

"Gravestone Symbolism: The Iconography of Death in Ireland." History from Headstones. Accessed Aug. 31, 2017. http://www.historyfromheadstones.com/index.php?id=949.

Grovier, Kelly. "Are These the Strangest Relics in History?" *BBC: Culture*, Sept. 15, 2016. http://www.bbc.com/culture/story/20160915-are-these-the-strangest-relics-in-history.

Guggenheim. New York: Solomon R. Guggenheim Foundation, 1992.

Gutierrez, Cathy, ed. *The Occult in Nineteenth-Century America*. Aurora, CO: Davies Group, 2005.

Hartley, Florence. *The Ladies' Book of Etiquette, and Manual of Politeness: A Complete Handbook for the Use of Ladies in Polite Society*. Boston: Lee & Shepard, 1872.

Healey, Kenneth. "English Churchyard Memorials." *Journal of the Royal Society of Arts*, vol. 115, no. 5128 (Mar. 1967), 260–274.

Heindel, Max. *The Light Beyond Death*. Oceanside, CA: Rosicrucian Fellowship, Mt. Ecclesia, 2001.

Herron, Jerry. "Facing Death: Modernity, Mortality, Postcards." *Qui Parle*, vol. 7, no. 2 (Spring–Summer 1994). 110–140.

Hesse, Rayner W. *Jewelrymaking Through History: An Encyclopedia*. Westport, CT: Greenwood, 2007.

Hijiya, James A. "American Gravestones and Attitudes Toward Death: A Brief History." *Proceedings of the American Philosophical Society*, vol. 127, no. 5 (Oct. 14, 1983). 339–363.

"Hilma af Klint: A Painter Possessed." *The Guardian*, U.S. ed., Art section, Feb. 21, 2016.

"A History of Diamond Cutting." Antique Jewelry University. Accessed Feb. 14, 2017. http://www.langantiques.com/university/A_History_Of_Diamond_Cutting.

"The History of Diamond Mining and Diamonds in South Africa." Cape Town Diamond Museum. Accessed Aug. 12, 2017. http://www.capetowndiamondmuseum.org/about-diamonds/south-african-diamond-history/.

"A History of Jewellery." Victoria and Albert Museum. Accessed Mar. 24, 2017. https://www.vam.ac.uk/articles/a-history-of-jewellery.

"History of Ostby & Barton Jewelry Co. and the Significance of the Historical Titantic Collision." Maejean Vintage, Apr. 30, 2016. http://www.maejeanvintage.com/blog/2016/1/25/history-of-ostby-barton-jewelry-co-the-significance-of-the-historical-titantic-collision.

HistoryNet. "Battle of Gettysburg: Facts, Summary and HistoryNet Articles about the Battle of Gettysburg during the American Civil War." Accessed Oct. 26, 2015. http://www.historynet.com/battle-of-gettysburg.

Holm, Christiane. "Sentimental Cuts: Eighteenth-Century Mourning Jewelry with Hair." *Eighteenth-Century Studies*, vol. 38, no. 1 (Fall 2004). 139–143.

Holmes, Oliver Wendell. "Sun Painting and Sun-Sculpture." *Atlantic Monthly*, July 1861.

Home, Daniel Dunglass. *Incidents in My Life*, 5th ed. New York, 1864.

Horowitz, Mitch. *Occult in America*. New York: Bantam, 2009.

Houdini, Harry. *Houdini Exposes the Tricks Used by the Boston Medium "Margery" to win the $2500 prize offered by the Scientific America; Also a complete exposure of Argamasilla the famous Spaniard who baffled noted Scientists of Europe and America with his claim to X-Ray Visiion*. New York: Adams, 1924.

_____. *A Magician Among the Spirits*. New York: Harper, 1924.

Husband, Julie, and Jim O'Loughlin. *Daily Life in the*

Industrial United States, 1870–1900. Westport, CT: Greenwood, 2004.

"The Impact of Lighting Poverty on Children." Lights for Life. Accessed Feb. 18, 2018. http://www.lightsforlife.org/impact_of_lighting_poverty_on_children.

Janson, Horst W. "The Putto with the Death's Head." *The Art Bulletin* (College Art Association), vol. 19, no. 2 (Sept. 1937). 423–449.

The Jeweler's Circular and Horological Review, vol. 9 (Nov. 1878). xxi–xxii.

John, Duke of Bedford. *Flower's Political Review and Monthly Register, Volume VIII, from July to January 1810–1811*. London: B. Flower, Horlow, 1811.

Joseph, J. W. "Editor's Preface." *Historical Archaeology* (Society for Historical Archaeology), vol. 43, no. 1 (2009). v–vi.

Kadish, Sharman. "Jewish Funerary Architecture in Britain and Ireland Since 1656." *Jewish Historical Studies*, vol. 43 (2011). 59–88.

Kahn, David M. "The Grant Monument." *Journal of the Society of Architectural Historians*, vol. 41, no. 3 (Oct. 1982). 212–231.

Kandinsky, Wassily. *Concerning the Spiritual in Art*. Translation by Michael T. H. Sadler, 1911. http://www.semantikon.com/art/kandinskyspiritualinart.pdf. Accessed Jan. 10, 2016.

Kaplan, Louis. *The Strange Case of William Mumler Spirit Photographer*. Minneapolis: University of Minnesota Press, 2008.

Keckley, Elizabeth. *Behind the Scenes: or Thirty Years a Slave, and Four Years in the White House*. New York, G. W. Carleton, 1868.

Kellogg, Ann T., Amy T. Person, et al. *In an Influential Fashion: An Encyclopedia of Nineteenth and Twentieth-Century Fashion Designers and Retailers Who Transformed Dress*. Westport, CT: Greenwood, 2002.

Kerr, Howard, and Charles, C., eds. *The Occult in America: New Historical Perspective*. Urbana and Chicago: University of Illinois Press, 1983.

Kete, Mary Louise. *Sentimental Collaborations*. Durham, NC: Duke University Press, 2000.

King, Charlotte. "Separated by Death and Color: The African American Cemetery of New Philadelphia, Illinois." *Historical Archaeology*, vol. 44, no. 1 (2010), 125–137.

Kivi, Rose. "How Does an Outhouse Work?" Hunker. Accessed Feb. 19, 2018. https://www.hunker.com/13425663/how-does-an-outhouse-work.

Kraft, Siv Ellen. "To Mix or Not to Mix: Syncretism/Anti-Syncretism in the History of Theosophy." *Numen*, vol. 49, no. 2 (2002), 142–177.

Kramer, Hilton. "Kandinsky's Spiritualism." *New York Times*, Arts and Leisure section, May 10, 1981.

Krick, Jessa. *Charles Frederick Worth (1825–1895) and the House of Worth*. The Costume Institute, Metropolitan Museum of Art, New York, 2004.

Kucich, John J. *Ghostly Communion: Cross-Cultural Spiritualism in Nineteenth-Century American Literature*. Dartmouth College Press, Hanover, NH, 2004.

Kucich, John. "Ghostly Communion: Spiritualism, Reform and Harriet Jacobs' Incident in the Life of a Slave Girl." In *The Occult in Nineteenth-Century America*, ed. Cathy Gutierrez. Aurora, CO: Davies Group, 2005. 31–82.

Kumar, Raj. "Annie Besant and Self-Government for India, 1914–1916." *Proceedings of the Indian History Congress*, vol. 41 (1980). 511–519.

Lachman, Gary. "Kandinsky's Thought Forms and the Occult Roots of Modern Art." *Quest*, Mar.–Apr. 2008. 57–61.

Laderman, Gary. *The Sacred Remains: American Attitude Toward Death 1799–1883*. New Haven, CT: Yale University Press, 1996.

Lavoie, Jeffrey. "The Spiritualism of Madame Blavatsky: An Introduction to Western Esotericism and the Life and Writings of a Victorian Occultist." University of Exeter. https://humanities.exeter.ac.uk/media/universityofexeter/collegeofhumanities/history/exhistoria/volume4/Supplement-Lavoie.pdf

Lake, Matthew, et al. *Weird Pennsylvania: Your Travel Guide to Pennsylvania's Local Legends and Best Kept Secrets*. New York: Sterling, 2005.

"Landmark Object: George Washington Statue, 1841." Smithsonian. Accessed Oct. 26, 2017. http://americanhistory.si.edu/press/fact-sheets/landmark-object-george-washington-statue-1841.

Laver, James. *Costume and Fashion*. London: Thames & Hudson, 1982.

Leadbeater, C. W. *The Astral Plane: Its Scenery, Inhabitants and Phenomena*. London: Theosophical Publishing Society, 1895.

_____. *Man Visible and Invisible: Examples of Different Types of Men as Seen by Means of Trained Clairvoyance*. Bodley Head, New York, 1902.

Lengel, Edward G., ed. *A Companion to George Washington*. Chichester, UK: Wiley-Blackwell Southern Gate, 2014.

"Leslie McVane, Member Highlights, Bartlett Adams Lecture." CTN Channel 5, MCMA, June 2, 2014.

"The Letters: From Vincent to Theo." http://www.vggallery.com/letters/to_theo_early.htm.

Lewis, Michael J. "How Art Became Irrelevant." *Commentary*, vol. 140, no. 1 (2015): 11. Accessed from Academic OneFile, Sept. 2, 2015.

Lichten, Frances. *Decorative Arts of Victoria's Era*. New York: Charles Scribner's Sons, 1950.

"Life After Death in Kamaloka (the Astral World)." Blavatsky Study Center, 2003. http://www.blavatskyarchives.com/morganafterdeath.htm.

Linden-Ward, Blanche M. G. *Silent City on a Hill: Picturesque Landscapes of Memory and Boston's Mount Auburn Cemetery*. Amherst: University of Massachusetts Press, 2007.

Linkman, Audrey. *Photography and Death*. London: Reaktin, 2011.

Lipsey, Roger. *The Spiritual in Twentieth-Century Art*. New York: Dover, 2004.

Llewellyn, Nigel. *The Art of Death*. London: Reaktion, in association with the Victoria and Albert Museum, 1997.

Lockwood, Rose. "Birth, Illness and Death in 18th-Century New England." *Journal of Social History*, vol. 12, no.1 (Autumn 1978). 111–128.

Long, Rose-Carol Washton. "Expressionism, Abstraction, and the Search for Utopia in Germany." In *The Spiritual in Art: Abstract Painting*

1890–1985, ed. Maurice Tuchman, Judi Freeman, and Los Angeles Museum of Art, 201–217. New York: Abbeville, 1987.

Longfellow, Henry Wadsworth. "Resignation." Bartleby.com. https://www.bartleby.com/102/67.html.

Loudon, John C. *On the Laying Out, Planting and Managing of Cemeteries and on the Improvement of Churchyards*. London: self-published, 1843.

"Louis-Nicolas Robert." Paper Discover Center. Accessed Oct. 18, 2017. https://www.paperdiscoverycenter.org/discovery-center/.

Love, Robert. "Houdini's Greatest Trick: Debunking Mina Crandon." Mental Foss, Oct. 31, 2013. http://mentalfloss.com/article/53424/houdinis-greatest-trick-debunking-medium-mina-crandon.

Ludwig, Allen I. *Graven Images: New England Stonecarving and Its Symbols, 1650–1815*. Hanover, NH: Wesleyan University Press, 1966.

Lutz, Deborah. "The Dead Still Among Us: Victorian Secular Relics, Hair Jewelry, and Death Culture." *Victorian Literature and Culture*, vol. 39, no. 1 (2011). 127–142.

Mackie, Norman Vardney, III. "The Social Aspects of Funerary Monuments in Colonial Tidewater Virginia." *Material Culture* (International Society for Landscape, Place and Material Culture), vol. 20, no. 2/3 (Summer/Fall 1988). 39–55.

Mallios, Seth, and David M. Caterino. "Mortality, Money and Commemoration: Social and Economic Factors in Southern California Grave-Marker Change During the Nineteenth and Twentieth Centuries." *International Journal of Historical Archaeology*, vol. 15, no. 3 (Sept. 2011). 429–460.

Manners and Rules of Good Society: or Solecisms to Be Avoided, by a Member of the Aristocracy. 38th ed. London: Frederick Warne, 1916.

"Marble." The Architect of the Capitol. Accessed Oct. 27, 2017. https://www.aoc.gov/capitol-hill/architecture/marble.

"Married Women's Property Laws." Library of Congress. Accessed Dec. 12, 2017. https://memory.loc.gov/ammem/awhhtml/awlaw3/property_law.html.

Marryatt, Florence. *There Is No Death*. New York: National Book, 1891.

Martin, William. *Peter Parley's Annual: A Christmas and New Year's Present for Young People*. London: Darton & Co., 1859.

Maskelyne, J. N. *The Fraud of Modern "Theosophy" Exposed*. London: George Routledge & Sons, 1912.

Maurer, Naomi Margolis. *The Pursuit of Spiritual Wisdom: The Thought and Art of Vincent Van Gogh and Paul Gauguin*. Vancouver: Fairleigh Dickinson University Press, 1998.

Maynard, Nettie Colburn. *Seances in Washington: Abraham Lincoln during the Civil War*. Irene, McGarvie, ed. First published in 1891 as: (*Was Abraham Lincoln a Spiritualist?*). Ontario, CA: Ancient Wisdom Publishing, 2009.

McCabe, Constance. "Preservation of 19th Century Negatives in the National Archives." *Journal of the American Institute for Conservation*, vol. 30, no. 1 (Spring 1991). 41–73.

McCauley, Mary Carole. "New Exhibit at Walters Art Museum Showcases the Statues of Maryland Artist William Rinehart." *The Baltimore Sun*, Entertainment/Arts section, Apr. 11, 2015.

McDannell, Colleen. "The Religious Symbolism of Lauren Hill Cemetery." *The Pennsylvania Magazine of History and Biography* (Historical Society of Pennsylvania), vol. 111, no. 3 (Jul. 1987). 275–303.

Mercer, G. E. "Correspondence." *Journal of the Royal Society of Arts*, vol. 125, no. 5250 (May 1977). 334.

Messer, Thomas M., and M. Mladek. *Frantisek Kupka 1871–1957 Retrospective*. New York: Solomon R. Guggenheim Foundation, 1975.

Metropolitan Museum of Art. "Henry Kirke Brown (1814–1886), John Quincy Adams Ward (1830–1910), and Realism in American Sculpture." Accessed November 10, 2017. https://www.metmuseum.org/toah/hd/reas/hd_reas.htm.

Metternich, Princess Pauline. *The Days That Are No More: Some Reminiscences*. London: Eveleigh Nash & Grayson, 1921.

Mikkelsen, Patti, and Richard Erwin. *Bartlett Adams: Stone Cutter*. New Gloucester Historical Society. Accessed July 28, 2017. https://archive.org/details/BartlettAdamsStoneCutter.

Miller, C. L. *Postmortem Collectibles*. Atglen, PA: Schiffer, 2001.

The Mirror of the Graces: or the English Lady's Costume (by a Lady of Distinction). London: North Bridge & Longman, 1830.

Moffett, Judith. *James Merrill: An Introduction to the Poetry*. New York: Columbia University Press, 1984.

Mondrian, Piet. *Neo Plasticism in Painting, 1917–18*. Hans Jaffé, trans. New York: H. N. Abrams, 1971.

_____. "The Realization of Neoplasticism in the Distant Future and in Architecture Today: Architecture, Conceived as Our Total Environment." *De Stijl*, 1922, Hans Jaffé, trans. New York: H. N. Abrams, 1971.

Moore, Jerry, Cynthia Blaker, and Grant Smith. "Cherished Are the Dead: Changing Social Dimensions in a Kansas Cemetery." *Plains Anthropologist*, vol. 36, no. 133 (Feb. 1991). 67–78.

Mott, Frank Luther. *A History of American Magazines, 1850–1865*. Cambridge, MA: Harvard University Press, 1938.

Mount Auburn Cemetery: Including Also a Brief History and Description of Cambridge Harvard University, and the Union Railway Company. 19th ed., Cambridge, MA: Moses King, 1883.

Mumler, William H. *The Personal Experiences of William H. Mumler in Spirit-Photography*, Boston: Colby & Rich, 1875.

Munich, Adrienne. *Queen Victoria's Secrets*. New York: Columbia University Press, 1996.

Mytum, H. C. *Mortuary Monument and Burial Grounds of the Historic Period*. New York: Springer-Science+Business Media, 2004.

Mytum, Harold. "Public Health and Private Sentiment: The Development of Cemetery Architecture and Funerary Monuments from the Eighteenth Century Onwards." *World Archaeology*, vol. 21, no. 2 (Oct. 1989). 283–297.

Nadis, Fred. "If Not Spirits, What Is it? Turn of the Century Magicians and the Anti-Spiritualistic Performance." In *The Occult in Nineteenth-Century America*, Cathy Gutierrez, ed. Aurora, CO: Davies Group, 2005. 183–214

Nagy, Ron. *Precipitated Spirit Paintings*. Lakeville, MN: Glade, 2006.

National Intelligencer, Washington, D.C., June 21, 1858.

Nelson, Louis P. *The Beauty of Holiness: Anglicanism and Architecture in Colonial South Carolina*. Chapel Hill: University of North Carolina Press, 2008.

"New England Native American Burial Customs." Access Genealogy. Accessed Aug. 28, 2017. https://www.accessgenealogy.com/native/new-england-native-american-burial-customs.htm.

Nickell, Joe. "A Skeleton's Tale: The Origins of Modern Spiritualism." *Skeptical Inquirer*, July–Aug. 2008. 17.

Nonestied, Mark, and Richard Veit. "Carrying on the Stone Cutting Business: Identifying New Jersey's Early Gravestone Carvers." *Gardenstate Legacy*, no. 11 (Mar. 2011).

Oberter, Rachel. "Esoteric Art Confronting the Public Eye: The Abstract Spirit Drawings of Georgiana Houghton." *Victorian Studies*, vol. 48, no. 2, Papers and Responses from the Third Annual Conference of the North American Victorian Studies Association (Winter 2006). 221–232.

Ogata, Amy F. "Viewing Souvenirs: Peepshows and the International Expositions." *Journal of Design History*, vol. 15, no. 2 (2002). 69–82.

Olcott, Henry S. "The Buddhist Catechism." Originally published 1908. Internet Sacred Text Archive. http://www.sacred-texts.com/bud/tbc/index.htm.

Olcott, Henry S. *People from the Other World*. American, Hartford, CT, 1875.

Owens, W.J.B., and Jane Worthington Smyser. *The Prose Works of William Wordsworth*, vol. 2. Oxford University Press, 1974.

"Pants? Queen Victoria's Underwear Sold for €12,000 at auction." *The Guardian*, July 11, 2015.

Pearsall, Ronald. *The Table Rappers*. New York: St. Martin's, 1972.

Peláez, Marina Watson. "Forget Kate's Dress: What's Behind William and Harry's Wedding Uniforms?" *Time*, Apr. 29, 2011. http://newsfeed.time.com/2011/04/29/forget-kates-dress-whats-behind-william-and-harrys-wedding-uniforms/.

Peres, Michael R., ed. *The Focal Encyclopedia of Photography*. 4th ed. Oxford: Focal, 2013.

Perrottet, Tony. "Gentlemen, Charge Your Indecent Props!" *Slate*, Dec. 18, 2009. https://slate.com/human-interest/2009/12/gentlemen-charge-your-indecent-props.html. Accessed Dec. 20, 2018.

Phillips, Clare, with contributions by Vivienne Becker, et al. *Bejewelled by Tiffany, 1837–1987*. New Haven, CT: Yale University Press, 2006.

Pike, Martha. "Memory of: Artifacts Relating to Mourning in Nineteenth Century America." *Journal of American Culture*, vol. 3, no. 4 (Winter 1980). 642–659.

Plante, Ellen M. *Women at Home in Victorian America: A Social History*. New York: Facts on File, 1997.

Plunkett, John. *Queen Victoria: First Media Monarch*. Oxford University Press, 2003.

Polidoro, Massimo. "The Charlie, Charlie Challenge?" *Skeptical Inquirer*, vol. 39, no. 6 (Nov.–Dec. 2015).

_____. "The Day Houdini (Almost) Came Back from the Dead." *Skeptical Inquirer*, Mar.–Apr. 2012. 23–25.

_____. *Final Séance: The Strange Friendship Between Houdini and Conan Doyle*. Amherst, NY: Prometheus, 2001.

Powers, Bill. "The Key to Any Good Performance Art Is Nudity: A Talk with Rob Pruitt." *ART News,* May 7, 2015. http://www.artnews.com/2015/05/07/the-key-to-any-good-performance-art-is-nudity-a-talk-with-rob-pruitt/.

"Queen Victoria's Bloomers Had a 50-inch waist." *The Telegraph*, July 11, 2008.

Radford, Tim. "Secrets of Human Hair Unlocked at Natural History Museum in London." *The Guardian*, U.S. ed., May 27, 2004.

Rahm, Virginia L. "MHS Collections: Human Hair Ornaments." *Minnesota History*, vol. 44, no. 2 (Summer 1974). 70–74.

Rainville, Lynn. "Mortuary Variability in New Hampshire, 1770–1920." *Ethnohistory*, vol. 46, no. 3 (Summer 1999). 541–597.

_____. "Protecting Our Shared Heritage in African-American Cemeteries." *Journal of Field Archaeology*, vol. 34, no. 2 (Summer 2009). 196–206.

Rappaport, Helen. "Magnificent Obsession: Victoria, Albert and the Death that Changed the Monarchy." *Daily Mail*, London, Oct. 29, 2011.

Rennell, Tony. *Last Days of Glory*. New York: St. Martin's, 2000.

"Revelation." Bible Hub. Accessed June 25, 2015. http://biblehub.com/revelation/7-9.htm.

Reynolds, Rebecca. "Boston's Outdoor Sculptural Garden: Forest Hills Cemetery." *Sculpture Review,* vol. 50, no. 4 (Winter 2001). 8–15.

Ringbom, Sixten. "Art in 'The Epoch of the Great Spiritual': Occult Elements in the Early Theory of Abstract Painting." *Journal of the Warburg and Courtauld Institutes*, vol. 29 (1966). 386–418.

_____. "Transcending the Visible: The Generation of the Abstract Pioneers." In *The Spiritual in Art: Abstract Painting 1890–1985*. Maurice Tuchman, and Judi Freeman, Los Angeles Museum of Art, eds. New York: Abbeville, 1987. 131–53

Roark, Elisabeth Louise. *Artists of Colonial America: Artists of an Era*. Westport, CT: Greenwood, 2003.

Romaine, Lawrence B. *A Guide to American Trade Catalogs, 1744–1900*. New Providence, NJ: R. R. Bowker, 1960.

Rondolat, Eric, "1.1 Billion Reasons Why Light Poverty Must Be Eradicated," *The Telegraph, Science News*, Sept. 11, 2015.

Rose, William Ganson. *Cleveland: The Making of a City*. Ohio: Kent State University Press, 1990.

Rosenberg, Charles E. "Sexuality, Class and Role in 19th-Century America." *American Quarterly*, vol. 25, no. 2 (May 1973), 131–153.

Rosenberg, Eli. "Ancient Burial Chamber Uncovered in Egypt, with 17 Mummies … So Far." *New York Times*, May 13, 2017.

Rosenthal, Angela. "Raising Hair." *Eighteenth-Century Studies*, vol. 38, no. 1 (Fall 2004). 1–16.

Russell, Vivian. "The Ugliest Place on Tweedside." *The Telegraph*, Oct. 11, 2003.

Rydell, Robert W. *All the World's a Fair: Visions of Empire at American International Expositions, 1876–1916*. University of Chicago Press, 1984.

Saint-Pierre. Jacques-Henri Benardin, trans. *St. Pierre's Studies of Nature*. London: Forgotten Books, 2016

Sample, Omar H. "Improving the Cemetery Monument." *Art and Progress*, vol. 3, no. 6 (Apr. 1912). 546–550.

Sandburg, Carl. *Mary Lincoln: Wife and Widow*. Bedford, MA: Applewood, 1932.

Sargent, Lucius M. *Dealings with the Dead*. Boston: Dutton & Wentworth, 1856.

Sayer, Duncan. "Death and the Dissenter: Group Identity and Stylistic Simplicity as Witnessed in Nineteenth-Century Nonconformist Gravestones." *Historical Archaeology*, vol. 45, no. 4 (2011). 115–143.

Schon, Marbeth. Review of "Bejewelled by Tiffany: 1837–1987." *Modern Silver*. Accessed Jan. 24, 2016. http://www.modernsilver.com/tiffany.htm.

Schorsch, Anita. *Mourning Becomes America—Mourning Art in the New Nation*. Exhibition catalog. William Penn Memorial Museum. Danbury, CT: Main Street Press, 1976.

Schultz, Martin. "Occupational Pursuits of Free American Women: An Analysis of Newspaper Ads, 1800–1849." *Sociological Forum*, vol. 7, no. 4 (Dec. 1992). 577–607.

Schuré, Édouard. *The Great Initiates—A Study of the Secret History of Religions*. San Francisco: Harper & Row, 1917.

Sears, Roebuck & Co. "Tombstones and Monuments." Chicago: Sears, Roebuck & Co., 1902.

Segrave, Kerry. *Women Swindlers in America, 1860–1920*. Jefferson, NC: McFarland, 2007.

Shepard, E. R. *True Manhood: A Manual for Young Men*, 8th ed. Chicago: A. B. Stockham, 1891.

Sheumaker, Helen. *Love Entwined: The Curious History of Hairwork in America*. Philadelphia: University of Pennsylvania Press, 2007.

Skinner, Charles M. "The Use of Precious Stones." *The Decorator and Furnisher*, vol. 14, no. 1 (Apr. 1889), 5–6.

Slater, James A., and Ernest Caulfield. *The Colonial Gravestone Carvings of Obadiah Wheeler*. Worcester, MA: American Antiquarian Society, 1978.

Smith, R. A. *Smith's Illustrated Guide to and Through Laurel Hill Cemetery*. Philadelphia: Willis P. Hazard, 1852.

Snell, K. D. M. "Gravestones, Belonging and Local Attachment in England 1700–2000." *Past & Present*, no. 179 (May 2003), 97–134.

Snodgrass, Mary Ellen. *World Clothing and Fashion: An Encyclopedia of History, Culture and Social Influence*, vols. 1–2. London: Routledge, 2014.

Southworth, Albert. "Comments at the National Photographic Association." *Philadelphia Photographer*, vol. 10 (Sept. 1873).

Speight, Alexanna. *The Lock of Hair: Its History, Ancient and Modern, Natural and Artistic*. London: A. Goates, Printer, 1871.

Steiner, Rudolf. *Theosophy: An Introduction to the Spiritual Processes in Human life and in the Cosmos*. Catherine E. Creeger, trans. Great Barrington, MA: Anthroposophic, 1994; first published by Rand McNally, Chicago, 1910.

Stone, Gaynell. "Sacred Landscapes: Material Evidence of Ideological and Ethnic Choice in Long Island, New York, Gravestones, 1680–1800." *Historical Archaeology*, vol. 43, no. 1 (2009), 142–159.

Stone: An Illustrated Magazine. Vol. 4 (May 1891–June 1892). Indianapolis: D. H. Ranck, 1892.

Strange, Julie-Marie. "She Cried a Very Little': Death, Grief and Mourning in Working Class Culture, c. 1880–1914." *Social History*, vol. 27, no. 2 (May 2002). 143–161.

Streeter, Burnett H. *"Immortality": An Essay in Discovery Co-ordination Scientific, Psychical, and Biblical Research*. London: MacMillan, 1917.

Stuart, Andrea. *Josephine: The Rose of Martinique*. New York: Grove, 2005.

Stulik, Dusan C., and Art Kaplan. "Photogravure," 2013. The Getty Conservation Institute. http://www.getty.edu/conservation/publications_resources/pdf_publications/pdf/atlas_photogravure.pdf.

Swartz, Anne. "A Redating of Kupka's 'Amorpha, Fugue in Two Colors II.'" *The Bulletin of the Cleveland Museum of Art*, vol. 80, no. 8 (Oct. 1993). 327–351.

Taft, Leonardo. *The History of American Sculpture*. New York: MacMillan, 1903.

Taylor, Lou. *Mourning Dress: A Costume and Social History*. Sydney: Allen & Unwin, 1983.

Theosophical Society. https://www.theosociety.org/.

Thieme, Otto Charles. "The Art of Dress in the Victorian and Edwardian Eras." *The Journal of Decorative and Propaganda Arts*, vol. 10 (Autumn 1988). 14–27.

Tolstoy, Leo. *What I Believe*. Constantine Popoff, trans. New York: William Gottsberger, 1886.

Tortora, Phyllis G., and Keith Eubank. *Survey of Historic Costume*. 5th ed. New York: Fairchild, 2010.

Trachtenberg, Alan. *Reading American Photographs*. New York: Hill & Wang, 1989.

Traverse, Alfred, and Roger W. Kolvoord. "Utah Jet: A Vitrinite with Aberrant Properties." *Science*, New Series, vol. 159, no. 3812 (Jan. 19, 1968). 302–305.

True Republican, Sycamore, IL, Feb. 18, 1891.

Trumback, Randolph. *The Rise of the Egalitarian Family: Aristocratic Kinship and Domestic Relations in Eighteenth-Century England*. New York: Academic Press, 1978.

Truong, Alain R. "Back at 'Death Becomes Her: A Century of Mourning Attire' at the Metropolitan Museum of Art's Costume Institute in New York." À Propos, Feb. 9, 2015. https://alaintruong2014.wordpress.com/tag/victorian-mourning-jewelry/.

Tuchman, Maurice, Judi Freeman, and Los Angeles Museum of Art, eds. *The Spiritual in Art: Abstract Painting 1890–1985*. Abbeville, New York, 1987.

Tuckerman, Henry Theodore. *Book of the Artist: American Artist Life*. G. P. Putnam, New York, 1867.

Turner, Christopher. "Mesmeromania, or, The Tale of the Tub." *Cabinet* no. 21 (Spring 2006). http://www.cabinetmagazine.org/issues/21/turner.php.

"The Twilight Years: The Deaths of George and Martha Washington." Martha Washington. Accessed

Feb. 2017. http://marthawashington.us/exhibits/show/martha-washington—a-life/the-twilight-years/deaths.

Urbino, Madame L. B. [Levina Buoncuore], Henry Day, et al. *Art Recreations: Being a Complete Guide to Pencil Drawing, Oil Painting…,* Boston: J. E. Tilden, 1871.

Veit, Richard F. "Resolved to Strike Out a New Path: Consumerism and Iconographic Change in New Jersey Gravestones, 1680–1820." *Historical Archaeology,* vol. 43, no. 1 (2009). 115–141.

Veit, Richard F., S. B. Baugher, et al. "Historical Archaeology of Religious Sites and Cemeteries." *Historical Archeology,* vol. 43, no. 1 (2009). 1–11.

Versluis, Arthur. "The 'Occult' in Nineteenth Century America." In *The Occult in Nineteenth-Century America,* ed. Cathy Gutierrez, 2005. Aurora, CO: Davies Group, 2005. 1–29

Walker's Hibernian Magazine, November 1786.

Wallace, Alfred Russel. *Miracles and Modern Spiritualism.* London: George Redway, 1874; reprint, New York: Arno, 1975.

Walvin, James. "Celebrations of Death in Victorian England." *Historical Reflections/Réflexions Historiques,* vol. 9, no. 3 (Fall 1982). 353–371.

Washington, Peter. *Madame Blavatsky's Baboon: A History of the Mystics, Mediums, and Misfits Who Brought Spiritualism to America.* New York: Shocken, 1996.

Watt, Melinda. "Textile Production in Europe: Silk, 1600–1800." The Met. Accessed Oct. 27, 2016. https://www.metmuseum.org/toah/hd/txt_s/hd_txt_s.htm.

Wecker, Menachem. "The Scadalous Story Behind the Provocative 19th-Century Sculpture 'Greek Slave.'" Smithsonian.com. Accessed July 24, 2015. https://www.smithsonianmag.com/smithsonian-institution/scandalous-story-behind-provocative-sculpture-greek-slave-19th-century-audiences-180956029/.

Weever, John. *Ancient Funeral Monuments, of Great-Britain, Ireland, and the Islands Adjacent.* London: John Weever Publishers, printed by W. Tooke, 1767.

"What Happens After a Person Dies?" The People of the United Methodist Church. Accessed June 25, 2015. http://www.umc.org/what-we-believe/what-happens-after-a-person-dies.

Wheeler, Tom. *Mr. Lincoln's T-Mails: The Untold Story of How Abraham Lincoln Used the Telegraph to Win the Civil War.* New York: HarperBusiness, reprint, 2008.

Whittaker, E. T. *Theories of Aether and Electricity: From the Age of Descartes to the Close of the Nineteenth Century.* London: Longmans, Green, & Co., 1910.

Whitefield, George. *Selected Sermons of George Whitefield: With an Introduction and Notes by the Rev. A. R. Buckland, M.A.* Philadelphia: Union Press, 1904.

Wilder, Laura Ingalls. *Laura Ingalls, Pioneer Girl.* Pamela Smith Hill, ed. Pierre: South Dakota Historical Society Press, 2014.

Wilkes, Sue. *A Visitor's Guide to Jane Austen's England.* Barnsley, UK: Pen and Sword, 2014.

Williams, Frank J. and M. Burkhimer, eds. *The Mary Lincoln Enigma.* Carbondale: Southern Illinois University Press, 2012.

Williams, Susan E. "Richmond Taken Again." *The Virginia Magazine of History and Biography,* vol. 110, no. 4 (2002). 427–460.

Zöllner, Johann Carl Friedrich. *Transcendental Physics: An Account of Experimental Investigations from the Scientific Treatises.* Charles Carleton Massey, trans. Edinburgh and London: Ballantyne Press, 1880.

Index

Numbers in *bold italics* indicate pages with illustrations

www.ingramcontent.com/pod-product-compliance
Ingram Content Group UK Ltd.
Pitfield, Milton Keynes, MK11 3LW, UK
UKHW051853150726
7214IPUK00021B/400